Marx, Engels, and Marxisms

Series Editors
Marcello Musto, York University, Toronto, ON, Canada
Terrell Carver, University of Bristol, Bristol, UK

The Marx renaissance is underway on a global scale. Wherever the critique of capitalism re-emerges, there is an intellectual and political demand for new, critical engagements with Marxism. The peer-reviewed series Marx, Engels and Marxisms (edited by Marcello Musto & Terrell Carver, with Babak Amini, Francesca Antonini, Paula Rauhala & Kohei Saito as Assistant Editors) publishes monographs, edited volumes, critical editions, reprints of old texts, as well as translations of books already published in other languages. Our volumes come from a wide range of political perspectives, subject matters, academic disciplines and geographical areas, producing an eclectic and informative collection that appeals to a diverse and international audience. Our main areas of focus include: the oeuvre of Marx and Engels, Marxist authors and traditions of the 19th and 20th centuries, labour and social movements, Marxist analyses of contemporary issues, and reception of Marxism in the world.

More information about this series at
https://link.springer.com/bookseries/14812

Achim Szepanski

Financial Capital in the 21st Century

A New Theory of Speculative Capital

Achim Szepanski
Frankfurt, Germany

ISSN 2524-7123 ISSN 2524-7131 (electronic)
Marx, Engels, and Marxisms
ISBN 978-3-030-93150-6 ISBN 978-3-030-93151-3 (eBook)
https://doi.org/10.1007/978-3-030-93151-3

The translation was done with the help of artificial intelligence (machine translation by the service DeepL.com). A subsequent human revision was done primarily in terms of content.
Translation from the German language edition: Kapital und Macht im 21.Jahrhundert by Achim Szepanski, © Achim Szepanski 2018. Published by Laika Verlag/NON.Derivate. All Rights Reserved.
© The Editor(s) (if applicable) and The Author(s), under exclusive license to Springer Nature Switzerland AG 2022
This work is subject to copyright. All rights are solely and exclusively licensed by the Publisher, whether the whole or part of the material is concerned, specifically the rights of reprinting, reuse of illustrations, recitation, broadcasting, reproduction on microfilms or in any other physical way, and transmission or information storage and retrieval, electronic adaptation, computer software, or by similar or dissimilar methodology now known or hereafter developed.
The use of general descriptive names, registered names, trademarks, service marks, etc. in this publication does not imply, even in the absence of a specific statement, that such names are exempt from the relevant protective laws and regulations and therefore free for general use.
The publisher, the authors and the editors are safe to assume that the advice and information in this book are believed to be true and accurate at the date of publication. Neither the publisher nor the authors or the editors give a warranty, expressed or implied, with respect to the material contained herein or for any errors or omissions that may have been made. The publisher remains neutral with regard to jurisdictional claims in published maps and institutional affiliations.

Cover credit: @Tetra Images

This Palgrave Macmillan imprint is published by the registered company Springer Nature Switzerland AG
The registered company address is: Gewerbestrasse 11, 6330 Cham, Switzerland

SERIES EDITOR'S FOREWORD

TITLES PUBLISHED

1. Terrell Carver & Daniel Blank, *A Political History of the Editions of Marx and Engels's "German Ideology" Manuscripts*, 2014.
2. Terrell Carver & Daniel Blank, *Marx and Engels's "German Ideology" Manuscripts: Presentation and Analysis of the "Feuerbach chapter,"* 2014.
3. Alfonso Maurizio Iacono, *The History and Theory of Fetishism*, 2015.
4. Paresh Chattopadhyay, *Marx's Associated Mode of Production: A Critique of Marxism*, 2016.
5. Domenico Losurdo, *Class Struggle: A Political and Philosophical History*, 2016.
6. Frederick Harry Pitts, *Critiquing Capitalism Today: New Ways to Read Marx*, 2017.
7. Ranabir Samaddar, *Karl Marx and the Postcolonial Age*, 2017.
8. George Comninel, *Alienation and Emancipation in the Work of Karl Marx*, 2018.
9. Jean-Numa Ducange & Razmig Keucheyan (Eds.), *The End of the Democratic State: Nicos Poulantzas, a Marxism for the 21st Century*, 2018.

v

vi   SERIES EDITOR'S FOREWORD

10. Robert X. Ware, *Marx on Emancipation and Socialist Goals: Retrieving Marx for the Future*, 2018.
11. Xavier LaFrance & Charles Post (Eds.), *Case Studies in the Origins of Capitalism*, 2018.
12. John Gregson, *Marxism, Ethics, and Politics: The Work of Alasdair MacIntyre*, 2018.
13. Vladimir Puzone & Luis Felipe Miguel (Eds.), *The Brazilian Left in the 21st Century: Conflict and Conciliation in Peripheral Capitalism*, 2019.
14. James Muldoon & Gaard Kets (Eds.), *The German Revolution and Political Theory*, 2019.
15. Michael Brie, *Rediscovering Lenin: Dialectics of Revolution and Metaphysics of Domination*, 2019.
16. August H. Nimtz, *Marxism versus Liberalism: Comparative Real-Time Political Analysis*, 2019.
17. Gustavo Moura de Cavalcanti Mello and Mauricio de Souza Sabadini (Eds.), *Financial Speculation and Fictitious Profits: A Marxist Analysis*, 2019.
18. Shaibal Gupta, Marcello Musto & Babak Amini (Eds), *Karl Marx's Life, Ideas, and Influences: A Critical Examination on the Bicentenary*, 2019.
19. Igor Shoikhedbrod, *Revisiting Marx's Critique of Liberalism: Rethinking Justice, Legality, and Rights*, 2019.
20. Juan Pablo Rodríguez, *Resisting Neoliberal Capitalism in Chile: The Possibility of Social Critique*, 2019.
21. Kaan Kangal, *Friedrich Engels and the Dialectics of Nature*, 2020.
22. Victor Wallis, *Socialist Practice: Histories and Theories*, 2020.
23. Alfonso Maurizio Iacono, *The Bourgeois and the Savage: A Marxian Critique of the Image of the Isolated Individual in Defoe, Turgot and Smith*, 2020.
24. Terrell Carver, *Engels before Marx*, 2020.
25. Jean-Numa Ducange, *Jules Guesde: The Birth of Socialism and Marxism in France*, 2020.
26. Antonio Oliva, Ivan Novara & Angel Oliva (Eds.), *Marx and Contemporary Critical Theory: The Philosophy of Real Abstraction*, 2020.
27. Francesco Biagi, *Henri Lefebvre's Critical Theory of Space*, 2020.
28. Stefano Petrucciani, *The Ideas of Karl Marx: A Critical Introduction*, 2020.

SERIES EDITOR'S FOREWORD   vii

29. Terrell Carver, *The Life and Thought of Friedrich Engels, 30th Anniversary Edition*, 2020.
30. Giuseppe Vacca, *Alternative Modernities: Antonio Gramsci's Twentieth Century*, 2020.
31. Kevin B. Anderson, Kieran Durkin & Heather Brown (Eds.), *Raya Dunayevskaya's Intersectional Marxism: Race, Gender, and the Dialectics of Liberation*, 2020.
32. Marco Di Maggio, *The Rise and Fall of Communist Parties in France and Italy*, 2020.
33. Ryuji Sasaki, *A New Introduction to Karl Marx: New Materialism, Critique of Political Economy, and the Concept of Metabolism*, 2020.
34. Kohei Saito (Ed.), *Reexamining Engels's Legacy in the 21st Century*, 2021.
35. Paresh Chattopadhyay, *Socialism in Marx's Capital: Towards a De-alienated World*, 2021.
36. Marcello Musto, *Karl Marx's Writings on Alienation*, 2021.
37. Michael Brie & Jörn Schütrumpf, *Rosa Luxemburg: A Revolutionary Marxist at the Limits of Marxism*, 2021.
38. Stefano Petrucciani, *Theodor W. Adorno's Philosophy, Society, and Aesthetics*, 2021.
39. Miguel Vedda, *Siegfried Kracauer, or, The Allegories of Improvisation: Critical Studies*, 2021.
40. Ronaldo Munck, *Rethinking Development: Marxist Perspectives*, 2021.
41. Jean-Numa Ducange & Elisa Marcobelli (Eds.), *Selected Writings of Jean Jaurès: On Socialism, Pacifism and Marxism*, 2021.
42. Elisa Marcobelli, *Internationalism Toward Diplomatic Crisis: The Second International and French, German and Italian Socialists*, 2021.
43. James Steinhoff, *Automation and Autonomy: Labour, Capital and Machines in the Artificial Intelligence Industry*, 2021.
44. Juan Dal Maso, *Hegemony and Class Struggle: Trotsky, Gramsci and Marxism*, 2021.
45. Gianfranco Ragona & Monica Quirico, *Frontier Socialism: Self-organisation and Anti-capitalism*, 2021.
46. Tsuyoshi Yuki, *Socialism, Markets and the Critique of Money: The Theory of "Labour Notes,"* 2021.

viii SERIES EDITOR'S FOREWORD

Titles Forthcoming

Vesa Oittinen, *Marx's Russian Moment*

Kolja Lindner, *Marx, Marxism and the Question of Eurocentrism*

Adriana Petra, *Intellectuals and Communist Culture: Itineraries, Problems and Debates in Post-war Argentina*

George C. Comninel, *The Feudal Foundations of Modern Europe*

Spencer A. Leonard, *Marx, the India Question, and the Crisis of Cosmopolitanism*

Joe Collins, *Applying Marx's Capital to the 21st century*

Levy del Aguila Marchena, *Communism, Political Power and Personal Freedom in Marx*

Jeong Seongjin, *Korean Capitalism in the 21st Century: Marxist Analysis and Alternatives*

Marcello Mustè, *Marxism and Philosophy of Praxis: An Italian Perspective from Labriola to Gramsci*

Satoshi Matsui, *Normative Theories of Liberalism and Socialism: Marxist Analysis of Values*

Shannon Brincat, *Dialectical Dialogues in Contemporary World Politics: A Meeting of Traditions in Global Comparative Philosophy*

Francesca Antonini, *Reassessing Marx's Eighteenth Brumaire: Dictatorship, State, and Revolution*

Thomas Kemple, *Capital after Classical Sociology: The Faustian Lives of Social Theory*

V Geetha, *Bhimrao Ramji Ambedkar and the Question of Socialism in India*

Xavier Vigna, *A Political History of Factories in France: The Workers' Insubordination of 1968*

Attila Melegh, *Anti-Migrant Populism in Eastern Europe and Hungary: A Marxist Analysis*

Marie-Cecile Bouju, *A Political History of the Publishing Houses of the French Communist Party*

Gustavo Moura de Cavalcanti Mello & Henrique Pereira Braga (Eds.), *Wealth and Poverty in Contemporary Brazilian Capitalism*

Peter McMylor, Graeme Kirkpatrick & Simin Fadaee (Eds.), *Marxism, Religion, and Emancipatory Politics*

Mauro Buccheri, *Radical Humanism for the Left: The Quest for Meaning in Late Capitalism*

Rémy Herrera, *Confronting Mainstream Economics to Overcome Capitalism*

Tamás Krausz, Eszter Bartha (Eds.), *Socialist Experiences in Eastern Europe: A Hungarian Perspective*

Martin Cortés, *Marxism, Time and Politics: On the Autonomy of the Political*

João Antonio de Paula, Huga da Gama Cerqueira, Eduardo da Motta e Albuquer & Leonardo de Deus, *Marxian Economics for the 21st Century: Revaluating Marx's Critique of Political Economy*

Zhi Li, *The Concept of the Individual in the Thought of Karl Marx*

Lelio Demichelis, *Marx, Alienation and Techno-capitalism*

Dong-Min Rieu, *A Mathematical Approach to Marxian Value Theory: Time, Money, and Labor Productivity*

Salvatore Prinzi, *Representation, Expression, and Institution: The Philosophy of Merleau-Ponty and Castoriadis*

Agon Hamza, *Slavoj Žižek and the Reconstruction of Marxism*

Kei Ehara (Ed.), *Japanese Discourse on the Marxian Theory of Finance*

Éric Aunoble, *French Views on the Russian Revolution*

Paolo Favilli, *Historiography and Marxism: Innovations in Mid-Century Italy*

Terrell Carver, Smail Rapic (Eds.), *Friedrich Engels for the 21st Century: Perspectives and Problems*

Patrizia Dogliani, *A Political History of the International Union of Socialist Youth*

Alexandros Chrysis, *The Marx of Communism: Setting Limits in the Realm of Communism*

Stephen Maher, *Corporate Capitalism and the Integral State: General Electric and a Century of American Power*

Paul Raekstad, *Karl Marx's Realist Critique of Capitalism: Freedom, Alienation, and Socialism*

Alexis Cukier, *Democratic Work: Radical Democracy and the Future of Labour*

Christoph Henning, *Theories of Alienation: From Rousseau to the Present*

Daniel Egan, *Capitalism, War, and Revolution: A Marxist Analysis*

Genevieve Ritchie, Sara Carpenter & Shahrzad Mojab (Eds.), *Marxism and Migration*

Emanuela Conversano, *Capital from Afar: Anthropology and Critique of Political Economy in the Late Marx*

Marcello Musto, *Rethinking Alternatives with Marx*

Vincenzo Mele, *City and Modernity in George Simmel and Walter Benjamin: Fragments of Metropolis*

David Norman Smith, *Self-Emancipation: Marx's Unfinished Theory of the Working Class*

José Ricardo Villanueva Lira, *Marxism and the Origins of International Relations*

Bertel Nygaard, *Marxism, Labor Movements, and Historiography*

Fabio Perocco (Ed.), *Racism in and for the Welfare State*

Marcos Del Roio, *Gramsci and the Emancipation of the Subaltern Classes*

Marcelo Badaró, *The Working Class from Marx to Our Times*

Tomonaga Tairako, *A New Perspective on Marx's Philosophy and Political Economy*

Acknowledgments

I thank Eric-John Russell for his work on the translation.

Praise for *Financial Capital in the 21st Century*

"Achim Szepanski is a mad scientist of the left, fusing ferociously heterodox political economy with equally fierce erudition and theoretical verve, drawn from a breadth of critical traditions and pointing toward a future arriving at furious velocities. As if that were not enough, he spends his spare time translating and publishing critical contemporary thought across numerous disciplines; it seems too much for one person, and perhaps this is all the work of a revolutionary collective operating under the name—but either way the radical left is fortunate to have Achim Szepanski on its side."

—Joshua Clover, *Professor of Literature and Critical Theory, University of California Davis*

"To understand value and its valorization, we need to understand money; to understand money, we need to understand its capitalist form; and to understand this capitalist form, we need to understand finance. Achim Szenpanski is one of the few who recaptures the whole 'line of preconditions' from the first and last condition: actual finance and speculative capital as a social totality. The conception is informed by different strains of radical critique and avoids the narrowing of conventional economics— towards a finance theory of value and money, power and state."

—Frank Engster, Author of *Das Geld als Maß, Mittel und Methode*

"Achim Szepanski's work on Marx, political economy of the present era, and his close examination of the speculative or finance economy as that apex of what has always already been present in capitalism, even in its nascent form, is a rare example of rigorous scholarship of Marx's original oeuvre without recourse to the intermediary authority of the Marxist philosophy issuing from the foundations of the Leninist Diamat. Szepanski has promulgated the non-philosophical treatment of Marx proffered by François Laruelle, as well as other radical and heretical forms of reading Marx and materialism, not only through his writing but also through the intellectual community he has established around his outlet Non-Copyriot putting Berlin once again at the centre of the most interesting discussions in political philosophy, economy and culture stemming from a para-academic setup, and thus once again demonstrating that scholarly vigor can no longer be found in the conventional academia."

—Katerina Kolozova, *Professor of political philosophy at the Faculty of Media and Communications-Belgrade and co-director of the School of Materialist Research (Vienna TU /Skopje-ISSHS/Arizona State University/CIL-Eindhoven)*

CONTENTS

1	**Introduction**	1
	References	9
2	**Capital**	11
	2.1 *Commodity, Money and Capital*	11
	2.2 *Capital and Total Capital: The Quasi-Transcendentality of Capital and the Actualisation-Virtualisation Connection*	37
	References	55
3	**Credit**	59
	3.1 *Credit and Interest-Bearing Capital*	59
	References	74
4	**The Category of Capitalisation**	77
	References	87
5	**Fictitious Capital**	89
	5.1 *The General Term of Fictitious Capital*	89
	5.2 *Bonds and Shares*	97
	References	103
6	**Speculative Capital**	105
	6.1 *Derivatives*	105
	6.2 *Securitisation*	126

xv

xvi CONTENTS

6.3	*Derivatives as Forms of Speculative Capital and Power Technologies*	133
6.4	*The Derivative Market*	162
6.5	*Heterodox Positions*	167
6.6	*Portfolio Theory*	175
	References	177

7	**Private Banks**	179
7.1	*The Functions of Private Banks*	179
7.2	*Creation of Credit by Private Banks*	191
7.3	*Leverage*	209
7.4	*Investment Banks and Funds*	214
	References	217

8	**The Financial System and the State**	219
8.1	The State	219
8.2	*The Functions of Central Banks*	245
	References	265

9	**Capital and the World Market**	269
9.1	*Introduction*	269
9.2	*Capital Export*	279
9.3	*The Financial Industry and the World Market*	285
9.4	*Imperialism*	287
9.5	*The Dollar as Leading Currency*	295
9.6	*Global Value Chains and the Global Proletariat*	299
9.7	*The Global Proletariat and the Different Zones*	305
	References	311

10	**Technology and Finance**	313
	References	323

11	**The Functions of Financial Markets for the Capitalist Economy**	325
	References	336

12	**The Financialised Subject of Risk**	337
	References	347

13	**Financial System and Crisis**	349
	References	363
Index		367

CHAPTER 1

Introduction

The world economy is still in a phase of secular stagnation with persistently low growth rates of real gross domestic product.[1] The postwar litanies of boundless economic growth repeatedly preached by the representatives of capital and the imperialist states have literally run themselves into the sand. Since the 1980s, financialised capital increasingly drives and determines the global economy, which today operates at a high level of financial consumption, investment and speculation. As a result, debt has risen temporarily beyond the capacity of debtors to repay it at all. The assertion that an increase in inflation would lower the debt level by reducing its value has so far proved to be invalid. The financial problems surrounding debt apply to other critical facts, such as the weakening of accumulation rates, the decline in capital investment, insufficient renewal of the capital stock, chronic low interest rates, slower population growth and an ageing population, lower growth rates of productivity of capital accumulation[2] and a slowdown in innovation. Finally, with declining natural resources such as water, food and energy, climate change

[1] Secular stagnation implies that the supply of capital is greater than the demand, leading to a reduction in interest rates. Moreover, the lack of demand also affects the supply of goods, which leads to falling price levels.

[2] To the extent that the microeconomic use of surplus value for the increase of capital simultaneously expands total capital or is accompanied by an increase in productivity, a

© The Author(s), under exclusive license to Springer Nature Switzerland AG 2022
A. Szepanski, *Financial Capital in the 21st Century*, Marx, Engels, and Marxisms, https://doi.org/10.1007/978-3-030-93151-3_1

1

initiated by fossil capital is leading to the reduction of biodiversity, stratospheric ozone depletion, ocean acidification, extreme weather conditions, precarious drinking water supply, chemical pollution and changes in soil conditions, to name but a few consequences. Additionally, less growth in international trade for emerging markets and capital flows have taken place. The idea that increased government spending, low interest rates and the provision of liquidity and cash in the money and capital markets would generate higher economic growth has so far been refuted by reality.

In the countries that have recovered fairly after the financial crisis of 2008, we see again a growing financial industry, while even there, the standard of living and real wages for large parts of the population are stagnating or falling further. Public goods such as health, education and retirement provision continue to be privatised, and their quality standards are dropping, not to mention the standard of living of future generations. Youth unemployment is rising almost everywhere in the world. Simultaneously, debt has also been increased due to low interest rates and increased government spending, while the size and market power of private banks (together with the shadow banking system) continue to be of paramount economic importance. The policy of easy money or quantitative easing has increased the prices of shares and financial assets, destabilising the growth of emerging markets.

Already before the COVID-19 pandemic, many companies financed themselves with cheap credit as a result of the loose monetary policies of central banks, which led to an increase in corporate debt. In 2019, private debt had already reached dimensions that made it difficult for many companies to repay their loans. Although the aim of more favourable financing opportunities was to increase investment, it did not happen, nor was the expanded credit supply accompanied by an increase in aggregate demand. The purchasing power of households is stagnating. Companies in the industrial sector are still confronted with declining profit prospects, while shortly before the outbreak of the crises, major stock markets were at historic highs. Enormous sums of money circulated on finance markets and drove up asset prices. In the shadow banking system, liquidity buffers were reduced again. There was also an increase in highly leveraged financial transactions, with massive share paybacks and high dividends paid out. For more than 20 years, the shadow banking system (almost 50% of global

growth process of production in an economy takes place while gross domestic product rises.

credit trading takes place in this area) and the market for short-term repo agreements[3] have grown steadily. New debt structures like CLOs and all forms of loans have emerged since the last financial crisis.

In the beginning of the COVID-19 crisis in 2020, we saw a sharp decline in both supply and demand for industrial production worldwide. Besides the huge profits of Big Pharma, the Big Techno Platforms and some Big Banks, the total corporate profits in the U.S. dropped in 2020 by about 30%. Global measures to contain the COVID-19 pandemic triggered also another crisis in the global financial system. As discord over the economic impact of COVID-19 grew from February 2020, stock indices fell precipitously. Investors especially began to buy enormous amounts of U.S. government bonds. Their yields fell and their prices rose, while prices of assets on risky financial markets collapsed, since financial players tried to raise funds by selling securities. But since almost no one wanted to buy these securities at that moment, a sharp drop in prices followed. The flight into cash did not stop, while assets were liquidated. The run on the U.S. dollar increased activities on the exchange markets, while now even safe assets continued to be sold and algorithmic trading was reduced. Even safe government bonds were at the end sold to obtain cash. Volatility was extremely high in the markets.

Already in the years before COVID-19, central banks intervened massively in the shadow banking system and acted as a dealer by conducting repo transactions for banks of all kinds. They no longer served merely as liquidity providers, but became traders on the financial markets. When the COVID-19 financial crisis erupted, central banks worked stronger again with traditional measures like lowering key interest rates and providing liquidity, but also used massive measures like quantitative easing and repo actions and acted as dealers on the markets

---

[3] Repos represent an important instrument of the shadow banking system. With a rise of liquidity, repos were developed, contracts under which securities are sold (mostly overnight) at a certain price, plus interest and a premium (haircut). The buyer becomes the owner of the securities. If the seller cannot buy back the securities, they can be sold on the market by the buyer. The securities therefore act as collateral. If, during the term of the repo, the underlying securities lose value, additional securities have to be delivered (margin call). The price of the repo transaction is determined by the quality of the security. The preferred securities for hedging repos are mainly safe government bonds. The problem with repos is that this form of hedging has a crisis-reinforcing effect. If the value of the securities is downgraded in a crisis, we see higher margin calls and higher haircuts. In order to maintain liquidity, players on the market are forced to sell securities, so that their prices fall.

and organised foreign exchange swaps. Furthermore, they gave credit to nonfinancial actors. The Bank of England bought U.K. government bonds directly on the primary market. So the central banks decided to make substantial funds available, while governments launched additional investment programmes in enormous sums (Wullweber 2021).

Despite the collapse of the global economy with the COVID-19 crisis, asset prices started after the shortfall to rise again in 2020. In search of higher returns, financial investors again turned to risky financial products and junk bonds, while stock market indices rose to record levels. In order to achieve higher returns, many institutional funds once again invested in highly leveraged and less liquid assets. The money injected by central banks into the markets funded much more financial asset price growth than consumption and investments. At the moment, Joe Biden plans a huge investment package for the U.S. But government investments to GDP in developed economies are at about 3% of GDP, while private investment of capital is around 20% of GDP on average. So a revival of investment depends more on capitalist investment. Economists suggest that the "multiplier effect" of government spending on real GDP growth is not more than 1% point.

At the moment, the politics of cheap money continues to fuel the asset and credit crisis, since debt ratios are already high. We see, for example, already high price-to-earnings ratios, inflated housing assets and high-yield corporate debt. There might also be a new consumer price inflation, creating conditions for a kind of stagflation, while at the same time problems in the supply sector are expected with protectionism, further immigration restrictions and interruptions in the global supply chains.

If inflation rises over the next few years, central banks might have to raise key interest rates and will then risk a massive debt crisis. But if they maintain a politics of cheap money, stagflation could occur while, at the same time, problems in the supply sector continue. But even if they maintain the second strategy, a debt crisis could follow, since private debt in advanced economies might become unsustainable and their spreads relative to government bonds might rise. Highly indebted corporations would go bankrupt, followed by indebted households and part of the shadow banking and private banking system.

Fictitious and speculative capital (financial instruments and promises of payment) was present as a kind of embryo from the beginning of capitalism, especially when considering that the capitalist production of companies must, in principle, be pre-financed. Thus, debts quasi-insured with the goods produced in the future will arise *sui generis*. Therefore, capital ought not to be understood as an (absolute) positive value, as famous economist Joseph Schumpeter, for example, assumed. Instead, it must be understood as a socio-economic relation in which precisely the intentional negative (debt) is a favourable condition for capitalist production, as Peter Ruben, for example, has explained: capital or capitalisation is debt production *sui generis* (Ruben 1998: 53).

In many cases, except for the self-financing of large companies, capitalist production processes are set in motion *uno actu* with a credit contract. Furthermore, the possibility for capitalist enterprises to pledge their future goods as collateral implies that their products (the right to extract a surplus with them) are potentially commodity-capital even before anything is produced and then realised as goods. We must as such recognise a form of financialised capital production from the very beginning. This is why Marx named his book *Capital* and not, for instance, *Commodity* or *Money*.

Since interest-bearing, fictitious and speculative capital in the form of loans, bonds, stocks and derivatives increases today much faster and, at least in nominal terms, has taken on a much larger volume than priced-out industrial and commercial capital, the growth of assets cannot feed itself solely from the capital accumulation of the "real economy". Instead, it has to be assumed as endogenous, that is to say, a capital-immanent financial power for the construction of capital having both negative and positive effects on the real economy.[4] Financial capital today employs

---

[4] For Lohoff and Trenkle, from the 1980s at the latest, financial capital has been the motor for expanding global commodity production, which, since the 1960s, had already taken place at a high level of productivity and based on progressive process automation. The authors speak here of "induced value production" (Lohoff and Trenkle 2012: 147f.), or of "inverse capital". First, because value production is based on the extraction of surplus value added through the use of labour by capital. Second, because the growing accumulation of fictitious capital increasingly drives production, which is essential to capital accumulation. Without the production of fictitious capital, functioning capital (the capital invested in the "real economy") should have entered a cycle of significant devaluation long ago. Financial volumes have grown considerably in the context of global economic transactions. The corresponding figures reflect this financial deepening in the developed economies of Western countries: bank deposits have today on average a value of 200% of the gross domestic product (Sahr 2017: Kindle-Edition: 4902). The Global Wealth Report estimated financial assets (excluding derivatives) in 2010 at $231 trillion, four times the global GDP. The total volume of derivatives grew from $72 trillion in 1998 to $673 trillion in 2008, twelve times the global GDP at that time. Correspondingly, the debt of non-financial actors (states, companies and households) in the OECD countries

enormous loan sums, fictitious and speculative capital and other multiple capital equivalents characterised by high liquidity, mobility and commensurability. They therefore process particular forms of movement and are perhaps not dissimilar to those of the fashion and marketing industry. The increase of fictitious and speculative capital in relation to an economy's abstract wealth is specifically indicated by an ever-increasing proportion of financial profits within the pool of total corporate profits. Even the profits resulting from derivatives cannot be considered fictitious in a vulgar sense since derivatives are realised in money. Thus, they possess all the characteristics of the power of capital, especially with access to the abstract wealth produced in an economy. Although these profits (dividends, interest and the profitable realisation of assets in money) have a relation to industrial production and traditional commodity circulation, they are generated auto-referentially by financialised processes. They nevertheless have genuine effects on the "real economy".

The modern financial system is a social relation immanent to capital. This includes the multiplication of capital by redirecting monetary capital from the shrinking to the expanding sectors of the economy and the self-referential production of profits by the financial system, thus securing capitalist power relations in a comprehensive, albeit crisis-like manner. The permanent assessments, evaluations and calculations of the processes of capital reproduction, currently functioning primarily through the financial system, have significant consequences for national economies and the organisation of capitalist power relations as a whole. They strengthen

rose from 167% in 1980 to 314% of the economic output in 2009. The increase of 147% is distributed among the state with 49%, companies with 42% and households with 56% (ibid.: Kindle-Edition: 4916) Worldwide, the debt overhang in 2015 was compared to the global GDP of 286% (Pettifor 2017: Kindle-Edition: 85). At the same time, financial sector profits have doubled in relation to corporate profits in developed economies since 1980. These figures sound quite impressive: the total nominal value of derivatives was already $694.4 trillion at the end of 2012, while the global GDP value was $71.1 trillion. The "off-exchange derivatives markets" accounted for a total of $642.1 trillion (Bank of International Settlements 2013). Here, however, there are some limitations in assessing the statistical quantities because the reported sums of money only represent the derivatives' nominal value (the amounts that may be payable; they can also be called virtual because the derivatives are not yet here realised). In 2012, the "gross market value" of the derivatives (the market price of the derivative contracts) had been estimated at $24.7 trillion; it is thus approximately equal to the added GDP of the two major economies, the U.S. and China. Besides, the derivative contracts cancel each other out through hedging, so that the net credit volume of OCT derivatives was estimated at $3.6 trillion at the end of 2012, a sum roughly comparable to the GDP of Germany (ibid.).

hegemonic capitalist tendencies (within an economic cycle) into the entire antagonistic socio-economic field.

The present Marxist interpretation stands in opposition to several theoretical approaches going back to Ricardo, Veblen, Hilferding and, in part, Keynes. Our understanding also contrasts with "heterodox" positions like Post-Keynesianism and Accelerationism, but also with traditional Marxism. The modern financial system's emergence is here often understood as unrealistic, hypertrophic and dysfunctional, possibly even a distortion of ideal capitalist production. This is a position diametrically opposed to Marxism.

Financial markets today have a dual function: on the one hand, they are used to evaluate economic actors (companies, states and households) through statistical and stochastic power technologies. On the other hand, they function as an instance of the capitalisation of future promises of payment, which are now traded internationally at the speed of light. While accounting in the "real sector" proceeded for a long time in relation to the past, from the 1970s onwards, future-oriented capitalisation, i.e. the calculation or discounting of future expected payment flows and promises, mutated into the most crucial method of the capitalist financial system, with which the attainment of monetary profits takes place either in real terms or is at least financed. Derivatives and all other exotic financial instruments, which must be understood as both power technologies and as new speculative forms of capital with which profits are made, are today a necessary condition for the permanent implementation of financialisation in the entire economic field. They introduce a formative perspective on current concrete risks and make them mutually commensurable. They reduce the heterogeneity of concrete risks to a singular security, i.e. to a single social attribute, namely the abstract risk embodied by derivatives, which must always be realised in money.

As a result, an analysis of the financial system is not to be carried out as an independent financial sector or a specific type of institutionalisation. Instead, it must be assumed that today all large capitalist companies, without exception, carry out critical financial operations. In *Finance Capital Today*, French economist François Chesnais describes finance as a highly interconnected and interdependent conglomerate consisting of major banks, insurance companies, pension and investment funds, shadow and central banks, transnational industrial and commercial corporations and powerful wholesalers (the organisational level). He then makes a distinction of finance qua finance: the processes of expansion of fictitious capital and derivatives, which are held, designed and traded on the financial markets by large banks, investment funds and hedge funds (the procedural and functional level) (Chesnais 2016: 36). Concerning such factors characterising companies such as number, size, balance sheet, business volume, degree of interconnectedness, position in the capitalist reproduction process and position of power, there has been an important change in the global financial system and world markets in recent decades. In their analyses, Glattfelder, Vitali and Battiston demonstrate that 737 companies currently influence about 80% of the total global market, with a highly networked core-group of 147 companies controlling almost 40% of the market. This network consists almost exclusively of British and American banks and financial firms (cf. Sahr 2017: Kindle-Edition: 8621). At its peak, the financial industry of the U.S. generated 40% of all domestic corporate profits and represented 30% of the market price of the stock volume in the U.S. (Das 2015: Kindle Edition: 571). The financial system benefits from the asymmetries of the enormous amount of information generated by the actions of buyers and sellers of complex financial products, with which in turn discrepancies in rating are exploited to lower the cost of capital in general. Additionally, the practice of share buybacks and capital repatriations leads to rising share prices. In January 2008, major U.S. companies used 40% of their cash flow to buy back their own shares (ibid.: 604).

The metaphor of a "central nervous system of capital", employed by Tony Norfield to characterise the current financial system, correctly indicates this development of capitalist economies today. If the principle of capital is an engine of a breathing monster called total capital, then the financial system is its brain and central nervous system (Norfield 2016: Kindle Edition: 168).[5] Furthermore, Randy Martin has emphasised in this context that the financial system is immanent to all three volumes of Marx's *Capital* (Lee and Martin 2016: 190). It plays in the movements of production/circulation and the connected consequential need to anticipate risk as an important element for the reproduction of capital. The financial system (as at the same time a self-referential system) executes, to a considerable extent, the competition, coordination and regulation

---

[5] Here, however, one must avoid the danger of simply equating the economic system with an organism since capital is an immanently antagonistic system that cannot achieve the integration that an organism with its homeostasis can acquire.

of companies (in all sectors). In turn, they presuppose the a priori of total capital actualised through the real competition of companies not, for Marx, as a ballet but as a war. Financial capital continuously modulates and provokes the competition of all companies - it is thus an integral part of the capitalist economy and not a cancerous ulcer that a doctor removes in order to restore the healthy body of capital.[6]

For Norfield, the financial system's operations are by no means limited to the multiple strategies of banks, investment funds and other financial institutions. Instead, they affect the capitalist system and its enterprises as a whole since industrial and commercial enterprises must continuously carry out a multitude of financial transactions. Thus, internationally operating companies use private banks to obtain needed currencies to buy imported commodities or to exchange profits from their export transactions into local currencies. Companies borrow from private banks in the short-term to secure their cash flows, or they take out longer-term loans to finance their investments. They issue bonds or shares on financial markets to raise money from investors, and they use derivatives to hedge against adverse movements in interest rates that limit their profitability. For example, pending interest payments can reduce purchasing costs of raw materials, IT systems, buildings, machinery and labour to produce new goods to sell them at a profit. Moreover, the net profits of industrial companies are affected by all kinds of financial transactions, from currency hedging to interest rate risk. This occurs mainly when companies themselves invest in financial collateral. The financing of capitalist production and circulation is a crucial aspect of the reproduction of capital on an extended scale.

References

Bank of International Settlements (2013) in: www.bis.org/statistics/extderiv. htm.

Chesnais, Francois (2016) *Finance Capital Today: Corporations and Banks in the Lasting Global Slump*, Leiden.

---

[6] Nevertheless, Marx developed the financial system only rudimentarily as the controlling instance of capitalist accumulation in *Capital*, Vol. 3 (Marx 1998: 432ff. and 601), although he was already fully aware of the following facts in the *Grundrisse*: "In the money market, capital is posited in its totality; there it *determines price, provides work, regulates production*, in a word, *source of production*" (Marx 1986: 206). For more details, see Heinrich (2003: 299ff).

Das, Satyajit (2015) *A Banquet of Consequences. Have We Consumed Our Own Future?*, London.

Heinrich, Michael (2003) *Die Wissenschaft vom Wert. Die Marxsche Kritik der politischen Ökonomie zwischen wissenschaftlicher Revolution und klassischer Tradition*, Münster.

Lee, Benjamin and Martin, Randy (eds.) (2016) *Derivatives and the Wealth of Societies*, Chicago.

Lohoff, Ernst and Trenkle, Norbert (2012) *Die große Entwertung. Warum Spekulation und Staatsverschuldung nicht die Ursache der Krise sind*, Münster.

Marx, Karl (1986) *Economic Manuscripts of 1857–58*, in: *Marx and Engels Collected Works*, Vol. 28, London.

Marx, Karl (1998) *Capital*, Vol. 3, in: *Marx and Engels Collected Works*, Vol. 37, London.

Norfield, Tony (2016) *The City: London and the Global Power of Finance*, London.

Pettifor, Ann (2017) *The Production of Money: How to Break the Power of Bankers*, London.

Ruben, Peter (1998) *Was bleibt übrig von Marx' ökonomischer Theorie?* in: *Philosophische Schriften*. Online-Edition: www.peter-ruben.de.

Sahr, Aaron (2017) *Das Versprechen des Geldes. Eine Praxistheorie des Kredits*, Hamburg.

Wullweber, Joscha (2021) *Zentralbankkapitalismus. Transformation des globalen Finanzsystems in Krisenzeiten*, Berlin.

CHAPTER 2

Capital

2.1 Commodity, Money and Capital

Here we can only give a very brief outline of three categories, which are essential for Marx: commodity, money and capital. These Marxist concepts and their relations have been developed and discussed in detail in our book *Kapitalisierung Bd.1* (Szepanski 2014). Under the aspect of the relationship between the commodity and money, Marx speaks, in the first three chapters of *Capital*, Vol. 1, of the commodity as a *commodity form*. When the development of value itself *is* addressed here at the same time, he refers to the *value-form*. In this context, Marx is then concerned with "developing the expression of value implied in the value relation of commodities, from its simplest, almost imperceptible outline, to the dazzling money form" (Marx 1996: 58). The simple Marxian form of value "a quantity y of commodity A is worth a quantity x of commodity B" indicates the following: (1) Two quantities of material goods are related. (2) These quantities are qualitatively different products. (3) At the same time, it is presupposed that these products are commensurately valid within a specific relation which Marx understands as an equality relation or relation of value, the latter being at the same time the expression

© The Author(s), under exclusive license to Springer Nature
Switzerland AG 2022
A. Szepanski, *Financial Capital in the 21st Century*,
Marx, Engels, and Marxisms,
https://doi.org/10.1007/978-3-030-93151-3_2

11

of value, which, however, must not be understood as an equation.[1] On the question of the equation the following has to be said: the equals sign is both set and simultaneously carried out, thus containing a performative dimension, which takes place through the calculation with regard to an abstract unit of money. (4) The value of commodity A is expressed in the value expression b(a) by the use-value of commodity B. (5) Reversibility is also possible such that a new function a(b) arises (cf. Quaas 2016: 7).

Concerning the last point, the axiom of symmetry, which unfolds the portrayal [*Darstellung*] of the equivalence relation between commodities, proves to be necessary. The positional changes of commodities A and B in the expression of value are at least virtually given, but neither commodity A nor B can actualise themselves in simultaneously both positions (relative value-form and equivalent form).[2] Thus Marx already here addresses questions of measurement, which leads to the following distinctions with respect to the determination of the commodity: there is (a) a use-value; (b) the concrete product, which is understood as the material

---

[1] The problem at this point is that the expression of value, if it is written as an equation, needs some kind of dimensional equality, without which we immediately have to deal with a logical contradiction, because 20 cubits of canvas are not equal to 1 skirt any more than 5 apples are equal to 3 pears. The linguistic formulation explicating the equation "20 cubits of canvas are worth 1 skirt" can also be formulated as follows: "The value of 20 cubits of canvas = the value of 1 skirt", a formula which, however, again expresses nothing but a tautology, because what Marx wants to explain, namely the value, he already presupposes by fixing the equation (cf. Ruben 1998: 21f.). To put it differently, it would have to be shown through the analysis of the simple value form that commodities realise something like an ideal identity in a quantitative way. Putting the equation and the value expression into one seems to really pose a problem here, as long as one does not bring the differential (symbolic) determination of the value expression into play. And one would finally have to show that this equation can only be read against the background of a third party, because purely from the factors of representation and relation the "value of the commodity" cannot be extracted conceptually. Hans-Joachim Lenger has pointed out that already the proposition of identity A = A points to a third, to a difference that precedes the equation, insofar as A has already doubled itself before in A = A and therefore as the first A is at the same time a third, so that identity emerges from the repetition of difference. A is not simply identical with itself, but will have been identical with itself via a detour, with which A as origin or as first is ever already deleted (cf. Lenger 2004: 68f.).

[2] Commodity A takes the position of the relative value form and commodity B takes the position of the equivalent form. The value of commodity A is expressed in the units of the secondary use-value of commodity B, i.e. commodity B already takes the role of the equivalent. Or, to put it differently, its secondary use-value is counted [gilt] as a measure of the value of commodity A, which is in the relative value-form.

bearer of a quantity (commodity); (c) the abstract quantity assigned to the product [*Wertgröße*]; (d) the type of quantity under which the quantity's status is subsumed (value); and (e) the numerical expression of the abstract quantity (price) (Schlaudt 2011: 260).

According to the majority of Marxian theorists, Marx has little difficulty transitioning to the money-form within the analysis of the value-form - from the simple form of value over the expanded to the general form of value. Still logically located before the money form, the general form of value is characterised by a single general equivalent, in which all commodities express their value (they are always in the position of the relative form of value). Money, as far as it represents the general equivalent, is a very specific form of value, namely the form of money. However, the stringency of Marx's method [*Darstellung*] of value-forms, which leads to the form of money, is quite controversial among Marxists. According to the position of Michael Heinrich, which we share at this point, no money commodity is necessary as a value mirror of all commodities. Marx demonstrates that in the general form of value, an exclusive shape of value [*Wertgestalt*] must confront commodities, but this objective figuration need not take the shape of a material commodity, as this would mean to confuse the pure formal character of the equivalent (serving purely as a form of expression), in which the commodities express their value, with the primary characteristics of the commodity which is excluded as the general equivalent (Heinrich 2003: 233).[3]

The exclusion of a general equivalent which functions as money must, in order to ensure the stability of an economy, be constantly repeated and at the same time consolidated. Yet this must be done while the embodiment of money by gold can be safely denied. Rather, one must assume in principle that it is not gold that gives money its value, but conversely, it is money that gives gold an economic value. This also refers to the conclusion that money does not need any reference to a money commodity. The first "function" of money, according to Marx, is precisely that money, as the general equivalent, is the (external) measure of commodities. The measure function of money is indicated here in a medial sense (and not represented by metal money or a money commodity), whereby the abstract measure has to be distinguished from the scale (price) which

---

[3] For Marx, money only becomes a generalised social mediation when labour-power becomes a commodity.

is applied to different entities and contains metric and ordinal differences that are registered qua numbers (Mau 2019: 31–32). The relation of money and number implies here the establishment of a connection between equality (measure) and difference (scale).

For the Greek economist John Milios, money expresses the commensurability of commodities among themselves, without inventing that commensurability (Milios 2002). At the same time, however, money possesses the potential of being immediately exchangeable into any other kind of commodity. Thus the commodity, even before it enters circulation, is already set in relation to money and has, at least potentially, a price (yet it must still be sold to realise its price). The price of the commodities is ideal money. The price-form actualises the distribution of product quantities in the monetary form. Marx, similar to Keynes in this regard, insists on the endogenous character of money, whose significance is by no means merely to function as a universal medium of exchange that mediates between supply and demand and facilitates market transactions by lowering transaction costs. Money is not a veil over real economic processes, but the centre of these processes which could not be maintained without it.

However, the problem of the forms of value is a little more difficult. In order to demonstrate the instability of the economic constitution of form, when it takes place purely at the level of the value-form, Marx introduces, in the first edition of *Capital*, a fourth value-form as representative of this problem. He writes: "It is only in its opposition to other commodities that a commodity turns into the universal Equivalent-form; but every commodity turns into the universal Equivalent-form in its opposition to all other commodities. If every commodity confronts all other commodities with its own natural form as universal Equivalent-form, the result is that all commodities exclude themselves from the socially valid displaying of their amounts of value" (Marx 1976). The fourth value-form, which Marx introduces in the first edition of *Capital* and omits in the second edition, indicates that the derivation of money from pre-monetary forms of value must fail. In the fourth value-form, the commodity takes the place of the general equivalent and excludes all other commodities from the equivalent form, whereas the place of the general equivalent can be taken by any commodity, so that all commodities are excluded from the general equivalent form. Thus the fourth value-form remains conceptually underdetermined like all other value-forms. There exists neither a valid *numéraire*,[4] nor a general validity of money or stability of an economic relationship, which takes place purely through the development of value-forms.[5] Therefore, we should try to find a different manner for resolving the problem of money.

Money has to be understood as something without content (it is non-material; it is therefore rather an un-thing [*Un-Ding*] than a thing, and it exists as a form always also through representations), whereby all commodities and their contents are opposed to it. Thus commodities are not money and money is not a commodity (Bockelmann 2004: 180f.). Commodity and money exclude and condition themselves. *Gleichgültigkeit* of money towards commodities does not mean indifference here, but aims further to the fact that the qualitative variety of commodities is reduced, through their relation to money, to purely quantitative relations among themselves. Commodities are without exception as economic quantities related to money (price) and are validated as equal among themselves exclusively through this relation. The fact that money has no content refers to the point that it cannot be understood as an embodiment of abstract wealth (e.g. as a money thing or as a money commodity). It is rather the case that money remains in all its materialisations a disembodied body, i.e. an abstract unity or an abstract medial form. The material carrier or substance of money is not its most important aspect and can differ. Thus gold, coins, paper bills, numbers and bits and bytes can easily represent money, and this also means that no gram of value is stored in money. But neither is money completely intangible,

---

[4] Already a market with only three participants requires a third, known as a *numéraire* or money, compared to an original exchange with two participants. Circulation, insofar as it helps to regulate the reproduction of a complex economy, which is based on a division of labour, represents one of the conditions for modern capitalist money (which explicitly has an algebraic structure), so that this can mediate a multitude of transactions that go far beyond the mediation of the simple act of exchange (Strauß 2013: 336). Money cannot be derived from isolated, random acts of exchange. If one tries to do so, one implicitly presupposes money and categories that are already involved in the daily use of money. That what should be explained, money, is here already presupposed. Money is always and already implicit in the forms of thought of every scientific model, even if without being recognised.

[5] The significance of money in *Capital* is not limited to the connection between value and money developed in the context of the value-form analysis. As Michael Heinrich has noted, Marx makes a logical break when, after the value-form analysis, he introduces the owners of commodities to explain money, which incidentally is quite correct (Heinrich 2003).

16 A. SZEPANSKI

even if it is only numbers on data carriers. Money without carriers would be meaningless.

So money, as a social mediator, has no content, while all content is opposed to it as a set of commodities. All content here means that commodities are elements of a quotient set, whose property or quality is characterised by equivalence (symmetry, reflexivity, transitivity),[6] a somewhat empty quality which in turn refers to the pure quantitative reference of commodities to money. Despite their separation, money and commodities are always related to each other, whereby the commodity is defined by its relation to money and vice versa (the relation is external to its *relata*). The commodity and money are related to each other in so far as, on the one hand, the one forms a existence [*Dasein*] for the other (but the commodity and money must first be separated in order to transform themselves into purchase and sale, namely from commodity into money and from money into commodity). Yet, on the other hand, the commodity and money are parts of the reproduction process of capital (Marx 1998: 25: 321). But at the same time, the commodity and money are the negation of each other, i.e. money, by its relation to the commodity, is precisely a non-commodity, just as the commodity, in its relation to money, is precisely non-money.

In terms of capital, the commodity and money are always already latent capital, whereby the integration of the commodity and money is established via virtual value which exists in real terms in the components of the commodity and money.[7] The rationale is not thereby absent, but it

---

[6] Commodities, as parts of a quotient set, must always actualise themselves, while value has a purely virtual status. Commodities must be sold, otherwise they have only the status of potential commodities. However, commodities are already priced out before they are thrown into circulation, i.e. they are always in an assumed relation to money, although they are only potential commodities, because they have to be realised through sales, otherwise they are nothing but garbage.

[7] In this work, we assume that value is a paradoxical *un-ject*, insofar as it has the property of having no property (Fuchs 2001: 110); according to Fuchs, it is *quodditas* without *quidditas*. Thus, value cannot be attributed to any essence, subject or object, and therefore, it may only be considered as an indeterminate determinant, which, however, is in turn distinguished from an abyss, or rather a double abyss: that of not being and not being anymore. Value is nothing less than a social relation. We cannot discuss here if this relation can be founded on the concept of abstract labour. In the course of the history of Western metaphysics, which presents the being of existence as primary, this has been given a number of names: God, reason, logos, subject, objectivity, history, substance, will, proletariat, etc. However, tracing back all being to a first principle or to a ground has long

2 CAPITAL 17

is repeated by the effects in a non-representative and incommensurable manner. Commodity and money cannot exist autonomously, but neither is their relation to each other primary; rather, they depend on the special relation of capital and value. Similarly, the transformation of values into prices is not a quantitative but a conceptual matter.

Capitalist money acquires its validity as a marker that refers to purchasing power, inasmuch as money is already "socially" accepted as a algebraic system, a form of thought and as a social fact. This refers to rules and significances that are followed quasi-automatically by the economic actors, and at the same time, money is so desired that it includes the expectation of the desire of others. It is abstract purchasing power, a store of the power of value. Money is thus linked to the promise, if not the certainty, that one will get something, whatever, in return. It is precisely the lack of content or the indeterminacy of money, not to concrete services or commodities, that constitutes its functionality and potency. In a certain sense, it is also characterised as symbolic (the name alone is enough to indicate its social effectiveness), and in history, hardly an arbitrary material, gold, was used to embody it (rarity, necessary divisibility

since been insufficient for (philosophical) modernity. Thus, for example, deconstruction aims at the weakening of reason, more precisely at the abandonment of a final reason, so that at this point a contingency in consciousness arises, which in turn can assume many different transcendentalisms under the rubric of plural or contingent reasons (event, freedom, *différance*).

Value will always belatedly reveal itself, even if capital tries to occupy and offer representations of the future. Therefore, in relation to value, one can always already speak of a "transcendental homelessness" (Lenger 2004: 10) of economics, of its trauma, insofar as it is never certain whether any calculation and planning goals of capitalisation, however differentiated and fractalised, can be retained. Value can only be inscribed in the "time horizon" of the future, of "it-will-have-been"; for only a posteriori can price movements in the future also be subjected to a definitive valuation. Only a posteriori does value jump, does it indicate what it will have been. And at the same time, the non-presence of value is always already tied to a dynamics of futurised and futurising virtualisation-actualisation, whereby there is no guarantee whatsoever that money will realise any purchases and sales of commodities in circulation. And yet, capitalism is constantly about claiming the ubiquitous presence of value, because at every moment, valorisation is supposed to take place everywhere. The so-called law of value, however, is already threatened by risk, by contingency, which tends to eliminate the consistency and coherence of any planning generally, and this even at the level of organisation. Thus not only is the "blind spot" of the economic itself indicated, but also the impossibility of being able to say something definite about value, unless it turns out to be a circling around the unspoken. As an indeterminate reason, value would always have to be thwarted - even before value can be determined, it has already relinquished itself to indeterminacy.

and durability of the material, etc.). Today, however, money exists also as a promise of payment which is written or digitised in the balance sheets of commercial banks, as a promise to accept money in order to pay debts (credit). Bank deposits, too, are not then of course to be understood as commodities, but as specific social relations (Sahr 2017: Kindle-Edition: 500), wherein it must be taken into account that money does not merge with the function of credit, as some credit theorists assume. We will return to this point later.

Money inheres the weak and underdetermined power of a validity (underdetermined, inasmuch as it is in the last instance capital, which causes the power of money; weak, because it represents the capital relation with its validity). Money functions as a reliable social fact within a socio-economic relation (capital as a total complex) that has the potential to integrate any transaction and promise of payment. As such, money realises a kind of objectified social relationship.[8]

By virtue of its objective validity, money includes the potential "to have everything" precisely because it remains independent of the concrete means of satisfying needs and desires. This corresponds, on the one hand, to its validity as capitalist money and, on the other, to its peculiar positioning vis-à-vis (capitalist) commodities. With regard to the former, it is a matter of a very special "function" of representation since validity is not effective in itself, but always for something else, i.e. the validity of money explicates the structure of the representation of "absence", namely of capital and value (Strauß 2013: 129f.). As a part of economic reality, capitalist money realises validity quite explicitly. This is indicated by its convertibility or potential purchasing power (the exchangeability of money for commodities).

Validity is based on the fact that money is accepted by all social actors without exception, or, to put it differently, when the meaning "money" can be attributed to a certain thing in a however rudimentary thought process, which is at the same time a practical execution of computation

---

[8] Money comes etymologically from "to be valid", which this alludes to the fact that it must necessarily acquire meaning, no matter what it means or to which commodity it refers. With every validity, a claim or a kind of influence is indicated; what is valid should not only be observed, but it should also be unconditionally obeyed. The claim can proceed from a theory as well as from a social objectivity like money, whereby the latter asserts its claims "as if by itself". The logical validity of a proposition results in turn from the impossibility to affirm or deny it at the same time. Here validity belongs to a form of theoretical practice.

and calculation (Brodbeck 2009: 334ff.). By using money as a matter of course (calculating, measuring, buying, selling, saving, etc. - all performative acts), social actors have *uno actu* accepted money as money, and that means also its validity. Money cannot be separated from validity. And money must be universally valid, it must apply to all social actors or large populations that exchange money without exception, or, to put it another way, it must be universally common to all, inasmuch they accept money as money and its validity. Brodbeck describes this social reality as a circle that is always already given and quite real: because everyone computes with money and relies on everyone else also accepting money as money, everyone accepts money as money (ibid.). The substance of money is thus nothing but a socially and collectively generated and always already circulating social fiction of the validity of money, which is nevertheless real and compelling (fiction, insofar as money itself has no intrinsic value,[9] and as it solicits belief as a social imaginary sign). The validity of money, which cannot be separated from its meaning, is constantly recreated in a social process in which everyone participates.[10]

Money is recorded in numbers and sums on accounts, existing in these pure numbers. At the same time, however, money is endowed with a very special power, namely the power to be exchanged for anything. As a quantified non-substantial thing, money is the comprehensive power of access to anything. As Bockelmann writes: "It becomes rather itself the measure, a measure in itself, pure quantum as a purely for-itself existing

---

[9] Even if money has no intrinsic value, money can bear value. So it can be said that the owner of 100 € possesses exactly the value that this 100 € represents, for example, certain commodities totalling 100 €.

[10] This does not mean that money is an abstraction, insofar as all commodities have a common property that must be indicated by the general equivalent. Rather, it is the unit of measurement of a recognised and enforced value/price that results from the process of capital accumulation (and political developments). Money is particular, insofar it can represent an asset, and it is universal insofar as it is the representative of a general equivalent. Economist Geoffrey Ingham (Ingham 2020) identifies three main groups of actors - states, private financial companies and households - that struggle over money, its effects and its redistributive powers. The starting point is (a) money as a structural and systemic function in the context of capital accumulation; (b) money as a public–private hybrid of circulating credit-debt relations; and (c) money as monetary capital that realises assets of all kinds, derivatives and future promises to pay as returns. Ingham's theory of money thus analyses money in the context of a fluctuating relationship of three actors, with money being constantly negotiated between these three groups in a web of all-round and mutual dependencies. For Ingham, the current monetary system evolved by integrating commercial credit systems with government monetary systems.

quantity between commodities [...] Money, as the *one* and *pure* means of exchange to be exchanged for virtually any commodity, can itself be determined only *quantitatively*, as a *pure set*. And since it has to stand in for virtually all commodities, it has to appear itself in virtually every possible quantity; it must be able to take all *numerical values* in a freely scalable way. Its results: money as *each one*, exchanged for virtually *all* goods, and therefore as a *pure set* in freely scalable numerical values" (Bockelmann 2020: 215). It would be more precise to use, instead of the category "set", the category of "number" or "abstract unit".

Money inheres the reproduction of an abstract unit: it calculates and measures in the abstract unit, whose model is One, and in this abstract unit of calculation it is measuring. Because it serves as a measure, it cannot be measured again, which means that money has no intrinsic value. (Its value is virtual, a social imaginary which is as real as the capital relation.) It is the unit in which market participants calculate and compute, allowing it to establish relations to commodities. All prices must be expressed in a single currency, which includes the identity of the unit in which is calculated. And it's not only about the unit as an existing entity, but also about a relation that precedes its *relata*, or, to put it differently, the unity of the many (commodities) must take place as a process of social validity (the power of capital), which is in turn accepted by all monetary subjects (Brodbeck 2009: 918ff.).

As a multiplication of this abstract unit, money can take the form of an infinite series of numbers. Money must be distinguishable as a discrete entity, and there must be a kind of multiplicity of this entity. It "functions" thus always also as pure quantity. Money as an entity of abstract measurement is at the same time always related to something, which is to be measured as non-money or commodities. In calculating with money all things are measured in an abstract unit or with the same measure. However, this not only brings forth counting relations in real terms, but rather indicates the structure of quantitative relations, which then become mathematics as an arithmetic form of social thought. The phenomenon "money" is in its execution at the same time the thought form of an abstract unit, the One of a valid calculating system. In transactions, money subjects relate themselves to the validity of the money unit, which thereby appears as a pure number. The act of calculation carried out in turn sets what money is as a unit of calculation. This can only work because money is a social function based on the power of capital and state.

For the One, however, the zero must be added without fail, as Brodbeck has shown (ibid.). The zero first gives the numbers a position; it is an usher that leads to a classification of the numbers in a system of counting that is infinite (ibid.: 921). A number such as 3 receive a higher rank through the zero: 30, 300, 3000, etc. The zero multiplies the social fiction given in the unit of the calculation and grants the digit a higher rank in validity. Money indicates the structures, discovered in mathematics, as a social institution; its form of movement, as will be shown, is that of the "empty more" (ibid.).

Everything that exists in the money economy receives a price through money. The price is the sign/number of money on commodities. The practice of money calculation, which is always also calculating thought (*ratio*, not logic), is thus at the same time the practice of the elementary forms of arithmetic and algebra. The equality of all commodities appears as the identity of a number assigned to commodities in the price. The price has the dimension unit of commodities/unit of money. On the one hand, the money units must consist of elements of the same kind (numbers; abstract number of money units or pure quantity); yet, on the other hand, the commodities to which one refers the number of money must be already measured with special measures (e.g. weight). A measure here unites number and unit of measure. In the price, therefore, measurement is implicit. Calculating in money, relating money units to commodity units, is a very elementary measuring process. In this process, the quality of the commodity is abstracted as a general rule, so that for the thought of calculation, only the numerical value with reference to the monetary unit counts and is valid. Money is a kind of a measure, which is not measured by anything else, while the measured is a social unit of the multiplicity of products and needs. The measuring of products in money, which is the consummation of calculation, establishes this unity in the first place. The measuring, however, is not one of products as of their social or inner nature, no matter whether one assumes abstract working time or its use as intrinsic value, but is based on an act of social power that produces validity.

When Marx speaks of money as a "social relationship", this means that money has already achieved a supportive stability, a high degree of trust and acceptance and, at the same time, a high degree of distribution within the capitalist economy so that it is generally accepted, desired and acknowledge, or, to put it another way, that it has an inherent deep network quality that refers to comprehensive and yet fragile and, simultaneously, interdependent socio-economic relations and for this very reason plays an important role in the reproduction of the capital economy. All these monetary relations can only occur if there exist already large populations engaged in activities of exchange, which cannot occur at all without money. These populations organise themselves by means of money.

In order to be considered capitalist money, which is much "more" than just a numéraire, i.e. to which the excess of capital is already inscribed and which is thus related to deep money and capital markets, a highly developed and densely networked payment and credit system must be available, so that all money transactions, credits and promises of payment can be efficiently processed and, in particular, instructions for future payments and promises of payment (capitalisation) can be realised. Capitalist money does not have to have a 100% stable value standard as a measure (value standard is not equal to value), but the value standard must not be too volatile either, otherwise its asset protection quality or its function for credit becomes problematic (inflation/deflation). Therefore, private capitalist and state-owned institutionalised safety structures are necessary. These are economic-political ensembles that can convert assets into central bank money or into assets with higher collateral. The more the promise to hold an asset on par is secured (without loss of value), the higher the asset is in the credit hierarchy. These assets are almost as liquid as legal money.

A capital system, which is characterised by the differentiation into credit-financed capital investments, fictitious and speculative capital, needs a relatively stable valuation standard, which is related to money as measure and to the ability for transmission of money (means of circulation, in which the measure is practically realised), whereby a number of further monetary "functions", which only makes sense in a capitalist social structure, have not yet appeared - value storage, means of payment or repayment of the credit, withdrawal of the money supply as treasure, money as capital, etc. (cf. Bahr 1983: 406).[11] But money does not have, or it does not fulfil, however, a function that could be ascribed to it by a purpose outside of its social relevance; rather, it *is* a social function.

---

[11] The amount of money is determined by its "function" as a means of circulation and payment (Marx 1998: 443–444). Additionally, money is a legal means of payment in the sense of a general debt claim. As a means of payment, it is a generalized credit-debt relationship expressed in an abstract unit.

And function here is nothing else than the process of producing social relevance in a capitalist economy. This allows us also to understand how money could become an end in itself (Brodbeck 2009: 342).

What financial theory adds to the money functions is that in the money markets and capital markets, money serves as a measure of the gap between the liquidity or price of an asset and its liquidation value (monetisation of the asset), a gap which is measured by money. In general, the financial markets have the property of being liquid in so far as there is a pricing of assets that need not be immediately converted into money. In the event of a financial collapse, there is simply not enough money in the market to realise or liquidate all assets, or, to put it another way, not all debts can be repaid. Approximately 97% of the "money" in the UK economy today circulates exclusively in the financial sector, while only 3% is paper money and fiat money (the latter is lent to companies and individuals operating in the so-called real sector). The capital economy could not be kept sufficiently efficient without ensuring adequate and at the same time flexible operationality of all these monetary functions briefly mentioned here.

The validity of money also always marks a separation of money from commodities, whereby money is open for a development which aims at multiplying as a primary potency. This potency for multiplication is not given with exchange as such or in the circulation of money, but presupposes the capital relation. We are no longer talking about money here, but about money as capital. On the other hand, the potency for the multiplication of money lies also in the dynamic structure of the acts of exchange themselves. We are here, at a logical level, in a circle which is that of capital itself. Whoever buys a commodity loses his money and is thus forced to obtain money again in order to be able to buy on the market. Thus, the desire for money is immanent to the act of exchange. In this immanence is the potency of a striving for more money, for more of the abstract unit. The formula that describes the simple act of exchange, commodity-money-commodity (C-M-C), must therefore always linked to the Marxian formula M-C-M', whose process of multiplication must be always subjected to private ownership.[12]

---

[12] Brodbeck writes: "As with other forms of money, it is to be found in the structure of the use of money itself. Money is a transitory medium. It functions as a socialization of services and needs only, if money owners spend it again and again to acquire products. The state of temporary money-lessness is therefore part of the use of money. It is true that

How can this be justified provisionally? Money intrinsically possesses no value; rather the "value" of money consists in nothing other than the presence of the capital relation, which, according to Marx, can be described with the formula M-C-M'. (The "value" of money as capital consists precisely, as far as its optionality is concerned, in the fact that capital offers the possibility to hold money either as cash or to use it as a security, especially the use for industrial investments or for speculation.) The social relation of equality (the tautology of M-M), and at the same time the purely quantitative difference (M differs from M' purely quantitatively), forms the "substance" of capital, which Marx develops in Capital conceptually as the processual valorisation of capital. Value is now to be understood as virtuality, which coheres in the relation of capital.[13] Capital as capital (as an end in itself) can only function as a spiral-circulatory movement if it dominates the capitalist sphere of production and integrates it into the monetary circulation M-C-M', and if it functions primarily as monetary capital implemented in the capital relation itself. The extraction of surplus value in production constitutes a necessary condition for this movement.[14] Or, to put it another way, the production of surplus value cannot be understood without circulation, but it cannot be reduced to it and to its result. When you only look at circulation, you have the following problem: either equivalent commodities are exchanged and nothing is added, or the non-equivalence is compensated over time,

there are many ways to reduce the insecurity inherent in it – money hoards are the most common among these ways for those who can spare money temporarily. But sooner or later, everyone is forced to enter the market, to offer services or products (labour-power), for which money is acquired in return. The function of money itself as a dynamic means of socialization thus brings about the striving for money again and again. If one looks at the uncertainty associated with this process, one sees in it an endlessly renewed impulse to want to obtain money" (Brodbeck 2009: 321).

[13] Marxist theorists often pretend that the concept of capital is in actu a conceptual process and an economic reality. One thinks of the term "real abstraction", which not only operates as a kind of reflection theory, but also underestimates the independent virtual-conceptual dimension of capital/value. At the same time, it must be assumed that economic quantities are not defined in the concept, but only in the sign systems and algebra of calculation as real, and as such they have a very real effect on economic processes.

[14] In Marxist theory, value and money cannot be defined independently of capital; rather, they are contained in the capital concept *sui generis*. A monetary theory of value is thus always already a monetary theory of capital. Value and surplus value are not essences, but specific socio-economic relations that can only be expressed and measured in prices and profits (causality through relations).

because a seller, who sells a product at a higher price than the product is worth, simultaneously acts as a buyer and loses in an unequal exchange what he has gained. To understand capital, there must be something that is neither money nor commodity, but always both (as a transitory stage); that is, that capital is simultaneously inside and outside of circulation, and latter indicates that it is processed in production. That is the process of industrial capital and this leads Marx to an anomalous commodity, namely human labour-power, which, if consumed in the production process, generates surplus value. For Marx, the wage-labour relationship is the most important characteristic of capital. The capitalist enters the market as the owner of money, with which he buys means of production, raw materials, energy, etc., and hires labour. In the production process, these commodities are consumed productively to produce other commodities (output) that exceed the value of the input commodities.

Capital is set as a quasi-tautological relation to itself (equality), so that only the quantitative difference M-M′ counts, i.e. the multiplication (of money): since capital has the absolute capacity to set itself as an end in itself in the process of multiplication within this relationship, it is initially excessive.[15] (With the concept of total capital, however, the extreme/boundlessness [*Maßlosigkeit*] of individual capital is again put on the leash, insofar as limits are set to individual capital by the movement of competition.) The famous formula M-C-M′ means that the surplus is injected as a quantity into the tautological chain M-M. The hyphens of the formula M-C-M′ refer to a special kind of mediation, which for Marx is given with the purchase and use of a specific commodity by capital in production, namely labour-power, which actualises the difference between its exchange value (its reproduction costs for living) and its use-value (which consists in producing a surplus value reified in commodities, which goes beyond its reproduction costs) in the production process as labour. With the realisation of the produced commodities in circulation, as in the formula M-C-M′, more money exists than at the beginning.[16] The process of which money realises

---

[15] Money is not equal to capital; it functions as monetary capital precisely when it is implemented in the comprehensive capital relation and its circulation movements (money capital, commodity capital and productive capital). As such, money capital is to be distinguished from interest-bearing and fictitious capital.

[16] A conceptual distinction between capital and capitalism must be maintained. Capitalism is to be understood as - from an economic, political and cultural point of view - a

more money thus requires production, in which capital extracts surplus value from labour (labour-power creates more value than is necessary to reproduce it).

From the start, surplus value should be discussed as a result of a non-simultaneity in simultaneity, insofar as the use and the exchange of labour-power interlock here as the a-symmetry of a symmetry (Lenger 2004: 309). Equivalence exists, because labour-power is paid at its exchange value and commodities are sold at their exchange value, whereby asymmetry is added, which is redeemed by the exercising of labour-power, whose use-value is responsible for the production of surplus value, insofar as its use in the production process generates a greater value than it itself represents as exchange value. It is from this differential between Yes and No that surplus value erupts, emerging as asymmetry-in-the-symmetry. This is the concept of industrial capital. However, even here one still refers affirmatively to the Marxist dogma that understands surplus value exclusively as the result of the exploitation of living labour-power. Alternatives to the various Marxist positions are offered, for example, by the economic

heterogeneous historical formation, indeed even as a world ecology of capital, power and (re)production in the web of nature (cf. Moore 2015: 84ff.), which is, however, essentially determined by the production and circulation logic of capital. In addition to the dominant mode of production of capital, capitalism also includes non-capital-determined modes of production, be they neo-feudal, informal, slum-like, corrupt, purely need-oriented and criminal economies, but also cooperative economies that are only partially or not at all linked to capital (only about 40–50% of all work performed worldwide is directly subject to the capital relation; cf. Rendueles 2017).

Capital, on the other hand, we regard as a conceptual-semiotic and algebraic category or as a differential system whose cycles of production, allocation, distribution and circulation follow specific immanent rules and "laws" that keep it in balance as it throws itself into crisis (imbalance and turbulence is the "normality" of capital). It is here not a matter of confronting ahistorical laws with historical contingent events; rather, agents and laws exist in a multidimensional structure of influences, whereby the structure is hierarchically ordered, which means that certain forces, such as the profit motive, are more powerful than others. The resulting systemic order is generated in and by continuous disorder, and the latter is intrinsic to economic processes. If order cannot be equated with optimisation, disorder cannot be compared with the absence of order. For Anwar Shaikh, a wide range of economic phenomena can be explained by a small set of operational principles, while current events circulate around centres of gravity that are already in motion. This is what Shaikh calls "the systemic mode of turbulent regulation", whose characteristic expression takes the form of the repetition of patterns (Shaikh 2016).

Capital and its own model of capitalisation functions, so to speak, as the motor (inseparable from social relations) of the formation of "capitalism", in which the economy, in the last instance, determines all other areas such as politics, culture, art, science, etc.

analyses of Bichler and Nitzan who, in their book *Capital as Power*, focus less on the industrial accumulation of surplus value and instead clearly bring to the fore the monetary calculation of capitalisation, i.e. the calculation (discounting) of a present value (of an economic unit) of profits, which are expected in the future (cf. Bichler and Nitzan 2009: 188f.).

Capital has to be understood as a specific social relation which is expressed in the spiral movement of an increase of money,[17] whereby its only sense as a moving relation, leading from money to surplus money, resides in the differential quantity; or, to put it differently, this relation is about a unilateration, which is capable of quantitative addition.[18]

Capital must satisfy the determination of the pure quantitative surplus, which however, always remains scarce; or, to put it another way, scarcity is here only motivated by the surplus, and this precondition generally distinguishes Marxist theory from all other economic definitions of scarcity (infinite needs versus limited commodities) - and even from the more experienced system-theoretical definitions in the wake of Luhmann, in which scarcity is presented as an economic artefact with which access to something makes further access to something less likely. Instead, within the capital relation, accesses make further accesses possible. To put it another way: capital *is* axiom (and process), which signifies that the meaning of the relation M-C-M′ first of all contains a more [*Mehr*] that is always lacking (Schwengel 1978: 294f.). The presupposed significant (money), to express it linguistically (without, however, proposing a structural linguistic capital theory), points to an invisible signifier (surplus), which is indicated in further surplus-containing significants (M′). The signifier/surplus, which is contained in the chain of significants of (advanced and realised) money and yet remains invisible, is indicated in more and more significants, which represent the signifier of the surplus, meaning that we are dealing with a non-equivalent sliding figure [*Gleitfigur*], described as follows:

---

[17] It is important to note that, according to Marx, products only have a price because they function within the framework of capital relations, as quasi-products of capital. Value and surplus value exist in their effects as prices and profits.

[18] Following Laruelle's "equation" $n = n$, one could speak with regard to the tautological aspect of capital as the qualitative immanent identity of the one-in-one, the capital-in-capital. This by no means excludes the possibility that capital moves in and through differences.

28   A. SZEPANSKI

M M'
M' M'' etc.

Here, one should picture an arrow from M' in the lower left corner to M'' in the upper right corner (i.e. above the chain of the money significants, below the driving forces of money signifiers). It is a strange kind of incommensurability, one which takes place here beyond the mere bourgeois distribution of surplus product. It is not the exchange of equivalents, but the abstract monetary surplus that to be understood as the constitutive functioning of capital. The concept of *Geldmehrwert* causes here *sui generis* the (bourgeois) concept of surplus value, insofar as the former has completely emancipated itself from any content. And this fact implies, as a formal and turbulent sliding process [*Gleitprozess*], a systemic "lack", the "lack" of surplus or the famous boundlessness [*Maßlosigkeit*] of capital, whereby the anticipation of more, oriented to the future, dominates the lack and not vice versa. Such becomes the case that a definition of lack/scarcity based on Lacan's definition of lack or the representation of the economy (which is oriented to the explication of scarcity, whether conceived as contingent or non-contingent) is excluded from the beginning. The boundlessness [*Maßlosigkeit*] of capital (as the anticipation of more) dominates both the lack and absence of lack. In this procedure, capital as an absolute process not only sets itself to itself (as an auto-referential system and at the same time as an turbulent quantum-system), but also its environment and therefore attains its peculiar ultra-stability, which cannot be separated from its ultra-instability (cyclically moving and crisis-prone) (ibid.: 201). Processes of *ultra-stability-in-ultra-instability* (of capital) must be thought of as a super-position, actualised through pragmatism, strategies and subjects of money relations, which are in no way merely observers, but actors within the dispersion in a game of inter-subjectivity. Contrary to the exclusive foundation of surplus value in the exploitation of the living labour force, we also assume the possibility of a machine-driven, algorithmic and generally monetary and financial surplus that arises from the exploitation of differences and quantum super-positions, which flow into the pure addition of more [*Mehr*].

The surplus value of money [*Geldmehrwert*] implies, on the one hand, the differential repetition of the production of surplus value as a quantitative variation and, on the other hand, the self-referential setting (determination) of capital, which, however, does not lead to a fixed result and can only have a definite effect by permanently pushing valorisation forward (ibid.). Here Marx speaks of the "restless never-ending process of profit-making" (Marx 1996: 23: 164). The circulation of money as capital (as an end in itself) it is not aimed first and foremost at individual profit, but is the mode of the restless movement of profit-making. As a settlement, the monetary surplus value [*Geldmehrwert*] is *sui generis* compatible with quantified repetition, which must be expansive for capital. The individual capital does not simply want to realise more money than it has invested in the production process, but it must do it again and again, driven by competition with other individual capitals on a growing and spiralling scale, while it collides with other competitors that do the same. Thus, surplus value is a kind of (invisible) instance and process that "decides" future multiplication, and this takes place through the strategies of profit-driven, price-setting and cost-reducing companies that always try to penetrate the most profitable areas and sectors of the economy, in which they are forced at the same time to advance productivity and technological change.[19] To summarise it briefly: capital

[19] The investment of a (industrial) company is determined by the expected net profitability, which is different from the current net profitability (cf. Shaikh 2016: 607, et seq.). In a boom phase, the expected profitability will be higher than the current net profitability, and vice versa in a recession, so that the two rates will not only fluctuate closely around each other over long periods of time, but tend to balance each other out. Supply–demand ratios always remain related to this development of average profit rates.

In an expansive economic system the growth rate of nominal output increases when demand exceeds supply and at the same time the growth rate of the capital stock increases, output exceeds capacity and capital flows faster into the financial sector if the current interest rate exceeds the "normal" interest rate (ibid.). These processes always take place within the framework of turbulent balancing movements, where in the short term, the relationship between supply and demand can strongly influence various movements, but in the long term, the relationships between capacity and output, between current and normal interest rates and between current and expected profit rates are decisive. This fact synthesises Keynes' remark that demand (the generation of purchasing power) can be relatively autonomous, with Marx's thesis that capital accumulation is always dependent on net profitability and that expected profitability is always dependent on average profitability, and that current capacity utilization fluctuates around normal utilisation. The level of savings and investments (the savings rate is linked, but unequal to the investment rate) depends on the interest rate and the amount of output, whereas the interest rate is determined by the profit rate, according to Marx (ibid.). Even a temporary increase in the profit rate will increase the level of output and employment. This is the Marxist answer to Keynes' theory of the multiplier (ibid.).

In these processes, the expectations of economic actors effect current prices (which influence the economic fundamentals), while those expectations are also subject to the movements of current prices and economic fundamentals. The current prices oscillate in

30 A. SZEPANSKI

involves the settling *and* repetition of turbulent processes of quantitative multiplication. Settlement implies the destruction of any fixed result *qua*

a turbulent manner around values understood as centres of gravity. It is to be assumed that the future is not based on the stochastic reflection of the past, but is non-ergodic (ibid.: 446). Nevertheless, expectations can by no means autonomously generate economic reality; rather, the gravitationally oriented centres of capital, which are determined in the last instance by the movement of the general rate of profit (and the mass of profit), continue to function as the decisive regulators of current economic events, so that boom phases always end in recession, and vice versa.

In Marx's simple macroeconomic model, the accumulation rate (growth rate of capital) is related to the expected net profit rate (expected profit rate minus interest rate), and the savings rate refers to the difference between investment and savings. In the short term, the interest rate will increase if the financial difference is positive, but in the long term, the financial situation of the companies will correlate in particular with the equalization of profit rates and the normal interest rate will correlate with the price level and the normal profit rate. Furthermore, bank credit offers the possibility that the expenses exceed the given income of a company, since banks can generate new purchasing power, so that investments grow faster than savings and consumption grows faster than income. For Shaikh, however, the profit rate remains the lynchpin of the profit-driven capital system, although the strategies of banks can massively influence the relationship between the expected and current profit rate, supply and demand, and output and capacity (ibid.: 626ff.). In 2009, net investment as part of the capital stock fell to its lowest level since the end of World War II and even the nominal capital stock showed a downward trend. Although there was a slight recovery thereafter, the level remains below the historical average and has fallen slightly since 2015.

Shaikh sums up the movement of an individual capital: competition is the war of all against all (ibid.: 333). The naming of competition as a war contains the implication that every competitive enterprise has to worry about tactics, strategies and estimations of its investments also in the future, so that one can therefore neither assume a normal profit nor introduce interest purely as a part of the costs. The real competition between companies generates specific patterns and samples: the prices set by the different providers in the same industry roughly equalize - measured by the mobility of customers - and the profit rates related to new investments are also roughly equalized in the different industries - measured by the mobility of capital, which *sui generis* aims at higher profits. Both processes involve movements around a corresponding, common centre, while there is not only competition shaped by the movement of prices, but also competition based on power, which is carried out by companies in their function as political-financial actors, for example, by carrying out industrial espionage, the takeover other companies, the negotiation of special alliances with the state, poaching personnel, etc.

Companies are *sui generis* price-setting organisations, which must orient their prices with those of the price leaders in the sector. Extra profits generated in a sector stimulate the adaptation of the most efficient methods of technology by insiders and outsiders, while new companies tend to undercut average prices, thereby eliminating the extra profits in an industry. This competitive behaviour of companies also indicates that there are significant differences in the costs of each company. The companies with the highest productivity work with the most efficient technologies, although there is always a certain range of

2 CAPITAL 31

a potentially circulating structure (virtualisation) and repetition implies the commitment *qua* a potentially fixable circulation (actualisation). Both settlement and repetition are *sui generis* bound to the goal of achieving more | *Mehr* |.

In the analysis of capital, a virtual simultaneity, or a super-position of commodity, money and capital (and monetary capital), must be assumed from the beginning in relation to the a priori of total capital. Commodity and money, if they are understood as integrative "functions" of the capital process, where the starting point of money is at the same time the point of its return increased by a surplus, are to be understood as commodity capital and as money capital (Marx 1998: 321). This super-position is always already present in the primary functions of money - they overlap and are intertwined with the increase of capital. As Frank Engster writes: "Monetary functions are developed linearly in capital, but the first monetary function (measure) enters through its second as a medium of exchange, and both are, as it were, overlapped by the capital movement M-C-M′ and are included in it" (Engster 2014: 159). Money as money, money as capital and capital as money are intertwined, but also differentiated. Money "as such" is always potentially capital. Under certain conditions, insofar as it serves as a means of exploitation, it actually becomes capital. Finally, in the process of reproduction, capital passes through a cycle in which, in addition to the commodity form and the form of productive capital, it also assumes the money form, As such, it is only one moment in the capital cycle, capital as money.

To consider the limitation that Marx, like any other writer, must make - if one disregards the poetics that make non-linear writing possible - is to always think during reading on the linear process of the representation of the category of capital, the terms simultaneity and superposition. To go further and put it even more sharply, the three volumes of Capital should be quasi-read backwards, and thus not begin from the commodity-form or the money-form, both of which are often enough understood as germinating seeds (the dialectical rise from the abstract to the concrete), but

---

technologies in a sector. Changes in relative prices can usually be explained by changes in relative productivity, whereby the latter is stimulated by technological change. The necessity to sell commodities at a price independent of one's own current production costs requires the increase of productivity through technological innovation, with which more or cheaper products can be produced with the same amount of work.

32   A. SZEPANSKI

from the total capital, the quasi-transcendental total process of the reproduction of capital. In this process, the individual capitals must necessarily comprehend, in the first place, what is objectively given[20] - namely, they must replicate the a priori of surplus value production that is given by total capital, and at the same time, they must affirm their mutual dependence and comprehensive networking in and through competition, and this under the exclusive condition of having to achieve at least an average profit rate and/or to realise a sufficient mass of profit.[21] The reproduction process of total capital overlaps, as a genuine macroeconomic category, the regulation of the reproduction processes of individual capitals, which are now further determined as merely integrating and mutually complementary movements. But the total capital is itself not a real economic magnitude, but a real virtuality.[22]

If capital has the capacity to set itself as an end in an excessive, growth-oriented and spiral-shaped movement (the circle is a special case of the logarithmic spiral, namely a spiral whose growth is equal to zero) - the starting point here is in a certain sense the end point and vice versa - then, as a sui generis monetary process of circulation (capital in its universality), capital dominates the process of production in order to integrate it into the primary "monetary circulation and distribution" M-C-M′ (cf.

[20] We do not presuppose the concept of objectivity in order to naturalise it, but only to explain it, and this also means in no way neutralising the social work that is demonstrated by the strategies of agents and companies, risk management and class struggle. But we must assume that most corporate and individual strategies ensure the reproduction of the economy and re-objectify its forms, with only proletarian class struggles and riots being able to truly destabilise and undermine the objective economic process.

[21] Marx had originally insisted on publishing all three volumes of *Capital* at the same time. The sequence of publication of the volumes (the second volume was published 18 years and the third volume appeared 27 years after the first volume) has had an influence on the reception of *Capital* to this day that should not be underestimated. Of course, by the time the third volume was published, the first volume had already been discussed and strongly popularised through several introductions, which in fact gave the impression that the first volume already contained all the important categories for determining capital: commodity and money, value and abstract labour time, proof of the exploitation of labour-power despite the exchange of equivalents, the analysis of capitalist productivity, etc. The important definitions and categories thus seemed to have been developed by Marx already early as Volume 1 of *Capital*, and they related in particular to the analysis of capitalist production, while later in *Capital*, Volumes 2 and 3, Marx apparently dealt only with extensions and special problems.

[22] The determinations of economic forms, which designate the characteristic qualities of capital, are general determinations of capital or determinations of capital in general.

Sotiropoulos et al. 2013: 43). It is worth indicating here that we do not understand capital as a subject or as an automatic subject (it does nothing). The subject is, as Nietzsche said, inscribed in the grammar of language as a culprit, and is difficult to overcome. Production, allocation, distribution, circulation and productive consumption, in terms of their integration (both structural and temporary) into the general circulation of money-capital, must therefore necessarily be considered as "functions" of monetary capital (and its metamorphoses, as phases, aspects and moments.

In *Capital*, Vol. 2, Marx assumes three cycles of (industrial) capital, namely monetary capital, productive capital (constant and variable capital) and commodity capital, describing the entire, comprehensive and general cycle of capital in the process formula $M - C \ (PM, LP) \ldots P \ldots C' - M'$. In addition to the production time (P), this cycle comprises two special phases or parts of circulation, namely the preparation time (M-C) and the realisation time (C'-M'). The entire process of the circulation of capital Marx calls, with regard to time, "turnover time" [*Umschlagszeit*]. Marx therefore uses the term circulation not only for the two phases of the sale and purchase of commodities, but also for the entire and general process of (monetary) capital and its turnover which also integrates production. With respect to the latter, Marx speaks of the total circulation time of a given capital (Marx 1997: 156). The entire and general circulation of capital is at first the circulation of monetary capital, in so far as this structures, represents and integrates the particular circulatory movements, or more precisely, the comprehensively spiral movements of capital, just as it also implies disturbances and turbulences within the cycles, in so far as capital itself functions as a centre that is ever shifting (Marx 1997: 31ff.).[23] The general formula of the monetary circulation of capital is the primary process of the capital economy, which constantly accompanies and includes the production of commodities as the production for profit and the production for the circulation of capital. Although monetary capital is also a moment of the entire reproduction process of capital,

---

[23] Marx describes the co-existence in the mediation of the cycles first and foremost in their juxtaposition, although he comes to the following conclusion: "Co-existence is itself merely the result of succession" (Marx 1997: 109). This remark alludes to the temporality of capital movements, but co-existence and succession should be determined simultaneously, and this includes some difficulties for analysis, which we cannot more deeply however go into here.

once capitalisation has been set as the formation of fictitious capital (for Marx, the most developed form of capital), then in relation to it all, qualitative differences between industrial and commercial individual capitals, their production processes and their commodities are erased. Marx writes: "And all capital is, according to its expression of value, monetary capital" (ibid.: 406). Debt capital or equity capital in its monetary form is also the motor for industrial companies which buy commodities (means of production, buildings, energy, raw materials, software, etc.) and rent labour-power, so that products enriched with surplus value can be produced and, if possible, realised so that it comes to a new formation of money capital. Machinery, energy, products or production processes are not capital in themselves.[24] Marx has shown that the above formula is the decisive expression of all economic relations according to capital, and this of course includes production, but which serves as a purely functional process, a process for producing profit. Capital always already binds the production process to its monetary metamorphoses or rather to the (monetary) total circulation, i.e. production is to be understood as a function, part and a phase of the general circulation of capital, whose general form can be described by the following formula: $M\text{-}C\text{-}P\text{-}C'\text{-}M'$.

Accordingly the logic of capital is valid a priori for every individual capital. And under this aspect every capitalist corporation has to be considered equal to every other, and this equivalence refers to the corporation as a structural–functional "place" of capital, whereby every capitalist structurally acts, on the one hand, as a kind of trader who buys commodities with borrowed money or as an owner of money (input of the corporation) in order to sell a produced output for profit, and, on the other hand, as a manager, who balances, monitors and coordinates the production processes in order to make them more efficient. Prices are set in a company not only to achieve a monetary output higher than the

---

[24] The assets or the capital of corporations (non-financial and financial) consist of tangible assets (capital equipment and real estate) and financial assets, to which stand opposite loans and shares of other sectors, and from this difference results the net assets. In recent years, financial assets have grown faster than fixed assets, especially also in the case of non-financial corporations, where financial assets have at times been larger than tangible assets (normally more of a characteristic of financial companies). The growing importance of financial assets is most evident in the asset structure of financial corporations, whose gross assets tripled, but which also had a rapidly growing debt, so that net assets grew much less.

monetary input of a given period, but to realise at least an average profit rate in the market (and a sufficient mass of profit).

If one now extracts the most important cycle from the permanently running capital metamorphoses of money, commodity and productive capital, namely the movement of money capital itself, then at least two capital-subjects are present in it. The place of capital is occupied twice, namely by the money capitalist and the functioning capitalist, so that in the analysis of capital (relative to the money capitalist), one cannot abstract in the first place from the existence of interest-bearing capital or credit. (Embedded in the differentiated capital-subject is always the pure action of the money-subject, the striving for an abstract *more* of a presupposed money.)

Marxist economists from Greece have developed the following diagram (Sotiropoulos et al. 2013: 8):

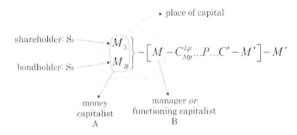

The money capitalist (A) is the owner of money capital and/or creates credits, i.e. advances abstract promises to pay, securities and debts (shares, bonds, securities, etc.). If specific transactions and/or the transfer of promises of payment to the functioning capitalist (B) take place, then these include the contingent promises (contingent, despite the provision of securities) of the latter, that payments will be made in the future. So the right is transferred to the functioning capitalist (B) to use the money capital (M) of the money capitalist (A) under specific conditions (e.g. payment of interest and repayment of the loan) for a certain period. If a corporation is listed on the stock exchange market, then the functioning capitalist (B) corresponds to the managers of the corporation and the money capitalist (A) corresponds to the legal owners (besides the lending banks). The functioning capitalist (B) uses the money (M) as money capital to buy the necessary means of production and raw materials, to rent labour-power and to organise the production process with the aim of generating profit (ibid.).

This has the following consequences: (1) The places of capital are occupied in parallel by the financial and by the functioning capitalists (with which we can reject Keynes' morally inspired distinction between a good and productive class of capitalists, located within the companies and directing the production processes, and an external and parasitic acting class of rentiers which seek exclusively for monetary profits).[25] (2) Fictitious capital and speculative capital are forms of capital. Prices here are to be understood as the result of the capitalisation of promises of payment. (3) The financial mode of capitalisation - promises and demands for the appropriation of a future surplus - opens up a terrain in which any and every flow of income and return tends to be placed in relation to fictitious and speculative capital and within these flows can be multiplied. (4) There

---

[25] The notion of the capitalist as a functionless owner, who draws his profit outside of the production process in the form of a pension by taking advantage of the scarcity of capital, goes back to Ricardo's work. Thus, the autonomy of the rentiers from the production process gives free access to the financial markets, profiting precisely by collecting rent and taking possession of a part of the income, which is created in the "real" sphere of production. In this sense, the modern rentier functions as an irresponsible usurer who obstructs even the production and accumulation of use-values by seeking and realising profit exclusively in the circulation sphere (through speculation and appropriation).

Correspondingly in Marxist literature, the formula of capital is often read in such a way that the profitability of capital can be secured by two different modes: a productive mode (M-C-M') and a parasitic or speculative mode (M' − M'', with M'' = ΔM'). Although Ricardo himself does not reach such conclusions, nevertheless he has significantly influenced much of the Marxist literature with his theory of pensions and labour value. If the rentier becomes dominant in the capitalist economy, the thesis is that the productive capacities of "society" are suppressed or sabotaged, as Thorsten Veblen for example says, while the speculative and predatory activities of the financiers will be the centre of economy. However, it must be countered that corruption, the manifold scandals in the financial system and generally the greed of the actors in financial markets are rather the results of an "objective opportunity structure" (Windolf 2017), i.e. of rather routine processes, rituals and linkages, which, however, promote the greed for money and opportunism of the actors.

According to Ricardian-inspired theorists the restless search for profits in financial circulation ultimately still needs the production processes of industrial capital and the exploitation of wage earners. Circulation would ultimately be purely a means of realising and absorbing profits that were previously generated in production or will have to be generated in the future to cover debts. It is precisely this economic situation that would today favour the stagnation and instability of the production of sustainable use-values. This is a position diametrically opposed to Marx's theory of value and capital.

is an increase in credits that are not only created by private banks. Additionally, there is risk management, which can be diversified into solvency, interest rates, liquidity and credit risks at the centre of the financial system and its decision-making problems (ibid.).

The industrial and financial systems possess a whole series of important mutual interdependencies; in fact, with regard to monetary speculation, there is initially no fundamental difference between productive investment and financial speculation, inasmuch as not only the purchase of shares or securities, but every investment in the capitalist production process involves a speculative moment. A distinction must then be made here not so much in terms of the concepts of financial speculation and industrial production, but rather in terms of the instruments, time periods and risks of speculation. (The speculative surplus value is sui generis a value without value; it is the zero point of the value that rises or falls, $+$ or $-$, with both symptoms oscillating around zero again and again.)

Moreover, it can be assumed that today especially all major capitalists are money capitalists. These are not only bankers, who lend to companies, but also rich individuals, who buy stocks and bonds, the directors of large companies, the managers of the big investment funds and of other financial companies. The money capitalists also include the new oligarchs from Eastern Europe, China and other emerging markets, the owners of large software and technology companies and the nouveau riche, who have simply moved up without leaving any significant traces in the history books of their class (cf. Norfield 2016: Kindle Edition: 1498).

2.2   Capital and Total Capital: The Quasi-Transcendentality of Capital and the Actualisation-Virtualisation Connection

For a further explanation of the concept of capital, we refer to French philosopher François Laruelle, who, in his conception of non-philosophy, speaks of "unilateral duality". He generally first assumes that two or more terms and their relations are always determined by one term. This is the principle of idempotency: $1 + 1 = 1$ (Laruelle 2010). The second term and the relation between the first and second term are immanent to the One, or, to put it differently, the second term is the clone of the first term, but at the same time the second term retains its contingency, in so far as the first term does not postulate the second term absolutely, but

38 A. SZEPANSKI

radically. This kind of causality always points to a non-relation between two or more events or relations and not between two or more things.

For a conceptual definition of capital, this allows us to analyse capital in the context of a unilateral "logic", i.e. *analogous to* the figure of "unilateral duality": if the first term stands for the capital relation and the second term encompasses the economic events and relations which are derived from capital, the two terms are not synthesised by a third, as is often assumed in Marxism, for example by abstract labour or value. Rather, the first term (capital in general as "logic" and as relation) uni-laterally determines in the last instance the second term (the third term, etc.) and the resulting relations, divisions and constellations between the terms. Both the second term (standing for commodity, money, production, labour, circulation, credit, forms of capital, etc.) and the relation between the first and the second term are immanent to the first term. This determination *is* the immanent mode or "logic" of capital, where capital in general has to be simultaneously defined as a logical construction and as a relation.

But there is another important aspect of capital, which can be described with the term "Quasi-Transcendentality" and relates to the notion of total capital [*Gesamtkapital*]. We have to differentiate between capital in general (the movement of categories) and total capital. With respect to total capital, the effects of connections between "effect-entities" have to be examined, without referring to an organic or Hegelian conception of totality (we refer here more to Latour's rejection of the relation between part and whole, cf. Latour 2017: 168, without, however, fully adopting his theoretical approach). Rather, the effects have to be related to the concept of quasi-transcendental total capital. Total capital is not to be thought of as a unifying system, but as a determination and, at the same time, as virtual potentiality, so that in respect to the latter it does not follow a plan, not even in the sense of the invisible hand of Adam Smith. A mathematical approach to this conception is the vectorial notation, where the single subsets, as a coordination of a vector x, are written in a n-dimensional mathematical space M' (cf. Quaas 2016: 215). The mathematical notation, however, ultimately remains an approximation, inasmuch as the virtual capacity of capital *sui generis* transforms the mathematical space.

It cannot be concluded from the linear successiveness of the conceptual representation of capital that the first form of appearance - the commodity which, in the opinion of many Marxists, Marx in *Capital*, Vol. 1 demonstrates to be an elementary form, after having previously introduced the capitalist mode of production as an immense collection of commodities in a single sentence - is a primary and elementary abstract form from which all further concepts are dialectically developed. It is rather the case that the decisive concept, as the title of the three volumes of *Capital* already indicates, simply capital, to which all other concepts, terms and categories stand in an immanent, yet not undifferentiated and unbroken relationship, so that the transitions between the various concepts and categories must always be problematised. We can now present the preliminary result in the following manner: unilateral duality of capital = logic of capital = virtual total capital = quasi-transcendentality of capital.

Let us now more closely examine the notion of the quasi-transcendentality of capital or the notion of total capital. Total capital is understood primarily in its transcendental constitution, namely as an a priori settlement to which individual capitals are passively related, inasmuch as they must follow the a priori of total capital and its axioms without exception. At the same time, total capital secondarily comprises the result of effects (the active price-setting and cost-reducing strategies of individual capitals which take place through competition) and even of contingent economic strategies which can always fail. To summarise, capital "flows in a field"[26] (Nail 2018) and it is double folded: first determination (capital) and second determination through the determinate (individual capitals). In consideration of the second moment, we speak only of the *quasi*-transcendentality of capital, whereby it must be added that the effects appear for many Marxist authors as causes (as quasi-causes), and in this lies also the possibility of the misjudgement of economic structures. The quasi-transcendental determination of capital is not a Kantian-inspired subjective transcendentalism, but must be understood *sui generis* as an objective or objectifying (and historical) determination.[27] Here economic events are given or effected, i.e. they

---

[26] Economic events can be conceptualised as relations between stocks and flows, which includes the relation of production (physical products) and circulation (flow of capital and value).

[27] The transcendental is not a condition of possibility because there are always actual processes. Possible conditions are therefore an idealistic abstraction. But the transcendental is also not an empirical condition, since its condition cannot itself be empirical. Otherwise there would be no difference between condition and conditional. The transcendental of capital is not a universal condition but necessarily historical. If a transcendental condition describes the rules or ordering of relations, these are relations of movements, insofar as motion here is neither ideational nor empirical. It is a process by which things and events

are the effects of objective economic structures (given-as-givenness), but this requires always the conceptual analysis of real or empirical economic events (given-without-givenness). The concept of total capital functions here not as a totality or even as a super-organsm, but rather as a setting and historical transcendentality. Moreover, the prefix "quasi" emphasises that there is no availability of structure without a genesis (and a set of contingent actions).

It should be noted that the economy as reality and the logic of theory are not identical, nor can they be so easily divided, since the economist is not an external subject of thought which constructs a theoretical object called "the economy". The thinker and their concepts are always already a part of real economy, in which one has to work, to count and to deal with money. But the discursive-conceptual dimension of the exposition [*Darstellung*] does not coincide 100% with economic reality,[28] which in turn means that, according to Althusser, the analysis of capital must always be based on a theoretically given (an object of knowledge and not a real object), although the economist is always, in its pragmatic dimension, a part of the daily economy of money.

The structural determination of capital is responsible for the transformation of the multiplicity of individual capitals as effect-entities of total capital insofar as they are placed in an economic milieu that exerts a real causal influence upon them. However, the concept of the quasi-transcendental total complex of capital (total capital) cannot be grasped if one does not take into account the war of individual capitals within competition and its correction processes. Competition is here to be understood as constitutive in the sense that, as an important relay for capital, it prescribes a very specific form of movement for individual capitals, within which, on the one hand, they must necessarily operate as functional entities of total capital precisely by actively employing price-setting and cost-reducing strategies, and on the other hand, institute contingent strategies which can always fail. As Marx writes: "Competition in general, this essential locomotive force of the bourgeois economy, does

themselves are ordered. Transcendentals of capital exist a priori, but include emergent material structures, patterns and circulations. For the concept of historic transcendentality, see Nail (2018).

[28] Thus, the term "real abstraction" often used by Marxist theorists can at best refer to a skewed analogy between concept and reality, i.e. concept and reality are ultimately always to be thought from their non-identity, insofar as reality always escapes the concept.

not establish its laws but is their executor. [...] Competition therefore does not *explain* these laws, nor does it produce them; it lets them *become manifest*" (Marx 1986: 475). Marx repeatedly writes that competition is the real function of capital.

The concept of total capital further implies that with respect to capitalist corporations, one must always speak of some (individual) *capital* and insofar as this is conceived as one, whatever it is, it is indicated that it always remains subject to the "logic" of capital, to what, again, the determination by total capital in the last instance refers. It is not only the quality and form of production of the respective individual capitals that is decisive here, but only the fact that each individual capital always already has to follow the axioms and processes of capital, whereby this transcendentality only prevails in the tendency - and "tendency" implies virtualisation (which "relativises" the determination of capital, similar to the movement and countermovement within the law of the general falling rate of profit) which the individual capitals constantly actualise by selling their products. Or, to put it differently, with regard to the concept of total capital, the interlocking of determination/necessity/settlement and virtualisation/actualisation/contingency must always be taken into account.[29] This aspect of virtualisation, which among other things consists in the fact that the realisation of the generated products is never guaranteed for the individual capital, always, in the last instance, remains linked to the aspect of determination. *One could also formulate it with more subtlety: the capitalist mode of production* does not *determine* absolutely - it performs

---

[29] What is at issue in this point is transcendentalism and abstract potency, contrary to Althusser's late philosophical-political determination of the necessity of contingency, which is not a necessity that has contingency, but rather necessity "is" contingency. We won't deny contingency, but rather situate it within an interdependency and relation to determination.

What holds capital together, which always follows the logic of profit, is a normalised quantum reality. Total capital is constituted by very specific interactions, namely those of competition which are placed in a quantum-field. This field of total capital includes virtual states and relations, which are energetic blank voids. The quantum reality of capital is non-empirical and virtual, a hidden reality. An empty and abstract quantum-structure prevails in the logic of capital. In the entities of capital all energy levels are never occupied, which are blank voids, but are quantum realities and effective. Total capital is under this aspect equal to an imaginary variety of formulas or an abstract numerical reality, whose potentiality is intensified by the probability of reality. For this reason, the Schröder equation must be normalised and squared: $\psi px(x, t)$ to the power of 2. This amount indicates how the probability of an individual capital can retrieve a power x at the time t.

42 A. SZEPANSKI

and sets a constituent framework.[30] On the other hand, in economic empirical reality we are always confronted with contingency: economic strategies remain unpredictable. One cannot even 100% predict the results of economic programmes and the actions of corporations and individuals, as economists try to do with their prognosis and always fail. The actions of a monetary subject or of a company even create uncertainty for many other economic actors. An economist can predict the falling prices for a product, but they cannot predict whether a company will not develop a new product, precisely on account of this price fall, which leads to a displacement of the old product and thus falsifies the prediction.

The systemic order of the capital economy is generated in and by continuous disorder: just as order cannot be equated with the optimum of regularity, disorder cannot be identified with the absence of order or with pure chaos. According to Anwar Shaikh, with the terms of Marxist

---

[30] On this point, Robert Kurz also takes a Marx-oriented position when he speaks of the a priori or transcendentality of capital. With regard to the concept of total capital, Kurz writes in his book *Geld ohne Wert*: "The real categories of capital theoretically presented by Marx are therefore from the beginning and at all levels of representation to be understood only as categories of the social whole, of total capital and its total movement as a total mass, which cannot be directly empirically grasped because it is qualitatively and quantitatively something different from the empirical movement of individual capitals" (Kurz 2012: 177). Marx's concept of total capital implies from the beginning the "total process". However, Kurz must be corrected insofar as the concept of total capital is neither a real category [*Realabstraktion*] nor a quantitative category. It is at the same time a transcendental category and a virtuality which cannot be expressed quantitatively.

John Milios also emphasises the importance of total capital. He refers in his book *Rethinking Imperialism* (Milios and Sotiropoulos 2009), co-authored by Dimitris P. Sotiropoulos, to an important passage of Marx, where he writes that "the immanent laws of capitalist production manifest themselves in the external movement of the individual capitals' and 'assert themselves as the coercive laws of competition, and therefore enter into the consciousness of the individual capitalist as the motives which drive him forward'" (Marx 1996: 433; Milios and Sotiropoulos 2009: 114). And as Marx writes further: "a scientific analysis of competition is not possible, before we have a conception of the inner nature of capital" (Marx 1996: 321). Milios and Sotiropoulos correctly conclude that the "immanent laws" of which Marx writes here can only be those of total capital (as social relation and national total capital), whereby the individual capitals appear as fragments or parts of an "external movement" (of competition) and can only take their place within the structure of total capital if they follow the "immanent laws" of capital. The concept of total capital is complex and was first introduced by Marx in *Capital*, Vol. 3. The structural determination of total capital transforms the individual capitals into entities insofar as companies are always already located in a "legislative" economic milieu. In these quasi-causal processes, competition as a specific inscription of the capital relationship into the differential accumulation includes an important "function".

economy, a wide range of economic phenomena can be explained by a small set of operative principles, which means that current economic events revolve around ever-moving centres of gravity that are *sui generis* those of the logic of capital and total capital (Shaikh 2016: 5). Shaikh, who uses here terms of relativity theory, describes these movements as the systemic mode of turbulent regulation, whose characteristic expression takes the form of a repetition of short, medium and long-term patterns.[31] Not only is there a continuous adaptation to averages and equilibria by changing from one state of equilibrium to another, but the movements of capital are in the last instance in a process of imbalance, which in turn are always bound to changing gravitational centres. This includes the system's permanent capacity to adapt to disturbances and extreme turbulences, and, last but not least, to cyclically occurring crisis by raising critical thresholds, expanding the scope for dealing with instability and keeping normalisation processes flexible (cf. Bröckling 2017: 128). The

---

[31] Turbulent regulation and the recurrence of patterns are considered as decisive gravitational tendencies of the economic system (Shaikh 2016: 5). Economic macro-analysis is first and foremost about the determination of commodity prices, profit rates, wage rates, interest rates and exchange rates (ibid.: 1946ff.). These processes have two tendencies: (1) balancing-out tendencies, which are characterised by the restless search of individual capitals for monetary advantages, whose unintended result consists precisely in the elimination of differences, which in turn motivates the pursuit again. While the average wage rate depends on productivity, profitability and on the class struggle between workers and capitalists, the average profit rate depends on wages, capital intensity and productivity. At the same time, the averages are the result of microeconomic projects and the interactions of individual capitals, whereby competition plays the decisive role. Shaikh subsumes both processes under the concept of real competition, whereby the profit motive plays the central role (ibid.: 6); (2) Formative tendencies that determine the path around which the balancing-out movements fluctuate. The second set of gravitational tendencies comprises the turbulent macro dynamics of the system, including processes of growth and stagnation. Here again, the profit motive is the dominant factor that is ultimately responsible for the regulation of investment, growth, cycles, employment and inflation.

The centrality of the profit motive has several implications. (1) A theory of profit and wages must be developed. (2) The role of profitability in real competition must be determined, insofar as all aspects of companies are affected, leading to a theory of price, which is determined by competition, and to the theory of endogenous technological change. (3) The expected rate of profit regulates investment and growth and also determines the relationship between aggregate demand and aggregate supply (ibid.: 6). The decisive factor here is not the actual profit rate of a company, but the regulating profit rate within an industry sector and the profit rate on future investment. Finally, the investment is driven by the difference between profit rates and interest rates, whereby the interest rate is the benchmark for the investment.

resulting economic growth is not only shown in terms of size, but also in the densification and the increase of connections.

The concept of total capital includes not only a structural determination (in a field), but also a dynamic-temporal (and contingent) process. Regarding the latter, through the process of competition in dynamic compensatory movements carried out through specific price fluctuations, the production of average profit rates of the different sectors initially takes place. This must be considered as an absolute necessity, because otherwise the most productive company would inexorably move ahead of less productive companies and form a permanent monopoly, which would eventually eliminate all competition between companies. Marxist theory has attempted to grasp the formation of monopolies with the concept of the centralisation of capital, in which small companies are either eliminated or integrated into large companies, thus reducing competition to the point where there exists a vertical integration of all the production processes in one company (monopoly) or a group of companies (oligopoly).[32] This development has not emerged in the historical course of capitalism in contrast to the concentration of capital, which concerns the increase in the size of a company. Thus, the process of the creation and split of companies always remains to be considered as a consequence of innovation, as the establishment of new business fields and of outsourcing, in which transnational companies separate from certain business fields or outsource elements of the global vertical supply chains. The identified current growth of the number of companies in Germany shows that, despite the recent waves of company takeover, a statistically reported degree of economic centralisation, measured by the share of large corporations or the 100 largest corporations in total economic output, has not increased, but in some cases even decreased. The share of the 100 largest corporations in the net value added of all companies decreased on average from 20% in 2000 to 16.4% in 2010. However, these figures also illustrate which high level has been reached in certain sectors with the concentration of capital, since only 50 companies produce half of Germany's total industrial output. In the sector of financial institutions, the business volume of the ten largest companies alone accounts for 50% of the total volume of the sector.

---

[32] Marx described the monopoly as a special individual capital that succeeds in systematically realising an extra profit over a long period of time; the monopoly is not opposed to free competition, but remains located within it.

Italian theorist Mimmo Porcaro characterises the current phase of accumulation of capital in the industrial sector as a period of "concentration without centralisation", a phase in which few companies grow enormously in size and, at the same time, the competition between these companies intensifies, while weakening all companies nationwide (Porcaro 2015: 24). These tendencies show themselves in the fact that in the developed countries in the 1990s, the most successful corporations were three times more profitable than the average company, and they are currently already eight times more profitable. Every second company with an above-average share of profits comes from the financial or technology sector. At the same time, however, small companies are now established, which, due to their extraordinary technological know-how, can no longer easily be taken over by large corporations. If, however, concentration in the large corporations continues to increase, integration and growth will today occur less through the use of new technologies, but more through the processes of the financial markets and the global supply chains and its financial networks, which in turn means that competition will have to develop in very specific ways. On the other hand, the highly dense financial networks today are characterised in such a way that an ever increasing number of payment promises and payment streams of the big financial companies flow through the networks, while the number of financial companies decreases, so that payment flows are constantly and recursively flowing back and forth between the same companies, leading both to a tremendous complexity and densification of the networks, including a high concentration of owners in the financial companies themselves, but also to a specific transformation of the competition between financial companies, but also between other companies (Sahr 2017: Kindle Edition: 6286).

Financial companies share the ritualised belief that the risks and complexity of their operations are regulated by what they call the "market", and this enables them to apply speculative capital profitably. If, due to the formation of oligopolies, competition in all sectors is weakened and uncertainty is reduced, then it is the task of the financial sector, to stimulate or simulate competition itself. If, for example, in many large stock corporations shareholders are identical, then competition is shifted to the management of corporations. (The networks that currently exist are characterised by a tripartite globalism where it becomes increasingly difficult to distinguish the economic, technological and ecological levels from one another.)

Within the framework of the compensatory movements for the production of average profit rates, each individual capital appropriates a certain share of the surplus value which is produced within a national economy, which, however, is not identical with its own surplus value that is produced in a certain period of time, but tends to be proportional to its share in the total capital, whereby it must always be taken into account that individual capitals attempt with the methods of labour intensification and relative surplus value production through technological innovation to increase the productivity of their labour and capital in order to achieve extra profits over their competitors.[33]

This type of differential capital movement is always oriented towards expected future profit rates. It is necessary here to strictly distinguish between average and incremental profit rates (the profit rates related to the new investment). Only the latter is relevant for the new investment and is adjusted over time by the movement of competition and the mobility of companies in different sectors. The profitability of the older and less efficient production equipment of companies no longer has a regulating power. What really counts now is the coming profitability of new investments (the incremental profit rate), whereby aggressive cost-saving investments are made even if they lower the profit rate of companies in the short term. But it has to be said that attempts to predict future price changes lead to alterations in economic strategies in anticipation of price changes, which, by altering the variables on which the prediction is based, change the real prices. In the objective total complexity of capital certain companies succeed in increasing their productivity in relation to others and thus distribute a calculated "value

---

[33] In extensively expanded reproduction, both the number of workers and the mass of means of production are increased, while in intensively expanded reproduction, an increased productivity is generated by technical and organisational progress and by increased qualification and rationalisation of labour-power. In most cases, it is not the inventors but the first imitators who introduce an innovation into the economy. Today, technological progress in industry tends to reduce capital expenditure in relation to the product, i.e. to the increase of capital productivity. The price of the means of production decreases while their performance increases. A decisive role is played here not only by the reduction in the price of electronic components through economies of scale (increased economies of scale are productivity improvements that result from intensive technology and improved organisation and rationalisation), but also by the use of information technology to increase the efficiency of existing processes, the planning, monitoring and controlling of production, and for the construction of products and plants from standardised modules.

quantum" (production price plus average profit rate) to more products against the previous production methods (the products become cheaper). The more efficient company is thus able to sell its commodities cheaper than the commodities of other companies due to technological innovations (cf. Bahr 1983: 434).[34] The more productive or more profitable company now earns an extra profit for a certain period of time, which remains related to the total macroeconomic value. However, this macroeconomic value cannot be a purely current size of stock (measured by GDP), but has, rather, as a flow figure a virtual-real dimension (virtual here also means that an absolute value quantum of total capital is ultimately not measurable). The calculating economist, however, continues to pretend, as if in a given period a fixed total value sum is produced in a national economy and also realised in circulation and can be clearly measured as GDP. But within a given period of time, the existing proportions (quantities, prices, values) between the companies are constantly shifted by further productions and possible realisations of profits as well as by technological innovations within the framework of capital as a total complex. Only as an ideal type are market values an average of the values created by individual producers with different technologies.

If profit is the central motive of capital, then the profit rate is its most important measure (at least for industrial capital). And if growth is an intrinsic aspect of the reproduction of capital, then the flow of money-capital takes place in the most profitable sectors, i.e. any new capital tends to flow faster into those sectors where the profit rates are higher than average, and it flows more slowly into those sectors where the profit rates are lower than average. This should be understood not only as an aspect of the entry and exit of companies into or out of markets, but also as a process of acceleration and deceleration of the capital flows. In

---

[34] Productivity is defined in Marxist economics in two ways that have different implications. On the one hand, the reduction of socially necessary labour-time through the increase in productivity which has other implications than the growth in the number of commodities produced by a company by a given quantity of labour. The increase in productivity can thus be expressed either in an increased production of commodities or in a reduced socially necessary labour-time. While the increased output of a company implies a material component and measurement, the reduced social labour-time refers to value or price variables. Although in the latter case productivity is not measured in physical entities, this concept for us also seems to be insufficient. We relate productivity to the surplus value in production, i e. to the total income or the nominal net income per working hour. Thus, the index of productivity refers to the quantum that the incomes can buy (wages, profits, pensions, interest) related to a working hour.

48   A. SZEPANSKI

the more productive sectors, the faster influx of capital will, over time, lead to a higher supply of goods, which will tend to bring prices and therefore profits down again, while the opposite will be true in the decelerated sectors. Thus, the realisation of extra profits is also reflected in their disappearance, while the tendency to equalise profit rates streams across all sectors. This is part of an emergent process (which is not consciously intended by any economic actor), whereby profit rates can undercut and exceed the already fluctuating centres of gravity in order to approach the average again in certain patterns (turbulent arbitrage within the framework of total capital). However, the equalisation of profit rates in no way refers to a state of equilibrium, but rather implies repetitive and at the same time turbulent movements of arbitrage around the centres of gravity of capital, which themselves are constantly changing (Shaikh 2016: 260). The average profit rate is thus not to be understood as a uniform profit rate, but as the result of a continuous distribution of profits around the average.[35] This is a result of price formation, not of production. Insofar as these periodic movements of companies, with their upswing and downswing and their circulation and circling around changing midpoints, which are related to the gravitation centres of capital, are driven by the calculation, prognosis and discounting of the profit rates of future production processes, the relevant profit rates that balance out over certain periods of time are those that relate to new investments (ibid.: 254). The incremental profit rates in turn fluctuate around the general profit rates and thus generate new average profit rates, which also in turn

---

[35] In their various writings, Bichler and Nitzan have repeatedly insisted that the functioning, the modes of operation and the strategies of capitalist corporations are not simply to maximise profits, but rather to beat or surpass the average, which is represented by the current average profit rates of corporations in the various sectors (cf. Bichler and Nitzan 2009). Average profit rates are influenced by a set of standard instruments such as loans granted to corporations and their interest rates, but especially by the "matching" of the organic composition of capital, accumulation rates and surplus value rates of companies, which are kept flexible by means of competition. The constantly fluctuating average profit rate may be considered the yardstick for the differential capital accumulation - it is the benchmark which indicates for the companies whether they can beat the average in their industry and other industries with their projects or not. It is this form of capital accumulation, which takes place through intra- and inter-capitalist competition ("beat-the-other") and is deeply inscribed in the social relations of capital, which Bichler and Nitzan call "differential accumulation" (ibid.). Of course, the benchmark also indicates if the economic activities of the companies have been able to provide sufficient social cohesion in various class struggles. Moreover, the dynamics of differential capital accumulation always depend on stable growth rates of the national economy.

fluctuate. Shaikh, in his recently published study *Capitalism: Competition, Conflict Crises*, emphasises that here, however, the growth rates of the profit masses (and thus the speed), and not only the profit rates, must be considered (ibid.: 593).

Accumulation refers to the transformation of surplus value into capital for the purpose of its expansion and exploitation. The (expected) profit rate of companies is central to capital accumulation because profit is the very purpose of all capitalist investment. Therefore, the profit rate together with the profit mass (and their relation) must be considered the decisive measure of the success of a company. The high-frequency trade with securities and currencies has shown that even with low profit rates or profit margins enormously high, profit masses can be realised if the moved sums of money capital are big enough. If the profit mass should be further increased, a decreasing profit rate requires an ever larger capital inflow and new forms of financing. The concentration of capital and its globalisation, as well as the strong influence of the financial sector on accumulation, has here in part their rationale.

The analysis of differential capital accumulation, which is only briefly and outlined as an ideal type here, coincides with what we call elsewhere "actualisation-virtualisation-interconnection" (Szepanski 2014). The term "entanglement" perhaps emphasises even more strongly than the term "interconnection" what happens in economic processes both simultaneously and over time. The problem here consists exactly in the fact that the dimensions of temporality and simultaneity - the problem of the temporalisation of time - has also to be thought as a constant passing (of time), so that simultaneity seems to have no place within time, for which simultaneity is the impossibility of time itself, but always contains the possibility of grasping time in itself (cf. Nozsicska 2009: 291f.). Time is virtuality, whereby differently running times are actualised without ever dissolving simultaneity. Precisely when time is actualised, it remains virtuality - a paradox that indicates the problematic nature of virtuality itself.[36]

---

[36] With regard to the mainstream economists' affirmation of a mathematical derivation of stable market equilibrium, one must always set virtuality equal to actuality, i.e. eliminate the factor of time altogether, so that the processes of realisation of capital (actualisation of the virtual), which here are always those of equilibrium, take place simultaneously and immediately (under the conditions preceding them). The (static) equilibrium theory is a normative standard that eliminates dynamic movement - and this is attempted to be demonstrated with simultaneous equations that imply that all significant quantities of the

50   A. SZEPANSKI

Let us briefly re-formulate the problem of the production of average profit rates in its ideal–typical way (which is important to state here) as follows: differential accumulation by means of the economic Mathem (through the price-money process and its numbers, a-significant signs and methods) orients unequal work, technologically different production processes, different qualifications of workers and unequal working hours within the tendency back to averages, which themselves vary over time. Tendency here also means that there exist constant counter-movements against the production of the average profit rate, which is expressed, among other things, in the search of individual capital for extra profits by means of technological innovation or the appropriation of cheap raw materials, energies and labour (cf. Moore 2015). The process is made first and foremost through money, but it also requires a whole range of other scales, techniques of measurement and a-significant signs/indicators to establish valuations, classifications, differentiations and, in general, accountability within and between companies. The mathematics (Mathem) of economics also possesses an assignative or performative aspect, since not only does it record valorisation processes, whose criteria are efficiency and rentability, but also stages certain allocations. The numerical objectivity, in which the comparisons between different sizes are written, in turn potentiates the competition between the evaluated companies, so that an almost incestuous relationship between differentiation, homogenisation and hierarchisation is created, in which the economic actors are inevitably involved with their contingent strategies. If capital is understood as a total complexity, then the informational entropy, which is inherent in the production and strategies of individual capitals, must necessarily be subject to a reduction that inevitably brings into play the Mathem of economics as a coding of a-significant signs, a formalisation with which the economic actors, by means of the specific systems of mathematics and probability theory, try permanently to correct and simultaneously exploit the uncertainty and elasticity of the various economic variables. This also means, however, that in the last instance, measurements by money take place, which verify that averages and deviations take place (Strauß 2013: 74f.). The mathematics (Mathem) of economics makes measurements possible and at the same

model are the same at the end of a given period as they are at the beginning. From all these equilibrium theories, it is hardly possible to prove crisis-like phenomena, which one would actually have to introduce here as endogenous features (Freeman 2021).

time provides an interpretation matrix oriented towards the measure of the successful market-mediated reproduction of capital. Bearing in mind that the structures of economics (building average) cannot express themselves directly in actualisation, the a-significant signs (math, tables, charts, algorithms, etc.) are necessary so that the Mathem of economy (ibid: 69f.) must necessarily be added to the concept of capital, i.e. (conceptual) capital and its economic Mathem (difference calculus) must be superposed.

From the point of view of individual capital, the economic procedure around virtualisation-actualisation-interconnection can be presented as follows (ibid.: 304f.): Firstly, in the given period $t0$, the production of a certain number of products takes place on the basis of the profit expectations of a company. This process is based on business calculations (quantities, cost calculation, market data, depreciation rates, etc.), which are based on semiotic, statistical and mathematical parameters and variables. Secondly, a virtualisation of the distribution of quantities of commodities takes place, starting from production and pricing, which should then lead to the realisation of quantities of commodities. Thirdly, the sale of products in the period $t1$ presents itself as a triple actualisation: (1) A part of the products is actualised in the given period as a realised quantity of commodities. (2) Only in the existing expectation and therefore quantitatively indeterminate is exploitation in the period $t0$ actualised quantitatively at time $t1$, as if it had already existed at $t0$. In real terms, the actualisation is characterised by a difference between expected and realised price masses. (3) An actualisation of the demand takes place with the limited means of the purchasing power of the masses or other companies in confrontation with the existing supply of commodities. The realised quantity of commodities in $t1$ in turn forms the starting point for adjusted profit expectations of the company for the period $t2$, reflected in changed investment ratios which in turn influence the respective investment and consumption funds. The average profit, which is realised by a company at time $t1$, is related to the actualised surplus value of the total capital at time $t0$, whereby in $t1$ the initially and purely virtual surplus value of the individual capital is locked to the "measure" that the number commodities can achieve in confrontation with purchasing power.

In the context of the conceptual exposition [*Darstellung*] of capital, it is assumed, as if despite its virtual character, total capital is quantifiable, whereby we are dealing at this level with an ever-changing number of actualisations at any given time, because the individual capitals produce and sell in different sequences, rhythms and tempos, ergo the flow sizes and variables dominate the stock sizes (ibid.: 305). The theory, however, continues to proceed as if the total capital as a value quantity at a given point in time (under the assumption of simultaneity) could be quantitatively written and fixed, whereas it must, in contrast, always be considered that a "value quantity" does not exist quantitatively on the total level, but is called up and withdrawn in an immense number of commodity-money transactions (in a period) and in a way, as if total value would just quantitatively exist. As Strauß writes: "The inscription of the differentiating value – and this is the validity of money in all registers, semio-economic value – actualises the virtual distributability of physical quantities [...] The inscription of prices actualises this virtual distributability of physical quantities in monetary form" (ibid.: 307). Production also creates certain amounts of value in a period, which are at the end, as we said, divided up so that the final results *differ* from the immediate results of production; total value cannot be quantified. Further, prices and values at the end of a period are not the same as those at the beginning, which would otherwise mean the economy is in stasis. But this is not the case. If prices would be the same at the beginning and end of a period, they would differ from prices at the start of the next period. As Alan Freeman writes: "But the end of the current period and the start of the next one are the same point in time, so two different sets of prices must apply at once [...] The fundamental difference between this and all temporal approaches is that in the latter, prices change during the period, that is, while production is going on" (Freeman 2021). This analysis, to repeat, concerns the economic processes in the industrial sector portrayed as an ideal type.

We can add here a few differentiations. Jason E. Smith refers, in his book *Smart Machines and Service Work*, extensively to the economist William Baumol, who assumes that developed industrial countries since 1960 are divided into two major economic sectors: the technologically progressive sector, whose production processes involve innovation, high rates of accumulation and large-scale processes, and the technologically stagnant sector (service sector), whose technological structures tend to prevent significant increases in labour productivity. At the same time, it can be precisely the dynamism of the first sector that causes stagnant productivity rates in the second sector, insofar as in the innovative sector over certain periods of time, machines are used that allow a higher output through the use of fewer workers (even if output remains constant, then the use of new machines definitely corresponds to the use of fewer workers), so that redundant workers have to find employment in other sectors, today especially in the service sector (Smith 2020: Kindle Edition: 1251).

Thus, the stagnant sector will tend to increase especially in terms of employment numbers, although income ratios are relatively elastic here. And because productivity in this sector remains low for several reasons,[37] the increase in output here leads to an increase in employment. Ultimately, this development, i.e. the differentiation in the growth rates of productivity, leads to a gap, whereby productivity in the first sector continues to rise, while in the second sector (services sectors), it tends to remain constant, which in turn leads to jobs that are lost in the dynamic sector and are absorbed by the stagnant sector. For Baumol, this trend leads to a growth rate in the economy that asymptotically tends towards zero. Solow's productivity paradox, which states that the computer is everywhere today except in the statistics on productivity, would today have to be corrected to the effect that the rapid computerisation of the innovative sector of the economy has led to declining growth rates in productivity throughout the whole economy.

In his book *Automation and the Future of Work* Aaron Benanav assumes an increasing deindustrialisation in the developed countries of the global North since the 1970s. To support this thesis, Benanav examines the development of productivity as the relationship between output

---

[37] A large number of labour-intensive jobs in the service sector are much less subject to competitive pressure or outsourcing to other countries because they have to be consumed close to the places of production. These jobs are often poorly paid, so there is often no reason for companies to replace these precarious occupations with the use of new machinery, which also takes years to pay off. And many of these jobs cannot (yet) be replaced by even the most intelligent AI machines because of their operational structure, such as nursing which requires intuitive complexity (from haptic to affective), emotional intelligence and dealing with uncertainty. Thus, and this is Smith's focus again, a polarisation between a highly mechanised, capital-intensive and productive sector and a much larger service sector with low productivity gains has become entrenched in developed countries in recent decades.

Smith further points out that the ubiquity of technological tools, such as the smartphone, which integrates telecommunications, shopping, video and sociality in one gadget, in the context of the rise of the big tech companies and the new platform companies, have far-reaching effects on finance, mobility, consumption, etc., but negligible effects on productivity in industrial workplaces. Moreover, there is a deep dichotomy between two separate service sectors; first the business sectors, which are often intermediary and supply products to industry, so service sectors belong to it, and the consumer sectors, which supply products to individuals and families.

and employment. The more output is produced per worker, the higher the labour productivity. For all sectors, then, the growth rate of output minus the growth rate of labour productivity is the growth rate of employment. According to Benanav, if the output of cars increases by 3% and labour productivity increases by 2% in the auto industry, then employment increases by 1% and vice versa. Whether changes in innovation result in job destruction depends on the relative speed of growth in productivity and growth in output. Benanav comes to an important thesis: if output grows more slowly than labour productivity, then the number of jobs will fall (Benanav 2002: 19).

While the growth rates of productivity since the 1970s in the U.S. were relatively high compared to those of output (leading to a decrease in employment growth), this was not because the former grew faster than before (which could be the sign of accelerating automation), but because output had grown much more slowly than before. For Benanav, this decline in output growth rates, as a sign of deindustrialisation, cannot be explained by technological terms alone. Since the end of the twentieth century, one could even speak of a global wave of deindustrialisation, as described by Benanav.

We cannot go deeper into the problems of growth, productivity and technology here. There are at least three main difficulties of the continuation of growth in a capitalist economy. At this point, the following however can be said: an economy that is to maintain a constant rate of return in the long term must grow at a constant rate. A growth rate of 3% corresponds to a doubling period of GDP of 23 years; a growth rate of 10% leads to a doubling of GDP after only 7 years. If the increase of the rate of return has become the general goal of the economy, this entails an acceleration of all processes dominated by the economy. Thus, if the world economy grows at three per cent per year from today, it would approach one quadrillion dollars of GDP by 2100.

Second, economic growth to date is still largely dependent on fossil fuels, and this type of energy is a non-renewable resource, whose cost is likely to increase over the course of the twenty-first century. The issue of possible renewable energy integration will not be discussed here.

Third, private money creation through credit/debt, whereby interest cannot be created through credit, means that there is always more debt in the system than the ability to repay it. For example, if a bank makes a $1,000 loan with 10% interest, it does not create the money to pay that interest - that would be $100. The bank just creates $1,000, not $1,100.

So the question must be: Where does the interest come from? The only possible solution is that the interest must come from the utilisation of capital in the future - that is, there is never enough money in the system currently to pay off all the debt. In this sense, the source of debt as a technology of power for creditors lies in its own permanence.

References

Bahr, Hans-Dieter (1983) *Über den Umgang mit Maschinen*, Tübingen.

Benanav, Aaron (2002) *Automation and the Future of Work*, London.

Bichler, Shimshon and Nitzan, Jonathan (2009) *Capital as Power. A Study of Order and Creoder*, Florence.

Bockelmann, Eske (2004) *Im Takt des Geldes. Zur Genese des Modernen Denkens*, Springe.

Bockelmann, Eske (2020) *Das Geld. Was es ist, das uns beherrscht*, Berlin.

Brodbeck, Karl-Heinz (2009) *Die Herrschaft des Geldes: Geschichte und Systematik*, Darmstadt.

Bröckling, Ulrich (2017) *Gute Hirten führen sanft*, Berlin.

Engster, Frank (2014) *Das Geld als Maß, Mittel und Methode. Das Rechnen mit der Identität der Zeit*, Berlin.

Freeman, Alan (2021) *A General Theory of Value and Money (Part 1: Foundations of an Axiomatic Theory)*, in: https://www.academia.edu/49503297/A_Gene ral_Theory_of_Value_and_Money_part_1.

Fuchs, Peter (2001) *Die Metapher des Systems*, Weilerswist.

Heinrich, Michael (2003) *Die Wissenschaft vom Wert. Die Marxsche Kritik der politischen Ökonomie zwischen wissenschaftlicher Revolution und klassischer Tradition*, Münster.

Ingham, Geoffrey (2020) *Money (What Is Political Economy?)*, Cambridge.

Kurz, Robert (2012) *Geld ohne Wert. Grundrisse zu einer Transformation der Kritik der politischen Ökonomie*, Berlin.

Laruelle, François (2010) *Philosophie Non-standard: générique, quantique, philofiction*, Paris.

Latour, Bruno (2017) *Kampf um Gaia. Acht Vorträge über das neue Klimaregime*, Berlin.

Lenger, Hans-Joachim (2004) *Marx zufolge. Die unmögliche Revolution*, Bielefeld.

Marx, Karl (1976) *The Commodity* [first chapter of the first German edition of *Capital*], trans. A. Dragstedt, https://www.marxists.org/archive/marx/works/1867-c1/ commodity.htm.

Marx, Karl (1986) *Economic Manuscripts of 1857–58*, in: *Marx and Engels Collected Works*, Vol. 28, London.

Marx, Karl (1996) *Capital*, Vol. 1 [1867], in: *Marx and Engels Collected Works*, Vol. 35, London.

Marx, Karl (1997) *Capital*, Vol. 2, in: *Marx and Engels Collected Works*, Vol. 36, London.

Marx, Karl (1998) *Capital*, Vol. 3, in: *Marx and Engels Collected Works*, Vol. 37, London.

Mau, Steffen (2019) *The Metric Society: On the Quantification of the Social*, trans. Sharon Howe, Cambridge.

Milios, John (2002) Theory of Value and Money: In Defence of the Endogeneity of Money, *Sixth International Conference in Economics*, Economic Research Center, METU, Ankara, September 11–14, http://content.csbs.utah.edu/~ehrbar/erc2002/pdf/i028.pdf.

Milios, John and Sotiropoulos, Dimitris (2009) *Rethinking Imperialism: A Study of Capitalist Rule*, London.

Moore, Jason W. (2015) *Capitalism in the Web of Life: Ecology and the Accumulation of Capital*, London.

Nail, Thomas (2018) *Being and Motion*, Oxford.

Norfield, Tony (2016) *The City: London and the Global Power of Finance*, London.

Nozsicska, Alfred (2009) *Die Zeichen, der Automat und die Freiheit des Subjekts*, Wien.

Porcaro, Mimmo (2015) *Tendenzen des Sozialismus im 21. Jahrhundert: Beiträge zur kritischen Transformationsforschung 4*, Hamburg.

Quaas, Georg (2016) *Die ökonomische Theorie von Karl Marx*, Marburg.

Rendueles, César (2017) *Sociophobia: Political Change in the Digital Utopia*, trans. Heather Cleary, New York.

Ruben, Peter (1998) *Was bleibt übrig von Marx' ökonomischer Theorie?*, in: *Philosophische Schriften*. Online-Edition: www.peter-ruben.de.

Sahr, Aaron (2017) *Das Versprechen des Geldes. Eine Praxistheorie des Kredits*, Hamburg.

Schlaudt, Oliver (2011) Marx als Messtheoretiker, In: Bonefeld, Werner and Heinrich, Michael (eds.), *Kapital & Kritik*, Hamburg.

Schwengel, Hermann (1978) *Jenseits der Ideologie des Zentrums. Eine strukturale Revision der Marx'schen Gesellschaftstheorie. Reihe Metro. Bd.1.*, Marburg.

Shaikh, Anwar (2016) *Capitalism: Competition, Conflict, Crises*, New York.

Smith, Jason E. (2020) *Smart Machines and Service Work: Automation in an Age of Stagnation*, Chicago.

Sotiropoulos, Dimitris P., Milios, John and Lapatsioras, Spyros (2013) *A Political Economy of Contemporary Capitalism and its Crisis*, New York.

Strauß, Harald (2013) *Signifikationen der Arbeit. Die Geltung des Differenzianten "Wert"*, Berlin.
Szepanski, Achim (2014) *Kapitalisierung Bd.1. Marx' Non-Ökonomie*, Hamburg.
Windolf, Paul (2017) *Was ist Finanzmarkt-Kapitalismus?*, in: https://www.uni-trier.de/fileadmin/fb4/prof/SOZ/APO/19-019_01.pdf.

CHAPTER 3

Credit

3.1 Credit and Interest-Bearing Capital

If Marx makes a distinction on the general level between credit and money - what Suzanne de Brunhoff claims in her book *Marx on Money* - he does so in order to develop a monetary theory of credit and not a theory of credit money (Brunhoff 2015: 51). One should therefore by no means set credit or debt identically with money, as it is often done in newer heterodox positions, but that money as well as money as capital should be related to credit where money as a means of payment comes into play. Lenders and borrowers must know the amounts of money used for credit, i.e. without money as number being presupposed, the credit and the concatenation of promises to pay (whose counterpart to the promise is trust) cannot be conceived within the capital-economy. At least this is Marx's position.

It must be noted here that credit does not represent money; rather, on the one hand, the credit agreement and, on the other hand, the disbursement of the credit amount in the form of bank deposits or cash are two different dimensions, or, to put it another way, money is recorded as debt and credit (Huber 2021). Credit is thus from the beginning also a legal relationship: while money enters the capitalist economy quasi-blindly, state law must in every case secure it. In the credit system, however, money is given another, quite decisive and qualitatively new

© The Author(s), under exclusive license to Springer Nature   59
Switzerland AG 2022
A. Szepanski, *Financial Capital in the 21st Century*,
Marx, Engels, and Marxisms,
https://doi.org/10.1007/978-3-030-93151-3_3

function, insofar as it is now used as a means of payment to settle debts with debts. Commodities are no longer exchanged directly and at the same time for money, but with credit they are traded against a legally fixed promise to pay at a time after the commodities have been already delivered (Marx 1998: 397). The surrender of commodities and payment can here fall apart in terms of time. Who receives a commodity without immediately paying enters into a debt relationship. A debt relationship is dissolved again by a payment. If one therefore describes money as means of payment, then a function is included, namely to cancel debt with it.

The logic and circulation of credit are different from that of money (as a means of circulation). Even the simple circulation of money is potentially infinite, while credit is a closed circuit, i.e. the terminated flow and reflux of money in its function as a means of payment. Finally, credit is about linking, stabilising, scheduling and expanding promises of payment or relationships of promise (and not relationships of exchange), whereby the money is here integrated into a system of relations of registered debt (Sahr 2017: Kindle-Edition: 3755). Promises to pay imply a promise (by the banks) to accept money in its function as an issued means of payment (debt), as at the same time it is also accepted to settle debt. Credited promises to pay are scheduled (fixed expiration dates) and require continuous payments of interest and repayments.

The analysis of the credit system requires an independent monetary theory of credit. Anyone who enters into a legal debt relationship and grants a buyer a deferred payment, grants a credit. Credit (from Latin *credere glauben*; *creditor*) implies that creditors are confronted with debtors, whereby creditors assume in good faith (trust) that debtors, if a loan is granted to them, would do everything in return to repay the loan and make additional interest payments. Due to the different forms of money, debt relationships can be fall apart in time. The form of money in use today, bank deposits, allows within certain limits to extend short-term debt relations. This is called credit. Whoever temporarily relinquishes a payment and grants a deferral of payment, grants a credit. Debt relations arise incessantly from buying and selling and are thus related to the concept of money. Only by understanding that credit and debt relations arise in monetary transactions can pre-forms of credit in history be recognised.

Let us first examine to Marx's theory of credit. It begins with the analysis of the general form of interest-bearing capital. In contrast to commodity capital, productive capital and monetary capital (three different forms of the reproductive cycle of industrial capital), interest-bearing capital circulates from the beginning and autonomously as capital. For Marx, however, credit itself is the specific form of the unspecific, that is, general interest-bearing capital (Marx 1989: 209). Marx examines interest-bearing capital in its general form between Chapters 21 and 24 of *Capital*, Vol. 3.[1] The credit system, its particular historical functions, forms and institutions in which interest-bearing capital portrays and executes itself, is then only analysed relatively briefly. For the analysis of the modern organisation and functioning of credit, Marx often uses the term "credit system". The credit system changes according to institutional conditions and historical cycles and patterns. In organisational terms, it includes today central and commercial banks as well as the money and capital markets.

The analysis of credit or credit relations is first of all that of the credit system in general, i.e. in Marx's view, this analysis occurs independent of the empirical-historical constellations. Yet, on the other hand, the credit system has to be understood as a constitutive part or as a specific form of the capitalist reproduction process, which is presupposed here in its general form. Capital requires a specific form of interest-bearing capital that is peculiar to it, namely that of the credit system. The credit system is for Marx the specifically capitalist form of interest-bearing capital. Since the reproduction of capital is financed and thus also structured through the credit system, it must be analysed as one of the constitutive elements of the capitalist mode of production. The basic functions of the credit system for capital, according to Marx, are to transform latent capital (treasure, accumulation and reserve funds) into interest-bearing capital, to finance with it investments and to accelerate the mobility of capital in the processes of producing average profit rates and to achieve an effective distribution of monetary capital to individual capitals (Marx 1997: 89–90). Thus, the growth of accumulation, both at the level of total capital and at the level of individual capital, is always dependent on the conditions under which the credit system offers money or promises to pay, and whether these are even demanded by companies. Michael Heinrich

---

[1] In the section on interest-bearing capital, Marx emphasises "a few particular points" about the credit system "required to characterise the capitalist mode production in general" (Marx 1998: 397). The concrete functioning of the credit system, in turn, according to Heinrich, changes with the monetary constitution, the organisation of the banking system, the establishment of a state central bank, etc. (Heinrich 2003: 407).

speaks at this point of the credit system as a structural control instance of capitalist accumulation. The dynamics of the credit system is therefore important, not so much for profits, which are made by companies in the past, but more decisive are the anticipations, promises, degrees of trust and expectations of future profits and the risk management corresponding to these conditions. This also means that the respective credit commitment refers to the anticipation and capitalisation of further contingent commitments. The specific financial processes that develop along the lines of capitalist production and circulation thus depend on the credit system, which Marx in turn distinguishes from the monetary system.[2]

Interest-bearing capital is thus to be understood as a constitutive part of the modern credit system; it is located outside the cycle of industrial capital, but is not completely decoupled from it. According to Marx, the cycle of interest-bearing capital can be described as $M-M'$. Here, money is not exchanged against other forms of money or against commodities, but rather, money, by lending a sum of money from the lender (against collateral) to the borrower, which will repay the sum plus a payment of interest, becomes potential capital.[3]

A relevant case of modern credit is the advance payment of a money capitalist to an industrial capitalist, who owns a company and uses the borrowed funds as money capital to finance profitable production processes. (However, credit can also be used to buy shares, government bonds or corporate bonds, or to finance consumer spending.) Acting as a lender and initiating the production process, the credit a financial company provides to the industrial company, which acts as a borrower and manages the production process, a sum of money is made available with the right to dispose of it for a limited period of time. The loan does not involve an exchange of equivalents, but rather the lender lends a

---

[2] The monetary system has three components: private banks and (industrial) corporations, and these two parts in relation to the central bank, which issues banknotes and which is supposed to guarantee the reciprocal convertibility of the different forms of money - besides the banknotes, the various flows of credit, which circulate between the banks themselves and between banks and companies. The credit system includes banks, money markets and capital markets. The money markets regulate the supply and demand for money, which is created in the interconnection between central bank, states and commercial banks. On the capital markets, money is transferred in capital, shares, bonds, derivatives, etc.

[3] Marx speaks of capital as capital as a commodity *sui generis*, which is "converted", i.e. lent and has a price, the interest (Marx 1998: 337).

sum of money to the borrower over an agreed period of time, for which the borrower must provide collateral and make a contractually codified promise to repay the sum of money within this period of time, rate for rate and to pay, in addition, interest. At the end of the contractually agreed period, after the monetary capital that has been invested into production has returned to the industrial capitalist with a surplus through the sale of commodities and then, as part of this surplus (interest), returned to the lending capitalist, the loan is considered to have been repaid and disappears. Credit is thus the closed circle of a financial promise.

The borrower, if acting as the embodiment of the functioning capital, has to carry out investments, services and projects, which are directed to the future, which the lender, however, only finances after the analysis and evaluation of the creditworthiness of the borrower, that is, in terms of the rentability, justifies investments in the future. The borrower must also provide collateral: in the case of corporate loans, machines, equipment and financial claims of the company are pledged to the bank as collateral. The perspective of profit that the company opens up also to the lending bank is part of the mutual investment, or, to put it another way, the expected profit of the company justifies the financial means, with which the company wants to realise future profits, or, to put it again in another way, the realised profit of the company has justified the anticipation, which the bank has made in the context of the lending and with which it has started the production process in the first place (Decker et al. 2016). Thus, the credit ultimately generates the investment and not vice versa. For Marx, in the course of the legal act of lending and repayment, the mediating production process, the "real cycle made of money as capital" (Marx 1998: 348) remains invisible.

The lending of financial companies to industrial companies includes a temporary doubling of capital, which is codified by contract law. When the monetary capital is lent by a bank to an industrial company, the capital is doubled, on the one hand, into a claim of the bank (fictitious deposit), which functions as capital, and, on the other hand, into investment capital (for the functioning capitalist), whereby this doubling remains related to an individual capital, or, to put it differently, the individual monetary capital receives a double existence, as an asset/liability and as investment capital (cf. Lohoff and Trenkle 2012: 121ff.). Marx sometimes denies this doubling and speaks only of a double functioning of capital, which is shown in the division of gross profit into interest and net profit (Marx 1997: 369), and he adds that (industrial) capital produces

64   A. SZEPANSKI

profit only once. Elsewhere he again speaks of capital that appears with double purpose, "as loanable capital in the lender's hands and as industrial, or commercial, capital in the hands of the functioning capitalist" (ibid.: 362).

Through the credit relation, a sum of money (with the potential for more) has doubled as capital for a given time interval, because, on the one hand, the borrowed sum of money, if it is used by the borrower for the extension of capitalist production processes, can set new capital cycles in motion, and, on the other hand, the lender can also regard their credit as a coming surplus, since they receive, as fixed in the credit contract, the repayment of the borrowed sum of money *plus* interest.[4] For industrial capital, this means that by taking out loans it can not only increase profitability, but also increase the variability of its projects and production processes, although it can also run into payment difficulties, if interest rates rise. This opens up the continuous iteration of payments, the movement of promises to pay, which resembles more of a spiral than a circle. If an individual credit relationship is integrated into an iterative chain with potentially ever-changing addressees, then a temporary expansion of the initial capital is created at each intermediate link. But this becomes precarious precisely when, in the chains of securitised lending, the sources and destinations of the credited sums of money are separated from each other in such a way that the lenders and borrowers no longer know anything about each other, thus exponentially increasing, above all, the possibility of camouflaging the debtor (cf. Rotman 2000: 146).

In many cases, capitalist production processes are set in motion uno actu with a credit contract. However, today, the large transnational corporations also rely heavily on self-financing, that is, they do not necessarily depend on bank loans or corporate bonds, but rather finance themselves by issuing new shares or by the profits they realise themselves and then reinvest. They also maintain, as the often quoted example of General Motors illustrates, their own financial institutions with differentiated departments, which are active on the financial markets with their own speculative projects and thus always invest more in financial assets than in constant capital and, in expanding their financial activities even

---

[4] Marx writes: "With the development of interest-bearing capital and the credit system, all capital seems to double itself, and sometimes treble itself, by the various modes in which the same capital, or perhaps even the same claim on a debt, appears in different forms in different hands" (Marx 1998: 470).

further, grant consumer loans to their customers so that the company's products can be purchased. In 2004, General Motors recorded 66% of its profits as bank profits, while only 34% were attributed to car sales. The large non-financial companies thus increasingly resemble, at least in regard to their financial departments, which could be qualified as non-bank banks, traditional financial companies when they enter the financial markets themselves, not only to realise traditional industry profits, but also to generate dividends and interest income, as well as income from securities trading. The BMW automobile group, for example, now generates 30% of its turnover with financial transactions. The Nike company increased its financial income by $1.2 billion between 2002 and 2005, while real investment fell by 12% in the same period (Sahr 2017: Kindle-Edition: 4928). In general, non-financial companies have increased both their payments to the financial markets (interest, dividends and share buybacks) and their profits from their own financial transactions, although the two processes are not causally related (Durand 2017: Kindle Edition: 2055).

Since 2002, there has also been a net financing surplus of non-financial corporations in the leading imperialist states, including Germany, which indicates a lack of profitable investment opportunities for companies in the industrial and commercial sectors.[5] This factor and the low rates of profit in the industrial sector make certain technological innovations for increasing productivity obsolete, so that, in contrast to industrial profit, which results from the difference between the cost of commodities and their selling prices, the growth of the market capitalisation of companies is becoming more and more the focus of corporate policies (which is also shown by the increase in mergers and acquisitions of companies) and certain strategies are sometimes completely geared towards influencing stock market prices. Over the last decades, many large companies have seen their share of global net profit and market capitalisation trend upward. That the latter share is higher than the former suggests that investors expect this profit share to continue rising.

---

[5] The net financing surplus is the profit of a company after the deduction of taxes, dividends, interest and investments. Since 2002, Germany has been accumulating such financing surpluses, while countries such as Spain and France have suffered deficits. At the same time, the ratio between the rate of portfolio income - interest, dividends and profits from investments in the capital markets - and cash flows (which can be considered as an indicator of financialisation) has increased from 20% in 1980 to 60% in 2001 (Chesnais 2016).

66   A. SZEPANSKI

Yet how does one define interest? The interest is the yield of money capital or the increase of a borrowed money sum. Already Aristotle knew the formula $M-M+\Delta M$. Here, the increase in money ΔM does appear as a consideration for lending.[6] ΔM in this form becomes interest and $\Delta M/M$ becomes the rate of interest, the "growth rate" of the original sum of money. The rate of interest measures thus the degree of the increase of the interest-bearing capital. Capital appears here not as a size but as a scale, indeed for Marx as a "meaningless condensation" (Marx 1997: 389), or, let us say, as a tautology. Capital does not appear with credit as a thing, as is often assumed with the use of the term reification. *It* must be taken into account *from the beginning* that the decisive point of the term "reification" is not that social relations appear as things, but that the regulations of social relations are understood as intrinsic qualities, that are due to things (Quaas 2016: 41).

In the case of a loan, the lending of money and repayment are separated by time. Therefore, we can give the original credit formula a time index "t", where t can stand for a week, a month or a year and the number "1" is supposed to mean such a time unit: $M(t)$ $M(t+1)$, where $M(t+1)-M(t) = \Delta M$. The interest ΔM is due at time t+1 and bridges the time difference of both money payments, while a change of ownership also takes place at each of these bridged times. The lender gives, the borrower takes money at time t and vice versa at time t+ (Brodbeck 2009: 984ff.).

Let's take a closer look at Marx's analysis of credit. For Marx, net profit/corporate profit and interest exist as quantitative different parts of the gross profit of a (industrial) company. One part of the gross profit takes the form of interest, which belongs to the financial capital, while the other part is the net profit (corporate profit) that belongs to the functioning capital. The common unit of the quantitative parts of the gross profit can change into a qualitative division, thus forming two fractions of capital (industrial and financial capital). On the one hand, the interest now seems to arise purely from the lending of monetary capital (as a result of the abrupt form of money multiplication $M\text{-}M'$, without considering that

---

[6] John Maynard Keynes in particular discovered here a new role of money: money is held as a collateral to guarantee solvency in a world of incessant market upheaval. Therefore, the money interest rate can also be described as the price for giving up security, as it is done in Keynes' theory of liquidity preference. The source of interest payments, however, are also for Keynes the profits generated by innovations.

interest is only a part of the gross profit, which is produced by the functioning capital); on the other hand, only the net profit/corporate profit seems to result purely from the capitalist production processes (and not the gross profit). The interest here functions as that part of the profit that the borrower, in its function as industrial capital, has to pay to the lender. For Marx, therefore, interest is always a part of the profit or average profit realised by individual industrial capital, so that the maximum limit of the interest rate is the average profit rate (Marx 1998: 360), while a minimum limit of the interest rate cannot be determined.

Qualitatively speaking, for Marx, interest is part of the surplus value, while quantitatively speaking, interest is related to the lent monetary capital and not to industrial capital, and this kind of self-referentiality is fixed by the interest rate (ibid.: 374). Although Marx refers over and over to the priority of the capitalist production process, in which the worker generates the surplus value for industrial capital, he also summarises that precisely because one part of the industrial gross profit turns into interest, the other part can now appear as the only corporate profit (ibid.: 376). The money capitalist does not confront the wage worker directly, but the functioning capitalist. As Marx writes: "Interesting-bearing capital is capital as *property* as distinct from capital as a *function*. But so long as capital does not perform its function, it does not exploit labourers and does not come into opposition to labour" (ibid.: 377). Even the profit of the company does not seem to arise from the exploitation of wage labour, but appears as the complementary part of interest, that rate which seems also to determine the profit of the company (and which is then no longer primarily influenced by the amount of the wage). Furthermore, the industrial capitalist can now actually imagine himself, compared to the independent money capitalist, to be only a highly qualified worker and thus without a conflict of interest with wage labour. It seems to be exclusively about the division of the gross profit into interest and corporate profit, while the gross profit itself remains presupposed without any further questioning about its origin. And if one then asks, the profit of the corporation seems to originate from the production process in general or, as Marx says, from the labour process in general, and not from a (re)production process initiated by capital. Marx thus shows that on the surface interest appears as the more important category compared to corporate profit, while profit, when transformed into the wages of the entrepreneur, appears as a mere "by-product" (ibid.: 390). At this point Marx speaks of the capital fetish. Interest here appears purely as the result of the relationship between two different capitalists (ibid.: 388). However, in his real definition of interest, which he fixes as part of the gross profit of the industrial company, Marx ignores the allocative function of the interest rate and credit for investment and capital accumulation, and thus also neglects the risks, expectations and promise relationships between creditors and debtors, which are of an extraordinary relevance for the regulation of the interest rate. Finally, he also largely ignores the process of credit creation, as the commercial banks do today. We will discuss credit creation in more detail later on.

According to Marx, the level of the interest rate is regulated by the existing relation between supply and demand on financial markets for monetary capital; it is always fixed at a certain point in time, even if it fluctuates over time. Certainly the interest rate does not hang freely in the air, as Marxist authors such as Anwar Shaikh or Samir Amin repeatedly point out (Shaikh 2016; Amin 2010: 62), because functioning capitalists with a specific demand for credit stand in opposition to financial institutions and to private banks with a specific supply of credit and the associated profit interests. Otherwise, Marx's theory of credit would actually be close to the theory of a natural interest rate, which is determined purely by the relation between supply and demand.

The financial markets can be divided according to the terms of the loan agreements into the money market (short-term money capital) and the capital market (long-term money capital).[7] Both markets also change capital in its fictitious and speculative form.[8]

---

[7] A distinction is made between a medium money market interest rate and a medium capital market interest rate, with the latter being higher than the former. Within the various sub-markets, in turn, the interest rates differ according to the creditworthiness of the respective borrowers. In contrast to the profit rate, whose empirical measurability has always been a problem for Marxists, the interest rate is a fixed size for a given maturity and the creditworthiness of the borrower. The production of a uniform interest rate is a purely empirical act. There is no general law to be reported here that determines the production of the interest rate, but rather the division of profit into interest and corporate profit takes place via the balance of power and the competition between the various capital fractions.

[8] Anwar Shaikh analyses in detail Marx's position on the determination of the interest rate and concludes that Marx held two different positions. On the one hand, the interest rate is determined, at least in the short-term, purely on the basis of the relationship between supply and demand on the financial markets. On the other hand, Marx assumes that financial capital enters into, or at least remains bound to, the compensatory movements for the production of average profit rates, and therefore the interest rates are

The interest payable on loans is calculated by the companies as a cost factor, i.e. the interest is subsumed under advance costs, even if the companies only use equity capital (in this case, the companies have to pay interest to themselves). On the liabilities side of the balance sheet, equity capital is opposed to that part of the assets to which no liabilities correspond, while the majority of the banks' assets consist of the debt of non-banks, which are claims of the banks against them. In accordance with the opportunity cost model, which is used for the planning of investment decisions, the interest that may be payable is, from the beginning, taken into account in the operational plans and balance sheets of the companies. However, at least in theory, companies have the choice to either let their monetary capital function productively or to lend it to debtors at an interest rate.[9] In the business calculation, interests therefore no longer appear only as a cost factor and as a constitutive element of the market price. The interest rate is instead considered now as an alternative possibility of exploitation of newly invested money capital and influences, in its allocative function, the future accumulation of capital. With the help of calculations, which one estimates in the business calculation as opportunity costs, the companies see themselves constantly forced to examine, when realising investments, if possibly more profitable opportunities of financial investments escape them.[10]

determined, in the last instance, by the movements of the profit rates, i.e. by structural factors (Shaikh 2016: 449). Financial profits, in turn, would arise from the difference between the interest rates at which banks borrow money and the interest rates at which they lend money (minus the costs in relation to the capital stock: fixed capital and reserves). The interest rate would in the end be defined by the integration of the financial companies in the equalisation movements of the profit rate and by the cost of inputs. However, Shaikh does not take into account that private banks have the potential to determine the interest rates in terms of the creditworthiness of customers within a certain framework, nor does he distinguish between the two completely different processes of industrial companies and banks in terms of the production and realisation of profits.

[9] On the level of total capital, of course, this choice does not exist, because not all the capital of an economy can be present as monetary capital. If money capital would not be borrowed at all for profit-making production processes, this would lead to a devaluation of money capital and to a total loss of interest.

[10] In order to calculate the rentability of investments, companies use mathematics of finance for investment calculation, i.e. the net present value method and/or the internal rate of return method. In business planning calculations, the net present value is usually used to estimate future investment projects. By setting a time t0, the net present value of an investment is calculated with the discount factor: $1/1$ + market rate of interest. This can be related to the Bichler/Nitzan capitalisation formula: with this one calculates

70 A. SZEPANSKI

Marx already sees here quite clearly that, on the one hand, the expanded reproduction of functioning capital sets some conditions and possibilities for modern credit, and that, on the other hand, the modern credit system at first allows the acceleration and expansion of the industrial accumulation of capital. This spiral movement prevails through the competition of companies, whereby they are forced, over time, to insert larger amounts of fixed capital, which must be financed by credit, and to accelerate the turnover period of their various capital circuits, precisely in order to ensure the continuity of their production processes (Marx 1998: 478ff.). In the history of industrial capitalism, the need for credit became more urgent the higher the proportion of fixed capital in a company (e.g. of railroad construction), thus making the permanent utilisation of production capacities over several periods a permanent necessity. This makes access to the credit and financial system for large corporations absolutely necessary, because now large sums of monetary capital must be advanced in the long term and the risk of devaluation of fixed capital increases due to its long amortisation periods. This is precisely what will later require the use of modern financial instruments, with which the many risks, including future production processes, can be hedged. When companies finance the renewal or expansion of fixed capital with loans and hedge these in turn with options, they are no longer dependent on making investments with full accumulation and amortisation funds.[11] These funds no longer need to be replenished; rather, the money accumulated in them can itself be reused as credit, thus permanently mobilising idle money capital. The growth of capital thus itself brings forth the necessity and potential of credit, whether it is used to mobilise unproductive capital, to shorten waiting times in production, to realise parts of the

the value of the respective investment (K) as relation between the interest rate (r) of the expected profits and current profit (E), so that one receives the following formula: $K = E/r$ (Bichler and Nitzan 2009: 185). According to this, capital is not to be understood as an (absolute) positive value, but as a relation, whereby the intentional negative (indebtedness qua credit) is to be understood as a positive condition for capitalist production, as Peter Ruben has explained - capital or capitalisation is debt production sui generis (Ruben 1998: 53).

[11] The accumulation fund is the accumulated surplus value that should be invested at a certain time in the future, insofar as a certain amount of money is needed for the investment. In the amortisation fund, the returning parts of the fixed capital are collected.

3 CREDIT   71

unused surplus value prematurely and to increase the speed of circulation, etc.[12]

The profit-enhancing movement of the credit system consists particularly in the fact that it accelerates both the production of average profit rates and the mobilisation of capital flows that can lead to extra profits for individual capitals. Marx writes the following on the equalisation of profit rates through the credit system: "We have seen that the average profit of the individual capitalist, or of every individual capital, is determined not by the surplus labour appropriated at first hand by each capital, but by the quantity of total surplus labour appropriated by the total capital, from which each individual capital receives its dividend only proportional to its aliquot part of the total capital. This social character of capital is first promoted and wholly realised through the full development of the credit and banking system" (Marx 1998: 601–602).

However, credit not only mediates and accelerates the production and circulation processes of companies, it also gives a certain elasticity to capitalist accumulation and reproduction, which in turn can lead to the acceleration of the entire reproduction process and thus to the growth of a national economy. The modern credit system also reduces the costs of circulation, including those of monetary transactions, while at the same time, increasing the speed of the circulation of money (ibid.: 433). Furthermore, the credit system provides large sums of money for investment and accelerates the mobility and circulation of commodities, labour and capital in the various branches of industry. In general, the functions of the modern credit system consist in regulating the imbalances and asynchronicities of the various cycles of capital. The credit system does not simply redistribute already existing amounts of money, but, as Marx also mentions in passing, allows the private banks to create potentially new capital with the credit (ibid.: 539). Provided that the factual preconditions for the accumulation process are realised, not only the accumulation rate of a company, but also the accumulation of total capital can be increased

---

[12] In general, taking a loan can also increase the company's profit rates. Take a simple example and assume that the average profit rate is 5% and the market interest rate is 4%. If a company invests now a million euro, then it realises a profit of 50,000 euro. If it takes then a credit of one million euro (and realises also the average profit of 50,000 euro), then the company must pay at the same time 40,000 euro interest to the bank. The total profit has now increased to 60,000 euro (50,000 plus 10,000 euro). The average profit rate is now 6% instead of 5% (cf. Heinrich 2003).

by credit. And if sufficient credit is available, then production and accumulation can be pushed "to the extreme limit", whereby credit becomes at the same time the "main lever of overproduction and overspeculation in commerce" (ibid.: 438). For this, however, the credit system itself requires a maximum of elasticity, which today in turn requires specific credit instruments, new forms of fictitious and speculative capital.

The private banks, when they grant their loans, do not rely on the savings and deposits of the customers and are therefore not necessarily dependent on the industrial corporations, but act with the granting of loans as autonomous and profit-oriented producers of money capital. The decisive criterion for granting loans is not their own scarcity of economic resources, but rather that the banks themselves can create credit and evaluate, at the same time, the potential of the debtors to create income, so that these can repay the loans and pay the interest. The different terminated promises of payment are entered into the balance sheets of the private banks, where they are balanced out as debts and credit. Thereby the private banks promise to accept their own promises of payment, which are given with the loan, also as a means of repayment. This means that they commit themselves to take back the amounts of money which they spend as deposits/liabilities, also again as money (repayment and interest). The deposits generated by the credit are thus bound to the promise of the debtor, to liquidate the credit by means of repayment and interest payment. With credit, a processual concatenation of promises to pay is activated, within which the credits simultaneously provide a means of repayment, with which the promises to pay can be terminated and liquidated, and this can only mean that the practice of granting credit is aligned to the expectation and anticipation of an open future. The disruption, interruption and crisis of the financial system are therefore possible at any time, just as the endless continuation of the chain structures of promises can be postponed, and here as an expectation of the production and linking of new payment promises, which are contingent to a certain extent, and by the stabilisation of already existing promises to pay (Sahr 2017: Kindle Edition: 754).

Apart from unsecured loans, the debtor must deposit securities, which he may have borrowed himself or, which in the case of houses, are not yet his property. This kind of mobilisation of collateral leads today to the production of new complex risks; for example, suppose that a government bond serves as collateral, which is transferred for a certain period of time to a new investor, who sells it for a shorter period of time and at a lower price than the original price to someone, who then transfers it again on modified terms, and so on.

In general, it can be assumed today that money does not have to exist independently of credit (which embodies a socio-economic construction), for example, as the transfer of property presupposed for credit. Rather, credit, which is created by private banks with the touch of a button, includes an immanent promise of payment, which exists precisely when it is trusted by both parties that at certain points in the future, amounts will be paid by the bank or repaid by the debtor, whereby the money and its price - the interest rate - thus become in a sense a measure of trust or promise (Pettifor 2017: Kindle-Edition: 447). The lender is not only concerned with the repayment of the loan, but wants to receive interest for lending the money in addition to the repayment. The interest is thus constitutive for the loan insofar as a lent sum of money has necessarily to flow back to the lender, i.e. increased by the interest, whereby the uncertainty of the payments increases for him if the value of the securities deposited by the borrower deteriorates over the limited period of time for which the loan is scheduled.

Already in the 1940s, as suggested by economist David Durand, the data collected by various institutional lenders about borrowers asking for consumer credit should be condensed into a probabilistic model in the U.S., which would decide who would and who would not receive credit in the future. By recording the solvency and payment patterns of the borrowers during the credit period, it became possible to calculate the future risk or credit default to a certain extent. This development continued in the electronically networked credit card payment system, which perfected the statistical imaginary through the use of increasingly bureaucratic, distanced and abstract procedures and extended it beyond consumption. This culminated in the Fico Score, whose function was to record the probability of an individual's loan default as a number. On the one hand, the credit score is based on the borrower's individual credit history and, on the other hand, it is the result of the evaluation of the data available from borrowers, so that, in the framework of a comparative analysis, the risk of lending to respective individuals can be calculated. In addition, data is made available to lenders that inform future lending by assessing and comparing the creditworthiness of different borrowers and will be related to its future risk potential. Creditworthiness now has a self-moving quality fixed by the statistics, whose subject is the aggregated population. For lenders, this means that they do not base the granting of

74   A. SZEPANSKI

loans solely on the creditworthiness of individual borrowers, but rather create a portfolio of assets that they can constantly modify in order to achieve the desired rates and amounts of risk management and recoveries. (The credit score was used in 1995 by state-subsidised companies, such as Freddie Mae, for mortgage lending.) This makes it possible not only to assess the risk, which is associated with the purchase of specific assets, but at the same time also to evaluate risks, which are associated with the purchase and transformation of an entire portfolio of assets. This allows the lender not only access to future value, but also the possibility of borrowing further sums of money on the financial markets themselves in order to lend them back at a higher interest rate. It is now possible to unify risk across platforms and to design risk at the different stages of the insurance processes and those of securitisation. If there is a unified metric for quantifying risk, then the primary and secondary markets can participate in an identical calculatory platform. If it becomes possible to measure the probability of an individual credit default, then one can also evaluate the risk within a pool of debt. The probability of the lender is now also that of a function as borrower, which allows him to diversify his own portfolio even more. Conversely, if the borrower, for example, takes out a consumer loan, he receives just enough credit to reproduce himself as a borrower at a given level of risk. The capitalist no longer meets only subjects willing to rent their labour-power for the payment of a wage, but neoliberal subjects, from whom it is expected to make their own choice in the future.

References

Amin, Samir (2010) *The Law of Worldwide Value*, New York.
Bichler, Shimshon and Nitzan, Jonathan (2009) *Capital as Power. A Study of Order and Creoder*, Florence.
Brodbeck, Karl-Heinz (2009) *Die Herrschaft des Geldes: Geschichte und Systematik*, Darmstadt.
Chesnais, Francois (2016) *Finance Capital Today: Corporations and Banks in the Lasting Global Slump*, Leiden.
De Brunhoff, Suzanne (2015) *Marx on Money*, London.
Decker, Peter, Hecker, Konrad and Patrick, Joseph (2016) *Das Finanzkapital*, Munich.
Durand, Cédric (2017) *Fictitious Capital: How Finance Is Appropriating Our Future*, London.

Heinrich, Michael (2003) *Die Wissenschaft vom Wert. Die Marxsche Kritik der politischen Ökonomie zwischen wissenschaftlicher Revolution und klassischer Tradition*, Münster.

Huber, Joseph (2021) *Modern Money Theorie – die falsche Verheißung*, in: https://vollgeld.page/mmt-falsche-verheissung#_ftn3.

Lohoff, Ernst and Trenkle, Norbert (2012) *Die große Entwertung. Warum Spekulation und Staatsverschuldung nicht die Ursache der Krise sind*, Münster.

Marx, Karl (1989) *Economic Manuscripts of 1861–63*, in: *Marx and Engels Collected Works*, Vol. 31, London.

Marx, Karl (1997) *Capital, Vol. 2*, in: *Marx and Engels Collected Works*, Vol. 36, London.

Marx, Karl (1998) *Capital*, Vol. 3, in: *Marx and Engels Collected Works*, Vol. 37, London.

Pettifor, Ann (2017) *The Production of Money: How to Break the Power of Bankers*, London.

Quaas, Georg (2016) *Die ökonomische Theorie von Karl Marx*, Marburg.

Rotman, Brian (2000) *Die Null und das Nichts. Eine Semiotik des Nullpunkts*, Berlin.

Ruben, Peter (1998) *Was bleibt übrig von Marx' ökonomischer Theorie?*, in: *Philosophische Schriften*. Online-Edition: www.peter-ruben.de.

Sahr, Aaron (2017) *Das Versprechen des Geldes. Eine Praxistheorie des Kredits*, Hamburg.

Shaikh, Anwar (2016) *Capitalism: Competition, Conflict, Crises*, New York.

CHAPTER 4

The Category of Capitalisation

Marx writes: "The formation of a fictitious capital is called capitalisation" (Marx 1998: 464). Fictitious capital is not fictitious in the trivial sense as it is effective, that is, operative (cf. Bourdieu 2014: 31). Bourdieu refers to the strong meaning of the word *fingere*, in the sense of "to produce" [*verfertigen*] and "prepare" [*zurechtmachen*], or in the sense of fabrication (ibid.: 574).

Capitalisation, which characterises the method of fictitious capital, is essentially distinguished by four parameters/variables: (a) the current stock of profits; (b) the hype coefficient; (c) the expected yield price; and (d) the risk-coefficient (Bichler and Nitzan 2009: 183ff.). For Bichler and Nitzan, the interplay of these four variables of capitalisation condenses and represents the power of the dominant capitalists, even indicating capital as power.

Let us go into more detail about the four parameters: (1) the actual profit produced in a production period starting from t0 and ascertainable *ex post* in t1 also results from the management of the future, which starts from the production period t0. The returns are unknown at time t0, but they are calculated and known with and in time, at the latest, when the incomes and profits are announced at time t1.

(2) With the hype coefficient, the expected profits are compared at a given time (present future) with the profits that are always only known

© The Author(s), under exclusive license to Springer Nature
Switzerland AG 2022
A. Szepanski, *Financial Capital in the 21st Century*,
Marx, Engels, and Marxisms,
https://doi.org/10.1007/978-3-030-93151-3_4

78   A. SZEPANSKI

ex post and on which one has speculated (future present). These two profit streams prove to be identical at best. As Bichler and Nitzan write: "By definition, *ex ante* expected future earnings are equal to the *ex post* product of actual future" (ibid.: 188). Of course, the relation between the *ex ante* expected returns and the returns of a future present, showing itself as an actualisation of the future, is variable. The following equation can be applied here:

$$Kt = EE = E \times H$$

(Kt) is the capitalisation in time, (EE) stands for the expected future profits, (E) for the current level of profits and (H) for the hype coefficient ($H = EE/E$) (ibid.: 189). The hype coefficient affects the collective error of the capitalists as a class and occurs already at the moment when the assets are priced out based on *ex ante* expectations, although it is of course only possible to determine *ex post* whether the expectations have been realised or not. If one expresses the hype coefficient in a number, it is articulated with it the question of whether the capitalists have estimated their future profits too optimistically or too pessimistically: if the expectations were excessively optimistic, then a hype factor greater than 1 is to be assumed, while if the expectations were excessively pessimistic, it is to be set less than 1; the hype coefficient is equal to 1 only if the projections of the capitalists are perfectly correct (ibid.: 188f.).[1]

---

[1] Bichler and Nitzan modify their basic capitalisation formula as follows: K: $E \times H/S \times Z$. Here we have two components in the numerator; first the realisation of the current profit (E). The future profit is unknown here and now and must be estimated by the capitalists. The optimism or the pessimism of the estimations is represented by the hype-coefficient H, which is equal to 1, when the estimations are correct, but which does not naturally occur in reality (Bichler and Nitzan 2009: 209).

The denominator, which represents the discount rate, also consists of two components: the first component is the normal rate of return (the profit on the investment) that capitalists believe they can earn by investing in risk-free assets such as government bonds (S). The second component is the scaling (stepped) factor - it represents the expected returns that capitalists demand when investing in higher risk assets (Z). If the normal rate S is 0.05% and the risk of buying stocks is twice as high as investing in government bonds, then Z will equal 2 and the discount rate will equal 0.1.

However, to simplify matters, one does not evaluate the expected profit, but takes the gross value of production in dollars GVA and introduces two additional conditions: one assumes that GVA will grow at a certain average rate and that the profit share will oscillate around a certain average in the future. One then reduces this estimation to the coefficient m and replaces E with GVA×m. The new equation is: $K = GVA \times m \times H/S \times Z$. Current

(3) For Bichler and Nitzan, capitalisation is based on the calculated (discounted) current value of the expected future, the risk-adjusted profits of an economic unit. The discount rate is used to estimate the current value towards future-orientated liabilities. The higher the discount rate, the lower the present value of the liabilities. The monetary return on long-term government bonds is used here as the norm for the calculation. The prices of assets are therefore based on market calculations of future monetary profit flows, which are discounted on the basis of market interest rates and the expectations of market players; or, to put it another way, they result from discounting expected future profits at the current market interest rate and a risk premium or discount (weighted interest rate) that depends on the quality of the security and the economic situation. This can also be referred to as a price fixing that is made in terms of expectations and promises of future profits, or it can simply be called the "yield price". Capitalisation means the fixation of a price that is related to the calculation or discounting of future promises of payment and thus always already related to the evaluation of the complexity of

economic variables have a relatively negligible impact on future incomes, and in fact, if we look at the third equation of capitalisation, it depends on the coefficient m, which in turn depends on the average future share of profits and the average future growth rate of profits. Current profits do not even appear there, although they are secretly assumed to exist (ibid.).

The equation can now be changed again with the formula $K = GVA: \times m \times H/\% \times \&$. The market capitalisation is then the product of two components: GVA, which is measured regularly, and the rate from the four remaining components, which are made up of estimates, beliefs and conventions. It is often argued that this type of uncertainty, which is shown in the oscillation of the four components, is not completely contingent, but rather, as statistics show, the self-correction process repeatedly produces middle values. However, it can be assumed that only 15% of the statistics and observations approach the normalised index of 100. Most evaluations deviate from the average, which in turn is interpreted by some economists (the dismatch thesis) in such a way that the market is economically a-chronic and irrational at times, for example through asymmetric information, errors in economic policy, imperfect markets and non-economic interventions, among others factors (ibid.). This asymmetric information situation does of course exist, for example, with regard to the practices of Goldman Sachs, which had concealed the amount of their rotten collateral before the financial crisis and bet on a financial collapse, while at the same time continuing to sell the same collateral to their investors.

If valuations are always out of tune, so to speak, and at the same time they are based solely on current power relations, then the question arises, according to Bichler and Nitzan, how evaluations can immediately target power relations, assuming that stock indices directly indicate the various forces and shifts in the economic power relations between classes.

80 A. SZEPANSKI

future production processes, which cannot be evaluated de facto by the financial markets (one has to think of the movement of stock prices), but always only fictitiously; the market is, insofar as prices are inscribed in it and are also realised by the actions of the buyers and sellers, an extremely flexible machine for the reduction of complexity.

With the calculated price of a security, the contingencies, which are always already included in complex capitalist production processes, are reduced to a number (Windolf 2017: 27). The capitalisation formula can be described as follows:

$$\text{Yield price: } E = G/r. \text{ (ibid.) } 10/5 \text{ x } 100 = 200$$

$$\text{Interest formula : } 200 \times 5/100 = 10$$

The yield price is the inverse of the interest formula (ibid.). While a sum of money is ultimately the starting point, the interest rate is fixed and the interest yield/capital value is the result; in the case of capitalisation, the interest yield, weighted by an interest rate (r), is the starting point (G) and the result is a price that a buyer is willing to pay for the promise of payment, which includes the security (ibid.). Here there are two unknowns to report, namely the anticipated profit, which cannot be calculated exactly because of the contingencies and complexity of future developments of production processes and projects, and the interest rate, which fluctuates on the markets and is supposed to be oriented on the companies' cost of capital.

The capitalisation formula therefore contains an *ex ante* valuation. The fundamental problem here is the prediction of future profits, whereby calculations can prove to be incorrect due to uncertainty (these are counterfactual or prospective statements). According to Bichler and Nitzan, they do not prove to be absolutely incorrect either, because over a sufficiently long period of time prices actually seem to oscillate around the average values and numbers. A certain constancy and stability can also be assumed for the interest rate/discount rate. However, it must be taken into account that the process of the production of relative surplus value qua technological innovation makes uncertainty an organising principle for capital, which means that the search of companies for innovation is a necessary result of profit production, making the system of capital accumulation first and foremost dynamic, but also uncertain. Even more, the strategies of companies for new innovation and products often fail.

Capitalisation is always oriented towards the future; one discounts the profits expected in the future, which should also be realised for all eternity. This approach to the future, which for LiPuma and Bichler and Nitzan is almost ritualised,[2] implies a systemic trust in the future potential of the capitalist economy, which is laid down in laws, regulations and contracts. It also demonstrates the belief of capitalists that income and profits will necessarily continue to grow at a certain rate in the future and that assets will find ever more buyers, i.e. that there will always be sufficient liquidity on the markets and that it will be liquidated through payments, or, to put it in other words, that the capitalist system will continue to run forever. This high degree of confidence in the functioning of the financial system is today based in particular on the unconditional affirmation of the objectivity of the respective risk models, on confidence in the state subsidisation of private banks in crisis situations (bailouts), on the positive effect of the intervention potential of central banks and on the confidence in the stability of the recursive payment flows mentioned above, which flow through the global networks of financial capital (Meister 2021: 44; Sahr 2017: Kindle-Edition: 6338). Thus, contemporary capitalists and analysts generally expect quarterly increases in profits, because short-term increases are supposedly more efficient than long-term increases. However, it must be remembered that capitalists are in a way forced into these tactics of thinking and acting, because capital accumulation touches upon certain asymptotes of economic cycles at ever-shorter intervals. The risk here is leverage, which requires short-term and favourable borrowing conditions in order to finance long-term projects. For example, homeowners in the U.S. expected from 2000 onward a leveraging of their homes as financial assets, while investments funds did the same with respect to their portfolios. The two intertwined markets developed after time in one direction, namely that of mutually enforced instability, whereby the possibility of falling yields was ignored. Today, on the financial markets, momentum trading dominates over long-term investment strategies. Remember that in high-frequency trading, the

---

[2] The financial market is a social imaginary, a deeply institutionalised imaginary that includes the people, who trust in this imaginary, and bodies, in which a knowledge is inscribed, plus ratified names, registered companies and a codified history. By constantly problematising belief and trust, the commentators of the markets invoke, without knowing it, a performativity, which normally is attributed to religion: ritual. For LiPuma, the market is thus a social totality, a practically relational construct and a kind of analytical object, which is constructed by the sciences (LiPuma 2017: 170).

holding of an asset is reduced to about ten seconds. The investment horizon of an institutional portfolio trader in the U.S. has shortened from seven years in 1940 to seven months in 2014 (Das 2015: 44). This shortening of time horizons is structurally inscribed in capitalisation. Financial securities imply an anticipation of future production, precisely by giving their holders the possibility of turning them into money at any given moment. But if this possibility is applied to the collective of market participants, liquidity ultimately turns out to be an illusion, because the totality of assets/promises of payment cannot, of course, be liquidated immediately. Nevertheless, any liquidation of liquidity or the realisation of assets in money remains a purpose of capitalisation (of an actor or a company, while the market as a whole always needs liquidity) and has very real effects on financial and other economic processes, whereby in boom periods investors liquidate or convert their securities into money over short periods, thus allowing the savings and monetary capital in the various portfolios to be flexibly managed, which is of enormous importance for insurance companies, pension funds and other funds today.

Bichler and Nitzan define power as an asymmetrical relationship between the owners of assets and the wage-earning population, and this relationship can be quantified by a rate that relates stock prices and wage rates (Bichler and Nitzan 2009: 217). Finally, the quantity of capitalist power expresses the confidence of the rulers against the economic inferiority of the governed, the confidence of the owners of the shares in contrast to the inferiority of the population who own little or no shares. In boom periods, capitalists seem to ignore current profit and focus entirely on the near future. When capitalised power is relatively low, the focus is also on increasing profits in the future, whereby wage-earning incomes are redistributed in favour of profits, pushing up the hype and reducing the volatility of profits. But if the index of power is very high, as at the beginning of the twenty-first century, then the confidence of one's own superiority must relate more strongly to the present, because it is then indicated that capitalist power is not limitless: the stronger the power, the stronger might be the resistance. Now, if in this case power reaches its asymptotes, that is, if the relation between profits and income is extremely divergent and the hype is still high, while the volatilities of income and returns are low, then power can hardly be increased. Bichler and Nitzan argue that any increase within the symbolic power machine then requires the use of capitalist sabotage politics that make the economic system more complex and, at the same time, more fragile (ibid.) Under these circumstances, capitalists are now forced to place their trust even more strongly in the fact that the system is held together precisely in the present, while trust in the future is increasingly dwindling.

(4) In order to implement capitalisation, uncertainty, which is involved in each investment, must be transformed into the calculation of risk, which is assigned to the different companies by the experts or analysts of the rating agencies and investment funds, for example, through the permanent monitoring and assessment of share prices. In practical terms, this appears as an always volatile spread between uncertainty and risk, which can only be reduced by something that even derivatives do not have, namely, such an extended time horizon that makes it possible to smooth the volatility and the spread. The future returns expected by companies must, since they are unknown, at least be weighed with specific risk factors, which in turn require a risk profile and special risk management. We will see especially in the discussion of the analysis of Greek economist John Milios that it is very important for the financial system today to transform uncertainty into a complex risk calculation, and this means that the prices for volatile future promises to pay (loans, share prices, securities, derivatives) are based on the assumption that future profit and income flows are weighed with specific risk factors and subject to risk management (portfolio theory); the risks can be quantified and consequently can be fixed in numbers.[3] (Specifically, derivatives capitalise on volatility that they themselves create.) Not only the profits of companies, but also their average costs are prognosticated on the financial markets. It is assumed that the exogenously determined development of interest rates has a certain influence on the companies' costs, which means that a fixed interest rate must be specified for the calculation of capitalisation. The commodity prices are thus also influenced by the current interest rates on the market, which in turn influence the interest

---

[3] The axiomatisation of the concept of probability assumes as basic requirements: (1) a result set; (2) events, i.e. a set of subsets of the result set; (3) probability as measure; (4) the result of a random experiment consists in the realisation of random variables. Each random variable is a function that assigns a real number to each element of the result set; (5) the expected value of a random experiment. In the case of dice, it is the sum of the numbers multiplied by the probability of their occurrence; (6) variance. The dispersion of random variables is a measure for the medium deviation from the expected value (cf. Mainzer 2014: 195).

rates with which future earnings are discounted. The prices of the securities/collateral will rise as the interest rates fall or the future prospects for dividends and returns improve.[4]

In economic reality, the degree of confidence of the various owners of monetary capital depends, in addition to the economic cycles of capital accumulation, on the processes of "normalisation" within the power relations, as Foucault has described in great detail. What explicitly counts here with regard to the quantifiable calculation of normalising power is the confidence in a future-oriented possibility of capitalising monetary capital in companies and on the financial markets. Already in the case of share prices, it is quite obvious that analysts have to deal with contingencies, which always also affect the course of future industrial production processes of companies and class conflicts. The following questions, for example, then arise for analysts and investors: will there be strikes in a company in the near future? Will there be interruptions in international supply chains due to political and military confrontations on a global level? Will new products even be approved by the state authorities and will the sales markets at home and abroad remain stable? In other words, any form of probability calculation of risk and risk weighing must by definition remain fictitious, because uncertainty can never be 100% translated into probability-based risk, even though risk management has very real effects on the economy.[5] The risk factor, defined by the probability that a future promise to pay (future profit flows) could occur, and the exogenously introduced interest rate, is *sui generis* linked to contingency. Prognosis here relates not only to future economic events and their effects, but also how other market participants assess the future chains of effects of economic events. All important participants in the

---

[4] Trading securities implies that profits are made through the spread between buying and selling, but the real profits are of course also dependent on the size of the respective transactions and less on the volatility of the securities prices, although higher prices can also lead to a higher volume of a deal.

[5] The conceptual distinction between uncertainty and risk goes back to Frank Knight, who, in contrast to apparently incalculable uncertainty, considers risk to be calculable (cf. Mazzucato 2014: 81). The risk is a measurable uncertainty, insofar as the outputs here have a known distribution, namely *qua* a prior calculation, which is based on statistical surveys (*ex-ante*). The risk thus knows calculable probabilities, which are those of a utility-maximising agent, and eliminates catastrophic events from the beginning. Knight is a little more precise at this point, however, and speaks in terms of uncertainty of unknown, unclassifiable, uninsurable and incalculable, but somehow assessable risks.

financial markets (speculators, investors, analysts, etc.) are integrated in a kind of mirror cabinet (Windolf 2017), which endlessly mirrors their prognosis, so that observations of price movements (also in the sense

Uncertainty then includes the intensive, non-measurable dimension of the risk, which cannot be measured, at least not with the usual instruments of probability theory, with which one measures the calculable risks. Uncertainty is the intensive or affective dimension of risk analysis. Where no group of instances can be constructed with sufficient homogeneity to make a quantitative determination of probability, there is definitely uncertainty, but yet at least certain expectations and estimations can be made because there are at least rates and ratios between assumed values. And if financial technologies serve to establish security, then it is also necessary to identify ever-new uncertainties, which in turn must be hedged. Knight then comes to a crucial conclusion: if all risks were known and calculated in advance, and if there would be for companies no barriers to market entry, then profits and losses would indeed converge towards zero. Not the calculable risk (quantity that can be measured), but the immeasurable uncertainty is consequently for Knight the condition for generating profits and especially extra profits in the future. For Knight, an important function of the entrepreneur is to face the uncertainty in order to profit from it; competition, which takes place under conditions of radical uncertainty, is an important machine of profit-driven capitalist economies, and this is an aspect that is simply absent, at least in the statistic models of neo-classical theory, in which the motivation to trade approaches zero when uncertainty is translated into risk (and the noise of the market disappears). With Foucault we can say that uncertainty is becoming productive, a power sign and a driver of the profit-machine. Where there is uncertainty and limits or market barriers, there are extra profits and extra losses. For the cycles M–M', which on the one hand contain multiple spirals and on the other are tautological at least in qualitative terms, uncertainty has a transformative function. We are dealing here with arbitrage and speculation, which recognise uncertainty as a correlation of intensities of divergent qualities. But in risk management, the translation of speculation into the extensive language of algebra takes place, i.e. into technical procedures which distinguish uncertainty from calculable risks. For Benjamin Lee, noise takes the role of uncertainty, insofar as it makes markets possible and at the same time makes them imperfect (Lee and Martin 2016: 99).

The concept of noise found its way into financial literature in the early 1980s, when the understanding of the market as an information processing system (Hayek), kept in balance by signals and "true" prices, gradually began to waver. From then on, the price of security can be based not only on information but also on noise generated by the less sophisticated traders. However, the "intelligent" traders and economists quickly learned how to make profits out of noise, which culminated in high frequency trading (HFT).

Adriana Knouf examines, from the point of materiality and interference between humans and machines, how certain forms and meanings justify the financial noise in various space times firstly, how the noisy activities of traders shake the models of the rationally acting and use-optimising trader; secondly, how the sonic noise accompanies the physical activities in conventional floor trading; thirdly, how the analysis of the relation between computerisation and trade demonstrates that material practices of the man-machine hybrid use noise as a means to make profits; and fourthly, how the problem of speed dramatically escalates, transforming the race for risk-free profits into a race to zero (Knouf 2016).

86   A. SZEPANSKI

of second-order observation) on the stock markets relate expectations to expectations, which can lead to a mimetic and self-reinforcing behaviour of the actors (herd instinct). However, it is necessary to contradict system theory and its theorem of second-order observation because these reflections remain bound to objective economic structures, contingent actions and class struggles, which the market participants - without even knowing it - either reproduce passively with the help of a various kind of representations[6] and/or, as is usually the case, affirm them performatively. Therefore, the trading of stocks and derivatives, for example, include the performative power of a ritual to collectively set in motion precisely what each individual agent presupposes (LiPuma 2017: 199).

The much-vaunted collective imitation structures on the stock markets, in which self-referential expectations respond to expectations, remain related to the objective structures of the economy, that is, to the exploitation imperatives of fictitious and speculative capital and its regulations. This is evident in the fact that companies must present balance sheets at a certain point in time and announce the profitability of past production periods, while at the same time they are always busy with prognoses about the future. Due to very specific transfer processes, promise relations and forms of control (consider, for example, factors such as markets for corporate control, of participations of institutional investors in industrial companies and of specific accounting rules), certain imperatives of fictitious capital become hard conditions, at which today the operations of any company are aligned.

The calculation of risk works at first with an *a priori* and then tries to prove this with inductive methods and statistical knowledge, just as it disguises the knowledge. With the calculation, the uncertainty is transformed into a calculable and measurable risk through specific analytical instruments or mathematically abstract and at the same time through physical systems, or, to put it differently, we find processes of non-uniform clustering and spatio-temporal variations. The corresponding risk management uses the conventional definition of discrete risks (rather than rates), which are provided with an external transcendental management. Thus, in conventional risk theory, uncertainty always appears as a deviation from the statistical average. Correlating risk analysis contains diagrams that bundle the different categories of risk (what is known in risk management as portfolio diversification) and illustrates the aggregation of quantities within a risk profile. The associated statistics do not exist without diagrams or sketches of populations and quantities.

[6] Technical analysis focuses on the trajectories and the volatility of the share; it works less with the fundamental data of companies, than with endogenous data such as stock market data or trends and temporal patterns in price movements on the markets.

At the same time, the functionality of the financial markets also depends on the willingness of market participants and corporations to produce a stream of liquidity in the face of uncertain volatility. The market is a real social fiction that agents produce and reproduce quasi-automatically through collective belief. The blending of the real and the fictional via the collective belief of the agents, as well as the trust in the functioning totality, indicates that markets always contain a performative dimension. Liquidity here consists in the representation of the social in the financial field, illustrated by the objectification of the counter-party on the one side of the deal, and the assumption of risk on the other side.

References

Bichler, Shimshon and Nitzan, Jonathan (2009) *Capital as Power. A Study of Order and Creoder*, Florence.

Bourdieu, Pierre (2014) *Über den Staat – Vorlesungen am College de France 1989–1992*, Berlin.

Das, Satyajit (2015) *A Banquet of Consequences. Have We Consumed Our Own Future?*, London.

Knouf, Nicholas A. (2016) *How Noise Matters to Finance*, Minneapolis.

Lee, Benjamin and Martin, Randy (eds.) (2016) *Derivatives and the Wealth of Societies*, Chicago.

LiPuma, Edward (2017) *The Social Life of Financial Derivatives: Markets, Risk, and Time*, Durham.

Mainzer, Klaus (2014) *Die Berechnung der Welt. Von der Weltformel zu Big Data*, Munich

Marx, Karl (1998) *Capital*, Vol. 3, in: *Marx and Engels Collected Works*, Vol. 37, London.

Mazzucato, Mariana (2014) *Das Kapital des Staates. Eine andere Geschichte von Innovation und Wachstum*, Munich.

Meister, Robert (2021) *Justice Is an Option: A Democratic Theory of Finance for the Twenty-First Century*, Chicago.

Sahr, Aaron (2017) *Das Versprechen des Geldes. Eine Praxistheorie des Kredits*, Hamburg.

Windolf, Paul (2017) *Was ist Finanzmarkt-Kapitalismus?*, in: https://www.uni-trier.de/fileadmin/fb4/prof/SOZ/APO/19-019_01.pdf.

CHAPTER 5

Fictitious Capital

5.1 THE GENERAL TERM OF FICTITIOUS CAPITAL

Fictitious capital is called fictitious not because it functions as imaginary or separated from the real conditions of production, but because it specifically operates the financing of capital's relations of production with respect to future multiplication: for Marx, it is the most developed form of capital, indeed its most important mode of existence (which, however, is today executed by speculative capital).

Marx develops the category of fictitious capital initially in the context of the emergence of interest, interest-bearing capital and credit. We already analysed credit and interest-bearing capital and will now go a step further. Shares, bonds and other securities, which are also called by Marx fictitious capital are constructed and distributed by the financial industry and traded in very specific financial places. The purchase of a bond entitles the reception of regular future payments to which the issuer of the bond is committed; he sells the legally binding promise, to make a sum of money function as monetary capital for the buyer of the bond. With a security, the debt relationship becomes tradable monetary capital, which serves the buyer as a financial investment, while the seller, who receives a certain sum of money for the security, which he uses to finance profitable production processes, is obliged to make payments. Speculation on the future increase of money realises itself here in trading with securities,

© The Author(s), under exclusive license to Springer Nature   89
Switzerland AG 2022
A. Szepanski, *Financial Capital in the 21st Century*,
Marx, Engels, and Marxisms,
https://doi.org/10.1007/978-3-030-93151-3_5

90 A. SZEPANSKI

with which buyers and sellers evaluate their future development differently and therefore come to a contract conclusion (Decker et al. 2016). Here the increase of capital presents itself also as an autonomous material existence.

For Marx, at this point of the development of the categories of the critique of political economy, fictitious capital consists mainly of shares and corporate and government bonds, whose purchase includes the legal right to participate in future income streams in the form of interest (bonds) or dividends (shares) (Marx 1998: 462ff.). Fictitious capital thus represents a claim (legal title) for future payments of certain sums of money, according to Marx "to future production whose money or capital value represents either no capital at all, as in the case of state debts, or is regulated independently of the value of real capital which it represents" (ibid.: 468). These are tradable claims for future payments based on the promises of the issuers of bonds. The economic power of fictitious capital also consists in the possibility of converting the security into money at any time at a certain price, which relates to future capitalisation. The security is a claim for future "value". The future becomes a present reality, in which value, from which future income should originate, has not yet been created or does not need to be created. If the risk of a share purchase is estimated as above average, then the current market value of a share is below the calculated value. If it is estimated as below average, then the market value is above it. Since the market interest rate and the risk assessments can strongly fluctuate, at least in the short term, there can be considerable outbreaks and changes in the prices and thus in the "value" of fictitious capital and, as such, financial crises can emerge if too many market players try to sell their securities simultaneously.

Today, fictitious capital is traded on the primary and secondary financial markets and therefore has a price. It's about financial assets or promises to pay, which are constructed and distributed in the distribution networks of the financial industry. The money that the buyers invest in securities is usually already there regardless of the contractual agreements of the respective securities trading, but not the security itself, which is actualised and fixes the claim for a surplus. As non-places where the prices of securities are fixed and differentiated based on promises, expectations and speculation, financial markets enable a quasi-autonomous form of movement of capitalisation that can be described as a "differential accumulation of fictitious capital". As Marx writes: "And by accumulation of money capital nothing more, in the main, is connoted than an accumulation of these claims" (ibid.: 469). With the existence of fictitious capital, no value is generated *in actu* in the Marxian sense, but is nevertheless really existing monetary capital, and this is, at least for Marx, in anticipation of a value to be generated in the future (ibid.: 468). There also occurs however an actualisation of virtual value, inasmuch as fictitious capital already now represents real claims on future assets and promises of payment. However, in the case of shares and bonds, the underlying price is the capitalised value in a company, to which the expected future incomes refer.[1]

The first function of the security is to be sold, whereby the agreement between buyer and seller first determines the price of the security, one that represents a capital advance for the seller and a promise of return for the buyer. The risk of whether the money will prove to be fictitious capital in the future is now shifted and carried into the security itself. The fictitious capital is risky in the hands of the respective buyer, and this is separated both from the first monetary sum, which was paid to the seller, and from the business project into which the money sum flowed. On financial markets, the security receives a new valuation with each subsequent sale. By trading fictitious capital, financial capital, on the one hand, opens up new investment opportunities for companies that urgently need money capital, and, on the other hand, delivers options for speculators who want to increase their money on the financial markets. Companies themselves can now act as issuers of securities and are thus classified as producers of fictitious capital, while speculators buy fictitious capital that can be redeemed in money at any time, i.e. it is very liquid. Private banks are active in both functions: they construct fictitious capital both for their clients and for themselves, and they act as buyers and sellers of securities for their own accounts and for the accounts of others.

The price of a security is of course not only dependent on the mutual agreement of the buyer and the seller, but a whole range of other economic factors such as the movements of discount rates and

---

[1] In the case of options, the holder does not receive any dividend, interest or payment before the option is exercised, since he does not have the collateral. All he owns is a contract to buy a security at a special price until the expiration date and the option is not exercised if the market price is lower than the price fixed in the option contract.

interest rates, the course of economic cycles and the forms of movement of differential capital accumulation are also taken into account in its determination.[2]

Fictitious capital in its different forms always already includes a speculative moment, insofar as the investors and speculators compare an expected, but by no means in the future 100% safe, future yield, which is related to a security with the height of the current market interest rates and the respective risk courses of other securities. A high return over two years (on a security) may be worthless to an investor than to receive a smaller amount already in the present, and how much less depends also on current and future interest rates, so that one tries to discount future returns, or reduce them to what they are worth today.

When profit expectations are high and interest rates are low, the value of fictitious capital, such as the value of shares, can increase. To illustrate the relationship between security prices and interest rates, we assume, in the following example, that someone owns a security worth €100, which makes a profit of €5 every year. If the interest rate is 5%, then you get the same return if you invest €100 at 5% interest. Now, if the interest rate falls to 2%, then this would correspond to a security price of €250 if a yield of 2% were realised (with an annual interest rate of 2%, €5 yield is realised at €250). If the interest rate rises to 10%, then this would correspond to a security price of €50 because one must invest €50 to get a €5 yield at 10%. In practice, the calculations are much more complicated, but in general, low market interest rates will cause the prices of securities to rise, while high market interest rates will cause the prices of securities to fall. The interest rate and the price of the security are therefore inverse to each other (ibid.: 464). When interest rates are low, investors will be able to

---

[2] David Harvey uses the term capitalisation exactly at this point, which for him denotes the formal process of forming fictitious capital, in which certain income flows, originating from the assets of land, real estate, bonds or shares, are assigned "fictitious" capital values, the determination of which depends not only on the expectations of the buyers and sellers for future returns, but also on the usual market discount rates and interest rates, which usually result from the play of supply and demand in money markets and capital markets (and of course are again based on expectations) (Harvey 2012: 41f.). With regard to the real estate sector, it should be noted that the purchase of condominiums is usually financed with loans. In the case of real estate, the expected resale price is the most important security with regard to the realisation of the payment obligation and is therefore considered a parameter for the production of fictitious capital. Borrowing for the purchase of condominiums is by far the most important item in household debt.

take out higher loans and invest in assets, be it derivatives, real estate, jewels, gold or stocks, which will of course further fuel asset inflation.

There is today an implicit guarantee by central banks for the protection of the trade with securities, which is equivalent to a put option, which means that asset prices cannot fall below a certain level. Interesting in this context is the current zero interest rate policy (with a simultaneous increase in state budget deficits), which in turn is causing the prices and rates of shares, bonds and real estate to rise. After the financial crisis of 2008, the U.S. reduced key interest rates to zero, with the government deficit rising to 12% of GDP in 2009. While the low-income population holds most of its savings as bank deposits and is adversely affected by low interest rates, those who invest their assets in stocks, real estate and bonds benefit from low interest rates. If the central bank charges negative interest on the deposits of commercial banks, so that they don't have give their money to the central bank but lend it to customers, this does not necessarily have to occur. Commercial banks do not even have to accept the cheap money from central banks. We will however come back to the policy of quantitative easing later.

Like loans, securities include a doubled increase for a limited period. This happens under very specific circumstances when an investor buys shares or bonds with the aim of making more money out of his money. Contrary to the purchase of standard commodities of industrial production, which serve either private or industrial consumption, the purchase of a security implies a promise of payment on the realisation of future returns. The seller of the security is also not excluded from capitalisation because he disposes the money that the sale of the security brings and can use it for profitable production processes (Lohoff and Trenkle 2012: 131f.). This type of business relationship by no means ensures a mere forwarding of already existing monetary capital because (a) in the concrete disposal of money capital, a company is the precondition for further profit-making production processes, and (b) the buyer can trade the share or bond with the aim of obtaining a surplus on the financial markets.[3]

---

[3] Lohoff and Trenkle summarise this point: "When a money capital owner gives away a certain amount of money in return for the securitised promise to receive an increased amount of money at a later date, not only has a new additional commodity been created, namely the respective title of ownership that can be traded on the financial market; this commodity increases the currently existing capitalist wealth because with it, additional

The multiplication of fictitious capital is never set identical to the productivity, production and increase of material wealth, which is of less importance to capital in the first instance, because the functions, parameters, variables and configurations of the flows of money capital are recorded that represent the abstract wealth of the capital economy, and to the extent of this wealth, the creation of fictitious capital has a direct and indirect influence. This kind of doubling through the creation of specific securities represents only a temporary increase in money capital, which does not at all mean that at the level of total capital, this is a zero-sum game that is exhausted in the redistribution of existing money capital sums. Rather, different types of investment can be initiated in the whole economy (while in the financial markets at the microeconomic level, the losses of one actor are in fact the profits of another actor). As long as the securities (shares, bonds, etc.) flow and are traded in the distribution channels and networks of industrial capital and the financial industry, as long as they are not 100% realised and thus devalued, they increase the (not unlimited) wealth of fictitious capital in addition to their possible use as productive capital.

Let us now take a closer look at the differences between interest-bearing and fictitious capital such as bonds and shares. While with credit, the lent money operates for the lender by means of a legal claim for interest and repayment of a future money increase, with fictitious capital an anticipated profit is fixed as a security, which contains the legal claim for future payments for the buyer and can furthermore be traded by him. While credit is about the potency of money, which can also function as a possible profit for the borrower for which he has to pay interest, fictitious capital is about future income streams that originate from a security that the investor buys for a sum of money, for which the expected income that the security is supposed to yield is like an interest payment. In the case of fictitious capital, the borrowers no longer appear as debtors suffering from a lack of money, but as issuers of securities (bonds) that in turn represent an increasing asset for the buyer, i.e. grant participation in the capital power of the issuer. While a debtor with the loan assumes the obligation to pay interest and deposit securities, the issuer/debtor of a security gives the promise that the realisation of the promise of payment will work for the investor in the future. Instead of providing financial

capital has been created that did not exist before the act of exchange" (Lohoff and Trenkle 2012: 128).

options for the companies through the granting of loans, the private banks provide the companies, which function here as issuers of securities, access to money and funds, so that they can expand their future projects and options. Creditworthiness mutates here into a secured condition that is traded with the security. Investors, in turn, no longer act on the capital market as mere creditors, but as speculators who buy securities in order to earn money by trading with them. For the buyer, the security functions as an investment, that is, as a sum of money capital which is objectified in the security and can also be resold. Where the creditor of a loan insists on punctual interest and redemption payments, with the security the payment of returns (and the repayment of the invested sum) is part of an investment that is checked for its robustness as a speculative capital investment using certain criteria (interest rates, comparison with other securities, etc.).

The large stock corporations certainly do not appear on the stock markets merely as debtors, which suffer from a lack of money and therefore are in need of potent lenders, but as issuers of securities, and these, as described above, represent an increase in capital in a double sense. Fictitious capital is thus an eminently important aspect of the modern financial system, but it is not exclusively controlled by the financial sector, since industrial and commercial companies today also trade extensively with financial collateral in order to consolidate and expand their market power. The scale of the market is extremely important for all companies, insofar being larger in terms of market capitalisation often means being able to offer or raise money capital or financial services at a lower cost than their competitors, or being in an influential position in the financial networks, depending not only on the constitution of the national markets, but also on international markets. In both cases, the politics and power of the national states still play a role that should not be underestimated. The leading companies of a nation receive permanent support from their state, for example, by having easier access to the national currency through the central bank, an important instrument with which they can gain advantages over foreign companies and financial institutions in particular. Financial companies can above all expand their foreign operations if they already occupy a dominant position in their own countries and their financial transactions on the world markets are conducted in their own currency.

It should be clear from the current state of the research on Marx's theory that only rudimentary a theory of fictitious capital is developed in *Capital*, Vol. 3, not to mention a theory of speculative capital or a theory of credit creation. But why does Marx call certain forms of capital fictitious at all? He gives three main reasons for this: (1) the claim for returns does not refer to the current profits of functioning capital, which are instead determined by the difference between costs and sales. The trade with securities serves in particular for access to future returns and is thus per se burdened with contingency. Marx calls these securities "fictitious capital", because they are based on the calculation of expected returns and profits. If the state should pay back the money it borrows plus interest, the creditor does not have claims on current capital, but on future tax revenues of the state or on other forms of state income (government bonds). (2) The claims thus relate to the future, but they include both expected and actual payments, and both are neither to be treated as equivalent. Unlike income that has already been realised, expectations of returns may not be fulfilled; on the contrary, they may turn out to be completely illusory. (3) A money capital flow, materialised in a security, creates different levels and scales of capitalisation depending on the movements of discount and interest rates in the markets. At the same time, the debtor, in his function as an abstract money-multiplying machine, should have sufficient monetary size and power. He should be able to run up debts in a proper amount and be considered solid in their repayment.

On the level of total capital, the problem around fictitious capital is as follows. While the covered accumulation of monetary capital (covered property titles) finds a correspondence in the accumulation of capital in the industrial and commercial sector or in the service sector, in the case of uncovered securities, money is used which either comes from future tax revenues, as in the case of the state, or from further fictitious capital, which in turn refers to future fictitious capital (cf. Lohoff and Trenkle 2012: 235f.). In the latter case, fictitious capital does not have to be covered by past exploitation of labour, nor realised through future exploitation processes in production in order to be retroactively covered. Therefore, certain sums of fictitious capital can circulate to a certain extent independently of the differentiated accumulation of industrial capital and service or commercial capital. And Marx was well aware of this autologic nature of financial capital: "The independent movement of the value of these titles of ownership, not only of government bonds but also of stocks, adds weight to the illusion that they constitute real capital alongside of the capital or claim to which they may have title. For they become commodities, whose price has its own characteristic movement and is established in its own way. Their market value is determined [*Bestimmung*] differently from their nominal value, without any change in the value (even though the expansion may change) of the actual capital" (Marx 1998: 467). For Marx, monetary capital shows itself to be a claim to future production: "All this paper is actually nothing more than accumulated claims, or legal titles, for future production whose money or capital value represents either no capital at all, as in the case of state debts, or is regulated independently of the value of real capital which it represents" (ibid.: 468). Here Marx implicitly ascribes to financial capital the power to increase money.

5.2   BONDS AND SHARES

By issuing bonds and shares, companies achieve a size and power based purely on equity and credit that they often hardly achieve at all. Bonds issued by potential borrowers - large corporations, governments, banks - guarantee the buyer in their simple form a fixed interest on a fixed investment amount and are redeemed at a fixed date at the nominal issue price. The issuers thus sell a promise and a claim for future income streams, which can then be resold by the buyer as an interest-bearing investment until the maturity date. Bonds are not in themselves values. Their value is rather a kind of calculated value, which, in the case of fixed interest securities, is based on the difference between the fixed interest rate of the bond and the current market interest rate. Take a simple example: an investor buys a fixed interest bond at a nominal value of €1000 and receives 3% interest per year for ten years. If the interest rate for fixed interest securities now rises to 5% the following year, the investor wanting to sell the security giving 3% interest per year will not find a buyer because its interest rate is fixed at 3%, although 5% interest on bonds can now be realised. The price of this security will therefore fall below the nominal value with the rise of the market interest rates. The economic quality of the bond is also decisive for the interest rate, or, to put it more precisely, the critical comparison taking place on financial markets between the quality of the bond, which is quantitatively measured in terms of expected future returns, and the anticipated future returns of alternative investments (size and security), determines its market value.

With the issue of shares, stock corporations want to convert foreign monetary amounts into their own capital. Money the company receives by issuing its shares is its equity capital. In this process, the company's stock capital is separated from the shares, from the future payments they imply and the participation in the company's profits (dividend). Ownership of shares includes the right to vote and the right to dividends. (Dividends, however, often play only a marginal role as only a small part of the company's profits is distributed to shareholders as dividends.) The equity capital of private banks in turn consists almost exclusively of financial assets, for example shares, which they do not produce themselves. But nevertheless, the equity capital of private banks is an endogenous product. Powerful shareholders have a certain influence on management decisions, especially if, like investment funds, they hold a high proportion of the company's shares or have voting rights. If the company then fails to meet certain expectations, the shares are sold and their price falls, making it more difficult for the company to issue new shares or bonds on the financial markets.

The market price of a share results from the many actions of the players, the buyers and the sellers on the stock markets. The major institutional players on the international stock markets today are investment, pension, fixed interest and hedge funds, asset managers such as Blackrock,[4] and the large private banks of the developed capitalist countries. The various financial institutions are in competition with each other, but it is also possible that the institutions may at times pursue joint strategies in order to survive together in competition. One might think, for example, of the strategies of investment funds, which do not dominate many stock corporations as a single majority shareholder, but as a whole or collectively. Through the shareholder value principle, a management and control instrument that functions by means of the shareholders' property rights, the investment funds have a direct influence on the management of the corporations, which, according to the specifications of the owners, should ensure that a highest possible and in the short-term realisable return on equity is generated. The rapid rate of share turnover that prevails on the stock markets today has also led to the reality that owners of stock companies are being replaced ever more quickly.

---

[4] Blackrock was founded in 1995 and today manages nearly $5 trillion in assets, more than any other financial company in the world. Blackrock holds only a relatively small stake at Deutsche Bank (5.17%), but no strategically important decisions can be made there without Blackrock.

For the movement of the share prices of a company, its expected future profit is decisive, i.e. future income flows should be capitalised. The stock prices still relate to the current business of the companies, but they refer in particular to the expectations and prognosis about the future economic development of the companies. As such, it is possible to speak of shares as fictitious capital as well. The stock markets constantly provide information, albeit always incompletely (money deals with the impossibility of complete information), on what the shares of a company are expected to yield in future payments in light of the prognosis of general economic trends, comparative assessment of the companies' profit prospects or the speculation on changes in interest rates. Calculations result from these evaluations and the corresponding trading activities with promises to pay the share price are calculated on the electronic stock exchanges every second. This development is always only relative to the company, its production processes and its capital assets. Thus, the share capital of the company has a separate existence from the capital forms of the production and circulation processes (productive and commodity capital). Nevertheless, today share price is to be understood as an eminently important economic parameter for companies listed on the stock exchange, since it ultimately represents what the company is "worth" (assets, production capacities, factory buildings, machines, warehouses, patents, market shares and jobs). Insofar as it has to be profitable in the future, the criterion for the valuation of the company is no longer capital productivity, which nevertheless satisfies the management and shareholders and is necessary for competition. Rather, it is the orientation towards market capitalisation, which can be significantly increased by the mergers and acquisitions of other companies.[5] The constantly fluctuating market capitalisation (the price of all the company's shares, i.e. the market value multiplied by the number of shares) quantifies important aspects of the economic performance of companies: on the one hand, those that the companies provide for the capital market, and, on the other, the market value (in addition to profit) represents a part of the capital power with which companies manage their production capacities, especially with regard to the

---

[5] Over the last years, stocks prices have risen much faster than corporate profits. In the first quarter of 2018, corporate profits in the U.S. were $1,948 billion; in the first quarter of 2021, they were $1,936 billion. Over the same period, the S&P 500 has risen by more than 50%, and the P/E ratio has increased by almost 80% over these three years.

100 A. SZEPANSKI

future (and which their owners and shareholders primarily have at their disposal).[6]

Shares and bonds are used by financial capital as instruments to increase the efficiency of capitalisation and to increase control over the money reserves of the economy. This concentration means that the value of a listed company is increasingly calculated according to the expectations of the financial markets, i.e. what returns it can achieve in the future and how lucrative the shares are for the investors who might buy them. And, if they inform themselves about the current prices of the shares and trade on them, institutional investors transform into speculators, insofar as they instrumentalise promises to pay, i.e. calculate according to financial mathematical formulas, equations and probabilistic models. However, to take probability as the measurable frequency of an apparently predictable event, especially if it is based on historical data, is an unjustified assumption, because the fact that something has happened in the past should not lead to the assumption that it will happen again in the future in exactly the same way. Therefore, with complicated models like the Monte Carlo Stochastics, one attempts to calculate all possible scenarios for the future, for example, by the invention of future stock prices, interest rates and economic cycles in simulation models, in order to then recognise how these factors affect the prices of the derivatives. But the models do not show what happens in the future as for example in physics, but only illustrate what can be expected in the future in terms of the realisation of promises to pay (the future generally remains uncertain or black).

In addition, stock prices on the financial markets also function as an index for the creditworthiness of companies and their competitive power as well as an informant of their capital size, i.e. their potency according to the capital size to initiate and realise sufficient profits through production processes. Thus, the operations of the "real economy" become the subject of permanent speculative and comparative calculations, evaluations and

---

[6] One deals in actualised virtual income before its creation in production (on over-trading, see Marazzi 2011: 74). If a stock rises from €200 to €220, the market value of a stock asset has risen by €20 without another market participant having lost €20. If many share owners were now trying to realise their capital gains as money, the prices would fall again. The shares themselves have no value, but they do have a book value, whereby the price movements of the shares have real economic effects. Share owners, who realise money, may save less and consume more, which increases effective demand and causes companies to expand production. However, shares can also be borrowed and what can be used to buy new shares causes share prices to rise.

controls by the financial markets and their institutions, which assess the effectiveness of the production processes of the companies by providing them with financial resources, while these amounts depend on the speculative expectations of the markets regarding the future profitability of companies. The potency of "real capital" thus becomes a dependent variable of the economic power of financial capital. However, this subordination of industrial and commercial companies to financial capital in no way reduces their business activity; rather, they in turn use external financial resources to increase their own effectiveness and capital size and thus also to improve their creditworthiness. The competitiveness of all companies is massively influenced by the use of the instruments of the financial industry, i.e. with the help of certain instruments, the financial institutions play a regulatory role in the projects of industrial companies, so that they can operate profitably and at the same time be considered a condition for increasing the turnover of securities. The large companies of the real economy today are themselves in turn to be seen as issuers of securities and as investors in fictitious capital, thus also participating in the business success of other companies. There is a fundamental identity between financial capital and real capital with regard to the increase of capital and the increase of capital power, and this leads to the tendency to subsume all economic processes under the processes of financial capitalisation. But this hardly means that competition between the two sectors has disappeared: while companies of the real sector use the capital market for their own competitiveness, financial capital regulates the competitive strategies of the real economy with the help of the instruments of fictitious and speculative capital, so that the interdependence and competition between the two sectors can be transferred into the evaluation and comparison of alternative investments and the resulting purchases and sales. The clash between the interests of industrial companies and the interests of financial capital now seems to have completely immersed itself in the price risks and price movements on the stock markets.

It is worth pointing out in this context that shareholder value is an important means of regulating companies, illustrating a shift from commodity production to fictitious and derivative (capital). Here there is the equation of a company's value with its market price, which implies continuous price-setting, while it is assumed that the market is an objective and non-personal judge of the company's value. Through its massive influence on credit, currencies and capital markets, fictitious capital embeds finance into the real economy and seeps into the ratio of the reproduction of production. The movement of a company's stock market price is now the key measure to generate shareholder value in particular. And this influences also the temporal compression of the horizon of investors, whose short-term perspectives now massively influence production, precisely by creating relative separations between the time of allocation of capital and the time of production processes.[7]

The period in which a stock is held, usually only from quarter to quarter, is much shorter than the cycles of product turnover in industrial production. This is also important, for example, in that financialisation has turned homeowners into passive investors who must now entrust their savings to institutional fund managers. Moreover, the income from shares often exceeds the profits that result from the sale of the related products. Thus, the quantity of money managed by the fund managers increases their influence and power in the companies, whose strategies must now be aligned with the pursuance of the strategies of fictitious and speculative capital regardless of the marketing of their products (long-term strategies or local ties to consumers).

Seen in this light, the logic of shareholder value consists in enabling the abstraction of fictitious and speculative capital from the industrial body of the company and, at the same time, radically reshaping it, that is, searching for a potential, in every aspect of the company, from which returns can be teased out. Day and night, an army of analysts around

---

[7] In the concept of shareholder value, profit is transformed from a differential size (profit is equal to the income that exceeds the costs) into a pure size of relations, known as return on investment, indicating the increase in value, which is valued on the stock exchange in short intervals between time t0 and time t1 (cf. Brodbeck 2009). With the so-called Sharpe ratio, one puts the increase in value of a company in relation to the risk, a definition with which one determines the return on a financial investment, insofar as it exceeds the risk-free interest rate. Return appears here as a function of risk, with the risk of an investor valid as a cost factor. In turn, the volatility of the return is taken as a measure of risk: one divides the expected profit of a portfolio (minus a risk-free interest rate) by its so-called standard deviation (ibid.). And thus, purely future-oriented sizes such as return on investment or Sharpe ratio serve as the current reference point for the decisions of the management, whereby the infinitesimal temporal maximisation of ratios or sizes of relation clearly move to the centre of corporate planning, which at the same time sets a process of acceleration in motion, so that on the part of management today, those decisions are always preferred that are oriented to the achievement of short-term returns. And this is copied from a specific stock market logic, which evaluates the increase in value of a company like that of a portfolio, i.e. profits must be realised in an interval between t0 and t1, and these are evaluated precisely with methods and models, which are supposed to function similarly to the diversification strategies of a portfolio (ibid.).

the world searches for hidden sources of exploitation, i.e. aspects of the company that can be monetised in the future, but have not yet been reflected in shareholder prices. Shareholder value is the ratio of the fictitious and the derivative when related to the company's environment. In this process, the distinction between capital and company is increasingly obliterated, insofar as every aspect of the company is directed towards monetisation, towards the transformation of the company as a social organisation into a machine for the increase of capital. The logic of shareholder value indicates the logic of the derivative: the directional and quantitative multiplication within a spiral movement, designed by fictitious and speculative capital.

In a sense, the share price itself can be now understood as a derivative, which is related to the underlying "company", with options running on the share price as derivatives on derivatives, so that the financial markets themselves transform into places where the future of companies is decided. Unlike fundamental analysis, which captures the fundamental business of a company, technical analysis generates based solely on the trajectories and volatility of the company's share price. Especially for a tech company, that is, not yet producing products, technical analysis is a welcome tool for measuring the risks implemented right now.

References

Brodbeck, Karl-Heinz (2009) *Die Herrschaft des Geldes: Geschichte und Systematik*, Darmstadt.

Decker, Peter, Hecker, Konrad and Patrick, Joseph (2016) *Das Finanzkapital*, Munich.

Harvey, David (2012) *Rebel Cities: From the Right to the City to the Urban Revolution*, London.

Lohoff, Ernst and Trenkle, Norbert (2012) *Die große Entwertung. Warum Spekulation und Staatsverschuldung nicht die Ursache der Krise sind*, Münster.

Marazzi, Christian (2011) *Verbranntes Geld*, Zürich.

Marx, Karl (1998) *Capital*, Vol. 3, in *Marx and Engels Collected Works*, Vol. 37, London.

CHAPTER 6

Speculative Capital

6.1 Derivatives

In recent decades, an ever-increasing proportion of the profits of private banks have been generated by financial activities that go far beyond simply borrowing and lending money. The commercial banks generate their profits through endogenous credit creation and through the trade of foreign exchange, especially securities and derivatives. In order to hedge or speculate, private banks themselves create complex collateral - derivatives such as credit default swaps, options and futures on interest rates and foreign exchange. Derivatives appear on the balance sheets of banks either positively as an asset or negatively as a liability. If the value of a derivative falls into negative, it is a liability, while a derivative as an asset is always a positive part of market value; that is, it is currently worth more than for which it was paid. Nevertheless, derivatives are not based on a pure accounting process, but rather have to be understood as speculative capital and at the same time, as a power technology. In general, derivatives are relations, or more precisely, relations about relations (the relative volatility of the derivative in relation to the volatility of the underlying asset, for example, the volatility of the relation between the euro and the dollar). There are two moving moments here: the speculation on the relation and the passage of time. The design and definition of a derivative

© The Author(s), under exclusive license to Springer Nature   105
Switzerland AG 2022
A. Szepanski, *Financial Capital in the 21st Century*,
Marx, Engels, and Marxisms,
https://doi.org/10.1007/978-3-030-93151-3_6

contract are determined especially by the variables of time, price fluctuation and volatility. Derivatives inscribe the use that a speculator makes of them, namely the socially instructed leveraging of speculative capital.

If the market price of a classical economic object (commodities such as clothes, food and computers) is directly affected by a loan, and this in turn can be massively influenced by the trade of a derivative, can one then really maintain the previous hierarchical order of three classes of economic objects (commodity, loan, derivative), whereby synthetic securities in particular are still referred to as purely derivative securities? How is the hierarchy between the economic objects to be understood? Classical exchange requires an immediate transfer of the physical object/commodity against money, and this has to be regarded as an invariant, symmetrical request of the economic property of the classical commodity-money relationship.[1] In the case of credit, this invariant requirement for immediate payment of the object is eliminated. Anyone who receives a commodity without paying immediately enters into a debt relationship. A debt relationship is dissolved again by payment. Money now has the potential to grow within the specific time horizon of a promise relationship. With the derivative, the invariant requirements, to which credit is still subject, dissolve further, whereby the economic properties of the object finally take on the freedom to fold, twist and bend or devour. The derivatives thus have a more powerful economic and topological reality than the other economic objects or services, and with respect to their reality, this also registers what can be described with Deleuze as potentiality, actuality and virtuality.[2] Moreover, the virtual

---

[1] Buying and selling consist precisely in the fact that a change of ownership takes place through the use of money: the buyer wants to become the owner of the commodity, the seller the owner of money. The use of money is thus an incessant process of change of ownership.

[2] Deleuze and Guattari discuss these registers in the context of the "quantum flow". This is a deterritorialised flow of financial money, which knows no segments and no stratified lines, but singularities and quanta. Singularities mean nominal liquid assets and quanta stand for processes, such as inflation, deflation and stagflation. The poles of the respective flows are regarded as condensations where money is created and destroyed. Through derivatives, certain distributions and corresponding *rhytmizations* of money capital flows can be observed in various forms and at the same time. For Deleuze and Guattari, each quantum flow is "deeper" than the money capital flows, whose metrics refer to elements of cardinal values: quantum flows are mutant, convulsive, creative, circulatory and material flows tied to desire and are always deeper than the solid lines and their segments (the latter determine, for example, interest rates and the relationship between supply and

6 SPECULATIVE CAPITAL   107

causality of the derivatives should be understood as determinant, performative and material; that is, the effects of derivatives virtually push for real material consequences. What must be added here is that capitalist companies are exposed to a whole range of risks, whether it is that they cannot find buyers for their products on the market, that the commodities they need for their own production processes are too expensive, or whether there are certain risks associated with the development of interest and exchange rates, which inevitably brings derivatives into play as forms of hedging (and not just speculation). Tony Norfield emphasises in particular the function of derivatives as instruments of hedging[3] (Norfield 2011: 110).

In this book, we refer to "assets" as specific forms of credit and as fictitious and speculative capital.[4] We assume a progressive differentiation of three different classes of financial assets: (a) the generic asset, (b) the synthetic asset and (c) the securitised synthetic asset. The category of generic asset includes forms of credit (loans, mortgages, etc.), fictitious capital (stocks and bonds) and vanilla derivatives (forwards, options,

---

demand). For Deleuze and Guattari then, there are two economic ways of thinking, (a) that of economic accounting (segments and solid lines of a molar organisation representing determinative metrics of cardinal value) and (b) that of financial-money, which today is called the flow of finance or just financial flows (Deleuze and Guattari 1992).

[3] Hedging means that certain economic actors use derivatives to hedge against the price fluctuations of their assets by selling the risks to speculators, who try to make a profit by anticipating future price movements, reducing the derivatives to a single characteristic: the changes in their prices. The speculative element of derivatives trading consists, among other things, in the fact that, to take an example, when the price of oil is expected to rise, not a barrel of oil is bought, but a derivative on the oil for a much smaller sum of money, which, if the price of oil rises accordingly, will pay off in a higher return than if a barrel of oil itself were purchased.

[4] Following Bichler and Nitzan, Jesus Suaste Cherizola develops the notion that assets are entitlements, which are exchanged in economic transactions (Cherizola 2021). To be more specific, assets are at first complex groups of sentences specifying a set of rights. They include an owner and a set of terms that specify what the owner is entitled to do. The set of rights that the asset grants must be materialised, which means that they must be recognised. This recognition gives the assets performative power. For the owner, an asset specifies a set of rights. For the subjects that validate it, an asset is a set of orders. An asset will have value only if someone expects that the set of rights/orders it grants will materialise. Assets are claims that can be sold, they can have a price and are exchanged in the market. The market is the system in which sets of rights/orders receive a price and are exchanged according to a unit of account called money. Not all transfers of entitlements are economic transactions, but all economic transactions are exchanges of rights/orders (ibid.).

futures), while the category of synthetic asset includes complex derivatives (CDS, TRS, etc.) (cf. Lozano 2014). Synthetic assets/derivatives are here generally understood as a form of speculative monetary capital in latency - latency or liquidity in the sense that derivatives still have to be realised in money. Securitised synthetic assets such as CDOs or CLOs can include securities, loans and credit default swaps (CDS).[5]

Investors can be divided into those who go long by profiting from the incoming payments of debtors and those who go short and profit from credit defaults. Derivatives do not simply involve investors, but rather one actor and one counteractor at a time, so that the loss of one is the gain of the other (this holds only for a single contract). But, as is the case with traditional insurance, the parties need not hold a claim via ownership of the underlying asset to hedge against the volatility of the CDO, but rather the CDO itself becomes a source of revenue and profit.

Completely contrary to the investment in industrial production processes, which must absolutely have a positive result for the company, with the speculation on derivatives, profits from economic events such as falling profit rates, insolvencies or scarcities can potentially be obtained if the conditions formulated in the derivative contracts occur in the future. Derivative contracts are intrinsically performative insofar as they themselves construct the terms of their own existence (including the speculation) (LiPuma 2017: 305). Short sales are a good example of this: one borrows a security in expectation of falling prices, then sells it and buys it back at a later date, when the price of the security has fallen, so that the price difference leads to a profit. Speculation can now be considered

---

[5] If the economic mode of existence of a classical object (clothing, computer, food, etc.) is directly affected by the generic asset (share, credit, etc.) and its value in turn by its synthetic replicant (CDO, CDS), then it seems indeed difficult to speak of only a derivative. It starts now from the derived: the chain of effects runs from the CDS to the option and to the credit. Already in general, that object has the highest power of effect, i.e. reality, which in its plurality comprises many variables and thus the most effective properties and components within a specific constellation. The real-virtual object of a third order is especially able to produce a differential self-referentiality with high speed and has no need for any externality to mediate its own self-referential movement.

The synthetic asset is created in the concurrence of what it is and what it is not. As speculative capital, it is what it is, a replicated embodiment of the generic asset (e.g. credit or government bond), but at the same time, it is more than it is, for it functions in a much more fungible way than the generic asset and possesses a much higher symmetry: it can radically affect, even determine, its trading, and it possesses a set of distinct, ever-changing different economic characteristics (cf. Lozano 2014).

an important operational category, a method that focuses on the future production of profits. Even the management of balance sheets, whereby the balance sheet is to be understood as a social, power-related production process with which numerical artefacts are addressed, is today to be understood as part of artificial speculation and is thus indispensably linked to the production of future profits. Speculation, arbitrage and hedging as characteristics of risk and portfolio management (a portfolio of stocks is efficient precisely when it produces the highest profit at the lowest risk; the aim is to distribute and spread profits, with losses capable of being more than compensated) are today directly linked to the organisation of capitalist production and circulation.

In principle, one can distinguish today between three forms and strategies of trading with fictitious and speculative capital: arbitrage, hedging and speculation (cf. Malik 2014: 336f.). Arbitrage aims to realise a risk-free profit by means of simultaneous execution of certain financial transactions in at least two or even more markets. One buys a share at one stock exchange (if it has different prices on two or more stock exchanges) at a certain price and sells it at once again at another stock exchange at a higher price (instantaneously), thus achieving a risk-free profit. Arbitrage is a means by which the volatile financial field in which the assets are traded remains liquid, but as soon as the arbitrage opportunity arises, it is immediately closed again by those very actors who have benefited from it.

Hedging uses derivatives to minimise risk. It is a strategy that compensates for risk by taking an opposite position to one already existing in the market. When a derivative contract is entered into, the position taken is intended to offset the risk arising from a change in the price of the underlying asset or liability. When the derivative contract is settled at maturity, its holder incurs a gain (or loss) that compensates (or does not compensate) for the loss (or gain) resulting from the price movement of the underlying asset or liability. Non-financial companies today tend to hedge much more than financial companies, which are particularly active in the field of speculation.

Even hedging already includes a speculative moment insofar as it refers to the trajectories of future volatility of the underlying. However, the correlation hypothesised in hedging - if y moves up, then x moves down - is not perceived by market participants as a parameter of the model, but as real. The hedge can therefore also mutate into speculation. In this case, it is not a matter of reducing the risks, but rather they are hedged only in order to increase the speculative capital, whereby the risk only counts quantitatively, as a calculation of a price, which is provided with a number. In this process, risks are separated from the conditions of their realisation, and this has certain implications: risk can now be defined in terms of volatility and measured as the probability of the relative variance of the derivative price. Volatility is itself measured into a logic of production. Derivatives now capitalise on the volatility they actively create.

Speculation means that derivative contracts are bought or sold to earn profits from the future operation of the difference between the fluctuating prices of the underlying and the prices of the derivative, i.e. to monetise the difference between the strike price (delivery price) and the spot price (market price) at maturity of the derivative contract. However, this is only half true since speculation (and hedging) operates mainly as the price movement of the derivatives themselves, where changes in the derivative prices result in a change in the speculator's profit-loss balance sheet (and not in the underlying assets).[6] The higher the volatility and the duration of a derivative, the higher the risk associated with it. Here, the return is endogenously related to volatility and time. Speculation is based on the affirmation of the risk that this endogenous relationship entails. Speculators must perform complex risk management when trading derivatives. In general, speculators have various options at their disposal to work with a higher leverage than a traditional investor, who invests in industrial production processes or trades the underlying at the respective market price. As will be shown in more detail, the speculator primarily trades the prices of the derivatives themselves, and thus speculation indicates that the derivative markets are by no means to be understood as markets,[7] where the primary objective is to buy or sell the underlying, which means that they are not considered as markets for those investments, where companies realise profits by managing the difference between the sales or selling price and the production costs of the commodities. Derivative markets are always tied to their own liquidity. The volume of speculative trading today

---

[6] Delta hedging, which is used to calculate the price of an option, means that profits can be made with an option, no matter in which direction the underlying asset moves, as long as there is sufficient volatility, which is measured as implied volatility, i.e. by the inversion of the Black–Scholes formula.

[7] One of the first institutionalised derivative markets was the Chicago Board Options Exchange (CBOE).

exceeds that of hedging many times over.[8] However, financial companies in particular are constantly mixing the three different strategies, i.e. speculation with hedging and arbitrage.

Usually, the generic asset (forward contracts, futures, options) is defined as a financial contract, whose value is derived from something else called an "underlying" or "underlying asset" (Esposito 2010: 152–153). This underlying can be the price of the financial instruments or derivatives themselves, or the prices of stocks, bonds, indices, interest rates, commodity prices, etc., can take on the function of the underlying, but also external factors such as the yields of wheat crops or bananas can take the function of the underlying. Basically, the number of possible underlyings is endless. In no case is the derivative identical with the underlying because the owner of a futures contract, who wants to buy a ton of copper at a certain point in time, is not the owner of the copper, but only becomes the owner if the contract is executed at a certain point in time. Until then, the derivative contract can be sold and gains or losses can be realised on it, depending on how the copper price develops. Thus, the writing of speculative derivative contracts seems to be entirely focused on capitalising the spread of strike price (fixed in the contract) and spot price (market price of the underlying) at maturity of the contract. We will, however, see that this is not the case.

A distinction must be made between derivatives which, as in the OCT markets, are negotiated directly between two partners and therefore do not require a standardised form (forward contracts) and derivatives integrated into complex chains of promise (options, futures), which circulate in the circuits of financial markets and are burdened with the inflexibility of standardisation and can only be typified and classified by very specific actors who have the economic power to do so.[9] Derivatives traded on the OTC markets are today the majority and are traded without exchange,

[8] It may be difficult for individual actors to find partners who take the opposite position in a contract, for which so-called market makers or speculators then step in to keep the markets liquid.

[9] Edward LiPuma sees derivatives as a generative scheme which involve a "bet" on volatility, enable the division and composition of capital and produce an amalgam of variable and incommensurable forms of risk and lead to an abstract number that functions as a social mediation (LiPuma 2017: 31). For derivatives, indexes such as gross domestic product are insignificant. Without the production of volatility, the derivative cannot exist; indeed, it motivates its replication and circulation; otherwise, it remains worthless.

and therefore do not require a standardised form.[10] Trade with derivatives requires an energetic and liquid market that makes the circulation of speculative capital possible, a market that is always already a practical, performative construct and a socially produced and real fiction - fiction, because it must be believed by the market participants and, at the same time, it is real and must be constantly recreated (liquidity in the face of uncertainty), and also an object of theory[11] (LiPuma 2017: 221ff.).

[10] Between 1999 and 2009, the volume of OCT derivatives increased from $2.63 to $21.6 trillion (Sahr 2017: Kindle Edition: 4972).

[11] In 2008, the volume of futures and options traded on a global scale was $2.4 trillion (Sahr 2017: Kindle-Edition 4972). It must be assumed that the decisions of rational agents, which neoclassical theory prefers, have strong points of reference to fiction. Rational agents are therefore those who want to maximise their utility, but do not necessarily know what strategy is needed to achieve their goal. And here fictions come into play that contain imaginations, images and narratives about future states of the world or future events that are cognitively accessible in the present through mental representations. This means that in the face of uncertainty the agents are motivated precisely by imagined future events and carry out their activities with the help of mental representations or fictional expectations - fictions which, in the economic sphere, take on the narrative form of beliefs, ideas, ideologies, fantasies, theories and discourses. Inasmuch as these narratives cannot be completely reduced to numerical quantification procedures, mathematical models or simply to empiricism, fiction always provides resources for a flourishing creativity industry. If the fictions are not bound to rational methods of calculation, they may not necessarily be true, but they still produce real economic effects. Fictional expectations represent future events, as if they were true and thus enable actors to act with some degree of intention in the face of an uncertain future, even though the future remains unpredictable and unknown.

Even Joseph Schumpeter insists that the construction of innovations is incompatible with those calculative behaviours that economic science claims, since the motivations cannot be rationally deduced from existing knowledge. Rather, it would be the contingent imaginations of the actors that motivate and guide their inherently partially calculable activities. The oscillation between open imaginations and rational calculations is based on relationships that require trust, i.e. the actors always try to obtain information about their respective cooperative partners and therefore interpret any signals that testify trustworthiness. Even the objective procedures that serve to enable the optimal choice must be seen from the point of view of uncertainty and therefore always contain fictional aspects, i.e. calculation as a form of fiction legitimises certain decisions apparently independent of the non-calculability of the results. Thus, in situations characterised by uncertainty, calculations are less to be understood as instruments that allow anticipation of the future, but rather as a kind of tranquiliser used against the effects of actions in unpredictable environments. They encounter the motivations of market participants, which are characterised by three features: incentives operate short-term, competitive and monetary. No one can turn down a short-term profitable investment, even if great dangers lurk in the future in which the investment will lose its value. LiPuma refers to this as the "treadmill effect" (LiPuma 2017: 147).

The simplest form of a derivative is the forward contract, an over-the-counter forward transaction which consists in the agreement to buy or sell an asset, item or commodity (underlying) at a fixed price and at a future date (cf. Malik 2014: 340f.; Hull 2011, specifically chapter 2). If one commits to buying the underlying at a certain price when the forward contract matures, one takes the long position; the sale (the delivery of the underlying asset) includes the short position. If at the fixed time the current market price (the spot price) of the underlying is higher than the contractually agreed delivery price (the strike price), then the long position makes a profit and the short position has to accept a loss. The delivery prices are regulated in over-the-counter clearing houses and certain costs are incurred at maturity.

Let us take a simple example and assume that K is the delivery price of the underlying commodity at maturity T, S is the market price at the delivery date and q is the quantity of the commodity that will be delivered at time t. The person who wants to buy takes the "long position" and the person who wants to sell takes the "short position". The former agrees to pay K tx q on a given day and will later receive something that has the value $S \times q$ (unknown until $t1$). This is a swap of cash flows. For the long position (purchase), the forward contract has the value F for the whole period t before maturity. If Ft is the current forward price in t, then the value can be written as follows (Sotiropoulos et al. 2013: 77):

$$f_t = (F_t - K)e^{-rt}$$

r is the interest rate and t is the time remaining time until maturity. If the price F in time t is higher than the price K originally set in the contract, the long position makes a profit, namely the discounted difference $F - K$. Ultimately, the "value" of the forward contract can be positive or negative. It indicates the profits and losses of both parties and includes the capitalisation of promises and risks and the corresponding future income. John Milios understands the forward contract as a commodity sui generis (capital as capital) (Milios 2019).

A future contract is a contractual agreement (on the stock market) between two parties to buy or sell a certain quantity of an item, commodities or indexes at a fixed future date and at a price fixed in the contract that differs from the current and future market price of the respective item. If the market price of the item rises, the buyer makes a profit and vice versa. In contrast to forward contracts, the success of future contracts does not depend exclusively on the agreements of the respective contracting parties, but also on the possible future exchange of contracts on the financial markets, which means that the prices of future contracts can vary according to the respective market trends and forces. They increase when more traders take a "long position" rather than a "short position" (cf. Hull 2011, specifically chapter 2.3).

Options are derivative contracts that include the right to buy (call) or sell (put) underlyings up to a certain point in time (maturity) and at a fixed price without having to execute the option. The price of a call option, with which one can buy a commodity or a security at a certain future price but need not, varies from zero to an infinite number. The use of options is mainly for hedging purposes (Malik 2014: 346f.). In contrast to forward and future contracts, costs are incurred when the option is purchased. There are two basic types of options: the right to buy something at a fixed price in the future is called a call option (call) and the right to sell is called a put option (put).[12] When you sell, you take the short position, and when you buy, you take the long position (cf. Hull 2011, specifically chapter 1). The relationship between strike price and maturity is called convexity. Options create a relationship between the future and the present so that future cash flows can have a calculated value already in the present, for example by comparing different risk profiles.

With the call option, speculation is made on the future development of the price of the underlying (the rise in the share price). It is redeemed if the price agreed in the contract is below the market price at maturity (European option), or even before that (American option). If the desired event occurs, the holder of the option has the right to buy at the fixed price. If he does not redeem the option due to certain other circumstances, the right expires and the small option fee is lost for him. Put options, on the other hand, will be redeemed by the holder if the price agreed in the contract is higher than the market price (ibid.). There are

---

[12] Put-call parity means that there is a fixed relationship between put and call options. The put and call must refer to the same underlying and have the same strike price and an identical maturity. Someone who holds the call option to buy a stock at the strike price must have the money to buy the stock if he exercises the option. On the side of the holder of the put option, the person who has the put already holds the stock to which the put relates. The price of the call option plus the cash needed to buy the share must be identical to the value of the put, plus the share price. The put-call parity measures whether there is an imbalance in market prices for options. If the put-call parity is not met, then there is an arbitrage opportunity, i.e. to be able to make a profit without risk.

two types of operators: the writer and the reader of an option, with the former writing optionality and selling it to the latter for a fee.

In general, it is important here to be able to rely not only on the price movements of shares, securities, currencies, etc., but also on the speculations that affect them, i.e. market fluctuations or volatilities of a higher order.[13] Most options, especially the exotic options, are to be classified as non-conventional, non-linear derivatives that include contingent claims (contracts between two persons where the pay-off is based on uncertain future events). This implies so-called non-linear delta hedging, where the delta measures the variable rate between the price of an option and the price of an underlying asset, a rate that is constant and invariant in the standard model. Delta hedging consists of an operator that determines "correctly" the delta of the portfolio, so that the price movements of the option and the price movements of the correlative reference position are close to equilibrium; the infinitesimal alignment of the two price movements implies that the delta of the portfolio is not strictly zero at any given point in time, but at least tends towards zero. The delta is constantly in a process of becoming zero. And this delta-neutrality is to be achieved by acceleration, i.e. the movement is to move ever faster towards zero. In order to dynamically hedge with such second-order derivatives, one has to recalibrate them continuously; that is, one has to find a financial method to force an endless deterritorialisation of the option towards zero, which can only be asymptotic; the continuous replication is always dynamic.

Swaps are highly complex futures contracts that are traded on the OTC markets. They agree on certain conditions for the exchange of future cash flows and money streams (cash capital flows, income or yield flows) and fix the respective dates on which future payments are to be made as well as the mode with which these payments are calculated in each case (cf. Malik 2014: 351; Hull 2011, chapter 5). Comparative cost advantages can be generated with the help of swap contracts, which were created in the early 1980s. For example, one exchanges uncertain cash flows with variable interest rates for sums of money with fixed interest rates, thus trading the risk of a price decline against the risk that a loan will

---

[13] The term volatility can be understood in general terms as the randomness in things, which is perceived as the intensity of change. In various models, current volatility is transformed into a statistical measure based on historical results, such as price movements over a one-year period. Volatility must be distinguished from the terms risk and uncertainty (Lee and Martin 2016: 203).

not be repaid. To illustrate this, take a simple example: a company that borrows money at a fixed interest rate for a long period of time wants to take advantage of the opportunity to borrow money at a variable interest rate, or for a shorter period of time than it is normally possible in the fixed-rate markets. A second company mainly involved in markets with floating interest is looking for long-term money or loans at an acceptable interest rate on the fixed-rate market. Now, the swapping of future interest amounts resulting from loans on the fixed-rate market and loans on the variable market favours both companies under certain circumstances, i.e. both companies pay lower interest rates in the future than they would have paid without the swapping deal. The result is a splitting of profits between the two parties. Interest rate swaps had a market value of \$12.6 trillion in 2009 (Sahr 2017: Kindle Edition: 4979).

The swap contracts do not necessarily have to meet the contractual requirements that are usual in conventional insurance markets, where, for example, the seller of an insurance policy must hold the corresponding amount of money in case of default. The liberation from the restrictions, which are found in the traditional insurance markets, has the consequence that there exist even more intensive networks, dependencies and entanglements between those financial companies (and their sizes; balance sheet sum) that provide loans and insurance. This in turn leads to lower prices for credit swap contracts and thus to a reduction in net costs and to the associated expansion of credit volumes.

Since 2000, a new type of synthetic securities, called credit default swaps (CDS), has been massively spreading in financial markets. These are contracts by which a policyholder insures himself with an insurer against the default of a reference debtor (of the former), for which the insurer receives a fee from the policyholder in the agreed period. The parties negotiate the risk of the reference debtor's default or a similar credit event. The greater the probability that the reference debtor will become insolvent, the higher the fee for the insurance, a fee that the insurers consider as a return.[14]

---

[14] In the case of the "Naked CDS", the CDS is characterised by the following points: (1) the seller of the CDS holds the risks of a loan default without holding the loan itself. (2) He can resell the insurance and therefore does not necessarily have to own the capital reserves that can compensate for the buyer's default. (3) The buyer does not have to be the owner of the underlying credit or even have any interest in it. The buyer and seller then construct the swap around a reference loan held by neither party in order to speculate precisely on its capacity.

Now, if the CDS is resold, the holder of a CDS can succeed to make a profit simply by managing time: the holder closes a contract as policyholder for the period $t0-t2$ and signs a second contract as a insurer at time $t1$, which is valid for the period $t1-t2$. He now speculates if the CDS, for example, has a government bond as a reference that the credit standing of state X will get worse over time, because then the fees (for him as the insurer) will increase, which means that he may earn higher insurance fees in the period $t1-t2$ than he has to pay in fees (as the policyholder) in the period $t0-t2$ (cf. Mühlmann 2013: 32). In the period $t0-t2$, the probability of a credit default or insolvency increases, whereby $t2$ can be regarded as a time segment that can be shifted, and at that end, insolvency may be possible. CDS transactions can be used to manipulate the interest rates that governments have to pay for their bonds; that is, these rates will rise if the prices for credit insurance are driven up. It is assumed that the probability of the occurrence of a credit event (e.g. insolvency of companies or states) increases over time, so that consequently the fees for insuring transactions increase the closer the event gets to the point of catastrophe, which radically breaks off the previous economic dynamics. This means that from the onset of the catastrophe, the kairos, we are confronted with qualitatively new time courses and structures (ibid.: 38). The risk of the speculator here is that if he acts both as policyholder and as insurer, he must also expect losses.

This type of insurance economics involves an asymmetric time machine, inasmuch as the irreversible time of risk (the insolvency of a debtor implies irreversibility; if it occurs, an insurer, who has negotiated a CDS with the creditor of a reference debtor, has to pay the creditor the full amount of the loan) is mixed with the reversible time of risk, in which the risk seems to be suspended, since an insurance company as a first-degree insurer that has sold a CDS to a bank can close a second insurance policy as the policyholder. If the first-degree insurer has to pay the full amount of the loan to the bank (due to the insolvency of one of its debtors), the same amount is reimbursed by a second-degree insurer, making the insolvency for the first-degree insurer a reversible event of time. An investor can also insure against the default of a securitised loan (CDO) by purchasing a CDS, whose price is higher the more likely it is expected that the CDO will default, which may occur at any point in the securitisation chain.

It is easy to see that with this type of concatenation of CDS viral effects can occur, because the actors behave simultaneously as insurer and insured, i.e. act within a combinatorics of inverse links (ibid.: 34f.). As

Mühlmann writes: "In the viral chain, all money is only borrowed from a lender, who in turn has borrowed it and insures his own lending, whereas the one who has borrowed the money from him also borrowed the money and insured himself, when he lent it to him" (ibid.: 186). The increase of chance up to catastrophe usually implies an increase of returns, without which entropies or losses can be excluded. After all, in the end, only those actors generate profits who drop out of the business shortly before the real catastrophe (e.g. the insolvency of a company/state) (ibid.: 116). CDSs are therefore always traded with a specific time structure and its contingency.

The extraordinary growth of the markets for CDS, which practically did not exist in the 1990s, is demonstrated by the fact that in 2007 these included contracts with a volume of $45.5 trillion (according to the *New York Times*, Arcane market is next to face a big credit test, 17 February 2008). In 2007, credit in the amount of $58.2 trillion was hedged through the CDS chains (Sahr 2017: Kindle-Edition: 4991). The reason for this enormous growth was the same as for CDOs: it enabled private banks, shadow banks and other financial institutions to realise high profitability, albeit in a different way than CDOs. When banks sell CDSs, they receive fees, and more importantly, the purchase of CDSs allows them to save money capital, since the balance sheet debt instruments, which have a weak credit rating, require significant capital reserves to compensate for the risk that a debtor cannot pay. If now the default risk is reduced by a CDS contract, the capital reserves can also be reduced and thus new money funds can be released to expand the business. And even CDS risks are still hedged today and thus seemingly reduced.

These processes accelerated the growth of mortgage issuance by U.S. banks in the years prior to the financial crisis of 2008, so that volume of CDO and CDS transactions increased. The permanent under-rating of risks (in the context of the allocation of mortgages) also helped this mechanism to grow, while low interest rates of the central banks supported this process. This included the growing allocation of subprime loans, whereby from 2006 onwards, private banks increasingly lacked borrowers who had the ability to repay their loans. In this context, CDS can certainly be described as important catalysts for the growth of financial capital. Their function is, on the one hand, to hedge financial risks and, on the other hand, to adjust the banks' lending to customers in order to increase profitability again at a time when low interest rates are damaging businesses and returns, which result from certain investments.

Let us summarise and explain further. As we saw, the derivative is not a thing, but rather essentially relational, or even more, it is a relation of relations. First, the relative volatility of the derivative itself in relation to the volatility of the underlying has to be mentioned for characterising the derivative. This will be examined later. In turn, crucial for the replication of the derivative is its size, the time period and the speed of volatility. In a sense, according to LiPuma, "bets" (which we interpret differently) are made on these relations and a "tango is played with time" (LiPuma 2017: 28). So in a derivative contract, two counterparties "bet" on what will happen to an underlying asset in the future, such as interest rates or exchange rates between the dollar and the euro. This bet is to be valid for a specific period of time, which is clearly defined in the contract. It must already be assumed here that the price of the derivative itself can be traded too.

For LiPuma, derivative markets are, on the one hand, historically determined and, on the other, arbitrary means of capital for ascribing risk to value (ibid.: 29). Derivative markets in some ways separate circulation from production and generate new modes of interdependence and connectivity (ibid.: 60). This refers primarily to the fact that derivatives are not limited by or dependent on the structures of production. And at the end the derivative is a non-determinant form that can refer to all imponderables and uncertainties in the world. Because there are a myriad of underlyings, there are few limits to the ways derivatives can be written. The derivative involves a speculative ethos, which is constituted between a culture of calculation and the illegibility of chance (ibid.: 229ff.).

For LiPuma, moreover, the derivative is a generic design scheme, which implies a time-based bet on volatility, on the division and recomposition of capital and on the mixing of variable and incommensurable forms of risk, ultimately resulting in an abstract number, an abstract risk, that in turn functions as a social mediation (ibid.: 36; for an economy driven by derivatives, metrics like GDP are meaningless). Derivatives represent the economic "totality" as an indeterminate, disparate aggregation of replicating contracts on a global scale, which are based on abstract risk. (The size and in principle boundlessness of derivatives today have enormous consequences for the organisation of national labour markets and the conditions of collective reproduction of the economy. Speculation becomes the privileged dispositif when the profits that result from speculation exceed the profits that result from the application of productive labour. Consider the real estate market, where the profits that relate to the house as a financial asset have exceeded the value of the house as a material good or commodity; indeed, profits are increasingly decoupled from the cost of the classic house.) There is, similar to the movement of capital, the intrinsic need in derivative markets to constantly invent new exotic or synthetic derivatives, to identify and capitalise global money flows, that is, to subject them to the logic of leverage.

Derivatives monetise risk for a specific period of time. The Now (the beginning of the contract) is a virtual and spaceless moment, but crucially, the contract has a duration related to the future. Further, derivative contracts are intrinsically performative in that they produce the conditions of their own existence, just as saying the word "promise" produces the promise until it expires under certain conditions (ibid.: 37). The use-value of the derivative consists in its dynamic replication, or, to put it another way, derivatives exist in the interval between inception and expiration, and in doing so they continuously create a new Now and new wealth by opening and closing the gap between a realised price and a possible future. Derivatives fill a period in which wealth is created as a consequence of volatility, as a dispersion of what they represent as an imaginary centre of spreads. The design of the derivatives shapes the leveraging of these spreads and volatility.

Convexity here means that the variation in the price of the underlying and that of the derivative need not be symmetrical. A variation in the price of the underlying can lead to a disproportionate variation in the price of the derivative (while this price influences massively the prices of underlyings). Thus, even a small variation in the price of the underlying can lead to a huge increase in the price of the derivative; recall, that in the subprime crisis, a small number of defaults, which are related to falling house prices, led to large losses on CDOs. In this context, the derivative cannot only be reduced to an anticipated income stream or return, because the size and speed of its volatility help determine the size of the return. The price thus refers also to the expected future volatility of the derivative, measured as the degree of variance between the moment of the transaction and its maturity. The derivative price is thus centred around the relation between the expected volatility and the maturity.

Thus, the pricing of volatility takes place in time intervals; that is, time is compressed and contracted in the period between the inception and expiration of the derivative, although it should be noted that the speed of circulation is quite different from that of classical commodities.[15] From the constant flow of time, the derivative cuts out and shapes a certain interval of time, an interval that presents the future, which in turn interacts with the present, or, to put it differently, it is about the interpolation of the future, which leads at the same time to the expansion of the present, but also to its destabilisation (ibid.). Traders are condemned to anticipate a future they cannot know, and in doing so, they follow the guidelines of financial theory, which tries to determine the future as a probabilistic distribution. This use and determination of time distinguishes the derivative substantially from the classical exchange of commodities. The derivative has no transparent value in the here and now; the only measure that motivates the transaction lies in the calculation of its future value. The derivative aims at a future; it can only be priced out because market participants assume a bid-asked spread, insofar as they reach an agreement on the net value of the derivative, but differ in their expectations and speculative calculations regarding the future value of the derivative.

If the present future, that which is expected in the future, and the future present, that which is called the future, which actually occurs, are not congruent, then, as a result of trading in speculative capital, a future present always occurs with which the difference from that expected and,

---

[15] Even the commodity must be considered in a more differentiated way today. Traditional Marxism continues to insist that only the object is to be conceived as a commodity, and that something that is not an object cannot ultimately take the commodity form. However, the digitally composed derivatives of synthetic finance contradict this idea of a commodity object, and one can now say that the object is a node in a web of relations, or an interface with the sociality that appears as an object (the nodeness of an object is a composed position). Jonathan Beller speaks of the transition of the singular commodity object to the dispersed and distributed commodity (the digital object), the transition from the movement of factory production to the distributed production of the network commodity in the social factory (Beller 2021). Industrial production creates commodified objects in the factory that are sold in markets, while distributed (digital) production creates digital objects that are effectively derivative "objects" in the imaginary and social factory network and are sold in attention markets. The new distributed image-objects are inextricably linked to franchising, platforms, brands and other modes of associative transmission. Owning a piece of a network, whether as a share, infrastructure or token, or even as a "commodity", can be defined as a network derivative because it provides a return on an underlying asset, namely traffic, which is the benefit of the network as a whole. A commodity is thus a part in a network of relationships - a node or, in normal parlance, a distributed object. But in the light of today's digital composition capability, even the traditional commodity object is a derivative, a structured, composable position on the tradable exchange value, and its base value is in the market.

122   A. SZEPANSKI

to a certain extent, calculated or fixed future, and whose potentials one may also have used, becomes actualised. As Elena Esposito writes: "The future is neither in the present future, nor in the future present, but in the difference between the two, and therefore includes both in itself" (Esposito 2010: 178). Now, according to Esposito, the temporal circularity of financial economics consists precisely in the fact that the present depends on the future, "which in turn depends on the present, which depends on it" (ibid.: 28). For Esposito, the derivative market or synthetic finance represents a "great apparatus for creating the future" (ibid.: 179) that effectively executes the financial system with its artificial reference on the contentless sign of money.

6.1.1   Excursus 1: The Black–Scholes Formula

The Black–Scholes formula, a performative mathematical method and a model for calculating the price of an option, became famous because it can be used to deduce the gains and losses of options through recursive adaptation or dynamic-hedging strategies, or, to put it another way, to neutralise directional risks in financial markets. Therefore, the two inventors of the formula assume that events will occur in the future with a similarly dispersion as events in the past, which means that risks should be predictable to a certain extent, insofar they can be derived from past developments. Another one of the prerequisites established by Black/Scholes is that rational investors behave like particles in a liquid (Brownian motion), whose exact location cannot be predicted, although the dispersion of their motion and its realisation can. Thus, creditors and debtors seem to be able to decide on their preferred risk structure without risk. Under these conditions, the cash flows of different assets (options and shares) are compared; that is, current volatility and future volatility are equalled.

In the Black–Scholes formula, the price of an option is calculated by a differential equation, which contains five variables: strike price, option expiration, risk-free interest rate, and the price and volatility of the underlying asset.[16] The unknown in the equation is the volatility

---

[16] For Robert Meister, the achievement of Black/Scholes is to have broken down financial assets into even more basic components of options and risk-free debt, at least as far as calls are concerned. If one pays the amount for an option to buy a house in the future at a price one sets today, one can potentially profit from a future rise in house

of the underlying asset (and thus the time), but it can at least be estimated by historical data. So the expected volatility of the underlying of the option and its future changes over the life of the option are, according to Black/Scholes, the first key to pricing the options, and volatility is the only parameter that has an exponential effect. What is not taken into account here is that the value of the option itself can also vary and exerts a decisive influence on the prices. Derivatives construct time as a resource and quantifiable dimension of risk. The longer the term of the option, the higher the potency of volatility. Therefore, a calculus must be developed that measures and predicts volatility. It can be calculated by the implied volatility. It is then not at first anymore about the value which is subsisted by the volatility of the price. The value of the option is now derived from the movement of price and the movement of the market (of the underlying asset), which means volatility. The volatility is now the "value" of the market as a quality and is as such unquantified. The normal way of quantifying it by economists is by the asset's volatility (underlying). But a number can also be put on the unquantified volatility through the option price or implied volatility.

$$\frac{\partial DT}{\partial t} + rS \frac{\partial DT}{\partial s} + \frac{1}{2}\sigma^2 S^2 \frac{\partial^2 DT}{\partial S^2} = rDT$$

1. The duration of the option contract until maturity
2. The risk free interest rate r
3. The reference price ($S0$)
4. The volatility of the reference price (σ).

Risk neutrality is a non-mathematical parameter designed to guarantee a derivative market that is sui generis free and immune to all socio-economic variations and events that might allow derivatives to be priced differently. This excludes arbitrage; that is, the same derivative cannot have a different price in Frankfurt than in London, and on this basis, it is then further assumed that the model allows a derivative to be perfectly hedged. A collateral cannot then have more than one price (law of one price). The law seems to be confirmed by the axiom that arbitrage is impossible in a sufficient market, and if arbitrage opportunities arise due

prices by selling the option at a profit, while limiting the potential loss relative to the original amount one paid, in the event that house prices fall (Meister 2021: 6).

to market anomalies, the spread between two different prices is immediately closed, although in reality arbitrage is always present in financial markets. There is a gap to report here between the economic model that designs reality and the reality of the model, which in turn is related to the difference between the certainty presupposed by financial theory and the uncertainties that financial actors face in their practice.

In the name of pure mathematics, an idealised perfect homogeneous space must be assumed which prevents arbitrage and conceives it as a purely external matter, where it then cannot do more than what it often does, namely to inflect or bend the prices. The Standard Model excludes that an option not only gives the holder the possibility to do something at a certain point in the future, but also opens up optionality. But today it is not only about the optimisation of the yield, but also about the increase of optionality. The holding of an option gives the owner the right (not the obligation) to do something at a certain time or also not to - it thus makes possible for him a choice, or, differently said, the option gives him optionality. This always includes social demands that exist in social relationships and networks and are related to future money flows, something that is often neglected in financial theory. Nevertheless, for Robert Meister, the "value" of financial theory, as Black/Scholes demonstrated, includes that it allows options to be priced out, doing so through texts, often enough standardised contracts that co-reference certain sequences of financial events and points of parity between them. Such a point of parity can be a spread between the prices of two commodities at a given time. It can also be a point of parity between non-comparable units such as an average price and the measurement of an average temperature. This moment of co-referentiality, found in derivative contracts, is priced out and traded in markets (Meister 2021: 14).

The Black–Scholes formula implies that the pay-off is specified at maturity and then runs backwards in time to determine the current values. It does not take into account that deflationary or inflationary processes may occur, and it assumes that counterparties can never be insolvent. When factors and changes in liquidity, changes in the supply and demand relationship, disturbances in the risk-free interest rate, arbitrage opportunities, etc., are taken into account, the formula quickly becomes too complex and hardly applicable in practice. The formula rather installs[17] a clean financial mathematics of rational agents; that is, it assumes the totality of the market as a mathematical representation and as a natural institution, thus losing sight of the market as part of the construction of a socio-economic form that makes capital circulate even today through the financialisation of life. Mathematisation reinforces this assumption when the agents simultaneously assume the market as an imaginary totality - the market as a continuous set of transactions that maintain liquidity.

The implied volatility is used to compare the risk profile of the underlying and the option, which is called a dynamic replication (the comparison of a known instrument with an unknown instrument). There are always options on the market with market prices. If the market moves in a random walk, then the prices of the assets move in the same progressions; that is, the volatility is stochastic and non-constant, and therefore, the parameter volatility requires an operator that is both deterministic and chaotic. Therefore, every operator, which tries to establish the future volatility, needs differential equations, which work with non-linear functions. Therefore, the Black–Scholes equation is inverted and the market price of the option is introduced to calculate the implied volatility, i.e. to determine the future price movements of the option. This practice leads to different volatilities and not, as assumed by Black–Scholes, to constant volatilities (unforeseen events in the future do not occur with the same dispersion as comparable events in the past when volatilities fluctuate). With the assumptions made by Black–Scholes, no market, in which volatility and uncertainty play an important role, could actually exist. Nevertheless, the model possessed and still possesses an extraordinarily high performance, inasmuch as the widespread use of the model in particular generated the price movements constructed with it, and did not simply map them; the data did not correspond to the model at the beginning of its use.

Option pricing theory with different volatilities then includes that the current value of making a decision later depends on how one expects that future scenarios will change. So a purchased option should insure us against the volatility of spreads, which is called the volatility of volatility (Meister 2021: 8).

---

[17] Due to the large number of buyers and sellers on the markets, it is extremely important to find a suitable partner for a contract from which one of course expects high returns.

Volatility, which is itself volatile, is an important statement of financial theory. First, there are two ways of measuring the movement of a future-oriented derivative: either the measurement of historical volatility by tracking how the derivative and its price fluctuated in the past, or by reading the implied volatility, assuming an anticipated price and tracking this back to the present (discounting). Here, one then calculates the leverage of a given derivative using the Black–Scholes formula.

One mainly only trades in volatilities. Instead of taking volatility as given and thus determining the option price, one takes the price as given and determines the expected volatility, which retrospectively makes the price form true. The value now added by optionality is a product of unexpected changes in expected volatility. In this respect, financial theory trades its own doubts about its risk models. It is about the reflexivity of the paradoxical effects of our predictions on the future, and indeed on what the future will be. However, trading with these predictive models can fail, since the actions of the participants falsify the assumptions of the models. When financial participants price out the volatility of their own expectations about volatility, they are implicitly trading their doubts about the models. This recognises that valuations are in the end based on future uncertainty, which also includes the constantly updating of data about the past to revise one's assumptions about future volatility. It is a matter of questioning what degree the future will be like the past. But this is a question of risk rather than uncertainty, and it is precisely because this difference is often ignored that prognoses of economists repeatedly and miserably fail.

6.2   Securitisation

In addition to classical derivatives (options, futures, etc.), synthetic derivatives (CDO, CDS, etc.) have been introduced since the 1990s. The securitisation of CDOs (collateralised debt obligations) involves the aggregation of a heterogeneous set of loans/securities, which consists of different cash flows and risks into a single security, a single homogeneous pool, which then functions as a single cash flow and single risk that can be traded on the financial markets.[18] This homogeneous pool can in turn

---

[18] The nominal value of classical derivatives in 2007 was over $2.4 trillion, most of which was constructed in the U.S., but also sold to Europe and Asia (Sahr 2017: Kindle Edition: 5015).

be divided into different classes of risks and cash flows, whereby both components change their quality with each division. The resulting classes are called tranches, which can be rearranged in various ways to produce a variety of specified risks and money flows associated with them. With each newly added tranche within a CDO, new dependencies on other tranches are created, which can trigger further series of additions, gradings and separations. New differentiation processes unfold and, at the same time, punctuations, which record, register and distribute the respective losses and gains of the various tranches. If the tranches are used for the essentially endless redifferentiation of risks, new levels of differentiation are constantly emerging, with which series of attachment points and detachment points are constituted (Lozano 2014). An "attachment point" is a point indicating that risks belong to a particular tranche, while with the achievement of a "detachment point", new risks are released, which from now on affect other tranches that belong to a higher level in the ranking of risks.[19]

Factors such as divisibility, maturity, risk and cash flow are important properties of these assets, or, to be more precise, the asset is these characteristics. Here, it is not the extensive actualisation of the asset that is its decisive component, but rather the fungible and intensive virtualisation potential of the asset, the possible change in its properties, which can lead to an at least theoretically endless, ad infinitum creation, which puts the risk and the future cash flows into a relationship that is as synchronous as possible, but without ever being able to eliminate the moments of desynchronisation. The simulation space market, in which synthetic securities such as CDS, CLO or CDO are traded today, is neither fixed nor flat, neither uniform nor homogeneous, but rather has to be considered non-Euclidean or topological, and is only moderately limited by the various reference classes to which the asset refers. In this context, CDO derivatives are to be understood as dynamically composed un-orders that intrinsically possess different economic properties such as maturity, yield, price, risk and cash flow, which can be plastically and non-linearly expanded and injected elsewhere; that is, they are created and can

---

[19] During the 2007 subprime crisis, price movements in CDS insurance policies related to mortgage loans, among other things, led to huge write-downs on these loans, ultimately resulting in higher interest rates on variable-rate mortgages, falling prices for houses and subsequently in massive defaults on the loans themselves.

128   A. SZEPANSKI

be suddenly destroyed again, and they circulate ad infinitum and as non-linearly swarms, vortices and fractals of differential repetition, thousand plateaus of concentration, condensation and resolution.

The distribution of securitised CDOs was organised at the beginning of the 2000s on the basis of the principle of "originate and distribute" (cf. Marazzi 2011: 36). This form of chain began in the financial markets in the U.S., from where it spread globally, proceeding as follows: since 2001, issued loans/real estate loans increasingly disappeared from the balance sheets of the major credit institutions by securitising them according to special rules. Private banks, or special purpose vehicles which were created by the banks, issued securitised promissory notes bought by rich investors. The payments related to these securities were served from the original loans (principal and interest payments). These securities were tranched from the beginning; that is, they represented staggered entitlements to incoming payments, with the uppermost tranche with the lowest risk (here many of the special purpose company's debtors must default on this paper) being serviced first, if there was just enough cash flow from the thus far saved loans (Sahr 2017: Kindle Edition: 5028).

The chain of securitisation thus begins with the issuance of asset-backed securities, in this case in the form of mortgage-backed securities. These debt securities were initially passed on or sold by private banks to off-balance sheet special purpose vehicles, often located in offshore centres, which in turn sold them to investors. The principle of "pooling" and "tranching" - the bundling and tranching of a security or portfolio discussed above - can then be repeated several times to create complex CDOs from simple debt instruments or to construct new tranches of securities in new special purpose vehicles.[20]

The CDOs, which consisted of mortgage-backed loans and other financial products, were also sold by the banks' special purpose vehicles on the secondary markets to investment funds, which in turn generated new loan portfolios or CDOs with different levels of risk, to pass them in packages to potent investors. The combination of secured loans

---

[20] Already in the early 1990s, some U.S. banks began to develop the mortgage business with their own special purpose vehicles (SPVs). Even then, the business model could not be had without risk, because the assets of these special purpose vehicles were tied up for the long term (these were mostly mortgages with terms of 10, 15 or even 30 years), whereas the liabilities consisted largely of short-term corporate bonds. The interest gains resulting from these transactions were passed on to the banks.

with unsecured loans was part of a credit rating structure where statistically independent risks were calculated, which should always lead to a normal distribution of risks as known from the Gaussian Curve, where events are most likely to be spread around a middle value. CDOs therefore contain hierarchically structured claims for payments from tranches that are assumed to be safe to the uncertain tranches at the end. And even these risky securities were bought up again before the financial crisis of 2008 and packaged into new payment promises. If a company buys the risky and defaulting securities in sufficient quantity, the risks can be bundled and financed by further tranched securities, thus creating third-degree CDOs, etc. The patterns of cash flows of certain debt pools are copied and traded with the help of swaps, thus multiplying and only seemingly reducing the risks - and of course, profits are realised when a loan is sold. The amazing aspect really was that most CDOs were considered to be less risky than their original material, whereby they were valued with certain ratings depending on the tranches. For the investors, CDOs seemed to be a lucrative investment, an attractive security and an efficient way of handling monetary capital, while for the creditors, the credit risk seemed to be reduced. The reasons for this development were repeatedly cited by the fact that risks were diversified (different promises of payment in a portfolio) and the fact that the value of the securities issued did not match the value of the portfolio of assets. In addition, the securities and their credit tranches could be insured by means of CDSs with special companies, called "financial guarantors", depending on their business models.

CDOs were often sold at a price lower than the nominal price in order to account for a certain number of insolvencies from the beginning, and at the same time, the number of possible insolvencies should be spread over as many subjects as possible, as if it were possible to dilute the risks to the point of irrelevance. Not only did this allow that investors could be served satisfactorily for a certain period of time, but the high fees generated by these sales also made it possible to better secure the CDO business of the banks themselves. However, it was precisely the packaging of CDOs into CDOs of CDOs and into CDOs of the third order that did not eliminate the alinearity and diachronic of the structuring of risks, but instead led to an implosion of the CDOs and at the same time intensified the dependency of the financial institutions on each other by successively increasing mutual credit claims.

Currently, financial markets are facing a new wave of CLOs (collateralised loan obligations). The CLO is a fixed or floating rate asset, a type of securitisation covered by collateralised loans, especially that of corporations. Banks are increasingly creating with loan differentiated CLOs, which can contain between 100 and 200 corporate loans from various industries. In this case, a commercial bank acts as a trustee that manages the process of conducting the corporate loans (collateralisation, payment, documentation) and prepares a monthly report for the investors. The loan portfolios of CLOs are divided into different classes (A to equity) and are evaluated by at least one rating agency and traded as listed assets.

Like the CDOs, a CLO bundles high-quality loans and risky low-quality loans into attractive packages with a high credit rating. In May 2017, there were two deals with a price of $1 billion and experts estimate that in 2017, CLOs were traded at $75 billion. Although many of the loans used as collateral in these deals have junk status, CLOs are rated Triple A up to 50%. As credit defaults are now expected to increase in waves, the mathematical models would also have to assess the correlation risks, i.e. the chance that defaults will occur simultaneously. However, most of the models, which are used to evaluate CLOs, assume that the correlations are low. But if many defaults occur at the same time, the expected Triple-A investments will disappear. CLOs are merely CDOs in a new guise.

6.2.1 Excursus 2: Rating Agencies

Financial events, which are structured by capitalisation, companies, states and households, are interpreted and quantified in the financial markets by special institutions, namely the well-known rating agencies and investment fund analysts, by using scientific discourses, measurement concepts, indicators, evaluations, charts, diagrams, mathematical models, political events, etc. The economic events are converted into monetary symbols and prices to identify the creditworthiness and investment security of projects. The creditworthiness of different actors can be compared and evaluated through the use of algorithms, which allow for the execution of data and through corresponding credit scoring procedures.

The rating agencies value against the payment of fees, loans and securities with grades (from AAA to d-d for default), which should reflect the risk of the respective investment. By means of differentiated analyses and the order of information, judgements are produced that include the evaluation of the creditworthiness and risk of the objects, a high significance and an enormous signal value for the global financial markets and finally construct universal comparability. The importance of this practice of credit evaluation and surveillance of the creditworthiness of borrowers is demonstrated by the fact that in 2001, the rating agencies valued payment promises worth $30 trillion, which already made it clear at that time that lending was hardly possible without the large agencies Moody's, Standard & Poor and Fitch, which together have a market share of 95% (Sahr 2017: Kindle-Edition: 5414). On the one hand, the rating agencies are private companies and on the other, the state permanently delegates tasks to them. For the ratings, the quantitative analysts, who mostly come from the natural sciences, combine indicators and mathematical models in a specific way with the use of information technologies to condense the information and at the same time make distinctions between unprofitable and profitable investments. It must always be held in mind that institutional investors often enough have exclusive access to certain information, which at first makes the realisation of high returns possible. In general, ratings, which include very special evaluation procedures on the productivity, performance and efficiency levels of economic players, are valued by means of standardised scores, whereby, in contrast to rankings, no exclusive places are assigned (Mau 2019: 56). Today, many credit and derivative contracts contain so-called rating triggers, which come into effect when the ratings of the companies or the contracts fall below a certain level, with which premiums then have to be paid (ibid.). However, rating agencies not only act as piloting and control instances, by comparing and evaluating risks and potential returns, but their function is also to fuel competition between companies and thus achieve new levels of acceleration in the construction of competitive processes in the context of capital accumulation.

The task of the rating agencies was and is to evaluate the securities, which are bundled in packages (assessments of the respective risk potential of a security and determination of the interest rate). In the case of CDOs, this implies the assessment of the risk itself. At this point, Sahr prominently mentions the example of the rating agency Moody's, which between 2000 and 2007 rated an incredible 72,461 tranches with mortgage securitisations valued at $4.7 trillion (and also with the top rating AAA, which indicates a quasi-non-existing risk of default; however, such highly rated promises were also relatively scarce in supply) (Sahr 2017: Kindle-Edition: 5065). CDOs were often better valued than the initial portfolios due to specific constructions of risk, which are tied to averages and arithmetic means; that is, they were considered as relatively safe and were especially bought by institutional investors such as pension funds, which are only allowed to buy highly valued securities and are considered as an important producer of capital on the financial markets (in the U.S. they generate a turnover of $10 trillion). The yield of CDOs was often higher than that of AAA government bonds and was also considered by investors to be a relatively safe investment and a good security. The sufficient creditworthiness of the CDOs resulted from the diversification of the portfolios. However, as we have already mentioned, the transformation of uncertainty into risk cannot eliminate contingency; on the contrary, only certain orientation values and targets can be established through prognostic procedures.

In general, the decisive function of the rating agencies is not to demand a massive reduction in the debts of private banks, companies and states, but rather the regulation of systemic debt and promises of payment comes to the fore, because these remain the basis for systemic financial operations on the basis of which the rating agencies themselves realise their profits. This also makes it easier to understand the development of financial crises, which from the point of view of the rating agencies are among the most lucrative situations. Thus, it becomes clear that the ratings of the agencies are by no means "objective" evaluations, but rather denote the condensation of strategic instruments of powerful financial organisations, to which governments and legislative parliaments have assigned the sovereign task of evaluating, assessing and, in part, regulating the financial system. The specific cooperation of organisations, which act as creditors and/or debtors in the financial markets, with the major rating agencies, however, does not so much indicate them as a control instrument qua monitoring, but rather leads to a further overstretching of creditworthiness, i.e. to a reduction of the potential for intervention that is designed to regulate the credit activities of financial institutions on a far-reaching scale. One now speaks of a revolving door effect, insofar as companies as debtors on the world markets urgently need ratings and the rating agencies as customers of these companies and thus have an incentive for good ratings. Since customers can change rating agencies in the event of bad ratings, even though the market is oligopolistic or highly concentrated, the latter are forced to relativise their function as organisations that are supposed to keep the trust in the payment promises of financial institutions precarious, and therefore today tend to act as pro-cyclical trend intensifiers. There is a strong suspicion that risk assessment and the calculation of the capital cover of companies are more or less removed from the state authorities and are now privatised. Rating agencies are constantly feeding certain ideologies, guidelines and data on unemployment, monetary stability, debt and labour market flexibility, austerity and privatisation into the media in order to test companies, the state and households in terms of efficiency, competitiveness, profitability and accountability. And many companies absolutely need ratings (for which fees have to be paid) in order to gain access to the capital markets at all.

However, not only the rating agencies, but also the state, expert regimes, influential lobby groups and think tanks, financial capital actors and intellectuals are among the evaluating authorities. The quantifying economisation (by means of statistics and prognosis), even of areas that were previously removed from the logic of capital, takes place through the creation of quasi-markets in precisely these areas. There is a narrowing of the logic of profit with corresponding accounting procedures, input–output matrices and stochastics, in order to inscribe competition in the previously non-profit-oriented fields as objectivity, so to speak, i.e. through the creation of key figures, indicators and models that always set information and price signals. This requires specific parameters of efficiency, performance and profitability, which can only be implanted in the healthcare system, educational institutions and authorities, if measurable data are available that can be translated into ratings, rankings and scoring.

6.3 Derivatives as Forms of Speculative Capital and Power Technologies

For Edward LiPuma, the relationship between the financial economy and the real economy is one of a disruptive interdependence. While the real economy depends on avoiding disruption and volatility as much as possible, volatility (and liquidity) is the lifeblood of finance insofar as fictitious and speculative capital must necessarily be capitalised and increased, serving in turn the interests of the real economy, which benefits when volatility in financial markets is more gradual and predictable, while jumps in volatility can in turn advance financial markets if they do not restrict liquidity. Derivatives thus also reconfigure the values of classical commodities, re-pricing them not in terms of an intrinsic value to commodities, but in terms of their uncertain future value. And this, in turn, also effects the structures of labour markets and the capital distributed in production. If a commodity is sold and secured even before it is a materialised thing, then derivatives infiltrate circulation into production precisely by ascribing floating prices to the commodity. To speculate on a commodity, which is driven by the derivative, is to speculate on the spread between the directionality of prices and the spread produced by the derivative markets.

Edward LiPuma and Robert Meister constantly address the topic of liquidity. Liquidity in its macroeconomic aspects is more than just a metaphor for the monetary fluidity of the financial markets. Rather, it concerns the capacity and possibility of the economy to circulate capital; that is, the free-floating circulation of monetary capital is a necessary condition for the national and international existence of the capitalist economy in the twenty-first century (Meister 2021; LiPuma 2017).

In its microeconomic sense, we define liquidity as the relationship between the maturity and the value of an asset. If liquidity means money virtually fixed in a financial asset, this is only possible if it is currently not in its monetary form. If the liquidity is actualised or transformed into money, then the liquidity of the asset is liquidated. An asset is perfectly liquid if it can be traded at par as needed. A measure of liquidity is the spread between the highest bid price and the lowest asking price for a product. The lower the spread, the higher the liquidity. Consequently, the investment can never remain perfectly liquid. In this sense, liquidity appears to be an intense consequence of the extensive quality of the security, which is denominated in money. Liquidity is a functional relation between the time of delay and the time of realisation of the asset. Liquidity must therefore be understood as an endogenous moment of the financial system itself. Finally, money measures the gap between an asset's liquidity or price and its liquidation value (monetisability).

Thus, the financial system makes capital relations generally more effective, but they are now strongly dependent on liquidity, which is constantly increased by trading assets. A liquid market needs assets, which can be sold to actors which are interested and can pay the price while needing a legal framework. If the prices of assets rise on financial markets, derivatives are preferred in the search for new profitable revenue streams, as they are usually more flexible to use than traditional assets. So the task for investors is to have assets that are as liquid as possible and at the same time generate a high return. In times of crisis, things change, as the settlement of loans is, in the last instance, only possible with state money or bank deposits. In liquidity crisis, all people want money but not derivatives or credit. (Marx treated liquidity purely as a realisation problem, either as the monetary return on an investment or as the repayment of a loan, with little regard for the possibility that companies' risks can be hedged, which is precisely what increases liquidity in the financial markets.)

Constitutive of the capitalist economy today is the circulation of speculative capital, moreover, the use of the new information technologies to shape and accelerate the flows of money capital and, finally, to advance the technologically assisted production of knowledge that informs market participants in their decisions to trade speculatively and globally around the clock. Liquidity is often used as a synonym for the social relations that allow agents to construct the collective enterprise that is the market; a market that always has for a contracting partner a counterparty; a market that is homogeneous and permanently provides the volatility that first enables the recalibrations necessary for the market to continue. There is a necessary link between contingent and often unpredictable financial events and the construction of the market as a (open) totality. The derivative markets are necessarily dependent on liquidity, i.e. as a *possibility* of the circulation of assets.

The financial system makes capital relations generally more effective, but these are now themselves heavily dependent on liquidity, which is constantly increased by trading assets. Furthermore, a dynamic replication between volatility and liquidity is necessary for the derivative. The ability to exploit volatility is necessarily dependent on liquidity in the financial markets (LiPuma 2017). In general, derivatives follow a difficult path, namely to increase volatility without it becoming so excessive and uncontrollable that it leads to a loss of liquidity. The collective confidence of market participants in the future liquidity of the market is essential here. Therefore, derivatives inherit the performative power to collectively set in motion the very thing that each individual agent anticipates. But liquidity in the markets can evaporate because agents can't remember their past mistakes. There is a spread and difference between risk and uncertainty that is itself volatile. If the financial markets can create liquidity in the sense that they provide funds to hedge credit risks, which prevents illiquidity, they cannot provide instruments to hedge liquidity risks themselves. States can only provide a certain guarantee for this and simultaneously support the trading of derivatives on the financial markets with their exclusive political power by issuing currencies and operating the swapping of their government bonds with assets and with the payments of bonds through the distribution of new money, thus pumping new liquidity into the market to satisfy the demand for financial resources further.

In any case, the growth of financial markets reinforces the financialisation of money. In this process, derivative markets must be volatile enough to attract speculative capital, but they must know how to avoid the point at which the elasticity of volatility can become dangerous to themselves: they are, in effect, creating the disease against which they must immunise themselves (ibid.: 54). The logic of speculative capital consists in the perpetual reinforcement of the motive to create opportunities for differential monetisation, or, put differently, it must generate the capitalisation of difference. And this logic is necessarily a mode of circulation, which is based on risk in its derivative form, and it always refers to capital accumulation. The new circulatory regime of capital is not based on the power of states to issue legal money. It is instead based on the private accumulation of capital. It is culturally diffuse and contains a highly abstract violence that culminates in a speculative ethos, namely the production of risk, a monetised subjectivity and a reorganisation of the relations between production and circulation (ibid.: 66). While financial circulation cannot replace industrial production, it does give it a new shape. Financial and derivative interests increasingly dominate the allocation of capital. It is not the real economy that drives the financial economy; conversely, it is the financial economy that structures the real economy. That is, derivatives organise capital flows between different collaterals, currencies and money circulation, and they necessarily possess regulatory capacities and thus actually take over state tasks and functions and integrate politics into the economy. At the same time, the social in its contingency, which traverses the space–time of a social formation, remains a considerable resource for derivative markets and for the mosaic of uncertainties that allows derivative markets to generate a sustainable market in the first place. (The social, whether it relates to money flows, currencies or interest rates, remains the gap between the price and value of a derivative, as participants must always agree on a derivative price to close a spread in the future, but they differ in their views of the value of the derivative in a given time interval.)

The modern financial system employs the expected future flows of returns and income, which are condensed in derivatives, whether the derivatives are related to the extraction of surplus value of private companies, taxation by the state or the subtraction of wage shares (Sotiropoulos et al. 2013: 179). It must be taken into account here from the beginning that in these processes of capitalisation, the asset is not subordinated to the capitalist production process, but logically precedes it; that is, it does not exist primarily because surplus value has already been produced and realised as entrepreneurial profit and interest on the markets, but because financial capital is to a certain extent confident that the realisation of profits of any kind will take place in the future and will be repeated according to the standards of extended reproduction. This kind of capitalisation also means that today, class struggle and the power relations between the classes are always linked to monetary quantification (ibid.: 156).

Already for Marx, an important consequence resulting from the extraction of surplus value in the production of commodities is simply that the surplus value can be transformed into what we today call an asset. In this context, the asset is a means by which surplus value can be, on the one hand, preserved, and, on the other, accumulated. If this were not the case, it would not be produced in the first place. This is why Marx called his book *Capital*, not *Commodity*. Capital is the decisive category here.

A farmer could rent land from the feudal aristocracy and borrow money to buy seed, taking credit only if he assumed that the future harvest could serve as security for the debts incurred. Thus, the future harvest was a potential pledge even before it was transformed into a commodity in the marketplace. Thus, a consumer product's production created two financial products simultaneously: the debt and the security. If the capitalist appropriated the means of production in later historical phases, these functioned to preserve and accumulate the surplus value produced by the workers. However, the functioning of the production goods consisted not only in serving as a means of the production of surplus value, but also embodied financial assets that served as a security for raising future debts and thus as material for creating new financial products (Meister 2021: 16).

The fact that financial products are not only instruments of circulation, but also provide means for the accumulation of real wealth, is a problem that Marx briefly explores. It must be further demonstrated, however, what role financial capital and financial markets play in capitalist reproduction, firstly in the ongoing reproduction of commodity markets. Today, capital is a system whose accumulated real wealth is also dependent on the availability and organisation of liquidity by the financial system and its financial markets, where monetary prices of financial assets can independently rise from the output of consumer goods and far beyond their growth rates. Capitalist production has to be pre-financed *sui generis*, and the fact that asset markets grow faster than the material output of industrial production is a logical consequence of capitalisation, but is at the same time always bound to certain historical conditions.

Marx assigned financial instruments exclusively to the sphere of circulation and analysed their function separately from the functioning of the technologies or physical means of production that preserve past wealth. At the same time, financial instruments made possible a future demand for produced goods. In Marx, when it comes to value (analogous to energy and matter), it seems that there is often a kind of principle of conservation (substance), whereby the growth of real accumulated wealth can never be greater than the profits, which are produced and realised in industrial production in a given period (multiplied by the rate of surplus value, which gets discounted by the rate of investment), so that any increase in the value of constant capital through and in the form of the financial instruments does not come to its attention or is considered purely as fictitious wealth (cf. Meister 2016: 156ff.). For the exoteric Marx, therefore, an economy's real growth can never be greater than the profit produced by industry. But this can no longer be valid for contemporary capital and the financial system and its financial instruments because the assets themselves are now the financial means to initiate and expand investments in the so-called real industry.

Marx's esoteric argument regarding the cycle of reproduction of capital instead describes how the production of commodities and services always creates a demand from investors and namely for financial resources, which serve to maintain, accumulate and increase surplus value, in which financial resources are produced in the same process as the production of commodities and services. Thus, the production of commodities today must inevitably be linked at the same time to physical production *and* to the accumulation of the value of assets.

Concerning especially the functioning of the financial system, we now ask the following questions: what new types of financial assets must emerge today to secure and simultaneously expand capitalist reproduction as a whole? How can the variable relationship between asset markets and consumer and machine markets create conditions to which new movements in social conflicts respond? In *Capital*, Marx argues that the new types of financial assets used to accelerate capital accumulation have to be distinguished from money. For Marx, the general formula of capital cannot be simply $M-M'$, i.e. money that leads to more money. To produce real wealth, there must first be a monetary investment that functions differently from purely money and the exchange of commodities, since it must be invested in machines and working power. Marx takes note, of course, that surplus value is produced by workers for a wage, which has for capitalists the function to increase the effective demand for the commodities produced by the workers. However, Marx rarely registers that surplus value is maintained and accumulated by buying means of production that not only serve as means (constant capital), but also function as securities, which serve as a hedge against the danger that parts of the produced goods are not realised, so that the company can go bankrupt. The purchase of new production goods (constant capital) is only a partial solution to how wealth can be preserved and accumulated without hoarding money. The concept of constant capital is now also to be understood as a kind of security, insofar as capitalist production must be financed and the surplus resulting from it must be reinvested in new means of production (ibid.: 20).

The production of financial instruments must definitely be understood as an alternative to saving money, by preserving and accumulating real wealth. For a financial investor, this means that the purchase of financial assets as a "version" of the formula M-C-M′ must be compared to the formula M-M′ - the former now understood as a strategy of hedging the value. In the formula M-C-M′, there are two substitutes for C (commodity), namely the monetary capital, which is invested in the labour force, and the monetary capital, which is invested in the means of production, acting, and this is the crux of the matter, as a means of production *and* as more or less liquid securities used to generate new cash.

For Robert Meister (ibid.), the mode of relative[21] surplus value production immediately introduces the financial system's logic into the

---

[21] Relative surplus value production explains the effects of capital resulting from technological innovation that increases productivity in a company. A relatively more productive company can sell an individual commodity (due to their reduction in value) cheaper than other companies and thus realise a larger part of the social mass of value for itself. As the means of reproduction becomes cheaper, the value of the commodity labour-power decreases. The share of variable capital also decreases in relation to the constant part (increase in the organic composition of capital). Still, this price reduction also leads to the fact that the labour force must produce less value to reproduce itself, so that the share of surplus value in the product itself increases again. But this is only valid for an individual capital; for total capital, the compensatory effect is only valid if the amount of labour force used productively increases in absolute terms. This is an aspect of the labour force, but there is also the technological effect.

140   A. SZEPANSKI

mode of production (and circulation). His analysis investigates the effects that the financial system's operations and methods have on the proper reproduction of the social relations between labour and capital (Lee and Martin 2016: 155f.). Let us try the first explanation: the surplus value produced in a given production phase can on the one hand (if it is not

In this context, Hans-Dieter Bahr noted that Marx, in chapters twelve and thirteen of the second volume of *Capital*, analytically divides production time (of capital) into working time and functional time of machinery (cf. Bahr 1983: 434). According to Bahr, the same can be said of machines' functional time as of working time, the latter of which should be reduced by the methods of relative surplus value production per unit. Fixed capital or machinery has its own functional times, which, insofar as they are quantities bought by the company, must be reduced in the same way as the working time that goes into the individual product. And insofar as the functional time per unit of product decreases - this can happen through increased economies of scale, innovation, rationalisation and automation - there is no reason why the machinery or today's digital technology should be understood no less as a source of surplus value than human labour, if the new products, for a given labour input, realise a sales price higher than the purchase price of raw materials, means of production, wages, interest, etc. (insofar as this sales price is due to technologically induced rationalisation). Consequently, individual capital can also increase its share of the total social production if it succeeds in reducing its production times per unit by making the functional time of a machine more efficient - and not only by the condensation of working time - and thus reducing internal operational costs. A company achieves an extra profit compared to competing companies exactly when it succeeds in selling its products that have fallen in price per unit due to the application of new technologies, cheaper than those of other companies and therefore increases its market share. Production costs per unit fall faster in the most productive industries than in other industries due to the application of specific technological innovation. When new technologies are implemented in a whole sector of industry, then extra profits disappear, and socially necessary, valid working and functional time is condensed on a general level; according to Marx, average profit rates level off with a new quality, but these are repeatedly capped by new wave movements resulting from further technological innovations or disruptions. It must be added that technological innovations only take hold if sufficient profits and demand can be expected.

However, this represents an ideal process, which implies that efficiency (minimum material input per unit of output) means economic efficiency per se (minimum cost per unit of output). Economic efficiency means maximum profit. However, this may not always be true from several points of view: (a) because it may even be efficient for the individual capital to use inefficient techniques or even to sell inefficient products; (b) companies often make calculations in such a way that they determine average unit costs (costs at a given average level of output), to which they add an industry-standard mark-up in order to keep this price stable over longer periods or to adapt it to cyclical changes in demand, with the aim of achieving long-term profit rates at a constant level; (c) it also happens, of course, that in some companies there is almost no "real value creation" at all in terms of labour, but they still absorb and realise a part of the total input of so-called abstract labour at the level of total capital, so that the internal productivity standard is almost irrelevant.

simply hoarded as money) only be maintained in the next phase by an extended reinvestment in means of production and raw materials, and on the other hand, increased. Without multiplication, there is no preservation of capital. In expanding production capacities, capital invests in labour-power because it hopes for a spread between the labour force of money (the contribution of workers to GDP) and the monetary value of labour (wages). There are, however, different arbitrage possibilities to increase profits for companies, especially when they operate with different technologies and different productivities. Still, these arbitrage possibilities are also eliminated in the course of the equalisation movements, which generate average profit rates. Otherwise, a dominant company would maintain and expand the extra profit endlessly, ultimately ending up in its eternal monopoly position.

For Marx, there are two different arguments that play a role in his analysis of the general formula $M-C-M'$. Concerning absolute surplus value, the argument consists first of all in the claim that the application of the labour force enables the production of a surplus value created by the workers, who are paid, in comparison with the total value produced by them, a smaller share of wages, with which they can buy those consumer goods they produce themselves. Methods of increasing surplus value intensify the process of work and the extension of the working day.

In the case of relative surplus value, the argumentation is different; it includes the problems of technological innovation, productivity and the organic composition of capital. Marx gets especially close to the problem of representation of the relation between the production of commodities and the production of assets in his analysis of relative surplus value production in *Capital*, Vol. 1. When it comes to the financial system, relative surplus value production is based on its first maxim, the law of one price (Meister 2021: 20). This law states that two identical units of commodities should be sold at the same price regardless of the companies' respective costs, whatever the forms of production are and where raw materials are transformed into finished products with the help of machines and labour. However, the company is given a positive arbitrage opportunity regarding its investment in production if it can produce more or cheaper units of goods in a given working time than its competitors (through technological innovation). The creation of arbitrage via the more effective transformation of the raw material (one part of constant capital) is part of the increase in productivity through the investment in new machines (another part of constant capital). The extra surplus value for a company here is not generated by hiring new workers or by labour intensification, but by the fact that the finished product can be sold at a lower price (per unit) than the same product of other companies. This accumulation of wealth through relative surplus value production is quite real and material insofar as it derives from arbitrage over constant capital (and not from absolute surplus value, which corresponds to an increase in working hours or a growing number of jobs). Moreover, the esoteric Marxist argument remains related to the necessity of realising the final product on the market, which remains dependent on the consumer goods sector and the financial sector (consumer credit), which influences the former. Marx's concept of relative surplus value production leads to questions of real accumulation. In the last instance, it is the logic of financialisation that expresses itself in relative surplus value production and finally leads to the general law of capitalist accumulation. This law describes the creation of an increased production capacity (of constant capital) with the simultaneous growth of the surplus population, which can no longer be brought into wage labour at all due to the use of labour-saving techniques.

Two arguments play an important role in the presentation of the general formula of capital: M-C-M'. Besides the production of absolute surplus value, there is also relative surplus value production, where, first of all, the financialisation of producer goods and the workers allows the capitalists to increase the material output in production. This happens by investing in better machines, raw materials, energy, software, etc., and simultaneously by reducing the cost of labour-power and the number of workers. The problem of realisation that inevitably follows from this includes the question of how it is possible at all to actualise the commodities as prices and to monetise them, thus generating further monetary funds. Marx deals with this problem in *Capital*, Vol. 2, which is often understood as if it is only about the balance of reproductive processes in and between the two sectors of production and consumer goods. The possibility that the prices of commodities are not realised is evident here. It follows that no further monetary funds can then be created or realised in money (non-realisation is also inherent in financial assets, unlike money, whose secret is that it does not have to be spent). Marx does not really discuss the relationship between market and liquidity because he attributes the problem of liquidity to the storage of the value of money.

The middle term of the formula M-C-M' cannot be understood simply as a productively used commodity in the production process. Still, it must also be understood as a hedged portfolio that is priced out as capital (ibid.: 24). The hedge itself, which is a marketable contract, has no use-value other than its exchange-value. It is quite understandable that in large corporations such as General Motors, the production goods are part of the portfolio of the company, containing bonds or options on the production goods. At this point, Randy Martin registers a shift from M-C-M' to M-D-M', where D stands for the derivative, which has now essentially the same function as the productively consumed goods (in production) insofar it also drives the self-movement of capital (Lee and Martin 2016: 176). For example, buying options on raw materials that a company needs for its production processes can increase its own creditworthiness, which is now restricted against the risk of rising prices for raw materials. Simultaneously, the operations of a whole range of other players are influenced by this price index of this raw material. Risks are transferred, duplicated, multiplied and shifted to other spaces.

Marx shows in *Capital*, Vol. 3 that there has always been a problem of realisation for companies, among other things also when they invest by credit in the means of production, which can lose value during the production period (here because of the better innovations of other companies), so that the manufactured products can no longer be sold on the market at the historical average price. The credit can then possibly no longer be serviced (Meister 2021: 21). The non-realisation of the market price for an end product or its sale below the average price results for the company in decreased monetary funds and a reduced possibility of using all raw materials and utilising the capacities/machinery to generate new higher monetary funds. This is a problem indicating that the investment must be hedged. The realisation problem and the used financial assets for it differ now from pure financial instruments, insofar as assets here are related to production goods and not serve solely as financial vehicles. Insofar as the former assets have a utility value that goes beyond their pure liquidity, they are not pure financial products, whose utility value consists solely in realising a price in a differential-immanent movement that generates returns on the financial markets.

What Marx could not know is that the realisation of the produced commodities can be hedged by the fabrication of puts and calls on options, which are related to the means of production and raw materials; thus, they tend to preserve at least the value of the investment in machines and raw materials during the period in which they are transformed into finished products. Marx could still have not known that by fabricating

144 A. SZEPANSKI

options, it is possible to intervene in the price of a finished product that fluctuates on the market. The existence of a market for puts and calls - the continuous possibility of permanently pricing and monetising the option - generates today also enough liquidity for the underlying market of production and consumer goods, which is a trend to eliminate the risks of their realisation. The "value" of the products is now increasingly preserved and at the same time accumulated in the form of financial assets by trading the spread between the market value of the asset, if it remains liquid at all, and the liquidation value of the asset (ibid.: 16). A fully liquid asset is also as good as cash and is then an alternative to saving money, whereby there is little risk that the asset cannot be immediately realised at its market price. To finance an asset that is not fully liquid, a liquidity premium must then be paid, either by executing a hedge or buying a more liquid security than the asset itself. The liquidation value of the asset will, in turn, be the money that one gets when selling the pledged security, and the liquidity premium will reflect the extent to which the original value of the security exceeds the value of the financial asset used to hedge the security.

Thus, the capitalist portfolio of a company consists not only of bonds and debts, but also of the puts and calls of the options with which hedging is done. Without the correct design of the price movements of puts and calls, there can be no robust recycling of the bonds and debts (ibid.: 7). A call is here understood as the right to acquire a potentially infinite surplus, and a put is an instrument to limit the loss. Both are derivative means that indicate whether it is worthwhile for a company to invest in new capital stock to increase its capital storage and its profit, whereby the capital stock is just one of the means of increasing profit because the complementary form today is the financial asset, which shows that relative surplus production is just one way of exploiting the spreads in a particular market. Without pricing out the calls and puts and trading them on the derivative markets, it is impossible today to maintain a well-hedged portfolio, which consists of debts and bonds, in which the portfolio should have liquidity at all times (ibid.). Therefore, the M-C-M' formula describes C always as a portfolio consisting of debts and capital stock and puts and calls. Unlike money, these are here purely financial products. Their relation can be fixed in a financial formula, which describes the parity of debts and capital stock in terms which in turn are related to the parity of puts and calls. Therefore, the investment in C must, according to Meister, fulfil the following equation:

$$Stock + Put = Debt + Call. \quad (Ibid.: 24)$$

This formula involves a simple identity: if you have a capital stock and a put that includes a downward hedge, then you can replicate a return on an investment, which is equal to owning a call that fulfils the possibility of participating in a surplus based on the capital stock plus the current price of a loan. One can now use puts or calls to obtain a completely hedged portfolio, which in turn allows a return that is at least equal to the risk-free interest rate. The M-C-M' spiral thus includes a double arbitrage possibility, namely, on the one hand, playing with the spreads in the valuation of machines and labour, provided that the wage cannot be insured, and, on the other hand, a fully hedged portfolio based on call-put parity. The basis for hedging is the loan as well as the return on the investment. If this return of money, which always remains related to the credit taken by the company, is the paradigm of the portfolio side of M-C-M', and if it is also related to the investments in wages, then the effects of the financial system on the production processes of companies are more complicated than Marx ever imagined.

In the derivative markets, assets are not priced according to their existing values but rather in terms of an uncertain future value. When a commodity (e.g. a house) is sold before it physically exists, and derivatives (on the house) are taken, then the latter subordinate the production to circulation by giving an asset a floating and contingent value. However, every commodity other than consumer goods has liquidity and can serve as a vehicle for preserving and accumulating capital. Classical consumer commodities have no liquidity, insofar as no economically realisable options are embodied in them. The wageworker cannot invest; he must spend his money entirely on consumption and must therefore continuously offer his labour-power on the labour market to earn money for his consumption. And financial products such as health insurance, pension funds and student loans are today part of a household's cost of living, but instead of understanding them as an investment in one's own "human capital", they should rather be understood as a kind of tax, which is paid to financial capital.

To make it clearer: Marx accepts the worker, when he enters the labour market, as uncreditworthy and debt-free. It is precisely these characteristics that make him purely wage-dependent, and this means that he must buy his subsistence goods exclusively with his wages: for Marx, wage labour is a social relation in which the workers, beyond their exploitation, are forced to spend money immediately (after having received the wage) on consumer goods. Thus, the earned money (as a wage) cannot function as an asset that preserves and expands value. The question that arises here is how can capital guarantee the working class's consumption when it has to accelerate more and more accumulation through technological innovation which reduces jobs? Furthermore, neoliberalism has led to decreasing wages over the last few decades. Today, to reproduce themselves, it seems necessary for wageworkers, in addition to earning a wage, to enter into debt. The reproduction of the labour force has thus long ceased to take place solely through wages but also through various financial instruments such as student loans, mortgage loans, health care, insurance, automobiles, condominiums and consumer loans, which are allocated to households by special credit companies at sometimes exorbitant interest rates of up to 20%. The relation between income and borrowing (debt currently accounts for 5–10% of income in developed countries) is influenced by factors such as the level of debt, income development and the level of interest rates. For example, student loans are divided by the state into tranches to be sold to third parties, who manage them as future investments. Thus, student loans function like the infamous mortgage loans that were blamed for the 2008 financial crisis. Today, an increasing portion of the wage is being used to buy financial products, such as health insurance and real estate loans, which in turn are used by financial institutions to create new financial instruments acting as vehicles for accumulating further wealth. Today, however, in many cases, the wage is only a part of buying the means of reproduction. Various financial products are now needed to secure the consumption of private households and protect their members against illness, old age, etc. However, these possibilities remain uncertain - they must therefore be hedged and thus financed, and this is because their timelines and costs remain contingent on future events. Income streams that derive from aspects of everyday life, such as cell phone bills and household water and electricity bills, are fed as inputs into new financial instruments, and thus even the unsuspecting households with their small incomes are now dependent, through certain chains, on the trading of derivatives in global financial markets. Randy Martin has called this the financialisation of everyday life (Martin 2009). The various forms of everyday credit are broken down to a few attributes with financial instruments such as CDOs (securitisation, the bundling of various forms of credit) and then traded in multiple combinations on financial markets.

The precariat, in particular, is now dependent, in addition to wages, on credit and other financial funds to survive. On the other hand, the surplus population is excluded from the sale of labour-power as the sole means of securing their subsistence and participates in financial resources, which are generated in informal or state sectors. For Marx, according to the law of capitalist accumulation, it was quite clear that capital accumulation leads, in the last instance, to a huge global surplus population (besides the industrial reserve army, which is still related to official labour markets). Wage-earning workers in the global north usually still receive sufficient wages from capitalists, which at least secures their (culturally determined) subsistence and generates effective demand for the mass products of consumption, which was especially the case under Fordism.

Once economic events of the financial markets have been translated into the features, models and methods of mathematics/a-significant semiotics/linguistics, a specific design of economic risks and specific risk management is required. For this, today, the trading and the realisation of derivatives (in money) are necessary so that a relatively efficient construction for processing the (economic) risks can be achieved. In the same breath, there is also the attempt to translate and quantify class struggles and their respective power relations, their cycles and constellations into risks. In this context, the analysts of the major rating agencies and those of other financial institutions are to be understood as transformers who permanently try with their anticipations to translate uncertainty in the financial markets into risks: for example, one will recommend buying a share or a security exactly when the expected value of future profit flows is estimated to be higher than the current price; if it is valued lower than the current price, one will recommend selling. The anticipation of complex future economic events, which take place simultaneously in the companies and on the markets, is thus translated into binary information. If capitalisation as a motive and strategy of financial capital implies the pricing of future promises of payment or profit streams, analysts provide the necessary complementary evaluations of those risk factors that are constructed and employed through capitalisation. On the one hand, these anticipations must not fall below a certain degree of correctness and accuracy, but, on the other hand, they are usually characterised by the optimism of analysts about the future economic developments of companies, since the former are monetarily intertwined with the interest structures of the companies. As analysts anticipate the profits and share prices of companies, while conversely, however, when preparing their balance sheets, the companies usually already know the anticipation of the analysts, we are then dealing with systems of mutual reinforcement within second-order observations.

On the financial markets, capitalisation - the discounting of future expected profit flows of assets - is now increasingly taking place as a process of continuous evaluation of the risks of investments, therefore using precise financial instruments, namely derivatives. Since every future flow of returns is largely unknown and uncertain, capitalisation cannot take place without transforming the unknown uncertainty into an apparently known risk. Likewise, without its calculation, i.e. the evaluation of the chances of generating returns in the future, standard regulation is mostly done with theories of probability. Here, the risk is commonly understood as a dimension that refers to certain socio-economic events in the future, whose chance of being realised must be subject to an assessment and evaluation and statistical and mathematical instruments. These events are thus evaluated with the help of statistics, probability theory and specific mathematical models, which, for the economist John Milios, have an ideological character per se; that is, risk involves the anticipation of future trends from the ideological perspective of charts, models, statistics, theories and a-significant signs (Sotiropoulos et al. 2013: 160). All performative strategies of the actors, who constantly re-objectify the financial markets as a socially imagined totality, imply that the probability of corporate insolvency and crisis processes is reduced. This requires both the establishment of a specific trust and a certain misunderstanding of capital relations and of one's own economic positions. This misjudgement means that one believes in the market as a collective fiction, thus in recognising the market as real, the fiction exists, but it exists differently than one believes. In turn, confidence is organised and materialised in institutions and economic processes to such an extent that these are largely autonomous, constant and repetitive (Bourdieu 2014: 37).

Capitalisation thus requires a certain mode of identifying, evaluating and ordering economic entities, events and promises to pay (as perceived reality), which must first be distinguished from one another and then objectified as risk events. This requires specific techniques and instruments, with which the risks can be distinguished, compared and then acted upon, or, to put it another way, it requires specific power technologies, which today are constructed by institutions according to algorithmically ascertainable risks as derivatives. The associated risk management implies the attempt of financial capital, including its associated discourse systems, opinion industries and research departments, to anticipate, evaluate and then act on future economic events, promises to pay and trends, events that are continuously formulated by using statistical, algorithmic and probability models, all of which are part of economic math (Sotiropoulos et al. 2013: 161). Thus, capitalisation, a method of calculating and evaluating future promises of payment, always includes a specific mode of representing, regulating and anticipating future economic events, which must be distinguished from one another to identify them as concrete risks, then and finally to trade them as derivatives that embody abstract risks. There is no capitalisation without the specification and comparison of risks. Today, the concept of risk is *sui generis* integrated into the logic of capital.

Let us first illustrate the whole process with a simple formula: the use of fictitious or speculative capital generates the expectation (E1) of future income and profit flows ($Dt + 1$, $Dt + 2$, $Dt + 3$...), which should flow back continuously to the owner of the monetary capital. In the case of investment D (for simplifying reasons, it is assumed that there is a return flow of money with a constant interest rate up to (R10) - an interest rate that takes into account all risks involved), the capitalisation or price of expected future income flows can be written according to the following equation: (ibid.: 140)

$$Kt : \frac{(Gt + 1)}{(1 + r)} + \frac{(Gt + 2)}{(1 + r)2} + \frac{(Gt + n)}{(1 + r)n} \frac{G}{r}, \text{wenn } n \to Gt + 1 = Gt + n = G$$

In fixing the price (Pt), capitalisation includes calculating the expected value of future flows of returns or income. However, for a Marxist interpretation of the above formula, two problems must be taken into account: firstly, the materiality of price-setting already includes the complex articulation of social power relations that co-organise and reproduce the utilisation of monetary capital. Secondly, the structure of monetary utilisation (capitalisation) cannot be separated from the further concatenations of promises to pay or from the processes of the "real economy" (ibid.). Today, it can also be assumed that financial capital, as the dominant form of capital, has its most important instruments in the derivatives and the trade of payment promises. It is precisely through these relations that the "real economy" is dominated and controlled. Here, it is also necessary to

150   A. SZEPANSKI

understand the translation of the relations between capitalist power relations and price formation, which is indicated in the sizes $Et[Dt + i]$ and (R) when it comes to financialisation processes.

The economic sciences understand risk as an opportunity expressed in probabilities (in Luhmann's sense as an adaptation to opportunity) and at the same time as a measure of confidence that the future price of an income stream can be realised (ibid.: 157).

A widely used calculation model for this is the value-at-risk method. Provided a normal distribution of profit and loss (the Gaussian normal distribution curve spans an average arithmetic middle value, while the width is determined by the standard deviation, the probability that a possible event will deviate from the middle value), the risk of a financial asset X is defined here, taking into account a confidence level Z (oscillates between 0 and 1) as the smallest number S, whereby the probability of a loss may not be greater than the confidence level Z (Mainzer 2014: 207). Or, to put it another way, value-at-risk is a number that indicates, for a certain period of time, how much money will be lost on an investment with a certain probability. This is, so to speak, the worst case within a given probability scenario. In the practice of the rating agencies before the financial crisis of 2007, the probability of a loss was often roughly enough underestimated.[22] In the end, the risk of a payment default results from the price fluctuations of payment promises in the past. Thus, a project's creditworthiness is determined by the historical performance of payment promises, a probability-based pattern of price fluctuations. We can further assume that with the application of such risk models and algorithms, factors such as normality and business confidence in the history of socioeconomic realities are really implanted in the mindsets and practices of the actors, thus often enough underestimating the risk of loss.

Securities with high variance (in terms of prices) are considered riskier than those with low variance. If the price of the government bond A is only half as volatile as the price of a share B, this can be described as follows: $x + VjA = 2 + VjB$ - V is the variance and j refers to various subjective assessments (Sotiropoulos et al. 2013: 157). However, this

---

[22] According to Frank Knight, the calculable risk must be distinguished from the largely incalculable uncertainty. While risk management uses statistical methods, there is at least no discrete expected value for the uncertainty. Financial mathematics has several axiomatically defined and consistent risk measures. Therefore, the properties of monotonicity, subadditivity, homogeneity and translational invariance are necessary (Mainzer 2014: 210).

equation does not consider the fact that the subjective variance does not express an assessment of risk that must be accepted by all market participants, with which it can only be considered objective. This can be seen immediately if the following formula expresses the subjective expectations of a market participant j: $x - VjA = y - VjB = z - VjC\dots$ (ibid.). The expectations here are infinite: there is obviously no measure that standardises the expectations of the various market participants, and thus no relevant comparison of the various concrete risks and the prices corresponding to them can be made qua abstract risk, so that economic objectivity in the sense we have already described cannot be established (ibid.: 158).

Therefore, all processes of pricing derivatives require the construction and measure of concrete and abstract risks, whereby the former can be compared with the latter. These processes occur in the global financial markets, where the various market participants must first be identified as risk-takers to be assigned a specific risk profile by the rating agencies (ibid.: 168). Thus, financial capital and its institutions "normalise" market participants based on risks; accordingly, the financial machines enable the construction, distribution and dispersion of the various concrete risks among market participants (who are in heterogeneous market populations and competitive relationships with each other), as well as the bundling of concrete risks, which then receive a singular price and a singular cash flow as a singular risk, an abstract risk, that is traded as a derivative and exchanged for money. The abstract risk subsumes the concrete forms of risk and mediates connectivity and liquidity production, both of which are necessary (LiPuma 2017: 62).

Let us go further: the team of authors around John Milios introduces, in addition to the definition of derivatives as a specific commodity of capital (capital as capital), the concepts of "risk" and "governmentality", for which derivatives can then be conceptually defined not only as commodities but also as technologies of power that efficiently guarantee the reproduction of capitalist power relations. Regarding Foucault's studies of governmentality (Foucault 2011), the processes of financialisation are thus described as technologies of power, which require specific instruments, methods and strategies to articulate, regulate and stabilise economic, political and social power relations (Sotiropoulos et al. 2013: 155ff.). Derivatives are thus not exclusively concerned with the multiplication of capital, but with the representative reproduction of the capitalist power relations that prevail between the various classes and class factions.

Financial capital normalises the various market participants with the help of the rating agencies' strategies and evaluations, which permanently prepare and publish risk profiles of the various market participants globally. We are dealing here from the beginning with a specific formation of risk profiles: anticipation, evaluation and comparison of promises to pay and other possible financial events, which are related to specific market participants, and resulting opportunities for the successful realisation of the events in the context of a necessary evaluation of the respective risk-taker and its potential for the realisation of a successful business (ibid.). If all market participants without exception have to make use of a specific risk management to operate efficiently on the markets at all, they are by no means subject to subsumption under identical risk categories and classes. Although the players and the accepted concrete risk events have to be permanently compared, even those who are in environments of similar risks do not have the same financial possibilities for the successful realisation of certain risks (there are barriers of entry into the markets and different capital strengths) (ibid.: 161).

With Foucault, the creation of risk profiles can be interpreted as a process of normalisation; this insofar as market participants (doubled according to risks, which are assessed to them) get distinguished from one another and thus individualised by the creation of profiles, on the one hand, and, on the other hand, are compared with one another and thus homogenised (ibid.: 157ff.). Today, we are dealing with extremely flexible normalisation processes in financial markets, whereby each market participant without exception is considered a risk factor to be statistically recorded and permanently evaluated (ibid.: 161). However, the process of risk allocation and evaluation is by no means based on an invariant norm. Rather, normalisation has to be understood here as a variable process within a strongly interwoven network characterised by constellations and marked by diversity, flexible rules of modulation, feedback and hierarchies, whereby "differential normalities" (Foucault) are constantly being produced. But diversities at the end must be reduced to a few indicators through specific quantifications to achieve new homogenisations, units and adaptations. At this point, we can speak of a versity (equalisation), and this in the course of an inversion and mutation of the diversity of risks. However, this does not mean the elimination of difference; on the contrary, versity uses difference as its real substrate to continuously generate standardised organisational systems, statistical systems and power technologies that modulate or even absorb differences. Thus, it is also possible that different fictional expectations of certain processes can be operable simultaneously. These specific forms of normalisation refer to market populations that are heterogeneous and therefore need to be integrated through flexible technologies (ranking, rating, scoring, etc.) that make use of differences and at the same time unify them. This type of risk distribution and allocation to corresponding risk subjects and risk groups is a strictly quantifying and yet, to a certain extent, contingent phenomenon represented by a-signifying signs (numbers, tables, models, statistics, charts, etc.). Insofar as they involve non-linear risk allocations, the models refer to the fractal, networks, adaptations, complex systems of biology and, of course, the internet, which today is an important part of financial infrastructures that are becoming more or less mobile. These processes imply the exploitation, aggregation and automated analysis of data in enormous quantities to model and anticipate the possible actions of market participants.[23] In the course of algorithmic and mostly privatised governance, power technologies, based on mobile and at the same time automated statistics, are implemented in the financial economy, with which the possible should be reduced to the probable.

When corporations go to the financial markets to sell bonds or to enter into credit contracts and insurance, they must be provided with risk

[23] Algorithmic governance is a politico-economic field and a new regime of truth, which is characterised by technological performativity, the permanent capture of data, the digital operations that perform these data and the digital doubles that are the result of these operations, whereby these doubles (profiles) interact with those who generate them. These processes cause and intensify each other mutually in automated circuits, which in turn are driven by calculation and capitalisation. This concerns the sciences (Big Data) and every form of decision-making, from everyday life to the financial system and the military, like any governance in Foucault's sense; algorithmic governance implements power technologies based on statistics, which no longer refer only to the average and the norm. Instead, we deal with automated, atomic and probability-based statistics, which does its forensics and data mining without any medium. Automatic computing collects, captures and mobilises the methods of new statistics the market participants controlled by extracting Big Data correlations. These statistics which continuously collect data, read and utilise traces of data mobilise an a-normative and a-political rationality, which insists on the exploitation, aggregation and automatic analysis of enormous amounts of data to model, anticipate and influence the economic agents' behaviour preventively. This future-oriented influence installs a new regime of affects within a regime of truth, in which the power to act should be an automatic production, through which the possible is reduced to the probable. This transition from static governance to algorithmic governance simultaneously indicates the transition from the state's public governance, as the administration of public things, to privatisation, the kind of governance, which leads to the destruction of private life and the public sphere.

profiles. Arrangement, scale and taxonomy of these risk profiles depend on to what extent these corporations, in view of the major financial companies, such as the rating agencies, are able (in the context of competition with other corporations) to pursue effective strategies for realising profits and increasing market capitalisation in the future. However, both processes do not always necessarily run in the same direction. Also, the capitalist state, as a sovereign debtor, receives a risk profile (drawn up by the rating agencies), which, under the current economic conditions, often assesses its potential for the successful exercise of neoliberal hegemony qua austerity policies, without the outbreak of class confrontations which are anxiously feared by the ruling capitalist factions. The risk profile of wage earners is based on an evaluation of their ability to maintain the rules and norms of labour relations successfully. Within the framework of these normalisation processes, financial companies not only differentially spread the risk profiles in the financial markets based on risk, but also continuously conduct stress tests, especially among potential risk participants, to assess their risk effectiveness as accurately as possible.[24] Diversifying portfolios and integrating relative risk-free securities such as government bonds or hedging with derivatives can achieve hedging management and control of the risk.

Such normalisation processes, which must always be understood as a specific form of risk production, today require mathematised and algorithmised technologies to achieve, to some extent, a stable and broadly defined increase of economic efficiency of companies, states and households as an organisation of capitalist power relations.[25] In this context, the rating agencies need to recognise the turbulent movements and fluctuations of the various price movements, which oscillate around the

---

[24] For this purpose, a convex risk measure is used to calculate the worst-case expectation for different models summarised under Q, taking into account the so-called penalty q(Q). For all models Q and all portfolios X, the expected value is defined. The resulting class M of possible probability sets is a set of probability measures (Mainzer 2014: 212).

[25] In general, risk calculation implies a systemic evaluation of each market participant regarding the effectiveness of the respective risk management and the objectives implemented in it, which in turn means that each market participant has to live risk as a social reality and thus remains trapped in his role as a risk-taker. The shaping of power technologies requires an ensemble of different social institutions, knowledge arrangements, analytical discourses and tactics represented by banks, hedge funds and insurance companies with their highly specialised research departments, rating agencies, magazines, think tanks, etc.

gravitational centres of capital accumulation, and evaluate and anticipate them correctly. In financial theory, non-linear stochastic differential
equations are used for this purpose, which can be described as follows:

$$vXt = cXt\mathrm{d}t + aXt - \mathrm{d}ft$$

Here c stands for the expected return, v for the volatility and a for the
stochastic volatility as a time-dependent random function (Mainzer 2014:
205). The aim is to understand at least the dynamics of turbulent price
movements, even if they cannot be predicted with certainty.

Concerning risk calculation, no matter which mathematical or
stochastic model is used, there must be instruments that make the various
concrete risks comparable and measurable to maintain the stability and
robustness of corporations and financial markets. If the concrete risks
could not be compared with each other using a differential and, at
the same time, general "measure", then financialisation as a normalising
power technology would hardly be able to assert itself on the financial
markets. Therefore, the various concrete risks must be transformed into
a singular dimension - into an abstract risk embodied by the derivative,
which is realised with money (Sotiropoulos et al. 2013: 178). This also
means that abstract risks are objectified by mathematical modelling. One
thinks here of the Black–Scholes formula (the mathem of economics),
precisely in that the agents tend to use all similar models, only to outbid
or undercut each other in the competition as exchange partners. Here,
we see a superposition between overlapping models and, simultaneously,
the iteration of the models, which the agents share and/or assign to the
other market participants, whereby informational financial machines like
Bloomberg's rhythmise and syncopate the information in a 24/7 mode.
Each operation realises and emphasises the market that it presupposes
and that is presupposed by it. In contrast, market participants usually
believe that market will always be populated by reliable counterparties
or exchange partners (within a contractual constellation) so that liquidity
will necessarily remain secured through the construction and distribution
of derivatives. All agents believe that they are well-functioning parts of
a moving chain, albeit with different monetary capital sizes and power.
However, this pragmatism in applying mathematical models does not lead
to a 100% correct modelling of prices. Rather, the models are part of
crisis-like processes in and with which they are defined.

156   A. SZEPANSKI

Nevertheless, derivatives today represent a reasonably effective solution, which at least guarantees the commensurability of concrete risks through abstract risks, however, without turbulent price movements on the financial markets, which regularly lead to bubbles and crises within certain cycles being sufficiently excluded. Derivatives play a decisive role in the functioning of financialisation, in terms of both the technologies of power and the deepening of monetary capitalisation (ibid.: 155ff.).

The authors around Milios explain these processes using an example (ibid.: 170ff.): actor A buys a security S, which contains several concrete economic risks playing an important role in the price formation of the security. In this example, the concrete risks of securities are reduced to two risks: interest rate and default risk. Actor A enters into a relation with actor B, who holds a U.S. treasury bond. The two actors agree to exchange their securities. Actor A overwrites the security, including the default risk, with all its future claims and payments. In return, he receives a long-term bond with the same maturity within which all payments involved in the U.S. treasury bond take place, whereby actor B accepts the default risk for the security S. At the same time, actor A can sell an interest rate risk to actor C, who wants to buy an interest rate risk as a holder of a U.S. treasury bill. Until the 1980s, most financial transactions in the money markets were based on this type of trading.

In the course of the global expansion of financial capital and the financial markets, derivative trading has expanded enormously, not only in terms of scale but also in terms of the type and number of instruments. To illustrate this, let us stick to the above example (ibid.: 171): the three market participants now succeed in absorbing further risk potential by exchanging income streams, which their securities should deliver in the future including the risks. Instead of exchanging the ownership of the securities themselves, the players take on further risks by exchanging and crediting the future income streams, which are related to these securities. Actor A continues to hold the security S but exchanges the future cash flows related to it with the cash flows resulting from the treasury bonds and bills' future cash flows. Actor A holds the security S, while actors B and C, in isolation from each other, hold the respective default and interest rate risk. While actor B bears a default risk with the future cash flows, actor C must expect losses if the short-term interest rate increases. This type of agreement requires as an abstract risk, a CDS contract conclusion (credit default swap) and an IRS (interest rate swap) to design and hedge the risks (ibid.).

In the above example, with derivatives (concrete risks), the default and interest rate risk can be removed from the original security and then traded independently of the underlying instrument's price movement. This "repackaging" of concrete risks includes the trading of abstract risks using the derivatives. Although the interest rate and default risk can already be understood as the bundling of various concrete risk components, it seems more appropriate to understand these risks in its new derivative form (abstract risk). Thus, CDS and IRS can be seen as the condensation of certain spot market transactions into singular derivative instruments (ibid.).

Financialised risk is separated from its social contexts and relations such that a given situation is assumed to be risky; the risk must abstract from the social, economic and political conditions in order to translate it into an analytical and mathematical space, which is just assumed to be independent of the circumstances. In this process, generative and classificatory schemes (interest rate risk, credit risk, transaction risk, direct risk, counterparty risk, liquidity risk, etc.) have emerged over the last 40 years, whereby ultimately any variable that can be identified can become now at least a concrete risk. The latter implies that finance sets each type of risk as a real object. In doing so, the respective types of risk must be translated into an abstract form. The incommensurable and variable forms of concrete risk are transformed into a singular form: abstract risk (ibid.).

The team of authors around Milios introduces another example: assuming that the swap itself is considered an important form of derivatives, a fixed-for-floating-rate-swap is introduced (ibid.: 175). This swap is a contract that exchanges the future cash flows of assets based on risk. The contract agrees upon certain conditions to exchange future cash flows (cash flows, income or yield flows). Asset A is a government bond issued by a sovereign, developed capitalist state, guaranteeing a fixed rate of income Ra. At the same time, B is a loan, which a capitalist company holds with a variable interest rate Rb. The fixed-for-floating-rate-swap includes the comparison of two future money capital flows (two different return flows are swapped):

$$X - Ra = y - Rb \quad \text{(ibid.: 176)}$$

Here, two future flows of returns or income are exchanged, whereby it should be noted that within the equation, in contrast to the (simple) value-form developed by Marx, neither of the two income flows expresses its value in the other value because the value expression of the income flows is already established, since the future income flows are in principle exchanged for money. The future income streams Ra and Rb are therefore already commensurable at a monetary level. But how do we have to understand the economic relations necessary for a quantitative comparison of the rate x/y? The two income streams can only be exchanged in money if the economic relations, namely those of state governance in case A and those of private surplus value production in case B, are represented to financial capital and its analysts' satisfaction. A perfectly liquid and efficient market is assumed. This makes it possible to abstract from generative contexts such as political events and economic crisis to bundle, compare and price (abstract risk) the apparently incommensurable, i.e. different concrete risks. Therefore, derivatives are needed. The above equation is based on a fundamental condition: decontextualised economic structures and class conflicts, identified as abstract risks, are exposed to a comparison. Concrete risks and the corresponding probabilities become objective with the abstract risk in the form of the derivative and function largely independently of the market participants' subjective assessments (ibid.: 177). If derivatives compare and integrate concrete risks and incorporate abstract risks, then they must be considered as a comparison of the concrete risks and the capitalisation of the abstract risk. Capitalisation includes the speculation on the volatility function of the abstract risk.[26]

We can understand the abstract risk as a singular risk in so far as it is considered a risk from the point of view of a general comparison of concrete risks and the measurement of risk as risk, whereby it is realised in money by trading derivatives. Therefore, the form of the abstract risk or its incorporation as a derivative always includes the risk measured in money (ibid.: 178). Time and volatility are thereby constitutive for the form of abstract risk, insofar as the derivative is written at a certain point in time and has a maturity during which it changes its price. Along with

---

[26] For this, a trader must calibrate the historical data as input in his model. He sets for the equation $yi = f(xi)$ a series of data points $(xi, yi) = 1,..., n$, in order to find the value $f(x)$ for a given value x. To do this, a functional, mathematical form for f must be found. The singular derivative (fixed-for-floating-rate-swap) is thus a hypostatised aggregation of different securities or derivatives. Finally, it is assumed that capitalisation's circular logic is certain and applies to all market participants. Without exception, these are reciprocally integrated into the financial field, and the derivative contract is considered a legal obligation with which the counterparties do not take on any risk.

volatility or price fluctuations, time is thus one of the important variables that design and define the derivative contract. With their design, derivative contracts are within a predefined temporal parenthesis. Financial economics reduces temporality in financial markets to an abstract and formal time that is assumed to be reversible, certain and belonging to a transhistorical logic of maximising utility. However, this contrasts sharply with the current practices of actors in financial markets, who constantly overwrite and discount the temporality of mathematical models.

The distinction between concrete and abstract risks does not imply the existence of two risks but rather the presence of two inseparable dimensions of risk within a single risk complex. Thereby, the abstract risk also implies a quantitative dimension of concrete risks; the plurality of different types of risks is reduced to a singular level.

$$x - \text{IRS} = y - \text{CDS} = z - [F \times \text{future}] = \dots \quad (\text{ibid.: } 178)$$

Milios understands derivatives when they incorporate several known risks in a particular way as a commodification of risks. He considers two aspects to be essential in this context: on the one hand, in contrast to Hilferding, derivatives should not be categorised as money,[27] but as (fictitious) commodities as capital (capital as capital); as commodities, they are always already exchanged for money. For Milios, the derivatives take the form of a commodity *sui generis*, which has a price: C-M. The integration of this relation is the cycle of fictitious capital: M-M'. Here, Milios refers directly to Marx, who understood the secondary utility value of money if it presents itself as capital in the realisation of profit, whereby capital has to be considered as a special commodity. As Marx writes: "Or, what amounts to the same, capital as capital becomes a commodity" (Marx 1998: 337).

We do, however, raise concerns at this point. Marx defined the exchange of a commodity for money (if one disregards the exchange of the special "commodity" labour force, which in the final analysis is not an equivalent exchange despite all Marx's statements) as an equivalent exchange. But the exchange of derivatives is not an equivalent exchange because the aim of the management is clearly the achievement of profits,

---

[27] Dick Bryan and Michael Rafferty problematise the moneyness of derivatives. They should serve as a new form of global money, playing "a role that is parallel to that played by gold in the nineteenth century": the role of "anchor to the financial system" (Bryan and Rafferty 2006: 133).

160   A. SZEPANSKI

which are realised in money. When Milios writes that derivatives participate in the production of profit as duplicates of the capital relation, it seems appropriate to start from derivatives not as a specific commodity (nor as money), but as a specific form of capital, namely that of speculative capital. Unlike the commodity, the derivative has no transparent price in the here and now, but rather its price is related to a contingent time in the future. A derivative can be priced out because its contracting parties close the bid/ask spread by agreeing on a current price. But regarding the speculative calculation of its future price, they distinguish themselves.

To illustrate this, let us assume in another example that security A contains a variable interest loan, and security B contains a fixed interest loan. If a swap here realises the comparison between two resulting future flows of income, then this is not a comparison of the exchange values of two commodities (or between commodity and money), but rather a comparison or exchange of two future monetary capital flows, which in the best case are profitable for both parties if they both can realise future income streams. Consequently, derivatives have to be understood as a specific form of speculative money capital, as the currently most profitable form of money capital and, at the same time, as powerful instruments with which the conditions, structures and trajectories of current capitalist reproduction processes can be observed and shaped relative effectively without, however, leading to the long-term elimination of crisis-ridden processes in the capital economy. The derivatives are entities/relations of the above-mentioned movement M-D-M'. As entities within a relation, they could be indeed understood as a very special commodity (commodity as capital), but especially in the process and in the exchange they have the potential to receive the quality of speculative capital. Capital here is a virtual structure that makes the existence of derivatives possible. Capital exists through the derivatives that actualise it. Accumulating capital means increasing the value of derivatives. Derivatives are priced out by continuous recalibration movements between singular risk assessments (to buy or sell them at a given time) and the market's movement as a whole.

Derivatives are sui generis speculative capital - a form of capital that manages the fabric of nomadic, differential and opportunistic money capital that circulates self-referentially in its own markets. Capital here has the value of an instrument that connects derivatives as a parallax and creates a globally fluid market and synchronises derivatives for the increase of leverage (LiPuma 2017: 29). The derivative is an instrument whose anticipation of the future helps to generate the future it anticipates. This dynamic has a self-referential dimension of generating returns and a relative dimension: the latter includes that the volatility of the derivative can implement volatility in the underlying, what in turn increases the spread of the derivative. Without volatility, no derivative is conceivable, and if derivatives do not circulate, then they are simply worthless. In circulation, rather contingent events based on socio-economic conditions are reduced to contextless risks and thus naturalised, i.e. melted down to discrete, independent and liquid risks that are exterior to the social.

In this context, derivatives are not to be understood as a special commodity; rather, as LiPuma refers, they should be understood as non-commodity commodities; they do refer to the commodity form, insofar as each derivative is particular and realised in money, but they are also, without exception, social mediations of the circulation of speculative capital (ibid.). Speculative capital has the very effect of generating markets of increasing volatility and higher risks. In this process, the circulation of speculative capital achieves certain autonomy characterised by the invention of derivative instruments, the abstraction of risk, the transformation of uncertainty into quantifiable risks and the proliferation of speculative capital itself. These processes set in motion accelerating complexity and increasing connectivity, so that financial institutions become increasingly interdependent, although this very fact remains largely invisible.

Speculative capital generates an end in itself through the means of connectivity, the derivative; the derivative serves as a source of profits and its own reproduction. The resulting culture and economy of finance produce new social forms such as that of abstract risk, new technologies such as the pricing of derivatives through mathematical models and new self-referential contractual arrangements. Factors such as self-referentiality, the compression of time and the monetisation of risk generate derivative markets whose construction of time bears no necessary relation to the markets of the underlyings or, for that matter, to the temporality of institutions, including financial institutions.

Finally, derivatives differ not only from classical commodities, but also from other forms of capital. They differ from a bond, for example, in a significant way. Derivatives do not throw off accumulative gains over time like bonds do. Whereas bond profits accumulate over time, the value of a derivative declines over time or towards an expiration date. The price of a derivative is linked to an underlying, but it prices out aspects that the underlying itself cannot price out, such as the specific risks of the underlying in relation to the risks that relate to the market as a whole.

Derivatives can form prices that relate to clearinghouse errors, accelerating inflation or a descent of yield curves. Credit, in terms of temporality, has to generate and anticipate the creation of derivatives, which in turn serve as a hedge for credit, but also for the derivatives themselves or for the liquidity of an institution. And finally the size and the volatility of the derivative must be liquid or tradable.

6.4 The Derivative Market

How can the derivative market itself be problematised? How can the contingent transactions executed by the actors be analysed, the completion of which is predicted by the collectively assumed condition of the existence of a market that produces the transactions by means of these realisations? The dynamic recalibration of derivatives requires a socialised subjectivity that consists in the belief by market participants that there is a totality called the market, even if it is assumed only as an abstract space for calculations that stimulate their motivations and even still traverses their bodies. Derivative markets have no tradition; they are historically singular inventions whose existence cannot be separated from liquidity (LiPuma 2017: 176).

The burning question here is why economic determinations entail, at least temporarily, markets that are regular and rational, but only partially, insofar as rationality (as "normal" price movements) is repeatedly replaced by periods of heightened and irrational volatility, sometimes so high that liquidity evaporates and the systemic failures of markets emerge with all consequences. It is here important to point out that the market is not a category of objects, but a set of social relations. If this is ignored, as mainstream economic theory does, then there is a persistent non-reflexive naturalisation of the market, insofar as relational categories are treated as object categories, which is a kind of ontological error. An important feature that distinguishes relational categories from object categories is the existence of social and historical determinations (ibid.).

Thus, there is quite a bit more to investigate when grasping the market as a social relation than merely analysing it as an imagined totality. The creation of a collective, that is, socially imagined totality, requires the conjunction of quasi-transcendental forms of objectification and processes of institutionalisation in which the construction of the financial habitus also takes place. If derivative markets include specific instruments of circulating relations qua relations through entities such as contracts, then the market that conditions this must itself be a determinant.

The logic of speculative capital, on the one hand, creates the general form of the market as a totalising framework and specific sets of relations and, on the other hand, shapes the connectivity, which is necessary for specific markets, and in which the actions of the actors reproduce, even if they fail, the concept of the market with the production of these markets.

From the point of view of concrete social relations, derivative markets are to be understood as processes through which actors reflect and objectify the structures in which they participate. The question now is which invisible aspects reproduce the whole called the market. The reproduction of the market is always also an unintended consequence of actions whose effectiveness (and failure) presupposes in turn the existence of the market. Derivative markets do not only include a superficial performativity that can be observed in the processes that create derivatives, but they also have a deeply performative structure in which actions are grounded in a social imaginary that stabilises and reproduces the market with respect to the precondition of its totalisation (ibid.).

Finance retains the word exotic, in case derivatives are written for the purpose of an extremely risky profit maximisation that transcends the actors' notions of the limits of the market. What often seems like a surreal treadmill is the repair of a directional dynamic of derivative markets, not only in the direction of increasing leverage, but also towards increasing complexity, insofar as the marketing of the products of speculative capital requires constant expansion beyond the boundaries of the market. In this regard, large companies with high sums of monetary capital, the corresponding knowledge and high interconnectivity have a clear advantage.

Finally, there is a form of performativity in and with which each market participant imagines the market similar to everyone else. The technologies used in the financial system, from high-frequency trading to algorithms and mathematical models, have the effect of obscuring the underlying social that serves to reproduce markets, while at the same time, increasing the sensitivity of market participants to make only quantifying judgements about their behaviour. Technology connects actors to the extent that they understand the market as the epicentre of their social lives. Overall, this is an anonymous socialisation and at the same time involves an existential performativity, the attribution of a very specific socialisation, i.e. a mutually expected repertoire of beliefs, desires and strategic judgements concerning the market and also the behaviour of market participants, especially with respect to counterparties whose self-representation requires nothing more than the electronic trace of a trade on a screen. Market participants assume that these structures are reciprocal and recursive, insofar as others would frame their behaviour in the same way as theirs, no matter how anonymous the others may be. This occurs with regard to the fact that the transactions that appear on the screen are mostly generated by computers. Yet one simply assumes that trading programmes reflect the intentions of actors. Trading programmes and the ideas of their programmers have, however, a general and standard utility value that traders try to shape and make profit.

Derivative markets must design and deploy their own principles of formation. LiPuma speaks at this point of the performativity of a financial event as a ritual, which is successful if it at least reproduces the integrity of the form or structure of markets and thus maintains liquidity no matter what volatility is involved in the unfolding of circulation. It must now be clarified how the ritual inscribed in the social relations of buying and selling performatively objectifies the derivative market. This performativity is necessarily prospective and non-retrospective: prospective in sending bid and ask prices (which deploy liquidity), but retrospective in the execution of a trade (which deploys counterparties and new price movements). Therefore, the market and its determination must be conceived both as a kind of an open totality as relations and as a practice of reflexive actors. A derivative market is thus a specific social space designed for particular modes of practices by actors, i.e. behaviours which are held together by the connectivity of the cognitive and socially instructed motivational processes (competition, self-esteem, profit, risk) that in turn also drive these behaviours.

It has been noted often enough that market participants both reify and personalise the market and, moreover, describe market movements through a series of metaphors. But what is crucial at this point is simply that there is a discrepancy between an abstract, asocial agency and an everyday space of traders in which transactions and their utility are to be maximised, assuming here the social totality called the market. It is about how concrete financial relations in all their social specificity produce and reproduce a social imaginary totality. This is the market as a means for the rational agent maximising utility. But such a market has never existed because agents must adopt intelligent and institutionally coordinated concepts and dispositions to survive in markets. Markets are organised on a systemic level; they are necessarily more and different than the sum of their individual parts. One cannot capture the systemic properties of markets by merely analysing the actions of the participants. While it is not the case that the individual actions of actors are unimportant, it is precisely because they (re)produce a differentiated dimension of social reality that is presupposed to them, a certain socio-economic structure of the market.

The financial market is of course also a social imagination, but a deeply institutionalised imagination that includes persons who possess trust in this imagination, and bodies that inscribe a knowledge, plus ratified names, registered companies and a codified history. For LiPuma, the market is thus a social totality, a practically relational construct and a kind of analytical object constructed by the sciences (ibid.).

The totality (of the market) is nothing more than a real social fiction: fictional because it is contingent and socially created, and real because it grounds real-world events. In this, performativity is not limited to ritual or certain linguistic events, but is implicit in the reproduction of all social forms and structures of capital. The rise of the derivative logic as the principle of derivative production (based on the separation and recomposition of capital) determines the generative scheme (design of exotic derivatives) adopted by traders, which in turn serves to performatively reproduce derivative markets.

The ritual of a financial event is performatively successful if it reproduces the integrity of the form or structure of markets and thus maintains liquidity in the markets, no matter what volatility is involved in the unfolding of circulation. The problem here is to reproduce the shape of a form when risks/uncertainties of future volatility and the implemented strategies exist. Performativity re-objectifies the form of the form, which is now a transformed form that appears ideologically as maintaining the integrity and identity of the market. Insofar as financial circulation makes all social forms fluid, these forms must constantly re-objectify themselves. The unification of performativity and objectification together leads to a reconceptualisation of totality that moves from crystallised forms to ones that must be permanently re-objectified.

This continuous process of re-objectification has its own social consequences, i.e. the formation of form is positional, perspectival and provisional. A derivative market is provisional insofar as its financing, agents and liquidity are constantly changing; it is positional insofar as its definition as a market relates to other markets; and it is perspectival insofar as its integrity depends on the positions of the individuals who find themselves in the financial space. The objectified forms here serve as real and fictional spaces in which the flows of money are brought forth as well as destabilised by means of the performativity that they re-objectify. It is also necessary for agents to maintain their collective belief in the integrity of form despite the destabilising effects of circulatory forces.

LiPuma repeatedly emphasises the problem of the functionality of markets and the derivative. If the derivative is to function as a speculative process, then one needs an energetic market. The derivative has value only if there is a market in which it can circulate. Finally, the functionality of the market also depends on the willingness of market participants to produce a stream of liquidity in the face of uncertain volatility. The market is a real social fiction that agents produce and reproduce quasi-automatically through their collective belief in it. The blending of the real and the fictional via the collective belief of the agents, as well as the trust in the functioning totality, indicates that markets have a performative aspect. Liquidity here consists in the representation of the social in the financial field, indicated by the objectification of the counterparty on one side of the deal and the assumption of risk on the other side.

To understand the social, it is necessary to consider the extraordinary gap between the economic models used to model the market and their justificatory use. The paradox required by financial economics is, on the one hand, the investment and thus also the dependence on a set of financial models that are necessary to determine the risk (models that systematically clasp the forces of social insecurity), and, on the other hand, a performativity that is the prerequisite for the success of the models and for the continuation of the markets. The actions of the isolated agents are at the same time collective. Trading derivatives and speculating on their future value, assuming that agents recognise the unpredictable abstract risk, are only possible for the agents themselves if they take certain dispositions related to plural forms of rationality (maximising profit, competitive dynamics, self-esteem, speculative ethos and even a certain nationalism). These dispositions, which mediate every purchase and sale of derivatives and also the past with the future, are based on the relation between the organisation of these dispositions, which are constitutive for the habitus of the agents, and the structure of possibilities, which are constitutive for the financial field at every conceivable point in time.

6.5   Heterodox Positions

Regarding the analysis of derivatives, let us now turn to the heterodox positions of Elie Ayache and Suhail Malik.[28] We will first introduce the main features of Malik's position. For Malik, the price movements of the underlyings and the contingent pricing of the derivatives are to be understood as interdependent processes of capitalisation of payment promises in the context of differential capital accumulation. The contingent and, in principle, endless price movements of the derivatives, which primarily refer to themselves and only secondarily to the underlyings, must nevertheless always include the factor of finiteness, insofar as the pay-off of the derivative on the due date means the decline of the respective derivative contract (Malik 2014: 410). At the same time, however, the maturity also implies a shift that is possible up to the expiration of the contract, which is inherent in the differential pricing of derivatives per se. Pricing therefore has to be viewed primarily from the perspective of the immanent features of the derivatives themselves and not from the exogenous perspective of the underlying assets. Here, the principally endless contingency dominates, which is shown in the constantly possible revision of derivative contracts. It is important to note that the aspects of finiteness and contingency always remain tied to the price movements and structures of capital, whereby the way in which the capitalist economy is shaped in monetary terms enables the dynamics of the price movements of the derivatives and their future money flows, while capital's hunt for profit remains absolutely constitutive for the economy.

---

[28] A detailed discussion on the concepts of Ayache and Malik can be found in Szepanski (2014, 2016). *Kapitalisierung Bd.2*, develops a Deleuzian theory of the derivative. The synthetic asset is the production of pure difference articulated as a simulation. What is at stake here is a real illusion [*Trugbild*] that no longer bears any resemblance to the classical economic object, so that the immanent "copy" of the synthetic model in itself quickly destroys any symmetrical and purely illustrative relationship between the physical object and the value-creating imago. At this point, the synthetic diagram, which has to be considered as a germ of the order and rhythm of the synthetic assets, can be understood at best as a illusion-construction, not as an imaged one, but as a topological relation between the economic properties of the synthetic assets themselves, their nomadic distributions, and this in contrast to the conception of purely logistical distributions. In the diagram of a synthetic asset, the discrete elements, which are nothing more than the economic properties of the asset itself (cash flow, maturity, price, risk, volatility, etc.), are related to each other.

The variability of the price of the derivative thus depends, among other things, on the likewise variable finiteness of the contract (determination of the pay-off, schedule, duration, etc.), and at the same time, this remains related to the indefinite market variability of the derivative price movement. Derivatives shift prices according to a differential logic of temporalisation: the market price found at the end of the maturity of a derivative contract does not coincide with the price that was fixed in the contract, which means that without the temporal non-coincidence between the market price (spot price) and the fixed price (strike price), there can be no derivative at all, but only the purchase/sale of ordinary goods. Derivatives permanently open and close the gap between realised prices and possibly imminent futures. Whoever, for example, buys derivatives on raw materials, does not acquire the raw materials themselves, but rather, on a second level, trades a speculative capital that always fluctuates in price, which means that prices primarily refer to the prices of derivatives themselves and not the prices of the derivatives in relation to the underlying assets. (Malik also subsumes options and futures under derivatives.) The dual variability, which is primarily that of the immanent price movement of the derivatives themselves, is what Malik calls the "plasticity of the derivative contract" (ibid.: 406ff.). The term employs especially endogenous derivative pricing (in its contingency). Here, plasticity is to be understood as the constitutive condition for the uncertainty of the derivative price movement: a trader who hedges or speculates on the future markets can sell or dissolve the contract at any time or at least subject it to revision or recalibration by realising a deal (hedge) opposite to the original contract during the term of the contract. Then, the trader simultaneously takes a long position and a short position on the deal in question. With this type of double positioning, called "flat", where neither the delivery of the underlying is necessary, nor is the reference to the underlying decisive, the trader can realise either losses or gains. Here, the trader takes a recombinant subject-object position, characterised, on the one hand, by his subjective opportunism, which consists in constantly switching from one position to another, and, on the other hand, by the objective relativity of the derivative pricing itself (under the dominance of the latter). Finally, it must be taken into account that it is precisely the fact that one can hold more than one position on the same asset that has inflated the nominal sizes of transactions on the financial markets far beyond their current credit exposures. The virtual, unrealised or outstanding nominal value of derivative contracts was approximately

$700 trillion in 2014, while the actualised price was approximately $30 trillion and global gross domestic product was approximately $78 trillion (cf. Das 2015: 35).

According to Malik, four issues can be identified that are absolutely essential for the economy of differential pricing of derivatives (Malik 2014: 404):

1. The derivative contract includes conditions relating to the price movements of the external referent (underlying).
2. The constitution of derivatives involves complex modes of intrinsic temporal binding and splitting of the present, although the uncertainty of the future plays the decisive role, so that the risk must always be assessed, with which all pricing decisions regarding derivatives are continuously revised.
3. Derivative pricing generates a new mode of optionality, by which pricing intrinsically relates to the operations on its own derivative markets. This happens with counterperformative acts, which, while making explicit the singular conditions of the exogenous reference of the underlying for pricing, relate first and foremost to the immanent price movement of the derivatives themselves.
4. Derivative pricing requires the moment of contingency, with which the endogeneity of the pricing of derivatives is extended to all pricing processes - and Malik calls this fourth dimension the "a priori-financiality" of capitalisation.

In addition, the differential price movement of derivatives differs from the usual bet in that the endogenous operations of derivatives, which have an indefinite plasticity (at least until the expiry date of the respective contracts), imply that the exogenous referent (the underlying) is employed, whereas in the case of the bet, the exogenous betting-event remains separate from the bet itself. The derivative pricing - which not only takes place in an indefinite process, but also shapes it - integrates and determines the price movements of the underlying assets. What is ultimately priced out on the derivative markets is the pricing process of the derivatives themselves. This process should be described as an immanent process constituted by the "Infrawager" (ibid.: 417f.) and this means that the modes of derivative pricing are not primarily dependent on externally determined conditions, but rather on the internal movements of their own parameters, coefficients and variables. According to Malik, the reality of the Infrawager, which manifests itself in and with derivative pricing, exists within a twofold contingency: contingency of abstraction (variability of the derivative contract and general fungibility of the underlying) and contingency of revision (indefinite plasticity of the differential price movement itself, i.e. a constant possible shift of the price) (ibid.: 420). This extends the derivative, which is normally understood as a zero-sum game between two parties who, in this game, refer to external events. The contingent conditions of pricing derivatives always remain tied to the institutional-material power practices of financial capital that are found in the derivative markets and to the monetary architecture of quantitative capitalisation.

Accordingly, Malik considers the pricing of derivatives to be immanent and contingent, installing a speculative dimension to the expectation of an unknown future and the promise of payment that satisfies it. Under this aspect, the derivative constitutes the third component of contingency, the thetic contingency. Thetic contingency demonstrates the de-identification of the price movement not only in relation to the underlying, but within the derivative price formation process it contains above all the de-identification of the derivative price in itself, i.e. every price is possible here, but it could also be different. In this respect, the volatility of the derivative is then decisive, as the dispersion or spread, which refers to its own imaginary centre. The temporal shift of the price movements of the derivatives is by no means to be understood only as anticipation in the sense of a purely temporal extension of the present into the future, but rather it contains the endogenous splitting of the present itself. By tying the future to the present, it comes both to an extension and to a destabilisation of the present. At the same time, the price movement is part of the futuristic contingency, which, however, cannot take place without the actualisation of the derivative through its exchange into money. The maturity is the point in time when the price of the derivative is convertible with the price of the underlying, and this convergence, which is realised in money, could be called the valuation of the derivative contract. The valuation implies the conclusion and exhaustion of the process of pricing the derivatives; it articulates the elimination of the difference between strike price and spot price at the end of the contract period.

Precisely because of its exogenous referentiality, the underlying, which is already expressed in money, is at first the determining term compared to the endogenous derivative price in order to be able to record the fact of the writing of derivative contracts. However, the valuation of the derivative and the underlying asset is in the last instance determined by the derivative pricing itself, and this pricing is constantly modified in the course of the (implied) volatility of the derivatives. Conversely, the price change of the underlying asset can also result in a disproportionately higher price change of the derivative (convexity of the derivative). The relationship between derivative price and the price of the underlying is non-linear. Ultimately, in financial markets, it is the price that virtualises the value at any conceivable point in time, and this becomes manifest in the context of derivative pricing; that is, the price manifests the reality of derivative pricing (manifest without manifestation). One must take into account that with derivatives the price is nothing but the spread between bid and ask. Thus, with regard to derivatives, we can no longer assume that the price is "anchored" by or in the value. And this further means that precisely because of the endogenous constitution of the price qua Infrawager, value on the financial markets is not primarily determined by factors such as productivity, trade, scarcity, demand, utility, utility value and abstract labour.

Malik refers to this a prioritisation of the derivative price in the wake of Derrida as the "Arkhéderivative" (ibid.: 445ff.), and under the condition of the presence of triple contingency: variability of the derivative contract (contingency of abstraction), variability of the derivative price (contingency of revision) and absolute volatility of pricing (thetic contingency). According to Malik, absolute volatility in particular represents the power of capital today.

The French theorist and trader Elie Ayache also claims that derivatives trade contingency, inasmuch as the difference that is produced by their trade, which always remains related to the future, simultaneously marks a difference in the present. In the minimal definition (relative contingency), the term contingency means that something as it is (was or will be), can be, but it is also possible in another way (cf. Luhmann 2015: 152). Against it, Ayache understands the concept of contingency as absolute, unconditional and independent, not as exchangeable, as the thing-in-itself, so to speak, insofar as things are what they are, but, and this is decisive here, they could also always be different. For the traders of derivatives on financial markets, it is always also a matter of determining a tradable price from the many possibilities offered by the price movements of derivatives in the face of fundamental uncertainty. When traders write derivative contracts or, as Ayache says, contingent claims, they create forms of contingency, where the difference that is made in the future makes a difference now, because the price is here a differential itself.

In doing so, derivative traders do not primarily observe the time series of price movements of the underlyings of the derivatives, but primarily the movements of the derivative prices themselves. The derivative trade and its price fluctuations thus deviate in reality strongly from the methods of past-related statistics, since derivative traders are not primarily interested in the statistics of underlyings and their prices. Instead, the fluctuating prices of the derivatives produce a surface called market, on which the prices are written and the price movements of the derivatives are separated from the movements of the underlyings, which are the basis of the derivatives.

An important question for Ayache is how to fix the price of a derivative that is consistent with the trader's strategy. According to Ayache, any dynamic trading strategy should be equivalent to consistently pricing a derivative (cf. Ayache 2010a). What makes the matter even more complicated is simply that the price of the respective derivative is determined and at the same time shifted by a dynamic concatenation of derivatives and their price movements - derivatives related to derivatives related to derivatives. The term "market" here refers to the simulative space that makes the translation of contingent claims and promises to pay possible in the first place. It is the medium through which the contingent claims move during their fixed term until a questionable value is actualised and there is no future for the derivative. For Ayache, the market refers to a surface that is based much more on space than on time, a surface that serves to inscribe prices and on which quantities of meaningless, quantifiable signs circulate, permanently communicating with each other. The instantaneously generated market prices of synthetic derivatives are thus distributed on a surface that isolates the traders from the observation of the underlying assets.

But what is a contingent claim for Ayache? It is something that replaces the necessary transfer between the possible and the real, which is imperative in stochastics, with the help of a written contract that has a real, material status and is at the same time a contingent formula, which is directed towards the future, and that constantly crosses reality (Ayache 2010b: 45). Money is used to realise the contingent claim, although it always already exists parallel to the contingent claim; it functions itself as a material reality against which the liquid contingent claim of the derivative is redeemed, and this can happen during the term of the contract or at maturity. The prices of derivatives are produced in indefinite processes of counter-actualisation/virtualisation; the price is the result of the permanent translation services of contingent claims (cf. Ayache 2010a).

The difference between stock price and strike price also implies contingency, i.e. although an underlying asset is always actually given, the derivative, because of its permanently changing price, keeps the value de facto unstable; in other words, it could also be different (it is a price). Ayache comes to the conclusion that the derivative gets its value with the price. His theory is at first about pricing functions. For derivatives, there is in the end no need for value theory. The actualisation of the price remains dependent on the programmes of contingent claims within the framework of the various schedules and time periods on the markets. Ayache calls this the "last minute" instability of value, which is what makes the price productive, namely volatility (cf. Ayache 2010b). Absolute volatility, which is purely virtual, always remains beyond the chronological order of time, whereby, for Ayache, the dimension in which continuous virtualisation qua price unfolds is space; absolute volatility remains sewn to the term price, inasmuch as contingency finds in price the translation of its differential character, i.e. as volatility sees its indeterminism confirmed. Consequently, the concept of price has, on the one hand, a virtual component, but on the other, it also refers to the empirical-current aspect of derivative pricing. The price, which indicates anticipations and is future-oriented, thus remains at the same time in the actuality of the market (cf. Ayache 2005: 13).

Money is material and counts, while the probability theory models most traders work with don't count. It realises a difference inherent in the synthetic derivative sui generis, precisely when a financial event occurs. Usually, the difference inherent in contingent financial claims or prices is defined in relation to the prices of the underlyings, and thus contingency is integrated into a corset of identifiable probable cases under the rule of the One. The One stands for the totality of the cases that the differences could take. If, however, the cases are to be prices in the markets, then the contingent prices of the derivatives are also to be understood as cases with a certain independence from the underlying prices. Of course, there are the maturities of the derivatives in relation to their underlying, but a derivative contract is created before its maturity. Long before the contract expires, the prices of the derivatives relate not only to the underlying assets, but also to the volatility of the derivative prices themselves, the volatility of the volatility, etc. The rule of price-fixing then consists in the continuous recalibration of the models of risk assessment of derivatives in relation to new pricing.

Instead, however, stochastics continue to assume that traders will move from one day to the next via a passage, that is, with a certain probability. However, the unlikely assumption that the probable cases of today are commensurate with those of tomorrow can only ever capture contingent pricing as backward looking, while at the same time requiring the construction of a number of possible future cases under the aegis of the One (probability) to calculate the current price of derivatives as the discounted expectation of future cases/prices. This, however, already indicates the limits of the stochastic measure of volatility for Ayache, while the determining parameters of the derivative have to be constantly reinvented and fixed in the context of a dynamic "replication", so that no reiteration of already known prices or prices planned or fixed by risk models takes place, since measure is referring to a future that will never be present (uncertainty). Thus, there are no constant and stringent transitions between the probability-based cases of today and to those of tomorrow to be reported. Rather, we sleep in the intervals, and these are irritating quantities because the connecting link between the cases of today and those of tomorrow is missing; the intervals are empty in-between times in which anything or nothing could happen. For Ayache, the contingent claims in the financial markets represent the conversion of debt, insofar as those claims are the future and debt is past-oriented. Rather than folding back certain instruments to the known current models in the current hedging process, the broker would be more interested in upgrading to the next level of hedging by using parameters that are used in a particular stochastic model to create a "hedging ratio" that is contrary to the model, while a second option, which differs in price from the first option, would be hedged according to itself. Thirdly, it should also be considered that each time a deviation of the option price from the price predicted by the current model is detected, this should be interpreted as a signal to upgrade the current model to the next stochastic level, using the deviating option price as a hedging instrument against the next stochastic factor.

6.6 Portfolio Theory

Portfolio theory attempts to provide instructions for combining assets/financial positions, or for constructing an optimal portfolio taking into account risk, profit and liquidity. In particular, the risk of a portfolio should be minimised without reducing the expected return, for which the assets must not be fully correlated. If risky assets of different types are grouped together in a portfolio, it is important to reduce the overall risk of the portfolio, and the lower the covariance between the assets in terms of expected returns, the less risky the entire portfolio is (since the total variance is lower) (for the whole complex cf. Asher 2016). For example, the shares of an automobile company and those of its suppliers are strongly correlated. The covariance is high, so the returns on the investments will move in parallel. An unforeseen event affecting the first company will also affect the second company.

Investors always try to choose a portfolio composition that promises the highest return on investment at a given level of risk. One can already see here that Markowitz's famous portfolio theory only makes sense because of the comparability of the risks, because there are a multitude of often-invisible interactions between the risks, which, if correctly assessed and compared, should result in a low risk of the entire portfolio. Bonds, stocks and derivatives are therefore selected here in terms of their strategic importance for portfolio diversification. Thus, the investment in a single asset is not to be examined for its specific return, but rather the various investments in assets are to be examined with regard to their respective participation in the entire portfolio, which should yield the maximum return, and therefore, the risks and the returns must be calculated.

Nobel Prize winner William Sharpe, who wanted to make a performative statement that would allow the level of risk in a portfolio to be compared and measured, investigated the optimal relationship between risks in 1966. The higher the Sharpe Ratio, named after him, the better is the performance of the portfolio with respect to the treatment of risks. The Sharpe Ratio is calculated as follows: subtract the risk-free interest rate, e.g. that of a 10-year U.S. government bond, from the portfolio's yield and divide the result by the standard deviation of the portfolio's yield (which measures the volatility of the portfolio). The formula is then as follows: $(Rp-Rf)/\sigma$ (Rp = expected portfolio return; Rf = risk-free interest rate; σ = standard deviation of the portfolio).

It is first thus asked whether a portfolio has a higher return than the interest of the U.S. government bond, and the result is divided by the standard deviation (σp). If two portfolio managers, A and B, have achieved returns of 10% in the last 2 years, with A's Sharpe Ratio of 1.11 and B's Sharpe Ratio of 0.88, this then means that A took less risk than B to achieve the same profit. It is a matter of how much the return of a portfolio rises or falls in comparison with the average return in a given period. If the returns are very volatile, a portfolio is exposed to a higher risk. Now, rather than simply examining the covariance of each individual asset relative to the other assets in the portfolio, we look at how an asset moves in price relative to the market as a whole to create a perfectly diversified portfolio that achieves the desired levels of risk and returns on investments (ibid.).

Financial collateral now has the function of being a "value" for hedging, and this in terms of constructing a well-diversified portfolio. The assets are thus to be understood as material carriers for the "hedging value" of the portfolio; they are materialised speculative capital. It can be assumed that, for example, the derivatives subscribed are not only a function of the parties involved, but also of the speculative activities of all the players which are active on the market. The fluctuating prices resulting from the fact that assets are hedged against each other reflect the countless visions of expected futures, indeed the market as a whole (ibid.: 42f.). Financial securities or assets then refer to the mutual promises they represent, or to the amount of risk they contain. The "hedging value" depends on the quantity of risks necessary to replicate them. Investors do not only rely on the expected returns, but they also have to consider the uncertainty or variance of the returns. Here, desirable events always refer to undesirable events. Thus, in a portfolio, one has to consider not only the expected return on a single asset, but also the variance of the corresponding returns, i.e. the covariance of each return with all the other returns of the other assets in a portfolio (ibid.: 44). And this, in turn, has to be related to the most important indicator that influences the returns of the assets in a given situation (these can be price indices, GDP or the stock market index). For example, an asset newly added to the portfolio should be asked whether it adds new risks (the volatility of this asset would then be greater than that of the dominant asset), or whether it makes the portfolio less risky (the volatility of the asset would then be less than that of the dominant asset). Investors hold a whole range of stocks, bonds and derivatives in their portfolios that they want to sell as soon as possible, and this should of course not depend on long-term prospects, but on the respective level of volatility of the assets in their own portfolio in relation to that of all assets traded in the market.

References

Asher, Ivan (2016) *Portfolio Society: On the Capitalist Mode of Prediction*, New York.

Ayache, Elie (2005) *The "Non-Greek" Non-foundation of Derivative Pricing*, in: http://www.ito33.com/sites/default/files/articles/0509_ayache.pdf.

Ayache, Elie (2010a) *The Blank Swan: The End of Probability*, London.

Ayache, Elie (2010b) *The Turning*, in: http://www.ito33.com/sites/default/files/articles/1007_ayache.pdf.

Bahr, Hans-Dieter (1983) *Über den Umgang mit Maschinen*, Tübingen.

Beller, Jonathan (2021) *The World Computer: Derivative Conditions of Racial Capitalism*, Durham.

Bourdieu, Pierre (2014) *Über den Staat – Vorlesungen am College de France 1989–1992*, Berlin.

Bryan, Dick and Rafferty, Michael (2006) *Capitalism with Derivatives: A Political Economy of Financial Derivatives, Capital and Class*, London.

Cherizola, Jesus Suaste (2021) *From Commodities to Assets. Capital as Power and the Ontology of Finance*, in: https://capitalaspower.com/2021/05/cherizola-from-commodities-to-assets/.

Das, Satyajit (2015) *A Banquet of Consequences. Have We Consumed Our Own Future?*, London.

Deleuze, Gilles and Guattari, Félix (1992) *Tausend Plateaus. Kapitalismus und Schizophrenie*, Berlin.

Esposito, Elena (2010) *Die Zukunft der Futures. Die Zeit des Geldes in Finanzwelt und Gesellschaft*, Heidelberg.

Foucault, Michel (2011) *The Birth of Biopolitics: Lectures at the College De France, 1978–1979*, New York.

Hull, John C. (2011) *Options, Futures and Other Derivatives*, Upper Saddle River, NJ.

Lee, Benjamin and Martin, Randy (eds.) (2016) *Derivatives and the Wealth of Societies*, Chicago.

LiPuma, Edward (2017) *The Social Life of Financial Derivatives: Markets, Risk, and Time*, Durham.

Lozano, Benjamin (2014) *Of Synthetic Finance: 3 Essays of Speculative Materialism*, in: http://speculativematerialism.files.wordpress.com/2012/12/ofsynthetic-finance-complete-text.pdf.

Luhmann, Niklas (2015) *Wirtschaft der Gesellschaft*, Frankfurt/M.

178   A. SZEPANSKI

Mainzer, Klaus (2014) *Die Berechnung der Welt. Von der Weltformel zu Big Data*, Munich

Malik, Suhail (2014) *Ontology of Finance. Price, Power and the Arkhéderivative*, in: MacKay, Robin (ed.), *Collapse Vol. VIII: Casino Real*, Falmouth: 303–480.

Marazzi, Christian (2011) *Verbranntes Geld*, Zürich, Berlin.

Martin, Randy (2009) *The Twin Tower of Financialization: Entanglements of Political and Cultural Economies*, in: *The Global South* 3(1): 108–125.

Marx, Karl (1998) *Capital*, Vol. 3, in *Marx and Engels Collected Works*, Vol. 37, London.

Mau, Steffen (2019) *The Metric Society: On the Quantification of the Social*, trans. Sharon Howe, Cambridge.

Meister, Robert (2016) *Liquidity*, in: Lee, Benjamin and Martin, Randy (eds.), *Derivatives and the Wealth of Societies*, Chicago: 2702–3299.

Meister, Robert (2021) *Justice Is an Option: A Democratic Theory of Finance for the Twenty-First Century*, Chicago.

Milios, John (2019) *Value, Fictitious Capital and Finance: The Timeliness of Karl Marx's Capital*, in: http://users.ntua.gr/jmilios/8124-Article_Text-22400-1-10-20200311.pdf.

Mühlmann, Heiner (2013) *Europa im Weltwirtschaftskrieg. Philosophie der Blasenwirtschaft*, Paderborn.

Norfield, Tony (2011) *Derivatives and Capitalist Markets: The Speculative Heart of Capital*, Leiden.

Sahr, Aaron (2017) *Das Versprechen des Geldes. Eine Praxistheorie des Kredits*, Hamburg.

Sotiropoulos, Dimitris P., Milios, John and Lapatsioras, Spyros (2013) *A Political Economy of Contemporary Capitalism and Its Crisis*, New York.

Szepanski, Achim (2014) *Kapitalisierung Bd.2. Non-Ökonomie des gegenwärtigen Kapitalismus*, Hamburg.

Szepanski, Achim (2016) *Der Non-Marxismus – Finance, Maschinen, Dividuum*, Hamburg.

CHAPTER 7

Private Banks

7.1 The Functions of Private Banks

While financial capital employs loans, fictitious and speculative capital and other multiple capital equivalents (which are often very liquid, mobile and commensurable), and also provides the organisation of the national and international payment system, organises foreign exchange trading and provides the funds for short-term (cash flow) and long-term investment, commercial capital, in contrast, focuses more on buying and selling traditional commodities. Think here of the large Walmart corporations, Lidl and Aldi. Credit card companies such as Visa, American Express and MasterCard, in turn, specialise in the management of the cashless circulation of money, which is essential today for all kinds of commercial transactions. These companies mainly handle payments between households and businesses. While commercial capital usually exchanges commodities for money, financial capital mediates and capitalises forms of money, especially those related to the future.

With the operation of monetary capital qua credit creation, private banks make a decisive contribution to increase the sums of fictitious capital and thus stabilise and expand capital accumulation at the level of individual capital and total capital. It is important to remember that the expansion of credit creation by private banks is also an important resource of speculative capital, which in turn fuels the derivative markets

© The Author(s), under exclusive license to Springer Nature Switzerland AG 2022
A. Szepanski, *Financial Capital in the 21st Century,*
Marx, Engels, and Marxisms,
https://doi.org/10.1007/978-3-030-93151-3_7

179

180   A. SZEPANSKI

and may, but need not, also fuel the real economy. Companies in all industries and sectors absolutely need the various services of the financial system. Commercial banks are profit-oriented organisations that are now relatively independent of both the finite capital holdings of traditional companies and the control of central banks. Interest-bearing, fictitious and speculative capital, insofar as private banks encode, lend, consolidate and concentrate the flows of money capital, is given here a real, specifically material existence. The companies of all industries and sectors need the various services of the financial system. Today, however, all large companies, no matter what sector to which they belong, are involved in financial transactions to consolidate their economic power.

In their initial phase, the operations of private banks were mainly focused on the purchase of gold, bills of exchange, stocks and bonds, which was matched by the issuance of overdraft credits, credits and loans. Historically, this often occurred first in the form of the bill of exchange; in the bill of exchange business, the person using the bill as a means of payment is liable until the due date of the last holder of the bill with real money (Lohoff and Trenkle 2012: 164f.).[1] In the concatenations of this early form of commercial credit, money dealers gradually intervened by buying up bills of exchange, thereby realising a payment promised in the future in money ahead of time, wherein they are paid for this type of service with a portion of the sum of money calculated from the fixed interest rate on the bill of exchange and the remaining term of the paper.

The commercial banks function as institutions for the concentration of money and money capital by collecting and borrowing money from households, states and companies as debtors, and by lending money or granting loans as creditors. Commercial banks carry out financial services and speculative transactions that are profitable. The most important *modus operandi* of the commercial banks is at first solely aimed at borrowing as much money as possible in the economy and to lend it at a rate of interest higher than that which they pay for borrowing the money. As Marx writes about the bank: "Its profit is generally made by borrowing at lower rate of interest than it receives in loaning" (Marx 1998: 400). In heterodox financial theory, this is called the "distribution model of money" (Sahr 2017: Kindle-Edition: 3208). Thus, the profit mechanism of banks is fairly simple: they lend at higher interest rates (lending rate)

---

[1] The borrower can sell the bill of exchange receivable to the bank by the due date by discounting the bill, whereby he receives the equivalent value minus the discount.

than they themselves pay interest on borrowed loans or deposits (deposit rate). To put it more precisely, the income or profits of banks consists of nothing more than the fees for payment transactions and the interest rate differences resulting from the spread between financing and investment services (Seiffert 2016: 31). The positive difference (after the deduction of costs) then represents the bank's profit. But against this, it is important to note already here that with the creation of credits, i.e. the creation of promises to pay (the creative function of money), the actual business activity of a private bank begins.[2]

Commercial banks free companies to a certain extent from their lack of money, that is, from the barriers of their economic size, and at the same time, they intensify the competition between companies, insofar as, in their function as comprehensive creditors and debtors of monetary capital, they establish a relationship of interdependence between companies, which implies that companies must compete among themselves for credit in order to remain competitive with the use of credit in the markets (Decker et al. 2016: 21f.). By controlling the creation and distribution of credit, private banks place industrial and commercial companies, which are concerned solely about the continuous increase of their capital, in an interdependent relationship, with banks controlling the monetary cycles and managing both the shortage and the abundance of money in an economy. There are therefore structures of mutual interdependence within the dominant features. Additionally, regardless of the business success of their debtor, private banks have an absolute right to repayment and interest on the loan; that is, it takes precedence over the increase of capital by those companies that act as borrower or debtor towards the bank. A private bank will only enter into a loan agreement with a company if it expects that the profit generated by the company with the help of the loan will be higher than the interest to be paid by the company. However, if the profit of the company turns out smaller than the interest or the company realises high losses, then the company and the private bank do not divide the smaller profit or even the loss, but the

---

[2] Today, the payment transactions of banks, which are carried out with the granting of loans, are largely digitalised and deducted in accounting terms, i.e. with debit and credit notes. It should be noted that cashless payment transactions not only serve to speed up monetary transactions, but also strengthen the private banks' power of access to the sums of money parked in their accounts and to those sums of money that circulate in a capital economy and serve their speculative lending business.

interest (plus repayment) agreed upon by contract is further demanded by the bank without consideration of the actual economic development of the company. If the debtor (the company) has no financial reserves, the creditor (the bank) will impound the money transferred as loan security and/or the company will go bankrupt. Banks are not simply satisfied with a certain share of the profit, but relentlessly demand from companies the legally secured, previously contractually agreed (fixed) interest (and repayment) of the loan. Therefore, private banks, which usually negotiate a fixed interest rate with companies, are not exclusively interested in strongly risk-oriented and extra-profitable companies, because in their case of bankruptcy, the banks also suffer losses, while they participate in the extra profits of the companies only in very limited manner, or not at all. The private banks evaluate and calculate, to a certain extent, the prospects of success of the transactions of the companies, to which they lend money (and demand collateral for these transactions), but they also abstract from the operations that these companies carry out with the money lent. Although the business of companies is supposed to be profitable in their function as borrowers, the interest rate is calculated as a percentage of the sum of money lent, as if it were only up to it to grow.

Let us first summarise the most important tasks, divisions and functions of commercial banks: concentration of savings and investment services (deposits), payment services (the management of cash and non-cash payments from customers), financing services, credit creation, investment activity with the issue and employment of securities, trading fictitious capital and derivatives and the organisation of foreign exchange trading (spot, forward and swap transactions) for commercial and industrial companies, but also on their own account, risk transformation (between savers and borrowers) and services (leasing, factoring, broking and consulting business). The most important business activity of private banks today is credit creation, without which the maintenance of capital cycles as an extended reproduction would not be possible, investment activities in securities and derivatives trading and the minimisation of overall economic transaction costs. For private banks, some important parameters for their own business activities can thus be determined: factors of competition (oligopolisation of the banks), amount of cash payments, reserve management, credit creation potential, investment activity, security and derivatives trading, risk calculation, various forms of managing payments in interbank transactions and with central banks (cf. Baecker 2008: 140f.).

7 PRIVATE BANKS   **183**

Let us now examine bank deposits transactions: three levels can be named here (cf. Seiffert 2016: 23f.)[3]:

1) The customer level (households, companies, government). At this level, transactions are carried out between private banks and their customers, and between bank customers themselves, with the deposits digitally written on accounts as alphanumeric signs, in order to then circulate between the accounts of the bank customers, who use the balances as money for consumption or as monetary capital. Today, the customer deposits are often created through credit-generating writing processes as the input of numbers on the computer keyboard (keystroke capitalism) (Sahr 2017: Kindle Edition: 8462).

2) The level of commercial banks. While the internal monetary transactions of banks take place as pure writing processes between their own customers, their external transactions involve the customers of different private banks contacting each other, with the clearing of cash flows between the accounts of the participating banks. This affects the second level, namely the interbank credit market. The transfer from a customer account of commercial bank A to a customer account of commercial bank B represents an outgoing payment for the former and an incoming payment for the latter, whereby the mutual payment flows are offset on the interbank credit accounts. Commercial bank A maintains an interbank credit account with each commercial bank to whose customer accounts it transfers bank deposits, while conversely, each commercial bank that makes transfers to commercial bank A maintains an interbank credit account with the latter. The bilateral money mutually accepted by

---

[3] Cash is negligible at this point, since its share of the total money volume is low, at about 10%. With the recent abolition of cash in some countries (in some African countries and in Sweden it has already been enforced, but in the rest of Europe, too, there are constantly further restrictions on cash withdrawals), the ruling classes intend, besides making illegal activities more difficult (an argument that is usually the only one stated publically), to enforce negative interest rates, to increase the profits of credit card companies as well as of private banks, the total control payment transactions and, finally, to fix deposits when it comes to rescuing these banks (Häring 2016: 60f.). Meanwhile, states are increasingly prohibiting cash payments, which they themselves have declared to be the exclusive legal tender.

the commercial banks could be called "interbank money" (Seiffert 2016: 26).

Commercial banks act as lenders and borrowers on the money market, depending on the payment obligations and money inflows that occur on a given day; these are loans that are extended from one day to the next (overnight money), although the margins in these lending transactions are rather low (the terms of the loans are short, but the volumes are high). With regard to the liquidity management of banks, they have to hold little reserves for their payment obligations, since they can obtain the funds relatively easily on the money market[4] (cf. Zeise 2011: 100f.). At this point, it should be noted that in interbank trade not only are the interbank credit accounts smoothed out, but the private banks also grant each other large loans through these accounts; they trade securities among themselves or they conduct bilateral foreign exchange transactions. The importance of the interbank business implies that the liquidity risks (refinancing) of the banks are now accompanied by interest rate risks, making the refinancing of a bank dependent on the interest claims of other creditor banks as well, whereby the risks appear higher the more the volatility on money and capital markets fluctuates. Refusing short-term new refinancing can have catastrophic consequences for a bank. Today, the market for unsecured interbank loans has declined sharply, while the market for secured repo transactions is rising.

3) On the third level, money transactions take place between commercial banks and central banks. The commercial banks are obliged to maintain accounts with the central banks and receive central bank money from them. If there are significant differences between two private banks in their interbank credit accounts, the crediting bank can require the other to settle the debt with central bank money, so that there are payment flows between the central bank accounts of

---

[4] The accumulation of monetary capital inaugurates a specific structure of terms that must always be taken into account in terms of the availability of capital within the differential accumulation of capital, and which is articulated in all the investment decisions of banks, which have various options when calculating and speculating with different degrees of profitability and availability of liquidity.

the private banks and, at the same time, a correction in the inter-bank credit accounts. If a private bank has too little central bank money at its disposal, it must take out a loan from the central bank.

In this context for the banks, the following tasks arise: (1) to orient the granting of loans to the techniques of financing solvency and the risk assessment of payment promises. (2) To positively manage the risk calculation (price assessment of risks). (3) To coordinate the different maturities of deposits and loans, i.e. to secure higher-interest long-term loans with shorter, in part daily renewable and low interest deposits, thus guaranteeing lotsize transformation (balancing between loan supply and demand) and maturity transformation (temporary balancing between financial investments and loans). The refusal of short-term refinancing increases the danger of illiquidity for a private bank. (4) Evaluating and, if necessary, demanding the collateral of customers, wherein today various promises of payment can also be considered collateral, so that the expectations of future payments in turn secure the expectations of future payments. However, private banks also frequently grant unsecured loans to companies and households. (5) To address the risks broadly or to handle the risk compensation through hedging. (6) To engage in credit creation and profitable trading of fictitious/speculative capital. (7) In general, the ability to secure the extensions of money on time, which in certain economic situations can, of course, only be obtained at high cost.

In large private banks today, these functions are part of the integration of commercial and investment banking. With regard to the latter, the banks maintain extensive global shadow banking systems[5] in order to

---

[5] Shadow banks are financial companies that conduct credit business relatively independently and pursue bank-like business models, but do not have a banking license themselves. They are therefore not bound by banking regulation and supervision and can therefore take higher risks in order to achieve even higher profits than commercial banks. Investment funds, money market funds and hedge funds are considered to be shadow banks. Most shadow banks have their legal domicile in offshore centres and tax havens. According to a July 2016 report of the European Systemic Risk Board (ESRB), the shadow banks in the EU alone invested capital worth €37 trillion in the fourth quarter of 2015. This represented about 36% of the financial system's total assets.

Shadow banks cannot create bank deposits like commercial banks. Loans are mostly granted via repo transactions. The actors of shadow banks buy securities with funds they borrow themselves. In doing so, they exploit price spreads. They thus move the money available in the economy between actors. The loans issued by shadow banks are not

186 A. SZEPANSKI

carry out the largely invisible trade in synthetic securities, i.e. without the state and the various banking supervisory authorities having any greater scope for regulating the derivatives trade. Thus, large private banks themselves maintain numerous shadow banks in the form of off-balance sheet special purpose vehicles (SPV) in order to evade state banking regulation and taxation on their profits or to hide liabilities and losses from their shareholders, banking regulators and the public. Shadow banks are to be understood as poles and relations that function outside the accounting of regular commercial banks and thus also outside of state and transnational regulatory bodies, a result of the fact that global supply chains, in which complex derivative and securitisation chains are constantly taking place, are becoming increasingly important for capital. It is estimated that in 2011 shadow banks will have handled one-third of the global volume of financial relations (Sahr 2017: Kindle Edition: 5120).

Commercial banks rely on the anticipation of the future utilisation of so-called bank deposits money, which has payment functions like cash, so that the effectiveness of their means of payment is not limited by the given level of deposits, but more by the solvency of customers and the confidence that, and to what extent, a future positive economic development will take place within a country and on the international level. The credit management of commercial banks extends to the acquisition of borrowers, the examination of their creditworthiness or their credit rating (their collateral), as well as the smooth processing of payment transactions and the accumulation of profits through the collection of interest. The potential for credit creation is in turn linked to risk management. In this context, balance sheets should document that private banks can smoothly link their own promises to pay with those of others; private banks justify their own debts with the debts they have granted to others by lending. Indeed, creditors on the liabilities side of the balance sheet should know that the selection of borrowers on the assets side of the balance sheet will generate sufficient cash flows to service the creditors' debts, which in turn requires a continuous inflow of redemption funds to service the loans (ibid.: 5607). It is a primary goal of banks to synchronise different payment flows, which have different payment terms. The problem is that a large part of the assets of private banks consists of long-term claims

recognised as state money. They receive money from money market funds, but not from their own balance sheet transactions like private banks. Their repo transactions remain promises to trade at par on demand.

(bonds, loans, etc.) that are not realisable in the short term, while their liabilities are largely short term.

The financial potential of a private bank always depends on the quantity of potentially available funds in relation to the amount of its payment requirements. This requires liquidity management that also strives to permanently secure its own creditworthiness, whose function here is to represent and realise solvency. Liquidity risks have to be recognised in time and are best avoided, because if a bank actually encounters payment difficulties, restrictions in interbank transactions cannot be excluded and further collateral has to be mobilised to restore its own solvency. Therefore, the bank organises a management for collaterals to ensure its own solvency: cash stocks and reserves (credit balances at the central bank for settlement process with other banks or payments to the state), which are readily accepted by other banks as means of payment, as well as liquid assets that can be transferred into money at any time. At the same time, the ratio of debt to the own means of payment, i.e. the particularly liquid securities such as government bonds and central bank money, has risen sharply in recent decades, so that more and more risky securities are being used. Overall, the business with collateral and pledge has diversified and at the same time multiplied; for example, in 2007, a single pledge secured three different loans (ibid.: 5538). Relative safe debt instruments such as government bonds are now also increasingly used by creditors to secure debts, which can quickly lead to so-called collateral chains, chains of insurance and securities that are growing ever larger.

An important criterion for the solvency of a private bank is the power to create credit, which includes, among other things, the permanent exploration of the customers' sufficient monetary capacity to take out credit (evaluation of their economic performance with regard to their creditworthiness; financial standing of households, states and companies), so that the bank, as a creditor, can then carry out a selection and credit rationing as well as a operative concentration on the supposedly secure risk willingness of customers. In a private bank, the potency to settle debts results less from its equity capital than from the quality of its investments, and this also means from the creditworthiness and the financial power of the debtors, whereby the strategies of private banks today tend to move away from the selection of concrete debtors and towards the management of the general conditions of debt (one thinks here of the suitability of certain risk models, the volatility of ratings and of market prices). On the other hand, banks themselves are also forced to exist vis-à-vis other banks as producers of information and as liquidity organisations in order to be recognised as creditworthy debtors at all.

Finally, the design of the (expected) asset and (promised) liability transactions of private banks require a balance sheet structure management, for which the help of maturities and risks of what tend to be short-term liabilities are compared with what tend to be more long-term assets in simultaneous procedures. This balance sheet management is similar to a specific production process, whose result is always a numerical entry, whereby the entered price sums are today increasingly developed according to mathematical models that include a prognosis of the future (market-to-model) and at the same time take into account the social plasticity of accounting procedures.

Today, private banks also rely on the extraction of income of wage earners. In doing so, they have repeatedly developed new methods and strategies in recent decades during phases of significantly weak class struggle, which can be summarised under the heading of "capturing". Through the privatisation of education, housing and health, through the reduction of the social system and through various tax reforms, states have enabled private banks to gain new access to the purchasing power of wage earners. To an ever-increasing extent today, access to education, health, housing, apartments, houses and long-term consumer goods is being provided to customers through insurance, mortgage, student and consumer loans and other forms of credit, whereby not only insurance companies but also private banks generate profits directly or at least indirectly from the absorption of wage income. The gradual privatisation of the retirement provision is another means of integrating wage income into the financial industry (cf. Lapavitsas 2009). Credit is now an important source of the reproduction of wage slaves.

Even after the financial crisis of 2008, private banks continue to realise parts of their profits by granting consumer loans to households that are permanently struggling with restrictions on their own solvency. With consumer loans, the share of the basket of goods, which is financed by real wages, is reduced. It is therefore precisely the crediting and innovation of financial capital that lead to significant reductions in real wages (cf. Sotiropoulos et al. 2013: 57). Mortgage loans open up further potential for real wage cuts; but they should not be viewed solely from the point of debt, because with a mortgage loan a household not only borrows money, but at least potentially owns an asset. From this point of view, future wages now also appear as an asset in the households' financialised portfolios, and thus wages, even if they are only small sums, mutate into a form of fictitious capital. Thus today, parts of the money resources of households are subject to the movements of capitalisation and the corresponding market risks, in which an apparent identity of interest between labour and parts of capital can emerge, consisting above all in the increase of household assets.

Let's turn now to the question of how the loans issued by commercial banks are used by the borrowers:

1) They are used to finance the investments of industrial and commercial companies to purchase machinery, energy and raw materials, to hire workers and possibly to improve the production processes from a technological point of view, so that in the future the productivity of the companies increases and, in a given period of time, more or higher quality products and services compared to those of the previous period will be sold. This increases the overall economic supply and also the overall economic demand, while unrealised investment projects, on the other hand, can lead to inflation, since a surplus product does not match the expenditure. Mortgage loans can only be considered productive if they are used to build new homes.

2) Money is used to finance the purchase of already existing commodities and services and thus can have an inflationary effect under certain circumstances, insofar as the money supply increases without additional commodities being produced. Although demand increases, supply remains constant (consumer credit or the purchasing of government debt by companies).

3) There is a purchase of securities, real estate and derivatives and often, as a result, asset inflation in the financial markets. It can be assumed that since 1990, about three quarters of the bank deposits generated by commercial banks are used for the purchase of various financial assets, which has a self-reinforcing effect, because the more securities (and real estate) on the market rise in price, the easier it is for banks to grant new credit, which is used for the purchase of securities. Thus, the banks initiate a further increase in the prices of securities, which in turn leads to the creation of new loans and so on. This leads to constantly rising prices and rising real estate prices, and persistent price increases in the financial markets lead to

190 A. SZEPANSKI

bubbles. In 2016, loans used to purchase securities on Wall Street reached a new high with $551 billion.

The three possible uses of the loans also lead naturally to interdependencies between different economic sectors: a company expands its capacities because it expects an increase in the raising of consumer loans, or more shares are bought on credit because a rising real investment of companies is expected. The increase in the money supply can lead to price rises on the stock exchanges and on the real estate markets, but conversely, real estate prices can also rise first and then the price of collateral increases, leading to renewed lending, with which we have a reverse causality, because here real estate prices precede loans.

If the creation of credit leads to the purchase of securities or derivatives, then most leftist and heterodox economists assume that this has to be estimated as a purely unproductive use of money. While it is true that credit creation can lead to asset inflation and speculative bubbles in the financial markets, credit (and the trading of fictitious and speculative capital) definitely has productive effects on capital; indeed, credit precedes or enables investment in industrial capital, if one abandons the self-financing of large corporations, which is in the end self-crediting.

At present, private banks grant a large proportion of their loans as mortgage loans. According to Swiss economist Mathias Binswanger (based on a cited mortgage study carried out on lending in 17 developed countries - England, U.S., Switzerland, etc. - since 1990), this share can, on average, account for up to 60% of the banks' lending volume (Binswanger 2015: Kindle Edition: 3297). This is due, on the one hand, to the increased number of homeowners and, on the other, to the growing demand for increasingly expensive housing, especially in the urban centres of developed countries.[6] The large industrial and commercial companies, however, are no longer necessarily dependent on the granting of bank loans or even on the issuing of corporate bonds in order to obtain financial funds for their own investments; they rather issue new shares or finance themselves from the returns on their investments.

---

[6] Since the last real estate bubble burst in 2007, house and land prices have now risen sharply again in most industrialised countries and, after deducting the rate of inflation, are now mostly significantly higher than in 2007. Most recently, real estate prices have shot up, in some cases dramatically. In April 2021, the median house price (excluding new construction) in the U.S. rose by 19% year-on-year.

In 2011, according to Tony Norfield, only 15% of loans in the U.K. went to non-financial companies, and two-thirds of these loans were not capital investments, but short-term loans, mainly to service the short-term cash flow of companies (Norfield 2016: Kindle Edition: 2643). However, long-term loans to companies remain structurally important, even though only a small portion of the assets of private banks includes the allocation of loans for productive investments.

7.2 Creation of Credit by Private Banks

Let us now turn to credit creation of commercial banks. Already 400 years ago, English goldsmiths began to create paper money by managing their customers' gold coins and issuing a kind of certificate on them (on which the amount of stored gold was written down), which they then lent as quasi-money. Because it rarely made sense for the owners to claim their gold coins directly, the goldsmiths, who are to be understood as forerunners of private banks, were able to issue certificates, which functioned as paper money without any material value, to certain recipients - certificates, whose "value" was higher than that of their gold coins in stock. Profit-oriented private banks in the subsequent periods attempted to constantly increase the ratio between the amount of paper money and the amount of gold coins. But this does not yet quite match the decisive mode of banking activity: for some time now, commercial banks have been creating so-called bank deposits with their lending, which is digitally recorded in bank accounts. Commercial banks do not lend the money that customers previously deposited, but rather produce bank deposits themselves by granting loans to customers. Binswanger even claims that the invention of "money creation from nothing" precedes the industrial revolution. Our answer to this is, firstly, that banks do indeed create bank deposits by creating credit, but not from nothing, as Joseph Schumpeter also assumed. Rather, they create it, on the one hand, with a view to or in access to the increase of future capital, and, on the other hand, in relation to a borrower. In this respect, one could speak of an invention under structural compulsion set by capital. It should be noted here again that credit is not money; rather, the credit agreement and the disbursement of the credit amount in the form of bank deposits or cash are two different dimensions, or, to put it another way, the money is recorded as debt and credit.

Credit creation is not to be understood as a one-sided act in which, for example, a demiurge, "out of nothing", creates money; credit requires the specific interaction between the private bank as lender and the customer as borrower. Commercial banks can only create credit if they find suitable borrowers, whose number depends on the current state of an economy. When granting credit, the banks assess the borrower's creditworthiness and solvency very precisely (whether the borrowers are capable of repaying the loan and paying interest); they demand collateral and in some cases also check what the customers are using the credit for. This means that borrowers must provide collateral when they take a loan; think of a mortgage loan, where real estate (in relation to a certain loan amount) is pledged and only becomes the property of the borrower after the loan amount, including interest payments, has been paid in full by the borrower. The basis of loan creation is then a previously rendered service, the built house, which the bank values at a price. However, if the borrowers use their financial assets as collateral, the question of their valuation and complexity immediately arises. For example, a debenture bond can secure a loan between creditor A and debtor B and it can then be passed on from creditor A to creditor C and from him to creditor D. This obviously leads to long chains and machines of securitisation, which enormously increase the financing potential of financial institutions. For 2007, IMF economists registered that payment promises amounting to $10 trillion were attributable to this type of securitisation chain. For example, if the security is a government bond, implying in one year the amount of €1000 with €10 interest, and this is transferred by means of a repurchase agreement for one month at a lower amount and interest to a new investor, who in turn sells the bond for 14 days at an even lower price to a third party, who in turn transfers it for one week even cheaper to a fourth party - it then becomes immediately clear that the security tends to loose its function. If the promise to pay fails, the government bond can no longer be used in its place because it has been diluted. Each link in the chain now represents a new danger for the failure of the entire chain, whereby risks are not minimised as intended, but rather virtually multiplied; that is, complexity risks are first set in motion.

There is the widespread misinterpretation that commercial banks are pure financial intermediaries who borrow money from customers at a certain interest rate and only lend out these sums of money at higher interest rates; or that they function like a logistics company that moves money capital to different places. Rather, however, private banks are to be understood as generators of future promises of payment, whereby they firstly open up potential for all kinds of economic processes. What private banks spend as credit is not based on certain liabilities (deposits of customers and savers), whose basis they then grant credit. This means that the commercial banks are not pure money brokers. If it were otherwise, the more credit they grant, the more savings would be generated in an economy, and to that extent, the savings of the economic actors would end up in their bank accounts. All private banks in a country would then be unable to lend more than the customers are willing to provide as savings. As Binswanger writes: "The banks would then be comparable to a blood bank in a hospital. Just like a blood bank, the bank would then have to tell its customers from time to time: 'Unfortunately, we don't have any more savings at the moment, but you can put yourself on a waiting list and we will notify you when we receive savings again'"[7] (Binswanger 2015: Kindle-Edition: 330). However, thanks to the credit creation of private banks, new investments, higher employment and consumer spending and additional government spending can be financed without having previously made corresponding savings in an economy. Rather, saving itself is to be understood as an effect of credit creation and constitutes a claim that implies either a liability or an asset. Thus, credit is not simply a result of economic activity but conversely, it creates certain economic activities, acting as a catalyst for investment and innovation, for employment and income. If, however, private banks spend too much credit in relation to the supply of commodities and services in an economy, this can lead to inflationary developments, while the restriction of credit volume leads to deflationary processes. Deflation increases the cost and value of debt, thereby benefiting asset holders, lenders and financial institutions. In an over-indebted economy, the reduction of credit leads to a decreasing supply of money, thus increasing the "real value" of money and thus its importance, while the liabilities and debts can no longer be realised as money.

Thus, commercial banks do not need the savings of their customers for lending; rather, their "productivity" consists in the management of

---

[7] If commercial banks would really only lend money which they have previously received from savers, then this money would have to appear on the asset side of the balance sheets. But the larger parts of the money can be found on the liabilities side of the balance sheets, and here in particular with the assets of the bank customers. All the money in an economy is on the liabilities side of the bank's balance sheet; that is, it represents debt.

194   A. SZEPANSKI

the payment promises pointing to the future or the creation of loans, with which they finance and initiate, among other things, according to their own calculations, risk assessments and speculations and, if possible, profit-oriented investments and the production processes of companies. In this way, there is no mere redistribution of funds, but commercial banks themselves operate as an essential, growth-generating factor in the accumulation of capital in an economy. They can thus stimulate and drive growth also at the level of "real capital". If additional investments, however, had to be financed by more savings, this would not allow for economic growth, since higher savings would lead to a corresponding decline in demand and investment, and thus have a counterproductive effect on growth. Savings and consumption are inversely related, and consumption is in turn proportional to the income generated in production. Finally, it is financed production that ensures that savings coincide with investment.[8] This is Keynes' answer to Say's law. Financing investments purely through savings would be a zero-sum game that would only lead to the redistribution of financial resources. To generate economic growth, however, investment must be higher than savings, and additional investment can be stimulated by the lending of private banks. Keynes clearly sees that savings do not precede investment, but that conversely, higher investment leads to higher savings, provided that private banks lend additional credit at balanced, i.e. relatively low, interest rates, thereby creating new demand that makes investment grow faster than savings and consumption faster than income.[9]

---

[8] Savings depend on the investments and these in turn depend on the profit rate. The accumulation rate (growth rate of capital) is related to the expected net profit rate (expected profit rate minus interest) and the savings rate to the relative financial gap between investment and savings. In the short term, the interest rate will increase if the gap is positive, but in the long term, the financing needs of companies will always be related to the average profit rates and the corresponding price levels.

[9] Investments are financed through loans and flow back to the accounts of bank customers, who do not necessarily spend them in the same year as income. This is then defined by the national accounts as savings. No causality can be deduced from the *ex post* observations of the statistics, as it is done, for example, with GDP or national accounts, since the type of financing is not taken into account here. In addition, we must keep in mind that the financing of investments must lead to growth in wages and consumption; otherwise, the new products could not be sold at all. The total output of an economy must increase.

Let us take a closer look at the process of credit creation.[10] Whenever a commercial bank decides that a customer is creditworthy (he must hold collateral and preferably have the potential for future capital realisation), it provides a loan and thus a certain amount of money is credited to his account. These deposits, if they arise from the granting of the loan itself, are called "bank deposits" or "book money", which is written on an account as a number by striking a key (one speaks here of keystroke capitalism). Today, mostly only electronic payments are processed.[11] So with digital money, symbols are lent out, which represent the bank deposits and are written down as a number on current accounts and always also inhere a claim to legal cash on the part of the borrower, on the condition that he makes the contractually fixed promise to repay the loan within a certain time period plus a certain interest. When the commercial bank grants a loan, it has to deliver the money, which is a liability for it, directly to the client and at the same time it owns an asset insofar as it collects interest over a certain period of time, while the client also has an asset/credit on his bank account, but also incurs the liability to repay the loan plus interest. These balance sheet relationships are essential for the relationship between creditors and debtors. The credit balances on the debtors' accounts due to the loan can be called "fictitious deposits", as they do not depend on the current money holdings that a private bank currently has at its disposal. It is, however, incorrect when French economist Francois Chesnais calls the bank deposits fictitious capital (Chesnais 2016: 84). Fictitious capital is rather a security that is traded on the financial markets and has a price that is a function of interest rates and the expectations of the buyer of the security. This distinguishes assets from bank loans, which remain on the balance sheets

[10] Up to 90% of the money is created as bank deposits by private banks. The largest part of the money, i.e. bank deposits, is thus endogenous and cannot be seen as a tax credit, as Modern Money Theory suggests. The fact that the state is exclusively the origin of what is called money applies only to the "fiat money", i.e. the money that is created by a unilateral decision of the will of the central bank (as an organisation of the state).

It is true that without government money, no bank deposits can be created. The extent to which government money is used to create bank deposits is decided autonomously by companies and banks. This money creation circuit between banks and companies ensures that credit endogenises the money supply, i.e. decouples it from government money creation.

[11] Horst Seiffert calls this a "money-creating writing process" (Seiffert 2016: 31). When the credit note is made to the account (sight deposit), the money supply increases, which today consists to a large extent of deposits in bank accounts.

196   A. SZEPANSKI

of private banks. Only when bank deposits or bank loans are used by holders of tradable securities, do they transform into fictitious capital.[12]

With the granting of a loan, the commercial bank has a credit claim on the asset side of its balance sheet against the customer, which is matched on the liability side by the customer's deposit as a liability against the bank, but - and this is the decisive point - this liability is not balanced by another payment from the bank. Rather, money is created simply by the lending bank if it expands its assets (the debtor's promise to repay) and liabilities (to the debtor) on both sides of the balance sheet. Thus, no other account of the bank or an external account is reduced by the amount of credit granted; rather, the bank can always pay its loans with its own promises of payment. Throughout the entire term of the loan, the bank's promise to pay off the loan amount granted remains a promise, and only if the customer withdraws part of the amount as cash does the bank does have to reduce its cash reserves (cf. Seiffert 2016: 89f.). The bank registers a loan on the asset side of its balance sheet and a numerically identical credit note on the liability side or the current account of the borrower. So while on the liabilities side of the bank balance sheet the liability appears as a deposit from the loan, on the asset side the balance sheet total has increased by an amount roughly equal to the loan (minus reserves). In technical jargon, this is called "balance sheet extension" (cf. Schreyer 2016: 33f.). The liability simply appears on the bank's balance sheet as "customer deposits". The question of whether, when the amount is registered, it is deducted from another account, which leads to the reduction of other variables in the balance sheet - either reserves (partial reserve theory) or other funds (bank as financial intermediary) - can thus be answered as negative.

For the customer of the commercial bank, the situation is as follows: although he has now the credited sum of money for free order, i.e. he can use, at least as entrepreneurs, the use-value of the money for the production of more money, at the same time there exist, however, appropriate bank debts. Thus, both the bank (lender) and the customer (borrower)

---

[12] Provided that the borrower does not withdraw the amount in cash, the lending functions as a cashless payment transaction. This includes the mutual settlement of payments on bank accounts by means of internal transfers within a commercial bank or payment transactions between commercial banks (interbank market) qua bank deposits. If borrowers use their accounts directly as a means of payment without withdrawing cash, this process eludes the central bank.

act in the role of creditor and debtor. While the customer receives a new credit balance and at the same time promises to settle the debts (creditor and debtor of the bank), the private banks also act as debtors (they owe the customer the payments) and as creditors, the latter because they create their own promise of payment qua bank deposits and thus collect interest. In and with the acts of credit, commercial banks and customers mutually attest their creditworthiness (Sahr 2017: Kindle Edition: 3729). We have now arrived at structures of chains involving the permanent creation, linking and scheduling of payment promises or promise relationships.

Bank deposit creation means that the limits of lending initially lie entirely in the risk management of commercial banks. This is also confirmed by empirical analyses. Economist Richard A. Werner has examined whether a commercial bank, when it provides money to a borrower, transfers the funds to the borrower from other accounts (inside or outside the bank) (Werner 2017). He comes to the conclusion that commercial banks do not transfer the provided money to borrowers from other internal or external accounts, so that both partial reserve theory and financial intermediary theory must be rejected. Instead, the bank has created a new bank deposit by simply registering it on the borrower's account as a deposit, even though the customer or other customers did not make such a deposit. The loan amount is entered in the balance sheet, or written on to the account, twice, namely as a promise of repayment by the debtor *and* as a debt of the commercial bank to the customer.[13] New loans can then re-enter the process of credit creation as collateral and thus create further new loans.[14] Also, the purchase of securities (which the

---

[13] A bank, on the other hand, cannot pass on the deposit of customer Y as a loan to customer X, since the bank deposits represent a *liability* only for the bank, which is recorded on the liabilities side of the bank balance sheet and is not an asset that can be lent.

[14] In the case of bank loans, bank deposits are created by an entry that corresponds to a balance sheet extension. The loan amount is entered on both the asset and the liability side of the bank's business account. On the balance sheet, the liabilities indicate the origin of a sum of money, while the assets indicate its use. On the liabilities side, therefore, there are the bank's liabilities (bonds issued, account balances, equity) and on the assets side, among other things, the loans granted. The bank needs equity capital to cover the loans to a certain extent. The origin of the assets (borrowed capital) is the bank's debts, including its own capital, by which is meant those "debts" that the bank makes to itself and does not have to pay back (liabilities side). The interest is not created in the granting of loans, but the corresponding sums are withdrawn from players who are in competition with each other. Interest only appears on the balance sheet when

bank writes down as assets) is to be subsumed under the heading of book money creation as a destitute purchase, if the securities are bought with book money that did not exist before.

When the customer repays the loan, the money supply rate decreases again, rate for rate, by the corresponding amounts, whereby the money deposited by the customer is deducted from the bank balance without another account increases by this amount at the same time. The customer's liability is thus reduced by the same amount as the bank's claim. During the term of the loan, there are usually few or no cash payments to the customer, so that the loan remains a promise of payment from the bank until the end of the loan agreement, which is then dissolved again when the loan is repaid. There is already a limit to credit creation here, and this is in the (albeit small) cash reserves that the commercial bank has to hold in order to meet cash withdrawals. However, if the commercial bank experiences a crisis of confidence, many customers could simultaneously demand large sums of cash, which the commercial bank is not in a position to pay because it does not have the cash directly in stock, it is not insolvent, but merely illiquid if it still has assets (and receivables) that it can sell with a short delay or receives payment. Commercial banks can also resort to central banks to raise cash by depositing securities there that are accepted as collateral. However, a large part of the assets of commercial banks are claims that are not readily accepted by central banks as collateral because such relatively illiquid investments such as real estate,

repayment and interest payments are due for the borrower. There is never enough money to pay all interest in an economy.

The bank balance sheets point to a synchronisation effect, whereby the creditors on the liabilities side should be given the impression that the debtors on the assets side will generate sufficient cash flows to service the creditors (Sahr 2017: Kindle-Edition: 5608). The balance sheets indicate that the debts of others or credits as assets balance out in dynamic and interdependent networks of relationships with one's own debts or credits as obligations. But through new, settled or even failed relations, the balancing movements are constantly shifting, and at certain points in time the balance sheets must be balanced by new debts. All this happens on the assumption that the agents as risk carriers take the places of debtors and creditors. The problem of bank balance sheets, as a short-term snapshot of corporate activities, consists, among other things, in the fact that they are tied to a chain of promises of payment not registered in them or off-balance-sheet promises of payment, in the fact that self-reinforcing stochastic flow protocols are found in them and, finally, in the fact that the existence of political guarantees, which today protect the large banks per se, must be taken into account (ibid.: 5801).

bonds and loans cannot be made liquid quickly enough as money. Moreover, in crisis situations, the massive sale of securities and real estate by commercial banks would cause prices on the financial markets to collapse.

During the term of the loans granted, commercial banks realise profits, known in the technical jargon as "seigniorage". The profits of commercial banks are thus generated by granting loans and writing credit to the borrowers' accounts, for which interest is charged. There are no profits from the creation of credit itself, but when a bank demands interest.[15] Therefore, the bank must examine only the creditworthiness of the borrower, i.e. the probability that he makes repayment and interest payment. The production costs are deducted from the gross seigniorage (interest), especially administrative and infrastructural costs connected with the circulation of money (buildings, software, IT infrastructure and wages, at the ECB additionally the printing costs for paper money) (Häring 2016: 138).[16]

Let's illustrate the creation of credit using an example that includes from the beginning the interbank market. If commercial bank A grants a

---

[15] The fact that banks create money by issuing loans raises two questions: first, how much interest does the issuance of credit generate, and second, who essentially benefits from that interest? Australian economist Tim Di Muzio comes to the following conclusion: in 1969, interest as a share of GDP in the U.S. was about $126 billion, or a little less than 9% of national income. By 1982, interest payments amounted to over $1 trillion, or about 30% of the national income. Since the early 1980s, interest as a share of national wealth has fluctuated between 15 and 31%, but has averaged just over 25% of GDP since 1980. To illustrate the magnitude of this quite real transfer of wealth, it is important to keep in mind that the amount of interest paid annually in the U.S. has exceeded the amount of federal income taxes paid since 1978 (Di Muzio 2015; Di Muzio and Robbins 2016).

Di Muzio further assumes that today every economic transaction, be it the purchase of a commodity, a rent or a mortgage payment, or the payment for a service, must include interest on outstanding debt. The question that now further arises is who primarily benefits from the extension of credit and the increasing capitalisation of commercial banks? Here, Di Muzio draws on the distribution of appropriated assets and shows that the top 1% hold a significantly higher percentage of interest-bearing assets (53.2%) and a significantly lower percentage of debt (6.7%) than the bottom 90% (9.2% and 72.4%, respectively) (Di Muzio 2015). Thus, by issuing credit, first to governments as a form of "public" debt and then to individuals, private banks have created a financial system that provides them and private investors with a steady stream of capitalised income, which in turn conditions their power and influence with which to protect their various interests.

[16] The gross seigniorage of the banks in the Euro Zone is currently expected to be around €300 billion per year (Häring 2016: 139). After deducting administrative costs for employees and the IT infrastructure, the net profit is approximately €150 billion.

200   A. SZEPANSKI

credit to customer A, which is credited to his account, and if customer A initiates a cashless payment to customer B's account at commercial bank B, then bank A records an outgoing payment and bank B records an incoming payment. These two payment flows are settled by commercial banks on a daily basis on special interbank credit accounts, in which in the medium term the differences on these accounts are balanced. If, however, the practice of granting loans between banks differs greatly, for example, one bank has more claims to customers than another bank, then this leads to unequal payment flows between the banks, which affect their interbank credit accounts and thus their respective profits. It is now no longer the bank internal entry claims/liabilities to customers, but the entries claims/liabilities between at least two banks, which are then essential for the changes in the cash flows (Seiffert 2016: 46f.). It must be added that the commercial banks only accept each other's cashless payments because these are covered by central bank balances, which in turn are as good as cash.

In the case of a cash outflow from commercial bank A to commercial bank B, the former has debts to the latter, while for commercial bank B the amount of money represents a credit balance. At the same time, however, there are also incoming payments to the accounts of commercial bank A, so that there is a tendency for the balancing of debts and credit of commercial banks, which are involved in payment transactions - on the overall level exactly when all commercial banks provide credits in the same amount and all borrowers transfer the same amount to the respective commercial banks. However, taking into account the fact that the balances of the accounts in the daily business of banks are constantly fluctuating, the differences will tend to balance out over longer periods of time. Commercial banks also negotiate among themselves permissible differences (credit limits) in the balances and document this in the interbank credit accounts. The banks also grant each other interbank loans, which are short term and have low interest rates.[17] In the case of persistent payment differences, commercial banks are obliged to balance the

---

[17] Interest rates range between 0.5 and 1.5% are based on key interest rates such as Libor (London Interbank Offered Rate) or Eurobor (Euro Interbank Offered Rate), but are ultimately freely negotiated by commercial banks. The amounts held in the interbank credit accounts are called nostro balances; they are entered accordingly in the banks' double-entry bookkeeping. The convergence of data collection and documentation, originally limited to financial transactions on the markets, is enriched with more and more indicators, for which an integrated business software is needed. Since the 1970s,

different amounts of money. This, however, brings a new type of account into play, namely the central bank account, whereby each commercial bank is legally obliged to hold such an account at the central bank of the respective country. On this account, there must be credits (central bank money/money supply M0) of commercial banks in a certain amount, which the banks receive from the central bank through their submission of securities and through credits.

When the loan is repaid, a writing process takes place that reduces the bank deposits. For this purpose, the borrower provides corresponding amounts of money in his account, which are then deducted by the bank. This of course also leads to payment flows between various commercial banks. If the participating banks carry out loan repayments in the same amount, whereby the same amounts of money were transferred between the banks for this purpose in advance, then credits and debts on the interbank loan accounts neutralise each other. The greater the proportion of internal transfers at a bank, the more independent that bank is from other commercial banks.[18]

If commercial bank A grants more loans than commercial bank B, then the first problems arise. If the borrowers of commercial bank A pay with credit, namely invoices that result in transfers to commercial bank B, then there will be an imbalance on the interbank credit accounts of the participating commercial banks. Commercial bank A may have to balance this difference with central bank money, which will lower the balance on its central bank account. Commercial banks are obliged to hold certain amounts of money in the central bank accounts (although these are subordinated to their own credit creation). This forces them to deposit collaterals (securities, precious metals, assets) and to pay the central bank interest when they take out a loan, which is, however, rather low. Thus, if

---

double-entry bookkeeping has been carried out in companies with relational databases and programs.

[18] As a tendency, commercial banks have to balance payments on their interbank credit accounts. If payments are balanced, certain withdrawals are available to the banks virtually free of charge. Since the banks are integrated into dense and complex networks, especially those banks that are of a corresponding size and thus contain greater local, national and international interconnections have competitive advantages over the small and less networked banks. The banks are thus intensively interwoven with one another and depending on economic development, are dependent on either increasing or reducing lending, securities trading and withdrawals (due to unequal balance of payments on interbank loan accounts).

202   A. SZEPANSKI

a commercial bank creates an excessive amount of bank deposits through lending and at the same time has a constantly higher outflow of bank deposits through remittances than its bank deposits inflows, it is forced to take out regular (collateralised) central bank loans with the money flowing into the central bank accounts of other banks. The commercial bank could now raise its interest rates on loans, which would reduce the amount of its lending, but might result in higher interest income. However, the competition between banks does not allow this to happen in the long run; or the bank increases the number of its customers in order that an equilibrium of the flow of bank deposits between the banks can occur. The more customers a bank has, the greater the probability that the bank deposits money will circulate internally within the bank, so that no transactions are required on the interbank loan accounts or the central bank accounts.

This already provides a first answer to the question of why banks even bother with customers, when they can apparently draw on bank deposits "out of nowhere". Banks are initially interested in as many customers as possible, to whom large sums of money are transferred by the customers of other banks, since this provides reserves for which they would otherwise have to pay interest. For the transfers between commercial banks, which take place on the interbank market, they are dependent on reserves at the central banks.[19] The accounts of commercial banks, which they hold at central banks, serve as a clearing system between the commercial banks, i.e. the money streams that flow between the commercial banks are settled there. However, only the difference between the mutual transfers on one day has to be settled via reserves. A loss of customer money leads to a new need for reserves, which the bank cannot obtain for free, because it must provide services for the reserves, either by lending securities to the central bank or by borrowing the money from other banks. The outflow of customer funds and the lack of customer accounts therefore have a thoroughly negative effect on the profitability of the banks. However, since the central bank's interest rates are currently at zero and the commercial banks are swimming in reserves, the private banks' interest in customers' money has diminished sharply. Again, there is a difference between equity capital and reserves, which is expressed in the fact that missing reserves lead to a liquidity constraint in the banks, which

[19] Only central banks can create reserves or central bank money by lending it to commercial banks. These in turn are needed for their interbank business and for the purchase of government bonds.

today the central bank usually solves immediately, while the destruction of equity capital leads to their bankruptcy.

Bank deposits created by the commercial banks themselves circulate between them. If one bank makes a positive difference in the payments that its customers make, the difference between the incoming and outgoing payments at another bank must be negative. Mutually out balancing sums can also lead to profits for both banks involved (withdrawals). Seiffert subsumes these processes under the term "structurally conditioned cooperative creation of bank deposits" (Seiffert 2016: 46ff.). In contrast, we do not speak here of cooperative creation of bank deposits, but rather of competition-induced credit creation, which constantly fuels the compulsion of private banks to innovate new financial instruments within the framework of the complex internationally interwoven network chains. Since every commercial bank receives and issues a large number of payments every day, payments between banks tend to balance out over time. This is part of the competition between banks. It can be assumed that the banks operate in the same mode to a certain extent, for example by using large sums of money to buy securities and derivatives, which in turn can increase their lending and withdrawals. And it is precisely this that then leads to new imbalances in the banks' payment flows. Through the competition, which is recorded, among other things, on the interbank credit accounts, balancing movements are set in motion, which in turn are counteracted by new imbalances. These movements function differently from the balancing movements for the production of average profit rates, in which industrial and commercial companies, branches and sectors are involved. Also, the process of profit production is different from that of industrial and commercial companies. If commercial banks are able to generate returns through, among other things, the creation of credit, they are not at first dependent on "conventional profits" resulting from the management of the difference between revenues and costs. The ultimate goal for a private bank is, within the framework of the processes described above, to absorb a share as high as possible of all possible profits of all commercial banks within a certain period of time, which arise from, among other things, the granting of loans. However, a commercial bank should not push too far in the hunt for extra profits; otherwise, it will endanger itself. The competition among commercial banks, which is evident in the money and capital markets, always has a disciplinary effect and is quasi-transcendental. And it is not only the large traditional financial institutions that participate in these processes, but also the banks of multinational automobile corporations and the banks of other corporations such as Siemens. It must be noted, however, that there are also cooperative aspects in the relations between the banks, for example, when they give each other loans and thus accept each other as debtors and creditors of similar sums (recursive credit) in order to make further payment flows mutually possible. Today, these mutually granted credits can even be deposited as a pledge with the central bank.

To rephrase the problem: If bank A transfers, after having written a credit of €100,000, to the account of customer A, to the account of customer B of bank B, then bank B can assign a new credit, since it has a credit balance of €100,000, which is covered with central bank money. What bank A looses here the potential to create credit, the bank B wins in addition. At this point, the suspicion that banks are concerned only with holding as high a deposit as possible emerges. Then, smaller savings banks would indeed have relative advantages over large banks such as Commerzbank or Deutsche Bank. But there are firstly the compensatory movements between the banks that have already been described: if a bank permanently grants too high a loan and thus more bank deposits flow away than it receives, then it must increasingly act as a borrower on the money market. This can include other banks critically assessing or even losing confidence in its solvency and then stopping their lending to this bank. In this context, the concept of total financial capital and the corresponding competitive processes remain crucial.[20] Besides this, due to the high degree of their national and international networking, the big banks simply have much more solvent credit customers.

So where are the limits to the creation of bank deposits (and the realisation of profits) for banks? The first limitation is that banks do not collect the profits resulting from the creation of credit directly at the issuance of the loan, but are rather realised only over the term of the loan, namely when the borrowers regularly pay interest and repay the loans. If a borrower can no longer pay, losses are incurred by the lending bank (loss

---

[20] Banks also create bank deposits by purchasing assets (securities, foreign exchange, gold and land) from non-banks. If a bank buys a company's bonds, for example, it credits the company with a sum of money, just as it would if it were lending to the company. As long as banks buy more assets than they sell, they also create bank deposits. Securities are thus monetised by the bank; that is, money is created without anyone else losing it. Government bonds are doubly monetised, which can be sold by commercial banks to the central bank. When government bonds are sold, commercial banks receive reserves, thus monetising the government securities for commercial banks.

of central bank money and the equivalent value of the loan), although it should be noted that the borrower has at least put money into circulation for a certain period of time. In terms of the banks' total capital, losses mean that the banks' liabilities exceed their credit claims.[21]

A further distinction is made at this point between the limits that are created by the processes of credit creation itself, which is influenced by the competition between companies, and those that occur in the banks' balance sheets as a result of the documentation of cash flows generated by credit creation (ibid. 2016: 51ff.). The limitations of the first mode include the number of borrowers corresponding to the economic cycles of the economy and the monetary potential of their demand for bank deposits, as well as the volume of securities and fixed assets available on the financial markets. Even though private banks have, through the processes of influencing interest rates, lending and supply of money, enormous influence on industrial investment, other economic activities and employment, they remain dependent on the economic power of borrowers, which consists of being able to pay off debts, and deposit collateral, which is always also a question of the economic development of a country and the world economy as a whole. If private banks pay too little attention to the regulation of their liabilities in their balance sheets, dangerous situations up to insolvency cannot be excluded. Excessive differences in payment flows between commercial banks lead to further limitations. If a commercial bank grants too many or too high loans compared to other commercial banks and/or buys fixed assets and properties in too high amounts, then it must expect debts on the interbank loan accounts, since there are now more outflows of payments than incoming payments. In addition, it must be taken into account that the size of a commercial bank and the corresponding degree of its national and international networking have a considerable influence on the creation of credit.

With regard to the accounting and regulatory rules which must be obligatory executed by commercial banks, the following limits must be assumed (ibid.: 94ff.): (1) liquidity requirement and equity capital

---

[21] Since banks set aside only a small percentage of the profits already realised to increase their equity capital, the danger that banks could go bankrupt in crisis situations increases from this side as well (large parts of the profits, however, are distributed as bonuses and dividends). Finally, if the loss of confidence in the bank persists, there is the danger of a banking crisis (Häring 2016: 160).

requirement and minimum reserve requirement. The legal reserve is the amount that commercial banks must hold on their accounts at the central bank. The minimum reserve was set by the ECB for the Euro area at 1%, based on the amount of customer deposits with a maturity of up to 2 years and the debt securities issued by a bank with a maturity of up to 2 years (ibid.). The bank itself determines the technical minimum reserves, which are related to the cash balance. However, the minimum reserve requirements are today largely covered by the cash balance that the banks would hold anyway. It should also be noted that the reserve balances do not have to be proven before the credit is created, but only afterwards. Private banks can obtain the reserves either on the interbank market or, today, quite easily from central banks. In the interest of a smooth process of credit creation and in order to avoid bankruptcies, central banks can no longer allow themselves to refuse to pay reserves to commercial banks, since these are forced to sell their assets quickly in the event of shortages or the threat of illiquidity, which in turn has a negative impact on the market prices of securities and derivatives and thus on the balance sheets of other companies (not only financial companies). Consequently, the minimum reserve policy of central banks has to follow the business practices of private banks and is ultimately dependent on them. And thus, the reserves that commercial banks must hold are no longer really a limit to their lending, so that the money multiplier (the percentage that banks must hold as deposits in order to grant credit) no longer plays a significant role. Today, reserves are primarily a resource for private banks to keep the clearing processes among themselves running (the balancing of assets and liabilities at the end of the day on the interbank market).

(2) A further limit is certain capital requirements that are currently determined by the Basel III Agreements. According to these agreements, banks must subject the funds, which are written on the asset side of the balance sheet, to a default risk assessment and, depending on the amount, the items on the asset side must be matched by a certain amount of equity (ibid.). This is intended to moderate the losses that may arise from the banks' lending business so that they are at least in a position to continue to service their obligations. Today, commercial banks have to back credit, market and operational risks, whereby for the former, the assets from securities, lending and tangible assets are multiplied by a risk weight of 0.20 (the other risks are extrapolated according to the ratios of the former). The resulting sum is then multiplied by 8% (ibid.). However, commercial

banks today are constantly succeeding in inventing new forms of derivatives and loans whose risks are not yet even represented in the Basel III regulations.

A bank's equity ratio is calculated as follows: first, the ratio between equity capital (core capital or share capital, i.e. subscribed capital plus retained earnings and reserves, supplementary capital and tier three funds) and risk-weighted assets is determined (ibid.). There is a legally defined equity ratio, called the "core capital ratio", which fixes the ratio of equity to the total capital (the balance sheet total) of the bank. A core capital ratio of 6% is to be valid for German commercial banks since 2015 and is expected to increase by 1% point from 2019. Furthermore, supplementary capital is assumed to be 2%, so that the equity ratio will amount to 8% overall. It is also being discussed whether banks should build up cyclical capital maintenance buffers that are dependent on economic developments and can be reduced during a recession. Here again, it should be emphasised that banks can continue to apply their own risk assessments and can use either their own internal bank models or the ratings of the rating agencies when evaluating risks, which means that the total of their assets can continue to grow despite the maintenance of the nominal capital-asset ratio. In order to prevent such practices, it would be necessary to introduce a restriction on leverage or a maximum leverage ratio, at which point the assets would have to be imported without restriction.

It must also be taken into account that, in addition to real estate, IT infrastructure, software, etc., the equity capital of banks consists primarily of financial assets, i.e. promises to pay, and thus, it must be understood from the beginning as an endogenous product of the banking sector, which cannot be regulated today by legal regulations alone and can be increased, for example, through share issues and retained returns. In principle, private banks create their own assets and equity holdings. In addition, to expand their financial room for manoeuvre, they can obtain loans at any time on the OCT markets, where the contracts are concluded as payment promises between two legal persons and are largely withdrawn from the regulatory requirements of state authorities. The securitisations discussed elsewhere also belong to this type of financing. Finally, with regard to the elasticity of their lending policy, private banks must not only take into account the factor of scarcity of equity capital, but also calculate the creditworthiness of those debtors who are able to pay certain amounts of money over a certain period of time, which realise profits for the banks and thus justify the risk taken by granting the loan. (3) Certain liquidity

208   A. SZEPANSKI

requirements constitute a further limit, always bearing in mind that the probability of the repayment of a loan must be calculated.[22]

A further question follows this problem: why do we need central banks at all in the current financial system, which seems to be dominated by private banks and other financial institutions? First, commercial banks need reserves, because customers are constantly demanding cash (as the amount of bank deposits increases, so does the need for cash); for receiving cash, commercial banks need central banks, which have the legal monopoly to produce it. Second, commercial banks must hold minimum reserves, at least in certain countries (The ECB has, however, significantly reduced the minimum reserve ratios as part of its policy of "quantitative easing"). The more bank deposits the private banks create, the more reserves they must then call up at the central bank. Third, the reserves are needed primarily in interbank transactions, which are settled via the central banks' clearing system. Although individual banks can also borrow reserves from each other, the entire commercial banking system can only expand its stock of reserves if they are made available by central banks.[23] Fourth, central banks are responsible for stabilising the value of

---

[22] If the already low cash holdings of commercial banks are reduced for any reason, the credits built up on them in the form of demand deposits must be reduced many times over (at a ratio of 1:10 by ten times the cash outflow). This can cause a credit crunch in the banking system. If all holders of current accounts of a bank were to withdraw their credit balances in cash at the same time, it could turn out that only a fraction of their money is available at the bank. The bank in question would have to file for bankruptcy, and there would be a danger that other banks would then also be emptied of their customers.

[23] Cash and reserves are only created by central banks. Central bank money includes cash plus reserves (accounts of commercial banks at the central bank) and cash in circulation. The corresponding monetary aggregate M0 is only a fraction of the monetary aggregates M1, M2 and M3. It is on the liabilities side of central banks because it represents a liability to commercial banks and to non-banks. Today, cash no longer needs to be exchanged for gold.

Money is accepted as a means of payment even if it is not covered by precious metals or real values, but by the confidence that, for example, loans will be repaid in the future. Credit relationships as promises of payment only work if they are trusted by a broad section of the population. With trust as a practice that guides meaning and is at the same time performative, uncertainty, which certainly includes routines, is created and restricted in social processes.

The future profit perspective, which a company as a borrower opens up to the bank as a lender, is the starting point for mutual investment, and the realised profit of the company (which realises the interest payments to the bank, which are primary) justifies the anticipations made with the debts. In short, the expected profit generates the means by

a currency, which is always linked to the capacity of the state to tax its citizens sufficiently.

7.3   LEVERAGE

If today private banks play a leading and at the same time driving role in the allocation of monetary capital to the various branches and sectors of the economy, then there ought to be noticed some important differences between financial capital and industrial and commercial capital in terms of profit mechanisms and economic power. There is definitely no single process that leads to the equalisation of the rates of return of the financial companies with the rates of profit of the industrial and commercial companies, or, to put it differently, the profits of private banks have no strictly lawful relation to the investments and the profits of industrial capital. It's not that the profits of private banks cannot be calculated at all, or that they have no relation to the profits of industrial companies, but that it is not the same process of an equalising movement of the profit rates between the private banks, as it is found in the industrial sector, nor is there an integration of the bank profits in the processes of producing the (industrial) average profit rates. This has been demonstrated by examining the different forms of investment and speculative activities of private banks in detail. The financial capital advance that is necessary for industrial companies to buy technology, machinery, energy, raw materials, buildings and to hire workers does not have the same crucial importance for financial companies when it comes to generating their own profits. The returns of private banks are not primarily based on the use of trading screens, buildings, software and labour. The fixed capital and circulating capital of industrial capital have relatively little to do with credit creation and capital processes with which private banks create their profits in real terms, because, unlike industrial companies, they can create bank deposits themselves and produce fictitious/speculative capital as a profit and therefore

---

which it is generated. Thus, it no longer matters whether the banknotes on the liabilities side of the balance sheet are backed by gold, commercial bills or government debt; what matters is the confidence that the loans granted by the banks will be used productively or profitably, so that there will be sustained economic growth. Then, the state can also repay its debts because it generates higher tax revenues due to economic growth. Companies can then also repay the loans, since they are doing profitable business. If banks grant loans that increase the productive capacity of the economy, the money is covered by the future productions that will be made with this money.

210   A. SZEPANSKI

have a much higher leverage than industrial companies. The profit opportunities in the financial industry are mostly created by increasing leverage and thus risk becomes an important reference for the time structure of capital.

Let's look at the problem of leverage in general: leverage is used by commercial banks and other financial institutions as well as by industrial and commercial companies. The latter companies, however, have much less possibilities to capitalise foreign funds than private banks; they are not able to create loans themselves and are therefore more focused on the production, distribution and sale of conventional commodities and services. Therefore, industrial and commercial companies usually have a much lower leverage rate than private banks. For example, industrial companies in the U.S. had a leverage of less than 1 in 2001–2010 (Norfield 2016: Kindle-Edition: 2396).[24] The leverage of private banks, however, is very flexible; it is initially determined by what is considered "normal" in this industry. Various empirical studies have shown that a leverage rate of 20 is the standard, although the rate can also rise to 50 and 60 (which was the case to some extent until the financial crisis of 2008) (ibid.: 6226f.). This high leverage generates a completely different dynamic of profit development and capital accumulation compared to the movement and level of average profit rates in industrial and commercial companies.

Profitable transactions appear on the bank's balance sheet on the side of the assets. But if the bank wants to carry the transactions out, it must first provide monetary funds - consisting of equity capital or debt capital - with equity capital representing only a small part of the liabilities (that part which is not borrowed from other owners but held by the owners of the bank itself; it is to be understood as a debt of the company to its owners). This is where the leverage effect comes into play. Leverage is understood to be the leverage effect that can be achieved by managing the difference between the cost of financing the debt and the return (on debt capital

---

[24] In many cases, certain companies are assigned to manufacturing companies, whereas they are much more likely to be regarded as financial companies. Take the example of Apple. Apple has a market capitalisation of $750 billion. In terms of assets, Apple has $27 billion, which falls purely on equity, production facilities and equipment, while financial collateral is $170 billion. Apple's Braeburn, a Nevada-based company, is now the largest investment fund in the world. In addition, Apple has been massively buying back shares since 1998 to increase its share prices and dividends. The transactions from derivatives trading have a volume of $120 billion (nominal on the contracts) (cf. Norfield 2016).

and equity capital). Or, to put it another way, leverage indicates the real ratio between equity capital and debt financing of investments. By using debt capital, the return on capital can be increased precisely when the interest on debt capital is lower than the return on total capital. If the return on total capital rGK is higher than the interest rate on borrowed capital rFK, then with the increase of the debt ratio V (relation between the equity capital and borrowed capital), the return rEK on the equity capital employed rises (return on equity capital). If the interest rate on borrowed capital is constant, we get the following formula: rEK = rGK + V · (rGK − rFK).

Let us illustrate the facts of leverage with an example. We assume that a bank owns €5 million in equity and borrows another €95 million on the money market, so that its total assets amount is €100 million. In this case, the leverage rate (ratio of total assets to equity capital) is 20. Business is good for a bank exactly when the cost of its borrowed funds is less than the costs of its total assets. If the bank pays 4% interest on the borrowed funds, the interest payments are €3.8 million, and if it receives 5% return on its total assets, the income is €5 million. What initially looks like a small 1% margin of profit generates a net income of €1.2 million and this amount is offset against 5 million equity. According to this, the ratio of return to equity is 24% (€1.2 million divided by €5 million). However, the profit would be lower if the costs of the respective financial operations were added.

Now, if the bank's business expands through further lending, it can increase its profits enormously. If the bank lends €195 million - with an equity capital of €5 million - then it has generated 200 million in total assets. If the interest rate on the borrowed funds is still 4%, then the bank will have to pay €7.8 million in interest on the sum of €195 million, but it will also generate €10 million in income if the rate of return on €200 million is still 5%. This gives a net income of €2.2 million. The bank will achieve a leverage of 44% on €5 million of equity. Of course, the risks regarding the return on assets are now also increasing. (If the average return falls below 3.9%, then the bank must expect high losses.)

Until 2008, the big banks increased their borrowing and the production of their own loans on the financial markets immensely in order to generate ever-higher investments and achieve higher profits. This increased their leverage rates from around 20 to up to 50 and more. Deutsche Bank in particular had at times an average of up to 60. In 2007, the assets of German banks had a level of 270% of the national GDP. The

212   A. SZEPANSKI

high leverage of private banks was an important factor in the financial boom, but it also accentuated the financial collapse as the illusion of ever-higher returns quickly faded. In the crisis year of 2008, all major banks in the U.S., the U.K. and the rest of Europe registered a rapid fall in profits and have since cut their leverage rates by selling or writing off parts of their assets and increasing their equity capital ratios. In 2011, rates were again much closer to long-term averages. In the meantime, however, bank profits have recovered to a certain extent, supported by the low interest rate policy of central banks, and in addition, the explicit and implicit guarantees provided by governments enable many private banks to borrow funds on the financial markets at much lower rates than their financial power really allows.[25] Spreads between lending and borrowing rates have also widened again, increasing banks' interest income. Low spreads can in turn be compensated by the private banks by increasing the volume of loans granted. They can also accelerate their growth by creating credit and increasing financial transactions, but when the economic growth of the entire economy is weak and the returns of companies in an environment of low interest rates are also weak, then there are financial problems that cannot be compensated by leverage alone.

The high cost of the debt crisis has prompted some governments to propose reforms to regulate the financial sector. But with the financial

---

[25] The nominal value of global derivative markets was $683 trillion in 2008. Since 2008, the Federal Reserve has repeatedly issued neutral funding guarantees for these markets. It has protected not only the banking sector, but also the shadow banking system, and this even outside the U.S. The shadow banking system provided 43% of all global credit in 2003, and its total liabilities were $25 trillion, twice that of the traditional banking sector. The Fed's hedges were $3.6 trillion for global money markets and $2.6 trillion for global derivative markets (Meister 2021: 124).

The political conciseness of government hedging is indicated by the rate between total debt in credit markets relative to gross domestic product. In 2016, the former amounted to $63.5 trillion in the U.S. and gross domestic product was $18.6 trillion - so the rate was 340%.

The flight to good collateral during financial crises increases the demand for government-issued liquidity, while private-issued assets suddenly become less acceptable. In this situation of the shortage of credit and private financial instruments, there may also be a shortage of government-guaranteed liquidity, which is now greater in demand. It seems to be an illusion that newly created financial instruments are as liquid as the government's bonds. Here, however, it is important to distinguish between liquidity and moneyness. By this is meant that securities of any maturity can be highly liquid and stable in their prices, but only the shortest IOUs can really serve the demand for money quickly. Only these instruments are as liquid as government-issued money.

sector playing a leading role in the economic power of these imperialist states, especially in the U.S. and Great Britain, a reversal seems difficult to achieve. The liberalisation of interest rates, the conditions of production of derivatives and their trade cannot be easily scaled back. It is to be expected that the more the state relies on the efficiency of central bank policy, which consists in the unconditional avoidance of systemic risks, and on its own financial capacities in its budgetary policy, the more likely it is to turn against very specific forms of regulation of the financial markets. In general, it can be assumed that debt today is not only recycled, but is growing in a spiral, because even at the micro-level we can see that newly created promises of payment can be used again as collateral for further loans, thus endogenously extending the chain of lending. A transfer of creditworthiness takes place here.

The leverage of commercial banks is limited, among other things, by the legal equity capital regulations, which force them not to use exclusively foreign money for their business, but always to provide a proof of a certain amount of equity capital, currently based on the regulations of Basel III. The equity capital of banks consists, apart from real estate, software, computers, etc., mainly of financial assets (payment promises such as shares) and is therefore to be understood as an endogenous product of the banking sector itself. This is especially true because the calculation of risks, to which the necessary equity capital also refers, is subject to the banks themselves or the rating agencies. The granting of loans depends on the value-at-risk, i.e. on specific assessments of the risks associated with the lending, which are made by the banks themselves. Capital requirements can today be further reduced by outsourcing to the shadow banking systems in offshore centres. With securitisation practices and borrowing in the OCT markets, capital requirements can be further avoided. Retained profits or new share issues also lead to a higher part of equity capital. At the same time, the balance sheet regulations of private banks are constantly being relaxed. Because they are obliged to hold only a small proportion of their deposits as reserves and because they can also create bank deposits, the multiplication machinery of monetary capital can be set in motion. If the leverage increases, the banks also risk increasing losses on their investments (deleveraging means the reduction of debt; lending and borrowing simultaneously decrease).

214   A. SZEPANSKI

7.4   INVESTMENT BANKS AND FUNDS

As important players in the international financial markets, we have to consider not only major commercial banks, but also investment, pension and hedge funds, insurance companies, rating agencies and asset managers such as Blackrock. Investment funds and investment banks are financial companies that mainly engage in the manufacture and trading of derivatives, asset management and the distribution of debt (bonds, commercial papers) or they provide advice and support to certain companies. The at least politically unsecured deposits of investment funds, which come from various companies, institutional investors and wealthy individuals, have increased rapidly since the 1990s. The investment funds collect the widely distributed money of savers, share capital and, ultimately, potentially any capitalisable money, which they can then dispose of with a high degree of sovereignty in order to invest it strategically for themselves and their clients in a profitable manner. These companies, which are active in the global capital markets, enable their monetary potent investors to benefit from almost all the returns that can be achieved in these markets.

The investment banks, in turn, finance themselves mainly through repurchase agreements or repo transactions and short-term "commercial papers" (both of which are known as "wholesale funding"), as well as through long-term debt that they raise from institutional investors. In repo transactions, a security is sold and at the same time, usually at short notice, a repurchase is agreed. The commercial papers issued by investment banks are short-term or long-term debt instruments. Here, the provision of liquid funds includes, on the one hand, two separate legal acts of purchase, but on the other hand, in reality, a hedging structure created by interconnection. This means that today there are closely interwoven networks, concatenations and connections of many differently unsecured and secured promises of differently constituted promise takers and givers, which run through different legal spaces, guidelines and regulations on disclosure.

The investment funds, which are relatively highly fragmented in their own sector in contrast to companies in other sectors, i.e. they do not have oligopolistic structures, are in fierce competition among themselves for the deposits of investors and customers (Windolf 2017). Today, investment funds in the U.S. own the majority of the shares of the 100 largest corporations, but not a single investment fund is the majority shareholder in one company. However, investment funds, especially in their entirety, possess strategic power over the large industrial companies and their management, which should not be underestimated. The investment, pension and private equity funds, which are regarded as institutional investors, now often hold all or at least a large part of the ownership of the large companies (Porcaro 2015: 26). The competitive pressure that prevails in their own industry is thus directly transferred to the stock companies, most of whose shares are held only to make certain demands on the management of companies with regard to the level of return on equity capital (and capital market returns), i.e. to managers to recognise as a company's goal the maximisation of short-term returns on equity capital and to ensure that this goal is implemented accordingly.

Through the concept of shareholder value, respective investment funds today therefore have a direct influence on the management of companies, which should achieve the highest possible return on equity that can be realised in the short term. On the one hand, this is about the maximum capital multiplication of companies, but on the other hand, the growth of the stock market listing and the correlating capital market returns have increasingly the priority of corporate policies. With regard to the valuation of companies, the analyses carried out by the investment funds are based on some important factors that always keep an eye on the capital market returns of companies, such as the movement of market correlations between companies, the size of the company and the value factor, which indicates the difference between the market capitalisation and the book value of the company.

The strategies of business organisation, technological innovation and the management of production processes of companies are thus increasingly oriented towards short-term profit maximisation, and thus, the logic of financial capital, through the interventions of financial investors, is flowing even more massively into the microeconomic parameters, into the internal control structures of industrial companies and into the strategies of their management. The competition between investment funds for maximum profits also leads to the fragmentation, sale or takeover of individual parts of companies and, ultimately, entire companies are profitable, but cannot meet certain return expectations of investors. This leads to a series of organisational changes: on the one hand, the transformation of managers into shareholders who hold shares themselves is taking place, and on the other hand, technical management is increasingly not only influenced but also dominated by the major financial investors and chief financial officers (CFOs). In this context, the strategies that are supposed to generate successful performance in markets are combined with the methods of increasing efficiency in the companies themselves, whereby all flows of money, services and commodities are to be recorded, compared and evaluated as much as possible in order to produce adequate information and to quantify costs and efficiency in the sense of profit maximisation, i.e. to objectify them as figures that in turn serve to account to banks, investors and the state. In the course of this, the management structure in companies is also changing, with technical management losing weight and strategic importance compared to the financial management of the company (financial holding). The specific internal forms of organisation of financial companies now permeate all large industrial and commercial enterprises, so that the talk of financial capital becoming totally independent of real capital is proving to be more than blurred. Rather, there is an increasingly close interlocking or intertwining of the various areas and sectors of capital enterprises, with the dominance of financial capital. The global "free cash flow" repeatedly postulated by the financial industry is exerting pressure on the self-financing strategies of large companies, although these companies are responding to these new challenges by setting up their own banks and issuing new shares and bonds. The autonomy of the financial sector remains relative, consisting in the innovation of financial instruments, the transformation of uncertainty into quantitative risk and the proliferation of speculative capital, thus the complexity of the system accelerates and the connectivity among institutions increases.

Due to the relatively low share of a single investment fund in most cases in the share ownership of a company, investment funds are generally very flexible in their strategies and at the same time very liquid; that is, they can sell their blocks of shares on the stock markets relatively quickly if the rapid growth in the value of their shares in a company fails to materialise. The profit targets of investment funds are significantly higher than those of normal industrial companies; in certain phases, they can rise up to 25%. Although investment funds have an immense influence on the strategies of companies, they are also to be regarded as unstable owners who sell their share packages, which they hold in a company, on average after 1.5 years (Windolf 2017). The rapid turnover rate of shares on stock markets has led to the fact that the owners of a stock company change ever more quickly.

Investment funds differ among themselves by their different investment strategies and organisational forms, firstly in those organisations that pursue particularly aggressive growth strategies and take high risks, and in those that only take medium risks and are oriented towards secure "income", although most investment funds today are heterogeneous conglomerates that simultaneously incorporate different investment strategies into their business. Depositing investors are also divided by analysts of the investment funds in risk classes, with the aim of spreading the risks as widely as possible among investors, while at the same time concentrating and continuously trying to expand the control over stock companies in the function of the owner. Investment funds themselves must be seen as transformers that attempt to combine the risk appetite of their investors with specific investment strategies.

On the one hand, investment funds act as traders and then choose the "exit" option for their strategies towards companies. On the other hand, they act as owners of the companies when they choose the "voice" option (ibid.). With the exit strategy, investment funds can threaten stock companies with the sale of blocks of shares and also enforce further restrictive measures, while they work most effectively as owners in the collective, at least as far as their relationship to the stock companies is concerned. For the exit strategy, investment funds have to be particularly liquid, which is usually not a problem, since they only hold small portions of the shares of a single company (usually less than 10%) and usually do not hold the shares for more than one to two years. As a collective, a group of investment funds can have a very strong influence on the management of stock companies - it can, for example, threaten hostile takeovers, selectively penetrate the supervisory boards or directly influence the operational processes of companies.[26]

References

Baecker, Dirk (2008) *Womit handeln Banken? Eine Untersuchung zur Risikoverarbeitung*, in: *Der Wirtschaft*, Frankfurt/M.

Binswanger, Mathias (2015) *Geld aus dem Nichts. Wie Banken Wachstum ermöglichen und Krisen verursachen*, Weinheim.

---

[26] From 2000 onwards, investment and pension funds began to trade more in derivatives relating to traditional commodities, a reaction to the low returns on their other financial investments (bonds, shares) and not as a desire to play with or bet on the prices of commodities. The low returns are part of a falling profitability of the whole economic system. If the profit rates are low, so are the interest rates.

218   A. SZEPANSKI

Chesnais, Francois (2016) *Finance Capital Today: Corporations and Banks in the Lasting Global Slump*, Leiden.

Decker, Peter, Hecker, Konrad and Patrick, Joseph (2016) *Das Finanzkapital*, Munich.

Di Muzio, Tim (2015) *The Plutonomy of the 1%: Dominant Ownership and Conspicuous Consumption in the New Gilded Age*, in: https://journals.sag epub.com/doi/10.1177/0305829814557345.

Di Muzio, Tim and Robbins, Richard H. (2016) *Debt as Power: Theory for a Global Age*, Manchester.

Häring, Norbert (2016) *Die Abschaffung des Bargelds und die Folgen. Der Weg in die totale Kontrolle*, Cologne.

Lapavitsas, Costas (2009) *Financialisation or the Search for Profits in the Sphere of Circulation, Soas Research on Money and Finance working Paper*, in: www.soas.ac.uk/rmf.

Lohoff, Ernst and Trenkle, Norbert (2012) *Die große Entwertung. Warum Spekulation und Staatsverschuldung nicht die Ursache der Krise sind*, Münster.

Marx, Karl (1998) *Capital*, Vol. 3, in *Marx and Engels Collected Works*, Vol. 37, London.

Meister, Robert (2021) *Justice Is an Option: A Democratic Theory of Finance for the Twenty-First Century*, Chicago.

Norfield, Tony (2016) *The City: London and the Global Power of Finance*, London.

Porcaro, Mimmo (2015) *Tendenzen des Sozialismus im 21. Jahrhundert: Beiträge zur kritischen Transformationsforschung 4*, Hamburg.

Sahr, Aaron (2017) *Das Versprechen des Geldes. Eine Praxistheorie des Kredits*, Hamburg.

Schreyer, Paul (2016) *Wer regiert das Geld? Banken, Banken, Demokratie und Täuschung*, Frankfurt/M.

Seiffert, Horst (2016) *Geldschöpfung. Die verborgene Macht der Banken*, Nauen.

Sotiropoulos, Dimitris P., Milios, John and Lapatsioras, Spyros (2013) *A Political Economy of Contemporary Capitalism and its Crisis*, New York.

Werner, Richard A. (2017) *Can banks individually create money out of nothing? The theories and the empirical evidence*, in: http://www.sciencedirect.

Windolf, Paul (2017) *Was ist Finanzmarkt-Kapitalismus?*, in: https://www.uni-trier.de/fileadmin/fb4/prof/SOZ/APO/19-019_01.pdf.

Zeise, Lucas (2011) *Geld – der vertrackte Kern des Kapitalismus. Versuch über die politische Ökonomie des Finanzsektors*, Cologne.

CHAPTER 8

The Financial System and the State

8.1 The State

Important components of the modern sovereign nation-state are usually considered to be (a) the government, state authority, taxation and administration, and (b) the territory, nation and population.[1] Pierre Bourdieu writes that state A forms itself by forming state B, and then adds: "the construction of the state as a relatively autonomous field exerting a power of centralization of physical force and symbolic force, and constituted accordingly as a stake of struggle, is inseparably accompanied by the construction of the unified social space that is its foundation" (Bourdieu 2014: 123f.). In no way is the state an expression of the collective will of a nation. Rather, state institutions determine territorial boundaries, education, official languages and "neutral" legislation. The latter are in particular guaranteed in the last instance by state's monopoly on the use of force, which the state exercises as a *capitalist* state. The state is born through long processes of concentration, which start from the exercise of military power and the establishment of the tax system, and leads to the appropriation of the resulting capital of tax and physical violence, in other words, processes of concentration are at the same time processes of

---

[1] It's not our task here to develop a Marxist theory of the state. For a more detailed discussion, see (Szepanski 2018).

© The Author(s), under exclusive license to Springer Nature Switzerland AG 2022
A. Szepanski, *Financial Capital in the 21st Century*,
Marx, Engels, and Marxisms,
https://doi.org/10.1007/978-3-030-93151-3_8

219

separation that keep the population away from power (Ibid.: 199). The emergence of the capitalist state is also closely linked with public debt, particularly with the raising of funds to finance war. The state monopoly on the use of military and police force, which, however, cannot occur without the state's appropriation of symbolic capital, is thus formed on the basis of historical expropriations. The state was, so to speak, created in a long *coup d'état* that established, once and for all, that there is a single legitimate and dominant standpoint, which is the criterion for all other standpoints. One will therefore search in vain for an authority that should be able to legitimise the state's legitimising authorities.

For Bourdieu, the state is the materialisation of a field of force composed of oppositions. The designation power of the state is installed in all its fields and apparatuses, which determine the conditions for the articulation of political demands, the reproduction of the economy (especially the guarantee of property rights) and the installation of the bureaucracy.

Following the work of Althusser, Nicos Poulantzas, even more specifically than Bourdieu, described the state as the material condensation of a power relation of classes, as a complex public and also private "field" in which various organisations, apparatuses and institutions, especially those of the ruling classes, operate at national and regional levels (Poulantzas 2001: 153). In this sense, for Bourdieu as well as for Poulantzas, the state is neither an autonomous subject nor a mere instrument of the ruling class, nor, however, purely neutral, but rather a field of force with a dominant class. Today more than ever, the state is a reliable guarantor of the conditions of property rights and the reproduction of capital by aggressively pursuing class struggle in favour of capital, mostly through austerity policies while establishing certain functional conditions for the accumulation of capital (and the population), regulating the public monetary system and, finally, necessarily guaranteeing the ownership of private capitals. Although the state thus primarily asserts the interests of the ruling classes by installing a compatible bloc in power, which for Poulantzas is not a monolithic but rather a strategic field, it is not a mere executive organ of capital.[2]

---

[2] In *Capital Hates Everyone*, Maurizio Lazzarato argues that since the middle of the twentieth century, the state has increasingly supported the components and functions of a dominant capitalist war machine (Lazzarato 2021: 43). The transnational functioning of finance and logistics in particular would weaken the state in relation to capital.

Processes of standardisation and integration characterise the transformation of a local market to a national market. In this process, the state does not unify a pre-existing market, but institutionalises a completely new, homogeneous national market by establishing borders and laws. Thus, the state is in a very specific way constitutive of capitalist economy, that is, it creates, transforms and produces real relations of power. It does not *ex negativo* fix certain rules for the economy, as it is still thought, for example, in the conception of the state by Althusser and Gramsci, where the state is in the end reduced to a prohibitive, repressive state apparatuses and faith-making ideological state apparatuses, where the functions and positivity of an economic state apparatus are not even considered. Poulantzas has pointed this out and ascribed a dominant position to economic state apparatuses (Poulantzas 2001: 30). One thinks, for example, of the important function that ministries of finance (and tax offices) have in the state, whose management staff today is often interspersed with representatives of the big banks. The profits of banks

In *The Global Police State*, William I. Robinson argues in the same direction. For him, the main representatives of capital today are a new transnational capitalist class that has emerged from the leading capitalist groups in the industrialised world, which emphasises the importance of global markets, and thus represents the hegemonic faction of capital on a global scale. They are the owners and managers of the multinational corporations and financial companies that drive the global economy. These corporations have internationalised markets through networks that transcend national boundaries and they operate largely independent of their original states and territories. Although at the beginning of this development it was the "Atlantic Ruling Class", factions of capital from almost every continent have now achieved the status of this transnational class (Robinson 2020).

But beyond all neoliberal theories of market fundamentalism, capital still needs the capitalist state, while conversely the state is structurally dependent on capital. On the one hand, transnational capital and its representatives instrumentalise states all over the world, and on the other hand, every country is now dependent on the circuits of transnational capital. In this context, states must provide good conditions of location for this kind of capital accumulation, that is, create a climate for profits and repressive rules for the proletariat that serve capital. States, however, are not transnational political authorities, although the new transnationalist class continually attempts to translate the structural power of the global economy into a supranational political authority, a kind of transnational state apparatus that does not possess a global government, but can at least be understood as a loose network composed of transnational and supranational organisations that cooperate closely with nation-states to secure the conditions of transnational accumulation. This is an institutional network, whereby the nation-states do not disappear because, on the one hand, they have to produce the national conditions for global capital accumulation and, on the other, they should not loose their political legitimacy as a nation in the process (Ibid).

and the adequacy of their capitalisation become important variables in the policies of finance ministries, which want to act as regulators with the development of models that provide information on the likely future course of yields based on macroeconomic relations. Executive power in the form of a ministry of finance is an essential part of the state apparatus, to whose imperatives, other ministries and apparatuses are subordinated. The economic state apparatus is characterised in general by the fact that it invents a wide range of rules, projects and laws, in particular to counteract the tendency of the falling rate of profit in the economy.

In recent years, the state's strategic network, a dense network of government personnel, bureaucracies, secret services, the military and the financial industry, into which the bloc in power is integrated, has been further transformed and is discussed under the categories "deep state" and "permanent government". Thus the political potential of the state, which consists among other things in facing both capital and wage earners as a third force, is further limited, but is not entirely eliminated. For the functioning of companies in a national location, an independent state sector (as an informal functional system, cf. Gerstenberger 2017: 609) is, to a certain extent, still absolutely necessary; a state that provides a whole range of infrastructural services such as research, science, communication, environmental protection, energy, water supply, regional planning, health, and the construction and maintenance of the transportation network as a public authority and thus maintains the reproductive conditions for an entire national economy. The state sector also includes educational institutions, the media, and especially apparatuses and instances that set in motion objectifying and quantifying mechanisms of counting, statistics and classification of the population. Modes of operation have a hegemonic validity in the various social fields and are in fact considered common sense by the population, constructing everyday life, indeed the world as a normality, an everyday life that generally gets on without violence and in which one can seemingly and easily trust. To this end, the state uses its power of naming to bring governance into a specific conceptual structure and to open it up to permanent intervention, today, by increasingly intense inscriptions into the socio-economic field, an a-signifying semiotic[3] with numbers, algorithms, mathematical equations, tables, graphs, diagrams, indices, plans, notations, affects, etc. (cf. Szepanski 2016),

---

[3] Guattari separates the a-significant semiotics (algorithms, mathematical equations, diagrams, indices, plans, notations, affects, etc.) from encodings and semiologies (Guattari

8 THE FINANCIAL SYSTEM AND THE STATE   223

which play an important role especially in information technologies, economics, science and art. In this way, a naturalising construction of social processes is always set in motion, which condenses and objectifies social reality insofar as it is translated into mathematical relations, geometries and a-signifying semiotics, whose performative potential consists in offering, distributing and, if necessary, enforcing standardised perspectives and views that represent a specific rationality and classification. Today, actors are placed in a social space in which data, information and other indicators are arranged in a certain set such that the measurements, be it the recording of poverty, GDP and wealth, not only concern the representation of socio-economic fields, but also produce performative affects that attempt to establish the habit, imagination and experience of the population. The social metrics that the state stages and which today culminate in a nihilistic omnimetry (on the obsession to count everything, cf. Mau

2018). A-significant semiotics work as material gears in machine complexes. Mathematical models, algorithms, computer languages and diagrams participate not only in the processes of subjectification, but also in the creation of objects, interacting directly with material flows by making technical machines like the computer work, while as monetary signs activating the flows of money capital.

Deleuze and Guattari speak of a-signifying semiotics also with regard to economic math, whose most important operator is still money. Here, human and nonhuman agents function as moving parts within the material practices and connectivity of rhythmicised money-capital flows. Money, stock indices and unemployment statistics, algorithms and scientific diagrams, formulas and models, functions and computer languages – they all produce beyond significations (language, writing), neither discourses nor narratives, but operate and multiply the productive forces of machinery and its networks in a mathematical, that is, algebraic or stochastic mode of economic semioses. In the differential machine complexes of capital, which today function mostly diagrammatically to produce financial, recombinant or machine surplus value, agents are no longer constituted as purely subjective and semiotics is no longer to be understood as representational.

With Deleuze and Guattari, we can then report that the a-signifying semiotics in the field of the economy of capital are not language-centred *dispositifs* that serve, say, the reproduction of ideology, but more abstract modes, including binary or probabilistic codes. On the one hand, the "algorithm" (of capital) does not directly calculate particular works down to averages (average profit rates), but calculates precisely with the mathematics and signs of the code to produce average profit rates. On the other hand, the methods of capitalisation operate with a-signifying semiotics that do not represent anything, but anticipate something by producing, calculating and shaping it. As signs of power, that is, capitalisation form, the mathemes and semiotics permanently open up the game with the future. This remains a game oriented to the requirements of capital and the restrictions of the state, in which certain technological innovations are also deleted if they cannot precisely fulfil certain economic conditions.

224   A. SZEPANSKI

2017: 23ff.) are ultimately always tied to the constellation, periodicity and intensity of class struggle.

The state constitutes economic capital in addition to institutionalising the tax system, in the sense that it has the right to issue legal money, set exchange rates and initiate its own economic policy. It also contributes to the creation of a national economic space or national market, which it structures in a specific way. The state is directly involved in the accumulation of the fictitious capital of a nation through the issuance of government bonds, while the functions of the state with regard to the accumulation of national industrial capital are more closely related to establishing and ensuring the framework conditions and infrastructure for the production of surplus value. Today, the structure of capital's concentrated and concerted decision-making power in the form of the entanglement of capital and state governments is quite obvious, however not so easily recognisable at first glance. However, certain state apparatuses and functions are transferred entirely to private capital actors, who thus themselves transform into producers of law (Porcaro 2015: 59f.). The sovereignty of nation-states is not only reduced by neoliberal waves of privatisation, but is also transformed by their involvement in processes of globalisation - processes that are characterised by various forms of cooperation among states, such as special bilateral agreements, some of which have already been privatised, trade agreements and even military alliances. In order to stabilise the international financial system, bilateral contracts (free trade agreements, etc.) are always needed between imperialist states, but also between them and the emerging and developing countries. But here too, the trend is toward privatisation. In 2013, approximately 3200 bilateral trade and investment agreements were concluded, 90% of which were the so-called Investor-to-State Dispute Settlements (ISDS), which allow transnational corporations to sue certain signatory states for damages in secret court proceedings. Germany has signed more than 140 such agreements, and all of them contain ISDS provisions (ISW-Report 2014, No. 97: Economic-Nato TTIP STOP!, 4).[4]

---

[4] In *The Code of Capital*, Katharina Pistor demonstrates how representatives of capital can bring state power to their side - by influencing the law, i.e. the code of capital - without having to take over the state apparatus as such.

There are four attributes that ensure that a particular good or class of goods becomes capital. These must be secured by law in order to turn pure property into capital: (1) Priority over competing claims to possession. (2) Durability protection. The attribute of priority protects the owner of capital against the misfortunes of others. But misfortune can

International competition between states and their companies has always been about creating attractive locations for capital investment in their own countries, and this implies not only an economic policy that is concerned with the accumulation and concentration of productive industrial capital, but also with the supply of fictitious capital and other means of financing. International law, informal meetings of states and international institutions continue to be strongly influenced by national sovereignty, although Western governments have long since conceded the partial renunciation of the exercise of sovereignty in certain territories called "offshore centres" from which the internationally positioned financial industry in particular profits.

Let us now turn to the relationship between the state and financial capital. Today, the state affirms the financial industry, especially when the latter uses legal money as a component of its own liquidity reserves, through a series of laws and rules the legality and legitimacy of its operations. This type of affirmation is extended today by the fact that in times of financial crises, the state not only assumes liability for the solvency of private banks, but also rescues them with enormous sums of money (bailout). In doing so, states, especially in the Euro Zone, obtain the funds with which they rescue banks by borrowing from banks, while the latter continuing to base their balance sheets in part on government bonds. With the affirmation of the creation of credit by commercial banks, the state leaves an important function in the economy to financial capital; it affirms in principle that the monetary assets of the capitalist economy should be supplied to the multiplication of capital wherever possible and that private banks should throw fictitious and speculative capital into circulation at a profit. For the state, as the economic administrator of a budget, the national accumulation of capital is in fact a condition and

---

befall him as well. (3) Universality. Private contracts can establish priority and durability protection between contracting parties. However, as long as only the contracting parties are bound, there is a risk that a third party may claim the good. Generality ensures that claims and entitlements are not only valid between contracting parties - e.g. between buyer and seller - but that the state defends the corresponding claims against everyone. (4) Convertibility. This attribute gives owners the right to convert their goods into state money if no private buyer can be found. Since government money is the only means whose (nominal) purchasing power is certain, convertibility ensures that even if private demand is lost, capital will not loose its value completely. An example of this attribute is the willingness of central banks to accept certain securities and provide central bank money in exchange (Pistor 2020).

226   A. SZEPANSKI

resource for its own demand for money, for which the infrastructures, public goods and state apparatuses and their functions, institutions and operations are paid.

The state balances its expenditures first of all by making its citizens debtors, i.e. by collecting taxes from them. At the same time, the state pays its expenditures with the means it has created itself and which can pay off debts, namely money. By virtue of state power, legal money is, regardless of its own material worthlessness, also a means that legitimises the power of private property to access the capacities of an economy. And it should be noted that any money debt can be paid off with legal money. But this is only one side: the very determination of the price variables that are merely represented by legal tender primarily results from the movements of the circulation of commodities, money and capital itself. What the units of legal money are "worth", which are related to the prices of commodities, depends on the accumulation of capital and the ever changing sums of capital-induced commodities and services, whose prices/exchange-values in turn are written in legal units. It can therefore be argued that capitalist money is based more on the historically developed economic processes and conventions of the capital economy than on the money created by the law of the state.[5] Therefore, there is still no valid legal definition of money (Häring 2016: 115). In whatever quantity or form, throwing money into circulation cannot be legally prescribed by the state, and this can be recognised by the fact that the creation of bank deposits by private banks is not, to this day, subject to any adequate legal regulation. Indeed, the bank deposits of commercial banks are accepted by the state as a quasi-valid form of money, but are not officially legal tender, even though they function as legal tender by convention or in

---

[5] See here also John Milios' study of the emergence of capitalism in Venice (Milios 2018).

Modern Money Theory, on the other hand, assumes that in the last instance the state alone is capable of creating money. However, against Modern Money Theory, there is no question whether the state, by issuing money, cannot determine the extent of purchasing power, which is in the price form, or whether money can function as capital. This is decided in private capitalist competition between capitalist corporations. Whether money as a means of multiplication proves itself in the capital cycle, or whether it is accepted as money at all, this is decided in the last instance in the private capital economy, which in turn means that for its financing, the state, although it provides currency, must make money from the transactions of the private sector.

good faith.[6] Since the state guarantees that bank deposits can be traded at par with state money and can be used to pay taxes, they are almost as liquid as state money. But instruments must be found to safeguard the convertibility of private banks, deposit insurance, capital requirements and refinancing facilities.

In trading fictitious capital, the state is involved both as an issuer of bonds and as a buyer of securities. As an issuer of government bonds, the state is one of the most important providers of relatively secure future payment promises on the capital market. If the local authorities, the government and other state institutions today cover considerable parts of their own financing needs on the capital market themselves, they put fictitious capital into circulation at precise and regular intervals. The financing of the state apparatus, which takes place primarily through the collection of taxes and the issuance of government bonds, is the subject of continuous state strategies, debates and disputes between parliaments, the executive, political parties and the various capital factions, while the financial system requires the state and the legal security it constructs, which is employed through legislation, the dispensation of justice and the corresponding apparatuses that guarantee the validity of the laws.

A certain degree of regulation and, at the same time, legal protection of the commercial banks' modes of operation is part of the state's sovereign organisational tasks, i.e. the state issues commercial banks a legal license to utilise the sums of money and monetary capital of a national economy according to the rules and success criteria of the logic of financial capital and, at the same time, to create credit. In general, the regulations concern certain issues of corporate law, the control of capital movements and ownership, and finally the conditions of access to the markets.[7] The state thus legitimises the economic power of commercial banks, but does not produce it. The employment of solvency and future promises of payment, as well as the functionalisation of the entire capital economy today would be inconceivable without commercial banks and

---

[6] In 2013, the total amount of cash in circulation in the Euro Zone was € 0.9 trillion, while customer deposits at banks and bank guarantees amounted to around € 10 trillion.

[7] The owner is a person who is entitled to activate social procedures that protect private property, while a possessor only has control over an object. But the owner also has control over the action of other people. Economic theory must always focus on ownership, which is evident from the fact that in most transactions, especially financial ones, there is no object to be possessed.

228   A. SZEPANSKI

other financial institutions. However, in order to safeguard the operations of capital, the state must issue certain regulatory provisions: capital asset ratios, minimum reserves, registration of large loans by state supervisory authorities, insurance for demand deposit, time deposit and savings deposit, etc.

The law of private property affirms the equation of promises of payment, which are related to the future increase of capital, with the real financial assets. This affirmation also applies to the monetary signs of commercial banks, which serve for the execution of payment transactions and crediting, whereby the identity between credit and capital is at the same time affirmed. But this affirmation does not guarantee that the multiplication of capital will be realised: the state must leave the execution of the important parameters of capital accumulation, capitalisation, relative price movements, etc., to the divergent practices and strategies of capital in the context of competition. In this way, state money will ever remain tied to the functions of "capitalist" money, to the functions of money as a measure, to credit and monetary capital, to the private financial system and to the liquidity of the banks with which they settle their liabilities against each other. Conversely, for commercial banks, legal money is an indispensable reserve that undoubtedly functions as money and at the same time as security that the banks need for their credit creation, even if only to a small extent. For private banks, legal tender is first-order liquidity, the unconditional and immediate solvency they need to produce their promises of payment. The offer of central banks to lend legal tender against interest and securities is used by commercial banks to (partially) refinance their liabilities, for which liquid funds are required; they also transfer the management of the monetary transactions between commercial banks to the central bank, or, to put it another way, by lending money to refinance the credit operations of commercial banks, the central bank puts the state-owned legal security of money behind the services of financial capital, thus at the same time the creation of bank deposits by commercial banks is generally accepted by giving them precisely that legal tender, which is necessary for their liquidity needs. Legal tender is thus affected in its "value" by its use as a reserve fund of private credit institutions. The quantity of power over the legal tender results also from the transactions of private banks themselves. The release of credit business by means of the integration of legal tender into the credit system also has the tendency that the (industrial) accumulation of capital remains behind the increase of circulating credit money and fictitious and speculative capital.

For the state - the administrator of a budget - the growth of the national capital economy is a fundamental condition for its own financing, so that the state can pay in return the commodities and services it applies and uses to companies with money. In order to finance its infrastructure and management tasks, the state does not first obtain the money by credit, as capital companies do, but by means of tax collection, whereby the taxes that affect all citizens are regular, with fixed due dates and compulsory (Bourdieu 2014: 202). The violence of its access, however, quickly disappears behind the objective aspects, for which archives, accounting, prices and specific technologies are necessary, which make the state appear to the majority of the population as a neutral supplier of services, goods and infrastructures that are essential for an economy. At the same time, the state necessarily remains dependent on the successful and productive application of private capital in its territory, that is, on the one hand, that the accumulation of capital is sufficiently growing and, on the other, that the class struggle between labour and capital is sufficiently pacified or even stopped. Affirming in particular the imperatives of promoting capital accumulation, the state organises its own household budget, in which it not only balances income and expenditure, but orients the income side to the economic success of the national corporations with high efficiency, while the expenditure side serves to meet the physical and social infrastructural needs that are absolutely necessary for the capital accumulation of its corporations.

The monetary requirements of the state are primarily financed by taxes *and* government bonds (there can be in principle also direct financing by central bank); the state pursues a flexible policy of redistribution by raising or lowering certain types of taxes, reducing public spending, carrying out privatisations and issuing new government bonds. The tax system is *sui generis* a relationship of domination and exploitation. The state, supported by its monopoly on the use of force, can partly finance its expenditures by ordering and enforcing the collection of taxes from all members of the population, thus transforming citizens into debtors. The institutionalisation of taxes was the result of civil wars in which the exercise of physical violence by the state led to the taxation of the population, in which physical violence must always legitimise or mask itself with symbolic violence (Ibid.: 203). Between the military, tax administration and statistics, there is a kind of circular causality (Ibid.).

230   A. SZEPANSKI

Tax payments do not represent money in return for the government, as Modern Money Theory maintains, but should be understood as an inflow of funds for the government to finance, at least in part, current government spending. Government spending financed by taxes and the issuance of government bonds does not constitute money creation; rather, expanded government demand for money may entail expanded money creation by the private banking sector. Under certain conditions, of course, central banks also create money, albeit to a lesser extent than the private sector.

If the state collects taxes, then they are usually paid voluntarily despite the coercive relationship that implies them, and belong exclusively to it. The legal statute for this in Germany leaves no doubt about this: "Taxes are monetary benefits which do not represent a consideration for a special service" (Abgabenordnung §3,1) Only the state is able to finance itself through taxes, whereby these are initially to be regarded as a deduction from the profits of companies and from the wages of private households. Thus taxes represent the hinge between the economy and politics, or between money and law. Insofar as taxes are sums of money that do not directly function as an accumulation of capital, they are removed from the direct control of capital, which it recovers in part through the trade in government bonds.

The capitalist tax state, as an independent economic subject that does not participate directly in value creation as a capitalist corporation, secures the right of formally free and equal owners, but by establishing the framework conditions of capitalist production, it supports in particular the property rights of the ruling classes and class factions, thereby at best accelerating economic growth. The declared goal of the state is and remains the promotion of national economic growth (economic performance within its own territory; the nation as a capital location), which is today written with the (political) ratio of the Gross Domestic Product (GDP): GDP is the result of adding up the prices of the goods and services produced within an economy in a given period (as long as they are not used as intermediate inputs for the production of other goods and services).[8] It can be written as follows: GDP = AP/h × AZ ×

---

[8] The calculation of GDP is simply a summation of economic transactions in the economy. This means also that things that actually harm the body of society - like car accidents, diseases, oil spills and so on - are added to GDP. Moreover, economic growth tells us very little about how the potential benefits and harms of financial transactions

ET. (Et stands for employed persons, AZ for working time and Ap/h stands for labour productivity per working hour) (Leibiger 2016: 39f.). GDP grows if productivity and working time increase, the unemployment rate decreases and the participation of the population in the labour force increases. GDP growth quantifies the change in the price of current GDP compared to the price of GDP in a previous reference period; it is measured in percentage and is price-adjusted (inflation is excluded). Today, GDP figures have a very strong influence on the political actions of governments and the bloc in power; it is an important political figure, but its significance is quite limited, a point which cannot be explored here.

The level of taxes always remains related to the cyclical phases of capital accumulation and the respective level of national capital strength and is determined differentially according to the economic performance of companies and citizens. Parts of the citizens' income and the income and profits generated by companies are collected through direct and indirect taxes. The ministries of finance and economics constantly review certain projects for their growth effects and set priorities with respect to government spending, so that cuts and shortages are always to be expected in certain areas of the national budget that are in accordance with the productivity requirements of capital, merely classified as "consumable", while funds are constantly being mobilised for government spending that is considered "investive". Where the investments necessary for national growth are too risky for private capital, such as medium or long-term research spending and basic research, neither of which is profitable in the short-term, the state must itself assume the financing and the risks involved (cf. Mazzucato 2014). Today, the state is getting rid of a whole series of infrastructural services that are directly capitalised through neoliberal privatisation. In the neoliberal phase of capital, there is a strong wave of privatisation of public property and public tasks, a reduction in taxes for capital owners and those on high incomes, as well as deregulation of the labour market, which results in a stagnation or reduction in real wages and labour costs. In addition, an elaborate system of partial privatisations and public–private partnerships is emerging, led and planned by the large management consultancies, and which is useful for the further

---

are distributed among classes. It is difficult to prove empirically whether growth, the cornerstone of neoliberal logic, has lived up to its claims. If we go back to 1950, the world economy grew by more than six times. At this rate of growth, the promised social, economic and ecological improvements should actually have materialised long ago.

accumulation of fictitious capital. There is definitely a connection between the privatisation of infrastructure, the neoliberal policy of lowering taxes and reducing labour costs. At the same time, neoliberal government policies have specific effects on the financial system. Indeed, the privatisation of public property also creates incentives to produce securities, inasmuch as the companies, which take over state functions, issue shares to finance themselves, and thus this type of redistribution of income strengthens the demand for fictitious capital.

With the money that the state collects through the taxation of companies and private households, it thus produces material foundations for the continued existence of the national economy, including infrastructure, education, health and research. With subsidies, cheap loans and insurance services, the state supports specific investments under the project name "structural and regional policy", where the required capital advance is too large for private companies and the turnaround time of the capital is too long. The state does not normally make productive investments directly, but its expenditures can sometimes be considered productive, at least indirectly, insofar as they create the conditions and potential for the growth of private capital and increase its productivity. On the one hand, the expansion of infrastructure provides profitable business for certain capital factions and promotes employment, particularly in the construction industry. On the other hand, the state also offers favourable services and public goods for certain capital factions. Transport and communication systems, energy and infrastructure (built environments), which are part of the general conditions of production, are produced either by the state or in its commission to certain private companies, and are used by the latter collectively and/or temporarily. For the temporary use of the infrastructures, companies pay rents or user fees. David Harvey calls the provision of such infrastructures to capital the "fixed capital of the independent form" or the "secondary capital circulation", whereby this type of capital is often exploited analogous to interest-bearing capital (cf. Wiegand 2013: 42). If the state makes these systems and infrastructures available, larger funds, machines and workers are tied up over a longer period of time, the productivity of the economy is usually increased, effective demand is stimulated, and under certain circumstances, some singular companies also generate surplus value (in the case of user fees), although state expenditure in the form of taxes and duties is paid from the revenues of the economy. This, in turn, counteracts, to a certain extent, the positive effect on the economy, because the state taxes profits and income and thus burdens capital with deductions. However, the permanent issue of government bonds, which is not possible without financial capital, can open up new capital cycles, i.e. it can be used to make long-term investments in physical and social infrastructures to a greater extent. The investments made in the secondary capital cycle, which are mediated through the financial system, are thus part of the general circulation of capital. For Harvey, investments in physical (secondary capital circulation) and social infrastructures (tertiary capital circulation; education, research, health, etc.) are at least potentially productive, but this is not primarily because these government expenditures are used by companies to produce surplus value, but because they increase the productivity of the economy as a whole and thus improve the conditions for primary industrial capital circulation (Ibid.). Moreover, state investments remain integrated into the circulation of financial capital through the issue of government bonds and their trading on the financial markets. What financial capital treats here as monetary capital and what also functions as the purchasing power of the state, however, does not usually serve the direct production of surplus value by the state; rather, it serves to produce the general conditions of value-added production, thus setting the relationship between capital accumulation and state debt. Through its various policies, the state also creates new markets, which, contrary to what is often assumed, do not emerge spontaneously. Rather, the markets for water, education and healthcare must first be created through material, technological and legal structures provided by the state. To do this, property rights must also be rewritten or defended, a series of laws enacted and class struggle pushed back.

Whether the government's budgetary, economic, monetary and structural policies have promoted national capital accumulation and/or have essentially only increased the government's debt level is something that financial markets evaluate by, among other things, setting interest rates on government bonds. In any case, the economic policy of states and their governments with regard to financial markets must at least be designed to prove their own creditworthiness (including through the policies of central banks) on the financial markets and to support the financial companies of their own nation. So the national economy should survive in international competition and show corresponding success on the world markets, i.e. to strengthen national economic resources, for example, by granting licenses to exploit national raw materials, and to support the national financial system and promote the productivity of domestic companies by financing important research projects. The creditworthiness of financial companies is primarily determined by the quality of their financial assets, and, if loans are involved, by the creditworthiness of their debtors, which in turn is dependent on economic and cyclical processes in which the risk models, price movements and ratings of the financial industry are always integrated. The creditworthiness of states is also dependent on the financial industry, which paradoxically also leads to the fact that in the event of a state bailout of private banks, the state borrows the funds from these banks, which in turn base their creditworthiness in part precisely on trading in government bonds. Thus, the creditworthiness of states and financial companies is closely linked. There is now an implicit subsidisation of private banks by the state's rescue promises. To measure this subsidisation, the banks' financing costs (interest rates with which they pay their debts) are related to their costs that would be incurred without the implicit guarantees of the state. The Bank of England has found that between 2002 and 2007, the amount of annual government subsidies to those private banks that operate on a global scale was averaged £70 billion in the UK (Sahr 2017: Kindle-Edition: 5699). Only the expectation of state support in an emergency, which is already tantamount to informal and implicit subsidisation of private banks, massively boosted the trade in financial products.

There is a function of government debt to consider here, which is not to finance government spending, but to absorb private valuations of assets by offering adequate collateral to guarantee at least the risk-free interest rate regarding privately produced collaterals that are traded more strongly than government bonds. This process culminated in the bailouts of 2008 (Meister 2021: 11). In general, the decisive factor is how elastically the private economy and the state can respond to the demand for money and liquidity via historically developed security structures.

By providing liquidity, the states of big countries can revive financial markets no matter how catastrophic the bubbles (see, for example, the financial crisis in 2008). For financial theorists, this kind of bailout is not primarily about ensuring that those who are holding the assets preserve their wealth, but about preventing economic contagion through the financial sector and avoiding destructive effects on credit markets, and more importantly, about the negative effects in the market allocation of productive assets when, as markets fall, any investment in them must be priced out at their liquidation value. Finally, it is about preventing non-accumulation of already existing wealth. If bailouts are done too late or not at all, this can only increase the cost of future bailouts (Ibid.). Meister refers to a constitutive conditional relationship between the state and the financial system.

If private default risks are government-backed for large parts of the private credit markets, then interest rate spreads between government debt and private debt is far from reflecting the existence of formal and assumed government guarantees. Indeed, private lenders would then be paid an unnecessary insurance premium for debt that governments have long since insured. The biggest lenders, Wall Street banks, are encouraged by the certainty of government bailouts to undercharge the biggest borrowers, the Wall Street hedge funds, for the risks they take regarding the "too big too fail" policy. One estimates that the 18 largest banks held $30 trillion in 2008 of risky investments partly responsible for the crisis. This policy implies that lenders can issue a short put that is expected not to generate losses.

By issuing government bonds, the trading of which is co-organised by private banks, the state secures additional funds to finance consumer spending, infrastructure, education, subsidies, etc. This goes far beyond the sums of money that the state collects from households and companies through its tax offices. The capacity of financial capital to create current investment resources from future flows of money capital is used by the state when it continuously issues government bonds in anticipation of future tax revenues and transforms them into liquid financial resources on the capital markets. Only in this way can the state obtain the funds necessary to finance its tasks without overstraining companies and wage earners with taxes. At the same time, the practice of financing the state not only through taxes but also through government bonds creates important business opportunities for financial creditors, who constantly intend to book the debts of the state as their own assets.[9] The ever-increasing

---

[9] German government bonds must be paid for with central bank money, which commercial banks obtain from the Bundesbank by depositing securities as collateral for the money it issues (cf. Schreyer 2016: 72ff.). The criteria for this collateral are flexible. The Bundesbank issues the short-term loans (maturity one week) every week on Tuesday, with which commercial banks can then buy government bonds on Wednesday at the Federal Finance Agency, which organises the auctions online (in 2016, about €200 billion were auctioned off). In order to participate in the auctions, a commercial bank must be a member of the "Bund Issue Auction Group". In 2016, a total of 37 companies belonged to this group, all of them banks. No equity capital has to be deposited for the government bonds to be purchased, as they are considered to be largely risk-free securities, (provided that the

236 A. SZEPANSKI

debt of the leading imperialist states is now an integral part of the world financial system.

What are the possibilities for the state to accrue debt? First, the government can borrow from private banks by selling them securities, but this is in turn limited by how much government debt a private bank wants to hold. Since these investments generally yield lower returns than alternative financial assets (when the economic situation is good), banks limit the amount of government debt in their portfolios. Thus, it also depends on how much government debt commercial banks want to hold on their balance sheets and how creditworthy they think the government is. Nevertheless, some proponents of Modern Money Theory claim that government bonds cannot be a source of funding for the government, since banks can only lend the government the money they have previously received from it or its central bank (via minimum reserves). However, a private bank can in principle very well lend money to the government without having "received" the money from it, and it thus extends the balance sheet and creates new money, for which the central bank is also not required. A private bank can buy bonds and thus exchange assets, an additional mechanism of money creation only under special circumstances.

Another way of borrowing is to sell securities to the capital markets or to institutional investors such as pension, hedge, sovereign and mutual funds. These institutional investors may buy government bonds, but this transaction merely redistributes new money to the government from actors who have already saved. The first two options for government financing - commercial and central bank lending to governments and

state can at least pay the interest on the government bonds in the future by taxing the population and companies).

The state, in turn, does not pay interest directly to creditors (the banks and the investors they serve), but rather to the accounts of the company "Clearstream", a global financial services provider that passes on the amounts. These processes take place largely anonymously, i.e. the investor groups, which receive approximately €30 billion in interest payments annually, are not known to the public (Ibid.). It can be assumed that large parts of the interest payments end up not only with the banks, but also with the investor groups, which are composed of international insurance companies and financial groups that the states use as secure sources of investment. The permanent issuance of government bonds is explicitly desired by financial capital because they are relatively safe investments for the capital that today is desperately seeking returns globally, but at the same time, governments should not get too deeply in debt because then the risk potential on government bonds will increase enormously.

redistributed money flowing into the economy in the case of institutional investors - lead to rising government debt, which usually includes corresponding government austerity politics: higher taxes, cuts in public spending, privatisation of public assets, etc.

Since borrowing from commercial banks and institutional investors is limited, there is a third way to create new money, and this could be an important policy choice during severe financial and economic crises: the central bank could buy the government's debt directly. While the first two options are theoretically limited, the third option to buy government debt is not, at least in principle. The central bank could thus, for example, buy as much government debt as necessary to support the economy in times of crisis, as we see today.

In this process, central banks do not "print" money, since the vast majority of new money creation is digital, that is, central banks credit the government's account by making an entry into the computer. All the central bank has to do is accept the government's promissory notes and, in return, make the deposit of money into the government's account, which is held at the central bank because of the necessary balance sheet operations. However, in doing so, the balance sheet must be balanced: the crediting of money (extending the liability side at the central bank) corresponds to a claim on the asset side against the government as debtor.

Now, one can say, as Modern Money Theory theorists do, that it is clear from the beginning that these claims will never be collected, but this then raises the question of how long creditors will trust the government when debt is high. The central banks of the leading nations can theoretically create unlimited amounts of money, but there are practical limits if, for example, inflation sets in domestically and as a result the external value of the currency falls or confidence in the currency drops. The central bank will, of course, want to continue to monitor inflation as the government spends the newly created money. Today, however, direct financing in this form is not possible, at least for the ECB (Central banks have until recently focused on price stability and fighting inflation, i.e. safeguarding assets, but the Fed has also focused on fighting unemployment in 2020). The representatives of Modern Money Theory point out here that money is always made available in necessary quantity to a state by its central bank; one thinks, for example, of Japan, U.S., Canada, etc., but it must be specifically pointed out that bank deposits are mostly created via commercial banks.[10] Although, as we said, most central banks are prohibited from direct government financing, the Bank of England directly purchased up to 50% of the government bonds issued by the U.K. government during the COVID-19 pandemic. There is a blurring of monetary and fiscal policy here. And there is another problem to mention at this point: while fiscal policy is often still based on reducing government spending and borrowing, financial policy is supposed to stabilise and even strengthen the financial system and especially the shadow banking system, which cannot work without new issuance of government bonds and thus permanent government debt (During the COVID-19 pandemic, the Bank of England and the Biden administration step away from austerity politics by directly financing instruments against the pandemic and by the establishment of new economic stimulus programmes. Economists like Joseph Stieglitz have long been calling for a turn away from austerity policies and for the state to turn to an active economic policy). Ultimately, it is a matter of pursuing a mode of government that recognises and supports the logic of capital, but pursues an active crisis policy by means of new instruments of monetary policy.

At the economic level, government bonds can only be considered "values" to the extent that the state is able to repay the borrowed money from its own assets, i.e. through future tax revenues. Ultimately, however, the national debt is considered covered today as long as the states find, for the payment of old debts (interest), new creditors for the issue of new government bonds, who make further funds available to them, with which the states can then pay the existing creditors at least the interest

---

[10] Modern Money Theory claims that a sovereign state has only one source of financing, namely the money provided by its central bank on its account. But if 90% of the money is created today by the private banking system and it buys government bonds, how can the state be financed exclusively by the central bank? Arguably, it cannot. Theoretically, it could even be financed independently of its central bank, and this is at least partly the case; consider again Japan, where the central bank holds only about 50% of the government debt.

According to Modern Money Theory, it is the government that creates money when it issues government bonds or in the form of mortgage bonds. As a rule, however, when the government issues securities, it first increases its demand for money, which can lead to additional money creation by private banks (bank deposits) and the central bank (reserves, to a small extent exchanged for cash). Representatives of Modern Money Theory, however, do not see government bodies as actors that demand money in the same way as private companies, but insist that only the government creates money when it issues bonds.

on old debts. This procedure of follow-up financing implies the continuous issuance of government bonds, whereby the states secure additional budget funds under the title "net new debt".[11] What is here capitalised is not so much future tax revenues, but rather the money inflows that come from the future borrowing of the state.[12] At the same time, taxes continue to act as a certification of the state's power to borrow more. But if the current practice of indebtedness continues, by 2040 most capitalist states would have to use at least the tax revenues purely to pay the interest on their government bonds (Stelter 2013: Kindle-Edition: 689). For creditors, state debt is also partly covered by the potential value of the state-produced physical and social infrastructure, insofar as privatisation of this infrastructure is always within the realm of possibility. The dilemma here is generally the following: if the issue of new government bonds tends to serve increasingly only to repay the interest on old government debt, then the state generates less and less additional money, which it can use to fund and stimulate the accumulation of capital. If the state nevertheless constantly issues more government bonds (which in itself is not a problem, since government debt is not about repayment), in order to finance all its infrastructure measures and its administration, then it risks the creditors gradually losing their confidence in its ability to repay and only buy the government bonds at higher interest rates, which of course can enormously restrict the state's ability to pay. While it is true that as long as states are indebted in their own currency, they cannot, in principle, go bankrupt, they must take care that the growth of their expenditures (taking inflation rates into account) does not exceed the growth potential of the economy.

[11] Positive net new debt exists when the volume of new loans taken out by the state exceeds the volume of loan repayments. Negative net new debt exists if the volume of new loans taken out is lower than the loan repayments. The debt ratio, in turn, is the ratio between the level of government debt and GDP. It can be reduced if the growth rates of real GDP are higher than the real interest rates on government bonds, whereby deficits in the primary budget do not compensate for this positive effect.

[12] Germany has about 1100 billion debts with the federal government and pays about €30 billion in interest annually. The debts have increased tenfold over the last 40 years. The debts are not being repaid; instead, expiring government bonds are constantly being replaced by newly issued bonds. Although the interest rates for German government bonds are very low (or zero), the share of interest expenditure in the budget has increased from 3% forty years ago to 9% today (Schreyer 2016: 70).

In the financial markets, the economic "quality" of a state's bonds is permanently assessed by evaluating, among other things, the budget situation, the financial trustworthiness of the state and the security of its future income that justifies its borrowing (The rating agencies are responsible for assessing the creditworthiness of a state. They use complicated procedures to determine its creditworthiness). Investors thus expect from the state that it supports national economic growth when they buy government bonds, which in turn promises the state increasing tax revenues. The criteria here refer to the calculation of the relationship between the increase in the number of government securities and the growth of an economy that is always also tax-viable, which investors regard as sufficient and accordingly will be rewarded with further investment in government bonds. The state is therefore economically dependent not only on the taxes that flow to it from companies and households, but it also needs a sovereign handling of its government bonds, which, however, is determined, in the final instance, by the speculative calculations of private investors. The state thus participates in the operations of the financial industry in order to secure its financing relatively independently of the cycles to which its tax revenues are also subject, but it must also observe the restrictions that the financial industry imposes on borrowing. The state pays with debt that the private banks credit to themselves as claims and which they trade in the financial markets as securities/fictitious capital. By issuing bonds, the state subjects its future solidity and political effectiveness as well as its financial needs to permanent evaluation by the financial markets, and this is always done through investors, which compare government bonds with all possible alternative securities traded on the financial markets. This comparison, as well as the relationship between the supply and demand of government bonds on the financial markets, which reflects the economic performance of the state and the national total capital, regulates the level of the interest rate of government bonds and at the same time provides new indications for their ongoing evaluation. The lower the prospects of future growth in capital accumulation on a national scale and the greater the increase in government debt in relation to this, the higher the interest rate. In principle, the fact that the central bank, which is tied to the state and is practically incapable of going bankrupt, provides private banks with legal funds to refinance them and is itself increasingly buying back government bonds from private financial companies on the secondary markets, is proving to be positive for the valuation of government bonds and, in general, the creditworthiness of the state.

The future economic growth of an economy, to which the mass of government debt is related, is in principle based on speculation. If the increase in government debt and the future growth of the economy diverge too much according to the assessment of investors (because, for example, the rate of inflation is rising and government borrowing continues to increase anyway), then interest rates on government bonds will rise first, and later perhaps even sales of the papers will falter. However, it does not depend on the absolute level of government debt whether a country has to fight a debt crisis, since the success of the country as a location of capital also depends on whether or not it profits from the cycles of the formation of fictitious capital through debt. If a nation's economic growth, which is supported by various measures, projects and policies of the state, stagnates or if tax revenues fall during a recession, then the state's financial needs will also increase. With the use of government debt as fictitious capital and the use of credit as a means of payment, the relationship between the level of government debt and the economic growth of a country's companies must constantly be balanced.[13]

As one can easily see today, it is not only the absolute level of the national debt that is important for the state with regard to its financing, but that interest costs can drive the state close of insolvency. This interest charge is based on the absolute amount of debt and the respective interest rate. While governments can, to a certain extent, still regulate the amount of national debt themselves, the interest rate on government bonds is generated on the international financial markets. If certain states and their banks are now considered to be especially prone to crisis, the capital market risks of both increases and the interest rates on government bonds rise.

Government bonds are also traded on the stock exchanges during their maturity, but not necessarily at their nominal value. If, for example, a country's creditworthiness falls, it has to pay higher interest rates for a

---

[13] Yields on government bonds usually remain low due to the comparatively low risk of default; it is precisely the security of the securities that make them an important item in any portfolio and contributes to the operational nature of financial capital and to increasing its potential. Government bonds are relatively (but by no means absolutely) safe and therefore relatively easy to sell.

newly taken loan, so that older government bonds only are bought if they yield an identical return. To give an example: if for a newly issued bond of €200,000, the interest rate compared to an old bond doubles from two to four per cent, the owner of the bond now receives €8000 annually, twice as much as with the old bond. However, the old bond can no longer be sold at a nominal value of €200,000; it can only be traded for €100,000 and is considered to be equally profitable compared to a new bond. The fall in the price of a government bond appears to be a sure sign that the issuing state no longer has a satisfactory credit rating (creditworthiness) and therefore the interest rates on its government bonds are rising, while for the lenders this process can be quite advantageous. This is one of the reasons why crisis is evoked when it comes to debt refunding and refinancing negotiations, since in this way, long-term interest rates can be pushed up even further. Lenders therefore also have an interest in high public debt and high interest rates. The counter-tendency arises from the fact that above a certain level of public debt and interest rates, repayment of the loans or payment of interest by the state seems increasingly unlikely. It is precisely at this point that the lenders then have a strong interest in the notorious austerity measures of the state: securing monetary stability, reducing the national debt, consolidating the state budget, reducing state social expenditure and increasing tax revenues - insofar as the latter do not effect the owners of capital.

The national currency symbol, declared by law to be a compulsory means of payment, is internationalised by the agreements of states to the extent that their currencies are interchangeable or convertible. In this way, states enter into a positive relationship of interdependence, in which they simultaneously concede to the power of private capital and, at the same time, claim each other as autonomous powers that recognise the same capitalist laws. The promised exchange of foreign money for one's own money, and one's own for foreign money, must be achieved in real terms. This requires respective guarantees, which are negotiated today in business transactions between the national central banks (and commercial banks), whereby the former confirm the money quality of foreign currency and the use of one's own means of payment as cross-border valid money by acting as a liquidity reserve for the exchange of one's own for foreign currency and foreign for one's own currency. States do not make their currencies convertible because of their equivalence (this is produced in national markets), but to establish their similarity as binding equivalents, thus providing the financial industry with the security it needs to reconstruct the world market with the exchange of the now quasi-international loan money (Decker et al. 2016: 120). By making their currencies convertible, states see themselves as guarantors of the international credit system, as participants in the growth of international financial capital and, at the same time, as competitors for the quality of their national credit system vis-à-vis other states.

With government bonds, transnational financial capital has fictitious capital that implies a share in a country's tax revenues. This also has positive consequences for the liquidity management of private banks, because these are relatively safe yield transactions, since government bonds usually have liquidity available at all times (but this may change in the future). Thus, by issuing their bonds, governments always support the policies of commercial banks and other financial institutions, with central banks taking back government debt from commercial banks and giving them legal tender in return.[14] This prevents, to a certain extent, states from compensating their debts through direct recourse on the cash desk of central banks. It is also a matter of actively structuring the financial markets in the wake of neoliberal policies, by diversifying government bonds issued in the primary markets, and by increasing the volume of transactions in the secondary markets, while the index of the interest rate on government bonds remains a decisive reference for the pricing of synthetic securities. Governments in turn buy the government bonds of other countries to hold foreign currencies so that they can hedge their own currency.

[14] The importance of issuing government bonds and thus debt today is not primarily the Keynesian motivation of countercyclical fiscal and monetary policy, as Modern Money Theory also assumes, but the production of a supply of safe collaterals which are demanded by the money markets, on which in turn the financial markets are built. This could also mean that the government becomes a factory of collateral production for the shadow banking system. In this scenario, treasuries do for market-based finance what central banks do for bank-based finance, creating underlying assets that in turn drive the growth of liabilities in the shadow markets. The government eventually becomes a shadow central bank. Although the state has privatised banks and corporations and left macroeconomic governance to independent central banks, its role in finance has grown. Sovereign debt became the cornerstone of the modern financial system, serving as a benchmark for pricing out assets to hedge positions in income markets and producing insurance for the creation of credit through the shadow banking system (Meister 2021: 51).

244 A. SZEPANSKI

However, the fact that state loans must also be written off, as current developments in Europe, for example, show, threatens the financial institutions, while at the present time a further rescue of the banking sector by the state would severely damage its creditworthiness (cf. Lohoff and Trenkle 2012: 269). Many banks that were facing insolvency in 2008 were rescued by states after the financial crisis under the motto "too big to fail", i.e. because of their systemic relevance, their size and integration into a dense network of financial organisations, while temporary nationalisations of major banks also took place. With regard to the analysis of the systemic relevance of private banks, the Bank for International Settlements (BIS) examines the indicator's size, cross-border activities, networking, financial institution infrastructure and complexity. After the financial crisis of 2008, the U.S. spent about \$3.6 trillion on bank bailouts, the UK \$718 billion, Ireland \$613 billion and Germany \$334 billion (cf. Kallert 2017 165).[15] Thus, the socialisation of the losses of private banks caused public debt to rise dramatically.[16]

---

[15] Tim Di Muzio points to a 2015 report of the global consulting company McKinsey, which calculated the growth rates that are necessary for some selected countries to begin repaying their sovereign debt (other debtors such as consumer, corporate, municipal and financial were excluded from the study) (Di Muzio 2015). In doing so, the average growth rates (of a group of European countries, the U.S. and Japan) illustrated that the real average growth rate was 1.67%, while countries would have had to grow at an average rate of 3.46% just to start repaying their sovereign debt. Since sovereign debt accounts for less than one-third of total global debt, one must assume that servicing all outstanding debt would require growth rates approaching 15% per year. Yet virtually all estimations of national and global growth from the IMF to Piketty predict a further slowdown in growth rates accompanied by rising global debt.

[16] In Keynesianism, the calculus of countercyclical budget policy consists of generating government debt during periods of recession in order to stimulate capital accumulation and effective demand through government spending on infrastructure, while the state repays this debt in periods of prosperity through higher tax revenues. This mechanism appears to be suspended when states not only pay their old debts with new borrowings, but also use them to service new interest rates, whereby taxpayers are initially burdened little or not at all by this type of state debt policy. The creditors of the state debt benefit from continuing to credit not only the old debts of the state, but also new debts. The fact that the state does not have to pay its debt obligations in the long-run solely from the economic output of the national economy qua taxes and is instead granted new loans all the time, is the basis for the existence of a smoothly functioning private money multiplication machine, while at the same time, the state must send positive signals to private banks and international financial institutions, consisting in measures such as the installation of a low-wage sector, cuts in the welfare state, subsidies for companies that have ever been successful, etc.

8.2 The Functions of Central Banks

By imposing rules on commercial banks for the employment of legal tender (and guaranteeing their freedom for the creation of bank deposits) and granting itself certain rights to finance its own liquidity needs, the state identifies the money it creates by law with the promises of payment made by commercial banks by credit, and thus its state power accords with the economic power of capital. Commercial banks are able to create bank deposits, which are accepted as legal tender, while only the state through its central bank creates legal tender. Besides central banks, only commercial banks can create money. Although the state presupposes its defining sovereignty over legal money, it does subordinate it in the last instance to capital, which manages quasi-autonomous credit, fictitious and speculative capital. At this point, the state, which authorises money by law and issues legal tender, must already be differentiated from the process of capital, in which money is created by commercial banks. The money of commercial banks is an accepted promise to pay and can be enforced by political coercion if necessary. The idea that a central institution (central bank, state) can directly decree the validity of money is not correct and ultimately a relapse into a kind of instrumental thinking, insofar as the state or the central bank is here seen as a quasi-divine power to define values. But for the validity of money, it always needs a consensus, the general acceptance of money of the capitalist economy by all economic actors *and* the power of private capitalist calculation with money.

The money that central banks lend to commercial banks is in its *form* at first nothing other than a sign, which the latter organise parts of their payments. Its function, with which it enters into circulation, consists not only in realising the prices of commodities (prices actualise the virtual distribution of commodities in monetary form), but it is also always related to the economic power of commercial banks, which is based on the creation of credit and bank deposits. If a central bank supports the liquidity management of commercial banks with its money, it cannot eliminate the uncertainty of the credit operations of the latter, which is based, among other things, on the relation between the bank's operations oriented towards the future and the dependence on the success of the credited companies in the past, which always remains an uncertain future.

In contrast to the economic power of commercial banks, the power of central banks is not derived from their commercial success, but from their specific references to the sovereign power of the state. Central banks are secured by the state. At the dawn of capitalism, there was a reciprocal relationship between the state and central banks: the state was liable for the security of the assets of the central bank which provided the state with money. There are three functions of central banks to mention at this point: they influence the terms of money and credit (monetary policy of the state), regulate commercial banks (stability of the national financial system) and provide domestic and foreign financial services to the state and the private sector (stability of payment systems). They therefore maintain the stability of the financial system, providing it with liquidity especially in the event of crisis, and have to maintain confidence in the currency (We must additionally remark that central banks today also actively intervene in the shadow banking system, providing it with liquidity and become traders on the financial markets themselves).

In the vertical hierarchy of the national monetary system, the central bank seems to take the leading position when it issues cash (paper bills and coins) as legal tender, which is exchanged by it (it is written as a liability on its balance sheet) for the securities of commercial banks. Thus, when the central bank issues legal money by granting loans to commercial banks, it also accumulates the promises of payment of commercial banks and thus fictitious capital. Central bank money is thus formally understood as a liability, which is realised in the exchanges (of securities) with the private commercial banks. The available cash functions in the balance sheet of the central bank as a payment obligation, a debt of the central bank, which is constructed in exchange for the promises of repayment of commercial banks, which in turn are secured by the debt obligations of third parties. Paper bills or coins become money by being entered into the balance sheets of central banks and are issued when a commercial bank wants to have part of the held reserves at the central bank as cash.[17] Cash can be used to pay off practically all debts.

It can be assumed, however, that central bank balances ultimately function as the effects of private credit creation, i.e. they are first produced and reproduced on the basis of the credit decisions of commercial banks. This is in line with the fact that today, private commercial banks produce 90% of money in all its forms, while central banks only issue 10% of

---

[17] Central bank money is not a liability insofar as the person who submits it to the central bank would only receive central bank money again (the central bank only owes a new bank bill).

money as legal tender. It is correct to say that without government money, no bank deposits can be created. But companies and banks decide autonomously to what extent they want to create bank deposits from government money. The second money creation cycle between banks and companies (or, more generally, non-banks) ensures that credits endogenise the money supply, i.e. decouple it from government money creation. However, central banks give financial players, especially in times of crisis, access to more crisis-proof liquidity and safe securities. During the pandemic, massive loans were also extended to non-financial actors in the shadow banking system.

In the national currency sector, central bank money has long since replaced gold, i.e. it functions self-referentially, insofar as the claim for money is a claim on the central bank - on the money of the central bank (Weber 2015: 220). All this does not mean that the central bank functions as a "lender of last resort", because it remains fully integrated into private money capital movements, the credit creation processes of commercial banks and differential capital accumulation. Or, to put it another way, central banks issue banknotes (cash) as legal tender and, in the exchange of money for the securities of commercial banks, certify their credit signs as equivalent to legal money, thus making legal tender also a relative dependent variable of the credit operations of the private banks. In the second half of the twentieth century, an essential field of competence of central banks, which consisted in quasi-autonomous currency and monetary policy, was increasingly transferred to financial capital. As a result, central banks are no longer exactly informed about the amount of money that is currently in circulation, which private banks constantly reproduce, and how many risks are actually circulating due to the fact that new creditor and debtor relations constantly enter into the financial markets (although they try to control this procedure to a certain extent with instruments such as the key interest rates and minimum reserves).[18]

---

[18] High proportions of the national and transnational operations of financial capital (commercial, investment and shadow banks) are executed independently from the regulations of the state, so that governmental intervention remains dependent on the price movements of derivative monetary capital. However, it is precisely in times of economic crisis that the use of the security *dispositiv* "central bank" is called upon again by endangered financial capital. Central banks constantly link their operations such as minimum reserve formation, liquidity protection and interest rate policy with the strategies of private financial capital. Moreover, it is precisely the establishment of central banks as the "fourth estate in the state", the legal disengagement from the executive and legislative branches,

The issuance of legal money by central banks is not merely "money creation from nothing", as often said, but rather a credit relationship is created with commercial banks, whereby the latter undertake to "repay" the borrowed sums of money plus interest to central banks in the future. The so-called creation of money is here not a unilateral act, but the creation of legal money results from an interaction between the central bank and the commercial banks, i.e. the central bank mostly only "creates" money by establishing a relationship with commercial banks. Thus, central banks exchange legal tender with the securities of commercial banks according to the rules they enact and permanently modify, thus functioning as a reserve fund for their liquidity management, with which the commercial banks auto-referentially organise their promises to pay, create liquidity and solvency and thus realise creditworthiness. The state and the central bank can by no means eliminate the risks that commercial banks take with their financial operations and from which ultimately the savings deposits of their customers are not spared.[19]

Historically, state regulation of national money began before the existence of central banks, but later they became an important instrument for the management of a national monetary system, both in terms of issuing national currency and managing government bond funds.[20] Central banks not only made offers to commercial banks, but also obliged them to use

and the transformation of the central bank toward a quasi-autonomous practice of governance, that confirms the alignment of central banks with the dynamics and necessities of financial capital accumulation (Vogl 2017: Kindle-Edition: 275ff.). But still, central banks remain a part of the state, as a kind of independent part of the executive (In terms of share ownership, central banks are often hybrid state-private institutions). However, the policy of "quantitative easing" (QE), the decrease of central bank interest rates and new repo-policies have in particular strongly promoted and accelerated expansionary developments on the money markets, without any striking improvement in the investment dynamics of industrial capital being reported to date (for the relevant statistics, see Krüger 2015: 459).

[19] The unit of measurement for legal tender is not a monetary good with physically defined units of weight, but the price of a constructed shopping basket, which allows the comparison of the previous with the current purchasing power of the same amount of money.

[20] Worldwide, especially in the major industrialised nations and the Euro area, almost all central banks are not direct branches of the state, but a kind of independent institution that decides for themselves the extent to which they monetise government deficits, i.e. purchase government debt on the secondary market (from banks) and take it onto their balance sheets. In the Euro area (as in other currency areas), there is an explicit ban on buying or taking over government debt on the primary market (i.e. directly from the government). But nevertheless, central banks are part of the state.

these offers. Today, commercial banks are required to hold balances in certain accounts with the central bank, to settle payments through these accounts and to undergo controls, which, taking into account the mutual mistrust of the banks and the criteria of confidence building, are part of a specific supervisory regime of central banks. Commercial banks thus also have exclusive access to central bank credit, but they must meet certain criteria in order to obtain a state license for their financial operations, especially when they collect and manage deposits of the general public. For example, the authorisation to conduct banking business is subject

If there would be a kind of total identity between state/treasury and central banks, as Modern Money Theory suggests, then government debt, on the one hand, and government-issued securities held by the central bank, on the other, should correspond to each other. This is not the case. As economist Joseph Huber writes: "Public securities held by the Federal Reserve do not equal the national debt, nor do reserve balances held by the government and banks at the Federal Reserve. At the beginning of 2019, all reserve balances at the Federal Reserve were about $1600 billion; the value of government-issued securities held by the Federal Reserve was 2200 billion; but government debt was 22,500 billion. Banks' excess reserves were 3–4 times higher than the government's transaction balances at the Federal Reserve" (Huber 2021).

Modern Money Theory (MMT) assumes that, in the last instance, only the state is capable of creating money. As Randall Wray, one of the main proponents of MMT writes: "Money is, and always has been, a creature of the state" (Wray 2000: 12). Money serves the state by mobilising financial resources and labour, whereby the state neither needs credits nor must collect taxes; rather, the state itself issues money through the central bank. Thus, through law, the state determines the official currency for a country by accepting only that unit for the payment of taxes. The state simply has this money if the central bank influences the government's account, i.e. provides the money with which public expenditures are then made. Thus, the government provides the money as a credit creation that circulates (acting as a means of circulation or lent) and flows back to it through taxes. But it has to be said that if the money represents a tax credit, then there must be, at the same time, a tax liability that organises the acceptance of the money that the state issues.

A "monetarily sovereign" government can issue currency almost indefinitely. States can thus, in principle, get into indefinite debt, which is technically possible. But as soon as a state has, for example foreign debt, it cannot borrow infinitely, and thus can go bankrupt - think, for example, of Argentina or Greece. Even if a state is only indebted in domestic currency, this does not mean that it can create money indefinitely since it has to take care of his debts.

Additionally, there is no question that by issuing money the state cannot determine how far the private purchasing power expands, which is in price form, or whether money can function as capital, since that is decided in private capitalist competition between capitalist companies. Whether money as a means of multiplication proves itself in the cycle of capital, or whether it is accepted as money at all, is decided in the last instance in the private capitalist economy, which in turn means that the state, although it provides the currency, must finance itself from the transactions of the private sector.

to certain admission criteria (in Germany, a retail trader is not allowed to establish a bank), and for the operations of commercial banks there exists a comprehensive set of rules. The state requires commercial banks to back their issued loans with a certain percentage of equity capital; it demands that loans above a certain amount and above a certain ratio of equity capital have to be reported to state supervisory authorities, and it initiates rules for the banks' risk and liquidity management. In addition, commercial banks are required to hold a proportion of minimum reserves of legal tender in line with their liabilities, both as balances with the central bank and as cash holdings. As such, sums of money are illiquid from the point of view of private banks, i.e. they are not suitable for use as loans or trading derivatives, and the minimum reserve requirement is kept low. It also cannot be ruled out that commercial banks will become insolvent and that consequently, insolvencies are handled in accordance with a strict insolvency code. A legally prescribed deposit protection fund prevents or at least reduces private asset losses and thus confirms the function of commercial banks as the general administrative authority for the financial assets of a national economy.

A central bank's influence on the credit policy of commercial banks is due to the legal definition of conditions under which the latter can obtain cash and reserves to back their own issuance of loans with collateral. In return, commercial banks must pay interest (with central bank money), which is debited from the accounts they hold with the central bank. Commercial banks also obtain additional reserves from the central bank by receiving loans against the deposit of collateral or by selling assets such as securities to the central bank. Reserves are made available to commercial banks only for a short time and at a fixed interest rate (difference between the purchase and sale price). By setting an interest rate on reserves, central banks try to influence the lending of commercial banks, but they cannot control this process. Additional reserves can be made available by the central bank through short-term facilities at higher interest rates, but de facto today the reserves of commercial banks are no longer rationed, that is, they can constantly obtain new reserves from central banks because the latter must be careful to maintain the capitalist payment system and cannot and will not easily restrict the lending of the private banks, since otherwise there would be the danger of financial collapse or a liquidity or solvency problem of the private banks.

Liquidity on the markets can be increased by lowering interest key rates and can be decreased by raising them. The Fed conducts its interest rate policy through open market operations, buying and selling government bonds to regulate the quantity and price of central bank money. The Fed has long tried, albeit without much success, to influence the lending activities of private banks by changing interest rates (and by means of minimum reserve policy). Higher key interest rates usually reduce the lending activity of commercial banks, while lower ones are intended to force it. If interest rates are high, commercial banks should also pass on higher interest rates to their customers. Yet the low interest rate policies of central banks in the last years have not automatically led to lower (real) interest rates and to the higher lending of commercial banks, because the latter constantly evaluate and calculate the risk of lending and the creditworthiness of borrowers/customers (for which they operate a specific risk management) and therefore restrict lending especially in phases of recession (while sometimes keeping real interest rates high).[21] Monetary policy here is characterised by an asymmetry in terms of both central bank interest rates and commercial banks' real interest rates. The problems that commercial banks have, especially in times of crisis, is not a lack of access to cash, but a lack of lucrative investment opportunities, when the demand of households and companies for credits might be low. Companies that are affected by low profit rates during a recession also normally demand fewer loans. The potential for commercial banks to create credit is thus limited to the extent that companies in recession are more likely to reduce debt than to take out new loans, or because commercial banks themselves restrict lending due to the lack of profit expectations of their potential borrowers. Thus, credit creation by commercial banks remains at first tied to processes of private capital accumulation and the movements of profit rates.[22] The key interest rate policy, whose aim is the regulation

---

[21] The key interest rate is the price at which commercial banks can borrow money from the central bank and thus the latter, at least indirectly, control lending. We will not go into any further details here except to mention that commercial banks today obtain their funds in particular on the money market and also in the shadow banking system.

[22] Central banks also create money, albeit in smaller quantities than private banks. For example, between 2015 and 2018, the ECB created about €2.6 trillion with its bailouts by buying the securities of private investors and institutions on the secondary markets. The ECB can only issue the money to private companies, but not to government institutions, which means that direct financing of the government budget by central bank is not possible here. The situation is different in Canada, the U.S. and Japan.

Modern Money Theory theorists argue at this point that government debt is identical to money creation, with the central bank assuming the role of a cooperating government body. Private banks appear here merely as auxiliary organs of the central bank and the

of circulation of money, not of financial actors, has today lost much of its effect and is increasingly replaced by central banks balance sheet policies, the use of money creation and money destruction.

Without the Fed's policy, interest rates on U.S. government bonds would be significantly higher. By lowering interest rates (0 or 0.25%) and freezing them at a low level, the control effect of a central bank is reduced (below zero per cent means that commercial banks have to pay money for their borrowed liquidity). Such a low interest rate is an expression of a crisis, which is why other forms of monetary policy by central banks have to be invented. The low interest rate policy and the purchase of government securities from its own currency area can also lead to further money problems (inflation). As long as the financial sector absorbs the newly created money, the creation of credit only raises the prices of fictitious capital, not of industrial goods. The inflation potential of the latter is only realised when the private creation of fictitious capital declines and the central banks directly throw fresh money into the real economy.

The influence of central banks on the credit creation of commercial banks has, after the financial crisis of 2008, declined for some time. Commercial banks always had further possibilities for obtaining missing reserves from central banks, which in turn constantly lowered the interest rates and thus simplified the procurement of further reserves for the commercial banks, although their lending activity did not increase over certain periods. At an interest rate of zero, central banks can no longer use the interest rate as an instrument to induce commercial banks to grant

government, which clearly downplays the important role of commercial banks in money creation. In fact, within a doubled banking system, the central bank seeks to ensure the liquidity of the economy and monitor the money and credit system, with sufficient liquidity available to the economy, but money must also be scarce to be accepted. If confidence in money as a currency dwindles in a national currency area, then no matter how much money the state "prints", it flows as potential capital to another currency area, where the multiplication of the capital appears possible. But as long as economic growth is guaranteed and future taxes make government bonds a safe investment, the central bank can store government bonds on its books, write them down or offset them against future profits.

further loans[23] (During the financial crisis in 2008, not only did the confidence in the economy of private banks decrease, but also their confidence in each other; banks no longer lent each other reserves and therefore the risk premiums on the interbank market continued to rise despite central bank interest rate cuts. This almost brought the interbank market to a standstill).

The changes of liquidity in financial markets, which has risen sharply at times (including the constant possibility of liquidity problems arising in the short term), the multiplication of derivative instruments, expanded risk management and the commercial banks' credit creation together make a comprehensive money supply control (M1 to M3) by the central banks obsolete today.[24] Central banks can at least influence the money supply by buying and selling government bonds. For a certain period after the financial crisis of 2008, the Fed's purchasing programme of government bonds were no longer limited in terms of duration and volume. The Fed held 27% of all U.S. Treasuries in 2012 (Stelter 2013: Kindle-Edition: 2473). The money supply is here more like a credit supply, which is today elastic and dynamically changes. The policies of central banks must inevitably be oriented to price movements on the financial markets, with financial companies themselves trying to gain greater influence on

---

[23] The amount of central bank money is influenced via the buying and selling of government bonds and thus also influences the price at which banks borrow central bank money to settle their balances. Although the central bank can keep interest rates low, it can only do so to a limited extent, because the central bank only has direct influence on interest rates at the short end; long-term interest rates (which are relevant for investment activity) are determined by many factors that are beyond the control of central banks and the government.

In contrast, MMT theorists believe that the central bank can keep these factors largely under control and should keep the interest rate as close to zero as possible. Mysteriously, they talk about "the" interest rate, but there are in fact many interest rates. Long-term government bonds will almost always have higher interest rates than short-term ones, because the future is uncertain and thus unpredictable things can occur before the bond reaches maturity. Without higher interest rates to compensate for the higher risk of default or for the longer maturities, there is unlikely to be anyone willing to buy special securities or willing to lend. Interest rates, along with expected yields, are an important factor in the volume that can be mobilised on the money and capital markets for investment.

[24] The money stock M1 comprises cash and bank money, i.e. the means of payment that can be used directly and universally. M2 also includes fixed-interest savings deposits with a term of up to three months and time deposits with a term of up to two years, and M3 includes even more recent investments that can be converted into M1 balances in the short to medium term.

monetary and fiscal policy. If the European Central Bank can only buy government securities issued in Europe on the secondary markets, the EU member states and their fiscal policy will remain more closely tied to price movements on the financial markets, and this in turn will intensify debt competition between EU states (Varoufakis 2011: 185f.). On the other hand, central banks' new instruments in monetary policy and the knowledge that central banks could, at least in theory, extend credit indefinitely against collateral (promises to buy and promises to pay) includes that the system of speculative capital can, especially in times of crisis, temporarily stabilise again. But the stabilising politics of central banks can also lead to new destabilisation. Higher repo activity by central banks leads to more liquidity and expands repo activity overall. This in turn requires more collateral for repo transactions, which leads to an increase in its prices. The politics of central banks thus stimulate the entire financial system again and can set in motion new spirals of asset prices and bubbles.

The term "quantitative easing" (QE) describes measures taken by central banks, such as the permanent purchase of mostly long-term securities and government bonds, which are held by commercial banks, when interest rates are already at zero and an expansive monetary policy is to be continued. This will reduce the supply of government bonds on the financial markets themselves, thereby increasing their price, while profits and interest rates on them fall. QE is part of the open market policy of central banks, i.e. funds are made available for private institutions by the central banks through the purchase of securities (government bonds) and through repo transactions. At this point, the central bank engages in money creation. If the central bank buys government bonds of its own government from private investors, then on the right-hand side of its balance sheet are the government bonds, while on the left-hand side are liabilities to third parties. The sellers of the securities, so the idea goes, should now reinvest the money they've received, so that the real economy is stimulated; or they should grant more credit. But the sellers of long-dated government bonds used, in the last years, the cash much more to rebalance their portfolios. Because there was an increasing demand of central banks for government bonds, the yields on them fall. The rebalancing of the portfolios of private investors therefore included a higher demand on assets like equities, corporate bonds and real estate. In the U.S. after the financial crisis of 2008, cash was flooding into high yield corporate bonds especially, inflating corporate debt and leading to the existence of zombie corporations, which could only afford to service the interest payments on their outstanding debt. As such, it is realistic to assume new stimulations in financial market speculation with QE policies. Thus, QE policy does not automatically lead to higher real economic growth, but it does accelerate the rise of stocks and other asset prices and generally functions in times of recession as a monetary incentive system for speculative capital, which engages in increasingly risky business with the inflowing money flows. It also happens, however, that commercial banks do not want to sell any securities to the central bank because they currently have no money needs. In addition, central banks can hardly control the credit creation of commercial banks, the credit demand of the non-banks, the market interest rates and the money reserves of the commercial banks. Before the COVID-19 crisis, many central banks finished their QE programmes, but they were quickly reinstalled in 2020, selling safe government bonds, as the need for funds among private investors emerged because of the restrictions and lockdowns during the pandemic.

By keeping interest rates low as an (unsuccessful) attempt to generate economic growth, central banks have pushed companies and households to take on more debt. This creates a debt trap and rising instability. We can also now see a lot of zombie corporations due to favourable financing conditions, which produce overcapacities and therefore contribute to deflationary pressure. During the COVID-19 pandemic especially, there are thousands of smaller companies that are almost bankrupt and kept in business by cheap credits, but are unable to start large investments even if they can get loans at low interest rates. The number of these zombie companies is growing by the day. In 2020, more than 200 big U.S. corporations were identified as zombie corporations, with debts of $1.36 trillion. The granting of cheap loans is called "evergreening", which supports those companies that have hardly any chance on the market. For example, analysts at Deutsche Bank complain that the monetary policy of the ECB "has brought disproportionate benefits to borrowers with the lowest credit ratings" and prevented the process of creative destruction. In 2020 during the COVID-19 crisis, corporate profitability and profits fell sharply, with the exception of Big Tech, Big Finance and now Big Pharma. Wages also fell. These results were at first deflationary[25] (Low

---

[25] The profound deflationary impulse of the past three decades was primarily due to a huge increase in global labour supply resulting from favourable demographic trends and the entry of China and Eastern Europe into the global economic system. The urbanisation

256   A. SZEPANSKI

central bank interest rates can in general reduce the state's budgetary discipline, lead to asset inflation, the prolonged survival of unprofitable companies and the zombie banks, and finally to the dissatisfaction of savers[26].

of China, as well as other economies in Asia and Eastern Europe, and the incorporation of many millions of low-wage workers into the global economic system depressed global prices. Investment in fixed capital declined in the developed countries. Domestic demand also weakened in developed countries at the same time global supply increased. This combination exerted downward pressure on inflation and thus downward pressure on both nominal and real interest rates.

The question of inflation or deflation is today uncertain. If already increasing aging has an inflationary effect (retirees do not produce but consume), higher inflation may also be the result of high government deficits being increasingly financed by central banks. Former Treasury Secretary Larry Summers and former IMF Chief Economist Olivier Blanchard both warned that the proposed $1.9 billion spending package by the U.S. Congress, on top of last year's $900 billion stimulus package, risks inflation. Monetary inflation is first seen in money and capital markets, for example as a stock market boom. Prices of industrial products still temporarily stagnate while stock prices rise and interest rates fall. A rise in capital prices that exceeds the growth of real capital prices, and is not accompanied by falling prices in industrial product, might be a sign of inflationary danger. Most mainstream economists instead say that it does not matter if debt levels rise because interest is now really low and as the economy recovers, government revenues will rise, emergency spending will cease and the cost of debt servicing will be manageable for all actors. But even modest changes in interest rates can produce stronger movements in net interest as a share of the economy in the future. Average repayment terms on government are now falling, so that government might soon enter the territory of expanding debt to pay the cost and repayment of existing debt.

The combination of loose monetary policy accumulated consumer savings that have not been able to spend due to the COVID-19 pandemic and already falling unemployment may also contribute to rising inflationary pressures. The current inflationary pressures might also result from the short-term supply constraints that are inevitable when restarting a temporarily depressed economy. But there would be enough capacities to support supply again. At the moment, we see at least sharp rises in some commodity prices, which are the result of slow returns and partial breakdowns in the global supply chains of trade by lockdowns.

[26] Since 2015, the ECB has lowered the deposit rates for private banks to minus 0.4 and the key interest rates to zero, and has also launched an enormous bond purchase program of €80 billion per month, which was reduced to €60 billion. On the secondary markets, the ECB can buy the government bonds of EU countries, which are participating in the EMSF and ESM, without limit. So far, however, neither a strong increase in inflation nor higher corporate growth rates have been achieved. However, a further explosion of prices on the stock markets has been initiated, with very high price-earnings ratios (ratio of market capitalisation of companies to GDP) and further increases in Tobin Q (market asset value of the company). The real estate sector is now also clearly overheated due to the low interest rate policy of the central banks in Japan, China and parts of Asia and

During the COVID-19 pandemic, the Bank of England has bought government bonds directly. In 2020, central banks were quick to issue emergency loans to provide short-term liquidity for private investors. The Fed launched the purchase of loans from companies with US \$2.3 trillion. Central banks have pumped around \$9 trillion worth of new money into the global financial system. The firepower of central banks regarding their financial means is today immense. It is important to note that even players from the shadow banking system, such as large investment funds, can now receive central bank money in exchange for securities. They can also use central banks to liquidate securities, a privilege previously reserved for commercial banks. Central banks can thus create enormous sums of money as long as there is confidence in a stable monetary standard. But this in turn depends on the strength of the national economy, generally of capital accumulation.

In 2020, the Fed sold government bonds to financial actors who held cash and provided cash to hedge funds and securities dealers. The Fed thus secures a minimum price for the securities held as collateral and guarantees a maximum price for the provision of liquidity. The Fed bought treasuries and all kinds of securities for about a \$1 trillion and acted in repo transactions as a counterpart to creditors and borrowers on the money and capital markets. An expansion of open market operations occurred and a provision of liquidity. The Fed also reactivated the overnight repo facility for the shadow banking system (which was closed a few years after the crises of 2008). By hedging the repo market (government bonds are fundamental here), collateral should not lose excessive value and at the same time the circulation of money should be saved. Repo transactions grew immensely over the last years and gained new importance.

Repo means in this context that commercial banks sell securities to the central bank and buy them back after a certain period of time (mostly short-term), whereby the former now have additional cash for a certain period of time. The amount of interest on the repo is the difference between the sale and repurchase price of the security, both prices being set by the central bank (cf. Binswanger 2015: Kindle Edition: 759f.). Repo are therefore contracts in which securities are sold at a certain price in order to sell them back again after a certain period of time. The

Europe. In addition, the negative consequences of the low interest rate policy for savers, pension schemes and life insurance companies must be taken into account.

borrower has to pay a risk premium on the security, which depends on its quality. Repos involve the promise of a trade at par. In times of crisis, the repo rate, the risk premiums and the margin calls increase and the repo transactions can become expensive.

In Europe, the repo market is intended to link the various securities markets in the currency area and facilitate the ECB's monetary policy decisions. The amount of repos that the ECB settles each day has an impact on the amount of central bank money available. The establishment of a European domestic financial market, in which securities and foreign exchange are traded, is thus kept flexible. The repo market offers a wide range of investment and financial opportunities for private and governmental financial actors. The high demand for collateral for repo transactions enables governments to place their bonds on the financial markets. Central banks, in turn, use the repo market as an instrument for their monetary policy.

In their official policies before the crises 2008 and in 2020, the Fed assumed care for the liquidity risks in the short-term, but not necessarily for the insolvency risks of banks. The liquidity risk in the commercial banking sector is created by producing financial liquidity through payment promises. The central bank acts within this framework and provides liquidity if necessary (QE). To take care only of liquidity risk is not sufficient anymore for the shadow banking system to stabilise it during crises. In 2013, the Overnight-Reverse-Repo-Facility for government bonds was already transformed into a permanent facility for banks and shadow banks. Thus, the need for safe government bonds was met, while the need for central bank money was not yet satisfied with a permanent facility. When disagreements arise about the liquidity and solvency of financial institutions, the financial system becomes destabilised. If the price of the securities excessively falls in certain periods and has negative effects on the repo transactions (repo rate rises), the institutions in the shadow banking system do not have sufficient funds to meet their liabilities. Normally, these funds are then made available through the private banks, while the competition between banks keeps the repo rate low. It can even happen that there are enough securities held by the Fed, like in 2019, and enough reserves at the big banks, but the latter are not willing to lend their money, like such as at the end of 2019. The importance then of repo transactions is increasing. When the Fed sold a small portion of its securities (to reduce its balances) and did not renew repo transactions, the repo rate rose sharply in September 2019, reflecting a higher short-term demand for liquidity from private financial actors in the shadow banking system. This demonstrated that it was now necessary again to give the shadow banking system access not only to safe securities but also to money funds. A new crisis hit the repo market when the repo rate for overnight transactions rose sharply to such a high level, which it hadn't reached even during the crisis of 2008, and so the market came close to collapse. When the repo rate reached 10%, the Fed had to set a cap and was forced to reopen its repo facilities to commercial banks and shadow banks. These measures were also essential for stabilising the financial system during the COVID-19 crisis. To prevent a collapse of the repo market, the Fed pumped an additional $75 billion per day into the money market, calming the situation down after a while.

Central banks must now create market liquidity by issuing *promises to buy* (not promises to pay) and therefore take care on insolvency risks. Central banks are now themselves acting as dealers in the financial markets by buying and selling assets to stem the downward movements through their own money creation. Central banks offer financial actors in repo transactions a bid-ask spread, a buying and selling price for financial products to hedge a framework in which they can be traded. Uncertainties should be converted back into a calculable risk. The price of repo-funds is now increasingly determined by the market-based valuation of the collateral (not through interest policies), which fluctuates constantly. This takes place in the shadow banking system via repo transactions, which in turn is intended to stabilise the key interest rate policy for private banks. So with central banks and state policies, the logic of capital is still accepted; there is no hard regulation by laws, but in times of crisis this logic has to be adjusted by central banks. The circulation of money capital is now even increasingly secured by central banks. We can see here a new framing of the neoliberal laissez-faire.

QE policy was still oriented towards the provision of liquidity by exchanging government bonds, while central banks had to further intervene in the crises directly in the money and capital markets in the role of market makers, guaranteeing supply and demand for almost all securities. Bailouts, Emergency Liquidity Assistance and deposit insurance were previously used to protect the official banking sector. The shadow banking system, on the other hand, only had its own private security mechanisms, which were normally considered sufficient. But after the fall of Lehman Brothers, which was one of the most important broker dealers in the shadow banking system, and in the crisis 2008, the Fed created additional collateral structures, new facilities for the shadow banking system, so that it could obtain money and government bonds.

Central banks may have now strengthened their position as a central circulation point, while still guaranteeing at first the circulation flows of fictitious and speculative capital. Prices for derivatives, for example, are fluctuating on the markets and are not fixed, but an acceptable framework can only be set by central banks. It is about a policy that makes it possible to guarantee the logic of capital even during a crisis mode. The stabilisation of the financial system now also requires that securities in the whole banking system, and for this a liquid market for securities collateral is necessary, which in turn requires a functioning repo market. Shadow banks are becoming increasingly important in providing liquidity and central banks are increasingly fulfilling the function of securing this liquidity. Here, both private capital *and* central banks acquire stronger power relations.

Already in 2008, the Fed acted as a market maker and as a broker-dealer to restore market liquidity. The Fed gave loans or exchanged Treasury Bills for all available securities, regardless of their credit quality. Today there is an implicit guarantee of central banks for hedging the trade with securities, which is equivalent to a put option, with which the prices of assets cannot fall below a certain level. The Fed acted as a counterpart via the establishment of new facilities for both lenders and borrowers on the money and capital markets. It bought large amounts of mortgage-backed securities, providing liquidity and collateral to the shadow banking system. This helped re-launch the securitisation market and to support money market funds. The Fed's own repo transactions also revived this private sector. Parts of the money market were thus integrated into the balance sheets of the Fed. Already in 2009, commercial banks were so saturated with reserves that an active monetary policy of the central banks qua repo was more difficult and thus they have further lost their influence on the money creation of commercial banks. In addition, central banks continued to grant cheap loans to commercial banks, with which they in turn buy higher-interest securities or grant loans to the private sector at high interest rates, enabling them to recapitalise their companies and put their balance sheets in order. At the same time, the purchase of government bonds according to Basel III does not have to be backed by equity capital. The situation changed again in 2020 because of the COVID-19 pandemic.

With the swap lines (currency swap agreements), already in 2008, the Fed offered other major central banks a temporary reciprocal currency arrangement to guarantee liquidity in U.S. dollars. The Fed agreed to keep a supply of dollars available for trading with another central bank at a specified exchange rate. In return, Fed received an interest rate premium, so that the swap lines were only used when there was no liquidity left in the markets. The dollar amounts that other central banks received from the Fed were passed on to domestic illiquid banks (which also had to bear the cost of the swap line). On 3 October 2008, the Fed granted the ECB, the Bank of England, the Bank of Japan and the Swiss National Bank access to unlimited dollar liquidity. Within three years, the amount of credit extended under swap facilities grew to a staggering $10 trillion (cf. Tooze 2018: 252). In 2020, as many companies struggled to meet their dollar obligations due to a lack of revenue, the Fed even extended its existing currency swap lines across the previous participating central banks to ensure dollar liquidity. The Fed opened a temporary window of opportunity for foreign central banks to use their U.S. Treasury Bonds to close repos with the Fed. The Fed became again the world's central bank.

In the central banks, both the volumes of long-term refinancing transactions and the balance sheet totals have increased in recent years, and their purchases are partly covered by poor-quality collateral. Unsalable securities were stored in bad banks, which were founded by the state, and enormous bond-buying programmes were set in motion. As the balance sheets of private banks were cleared of bad assets and credit, these banks improved again. But not all banks made use of the Fed's facilities, as their creditworthiness in the financial markets would be affected. In the course of the financial crisis of 2008, a large proportion of the rotten mortgage-backed securities (MSB) were thus deposited on the central banks. The inflation of central bank balance sheets has been driven by measures to rescue the existing financial system in particular, while the quality of central bank assets has deteriorated significantly.[27] While central bank assets are not at a historical record level compared to GDP, the criteria for covering the money created by central banks (cash and reserves) have never been so precarious. In the past, central bank money was backed by gold, then by secure debt (government bonds), but today it is not even

---

[27] Between 2007 and 2012, the Fed increased its balance sheet total from $900 billion to $3.0 trillion (Stelter 2013: Kindle Edition: 2465).

262   A. SZEPANSKI

backed by secure debt because the assets of central banks include risky stocks, mortgages and non-tradable credit claims of commercial banks.

Debt always becomes a problem if it exceeds the capacity of companies, states and households to repay it in the long run.[28] Therefore, if one wants to follow Keynes at this point, the real interest rates of commercial banks should be low enough to allow continuous repayments, no matter whether they result from income, profits or taxes, and there should also be political control of lending, because too high (real) interest rates lead to intensification and extension of working hours, pressure on profit rates and higher taxes. Despite the low interest rate policy of central banks and the oversupply of money and money capital, the real interest rates of private banks have not fallen in the last decades, as mainstream economics would like to think, but have risen. The interest rates of central banks and commercial banks do not have to be synchronised. Only a few institutions can borrow money from the ECB at zero per cent interest rates, while commercial banks set their own interest rates for lending, always assessing the risk of the debtors, calculating their returns and observing the policy of their competitors in lending. It is also important to note that debtors do have the power to influence the supply of money and monetary policy.

Let us summarise: in a monetary system, which has replaced gold, legal money is created in the credit relationship between commercial banks and the central bank. The latter obtain fictitious capital when they grant loans to commercial banks that represent payment claims. Since the financial crisis of 2008, this relationship has shifted. The stability-oriented monetary policy, according to which commercial banks can only lend central

---

[28] Private banks create deposits when they make loans to borrowers, but they do not create the interest, so that there is always more outstanding debt in the system than there is potential to repay the debt. The only way to overcome this structural gap, at least temporarily, includes institutions taking out further loans with a later maturity date compared to the loans extended to earlier institutions. This structural feature of outstanding debt permanently fuels competition for larger yield differentials so that debt can be repaid in the first place.

Moreover, there can be a difference between the total price of commodities and services on the market and the available purchasing power, which in turn makes it necessary to expand lending if the economy is not to slide into recession. This in turn strengthens the power of commercial banks, since governments, most businesses and households can hardly survive without credit.

A third dimension concerns the growth rate of the world economy that would be necessary to repay the outstanding debt, or at least to sustain the debt-based money flows.

bank money against first-class collateral, has generally been abandoned: today, fictitious capital with a high probability of devaluation accumulates at the central banks instead of first-class monetary claims. In fact, it no longer matters what the central banks buy from commercial banks or even the shadow banks in order to provide them with additional reserves; it seems as though it is enough to hope for future economic growth, so that at some point the debts could perhaps be repaid.

With regard to the low interest rate policy of central banks, their supporters argue that it would encourage borrowing by companies and consumers. This has demonstrably failed to happen after the financial crisis of 2008. Instead, this policy is increasing the demand for derivatives, securities, shares, real estate, etc., and with it also the prices of assets. It is also known that the enormous credit money injections by the Fed and other central banks that we have seen since the global financial crash of 2008 have not led to consumer price inflation in any major economy, but instead have led to an increase in financial asset prices. Banks and financial institutions, awash in the largesse of the Fed and other central banks, did not excessively on-lend those funds (either because the large corporation did not need loans or the small ones were too risky to lend). Instead, companies and banks speculated more in the stock, derivative and bond markets, and in the face of low interest rates, borrowed even more, paid out increased shareholder dividends and bought back their own stock to boost prices.

Low interest rates generally reverse the relationship between savings and debt incentives: those who save money receive low amounts of money; those who take out loans, for example to speculate, receive "cheap money" and at least the option of high returns (Stelter 2013: Kindle-Edition: 834).[29] As we have already seen, interest rates and the prices of securities behave inversely to one another. The price increase of assets resulting from low interest rate policy makes those richer who already hold enough assets, such that they prefer all those who invest their assets in securities, shares, real estate and derivatives. This in turn benefits the financial industry, which not only collects fees, bonuses and commissions by trading the assets, but also creates credit and realises returns.[30]

---

[29] The savings rate in the U.S. fell from 11% at the beginning of the 1980s to 1% in 2015. Borrowed money was used mainly for speculation or even for consumption.

[30] In 2015, the majority of long-term corporate loans issued in the Euro zone served to purchase existing real estate, securities and derivatives (€2.4 trillion) (Häring 2016:

264 A. SZEPANSKI

Of course, the negative aspects of the zero interest rate policy for commercial banks must also be taken into account, as it reduces the spread between lending and deposit rates. Moreover, commercial banks today have to pay for parking money at the ECB. Due to the ECB's purchases of government bonds that are considered stable, interest rates are also falling, especially on German government bonds. Thus with 80% of all German government bonds, no more interest payments flow from the state to commercial banks; they must rather pay in order to acquire government bonds.[31]

The industrial companies, in turn, have to struggle with low profit rates and a lack of effective demand due to the over-accumulation crisis. And when the profits of companies rise again, because, for example, interest rates are low, they often buy enough of their own shares to increase their share price. New investments in production only take place when the profit rate on future investments is expected to increase and demand is expected to simultaneously rise.

For a short period, the Fed started to raise key interest rates, probably with a view to lowering them again in the next crisis. The measures introduced relate to short-term interest rates, the change of the central bank balance sheet (sales of government bonds) and the dosage of the adjustments. If central banks raise the short-term interest rate, other interest rates charged for borrowing money to invest and speculate can rise too.

Kindle-Edition; 144). With mortgage loans amounting to €3.9 trillion and consumer loans amounting to €1.2 trillion, private households were in debt, with €1.2 trillion going to other financial institutions; €2 trillion of loans went to countries outside the Euro Zone, €1.1 trillion to other Euro foreigners (Ibid.). With regard to mortgage loans, it can be said that as the price of real estate rises, the assets of homeowners also rise, which in turn serve as collateral for new loans, e.g. consumer loans. The low interest rate policy of central banks strengthens above all the raw material and capital markets, while the speed of money circulation decreases. These are deflationary processes.

[31] After the financial crisis of 2008, Germany in particular benefited from the generation of further fictitious capital, because countries such as China or Brazil made extensive investments with the help of the globally floating fictitious capital and a considerable proportion of their orders for the required capital goods went to German companies. Because the German capital market was not so badly affected by previous financial crises, financial capital seeking investment was also more strongly oriented towards Germany. In addition, German companies can obtain financial capital relatively easily and cheaply, while the German government can sell its government bonds at negative real interest rates, which, driven by both factors, means that the debt of the German national budget remains lower than in other countries and, in the course of this, government interest expenditure also falls.

8 THE FINANCIAL SYSTEM AND THE STATE 265

This effort to regain some space for manoeuvre in monetary policy can be a factor in monetary policy, although this in turn has negative effects on the financial markets and the real economy. If central banks end the low-interest-rate policy, and as a result of which real interest rates would also further rise, many industrial companies, households and many countries, including some of the industrialised countries, could become insolvent. Also, the state cannot make debts arbitrarily, since it is constantly evaluated on the secondary markets. Even cancelling the debt does not fix the problem; for example, the ECB has increased the liquidity of private banks by buying up government and corporate bonds in order to drive their power to create credit, and thus to create bank deposits. This money circulates even if the bonds are written off. At the moment, central banks again stopped raising interest rates.

It also remains unclear what significance the shrinking of the Federal Reserve balance sheet will have with regard to tighter monetary policy. At the same time, debt continues to grow and with it the possibility of external shocks, especially due to the sharp rise in asset prices in parallel with the increase in debt. If these prices fall rapidly, there will probably be a financial collapse, or at least a collapse in the markets, for which even more money will have to be made in response. Higher interest rates can also lead to a stronger dollar and to capital inflows from the emerging markets to the U.S. financial markets, making them even more crisis-prone.

REFERENCES

Binswanger, Mathias (2015) *Geld aus dem Nichts. Wie Banken Wachstum ermöglichen und Krisen verursachen*, Weinheim.

Bourdieu, Pierre (2014) *Über den Staat – Vorlesungen am College de France 1989–1992*, Berlin.

Decker, Peter, Hecker, Konrad and Patrick, Joseph (2016) *Das Finanzkapital*, Munich.

Di Muzio, Tim (2015) *The Plutonomy of the 1%: Dominant Ownership and Conspicuous Consumption in the New Gilded Age*, in: https://journals.sag epub.com/doi/10.1177/0305829814557345.

Gerstenberger, Heide (2017) *Markt und Gewalt. Die Funktionsweise des historischen Kapitalismus*, Münster.

Guattari, Félix (2018) *Planetarischer Kapitalismus*, Berlin.

Häring, Norbert (2016) *Die Abschaffung des Bargelds und die Folgen. Der Weg in die totale Kontrolle*, Cologne.

266 A. SZEPANSKI

Huber, Joseph (2021) *Modern Money Theorie – die falsche Verheißung*, in: https://vollgeld.page/mmt-falsche-verheissung#_ftn3.

ISW-Report (2014) Nr. 97: Wirtschafts-Nato TTIP STOP!.

Kallert, Andreas (2017) *Die Bankenrettungen während der Finanzkrise 2000–2009 in Deutschland*, Münster.

Krüger, Stephan (2015) *Entwicklung des deutschen Kapitalismus 1950–2013. Beschäftigung, Zyklus, Mehrwert, Kredit, Weltmarkt*, Hamburg.

Lazzarato, Maurizio (2021) *Capital Hates Everyone. Fascism or Revolution*, Cambridge.

Leibiger, Jürgen (2016) *Wirtschaftswachstum. Mechanismen, Widersprüche und Grenzen*, Cologne

Lohoff, Ernst and Trenkle, Norbert (2012) *Die große Entwertung. Warum Spekulation und Staatsverschuldung nicht die Ursache der Krise sind*, Münster.

Mau, Steffen (2017) *Das metrische Wir. Über die Quantifizierung des Sozialen*, Berlin.

Mazzucato, Mariana (2014) *Das Kapital des Staates. Eine andere Geschichte von Innovation und Wachstum*, München.

Meister, Robert (2021) *Justice Is an Option: A Democratic Theory of Finance for the Twenty-First Century*, Chicago.

Milios, John (2018) *The Origins of Capitalism as a Social System: The Prevalence of an Aleatory Encounter*, London.

Pistor, Katharina (2020) *The Code of Capital: How the Law Creates Wealth and Inequality*, Princeton.

Porcaro, Mimmo (2015) *Tendenzen des Sozialismus im 21. Jahrhundert: Beiträge zur kritischen Transformationsforschung 4*, Hamburg.

Poulantzas, Nicos (2001) *State, Power, Socialism*, London.

Robinson, William I. (2020) *The Global Police State*, London.

Sahr, Aaron (2017) *Das Versprechen des Geldes. Eine Praxistheorie des Kredits*, Hamburg.

Schreyer, Paul (2016) *Wer regiert das Geld? Banken, Banken, Demokratie und Täuschung*, Frankfurt/M.

Stelter, Daniel (2013) *Die Billionen-Schuldenbombe. Wie die Krise begann und warum sie noch lange nicht zu Ende ist*, Weinheim.

Szepanski, Achim (2016) *Der Non-Marxismus – Finance, Maschinen, Dividuum*, Hamburg.

Szepanski, Achim (2018) *Imperialismus, Staatsfaschisierung und die Kriegsmaschinen des Kapitals*, Hamburg.

Tooze, Adam (2018) *Crashed: Wie zehn Jahre Finanzkrise die Welt verändert haben*, Munich.

Varoufakis, Yanis (2011) *The Global Minotaur: America, The True Origins of the Financial Crisis and the Future of the Global Economy*, London.

Vogl, Joseph (2017) *The Ascendency of Finance*, Cambridge.

Weber, Beat (2015) *Geldreform als Weg aus der Krise? Ein kritischer Überblick auf Bitcoin, Regionalgeld, Vollgeld und die Modern Money Theory*, in: *Prokla 179. Illusion und Macht des Geldes*: 217–237.

Wiegand, Felix (2013) *David Harveys urbane Politische Ökonomie. Ausgrabungen der Zukunft marxistischer Stadtforschung*, Münster.

Wray, Randall I. (2000) *Modern Money Theory: A Primer on Macroeconomics for Sovereign Monetary Systems*, New York.

CHAPTER 9

Capital and the World Market

9.1 Introduction

While there are important parallels between the national market and the world market, the former is not simply a subcategory of the latter. A closer analysis of the world market, which must always be seen in connection with national economies, makes it evident that the world market is more than just an aggregation of states and companies. It is a complex structure, a chain of international relations, flows of commodities and money capital and monetary causal interconnections that are based on the various national states and the various systems of capital power. While the complex structure of the world market develops a certain autonomy, there is no uniform economic structure. The world economy is not simply the sum of its national parts, but is itself a hierarchically differentiated structure within which today the growth of capital exports of corporations of the leading imperialist states is supported, the space for the circulation of capital and the financial industry is expanded, and a complex relationship between leading and subaltern nations is established within the framework of complicated networks of information transmission. Furthermore, international credit relations are expanded, transnational corporations are formed, international trade in derivatives is expanded and peripheral countries are gradually integrated through from the resulting dynamics of capitalist centres into the capitalist world economy by developing the

© The Author(s), under exclusive license to Springer Nature Switzerland AG 2022
A. Szepanski, *Financial Capital in the 21st Century*,
Marx, Engels, and Marxisms,
https://doi.org/10.1007/978-3-030-93151-3_9

269

peripheral countries as markets or low-cost production places. There also exists a loose network, which is constituted by transnational and supranational organisations, which closely cooperate with nation-states to secure the conditions of a transnational accumulation of capital. This is an institutional network, whereby nation-states do not disappear since, on the one hand, they have to produce the conditions for global capital accumulation, and on the other hand, they cannot loose their political legitimacy as a nation.

The expansion of financial markets and the massive export of capital since the 1970s from the U.S., Western Europe and Japan to the peripheral states contributed to the partial deindustrialisation of these developed capitalist countries and led to the import of cheap consumer goods and enabled an export-oriented industrialisation of peripheral states. The foreign exchange reserves that China in particular has generated through its export-oriented growth model, flowed into U.S. government bonds and other financial assets, thus deepening the expansion of financial markets. The countries of the global south and their growth strategies remain dependent on a continuous influx of foreign capital and on foreign sales markets. If capital is withdrawn or the demand for raw materials or consumer goods declines, these countries will face economic problems because the strategies to stimulate domestic demand and thus to avoid foreign markets only work in the long-run. China and other emerging economies at present cannot welcome a decline of neoliberal strategies since they are economically integrated into the neoliberal world order. Today, the establishment of the world market has long since been achieved. Yet, China's entry into the WTO was the last step of integration thus far.

The deepening of the international division of labour and the integration of countries and companies on an economic level always requires corresponding political regulations. The nation-state remains an important regulatory authority, but with the increasing internationalisation of capital, transnational institutions for international regulation are being created, while informal agreements between governments are also taking place. It should be noted that a transformation of political processes that were still related to parliamentary democracy is occurring here, transforming these processes into supranational and expert-dominated institutions that largely elude democratic control - for example, the World Trade Organization (WTO), the International Monetary Fund (IMF), the World Bank, the EU and the European Central Bank. Thus, the cyclical forms of profit movement, especially the production of average profit rates and the tendency of the profit rate to fall and its counter tendencies, can no longer be discussed at the level of national economies alone. Nevertheless, international capital and price movements do not lead to average profit rates on the world market. Instead, national differences in productivity and the development of profit rates are modified in a specific way on the world market.

The financial system is an important economic factor in the world economy, within which companies in different sectors, industries and states are intertwined in a hierarchically organised network (as competitors). The global financial markets have differentiated themselves into complex, multidimensional systems that not only include the money, bond, stock or foreign exchange markets, but also the capital and derivative markets as well as markets for all types of collateral (cf. Sotiropoulos, Milios and Lapatsioras 2013: 118ff.). An important new characteristic of the international financial system is the rapid development of the shadow banking system. At the same time, it must be taken into account that since the cancellation of the Glass Steagall Act of 1933, the separation of commercial banking and investment banking no longer exists for all commercial banks.

From all these points of view, the financial system now accomplishes the following at the international, or rather transnational, level[1]: (1) overcoming the borders and frictions caused by national territorialisation and national restrictions; (2) opening national economies to foreign companies; (3) overcoming the cumbersome nature of traditional industrial production, which is now even becoming "easier" through integration into global supply chains; (4) promotion of international competition (Ibid.). The international financial system has the function of stabilising and strengthening the dominance of big corporations and imperialist states in the world system, while, conversely, the position of a country

---

[1] William I. Robinson assumes that between 1945 and 1973 the world economy remained international (large corporations operated from national territories), while from 1973 onwards, one can speak of a transnational economy, in which state territories are not the basis but rather a complicating factor for capital. For Robinson, here a shift from a world economy to a global economy takes place. Whereas in the stage of the world economy, countries and regions were interconnected through trade and financial flows in an international market, in the new global economy, nations are quasi-organically interconnected through the transnationalisation of production processes, finance and the circuits of capital accumulation (Robinson 2020).

in the world market, the use of its currency in international trade and its military power strengthens the ability of its corporations to increase their power and control over economic resources at the international level. Only few countries have an internationally functioning banking and financial system. Such countries must already have developed foreign trade and an extensive international investment business, which means intensive financial economic relations with other countries.

9.1.1 The Export of Commodities

The volume of exports and imports is currently growing only modestly on the world markets. In 2015, global exports increased by 1.4% and imports by 1.6% (UNCTAD, Trade and Development Report 2016: 5).

On the world market, the existence of different national currencies is reflected in the absence of a single international currency. While at the national level, commodity prices are expressed in the units of a national currency, a decisive transformation is taking place at the international level: the prices of a country's commodities that are exported or circulate in international markets must be transformed from its own currency into a foreign currency. The absence of a general money-equivalent at the international level requires the creation of regulated exchange relationships between the currencies of different countries. Ideally, these exchange relations express the real economic power positions of the various national capitals and their countries in international competition. The resulting deficits or surpluses in the trade and payment balances of the respective countries necessitate certain processes for adjusting exchange rates (revaluation and devaluation of a national currency), which should regulate the correlation between the economic power positions of the countries on the international scale of productivity and the international position of their currencies (but usually cannot do so for structural reasons). Since the 1990s, the international financial system has evolved in such a way that more and more dollar-denominated assets have been produced, with which further capital has been accumulated and which have allowed the financing of permanent balance of payments deficits and surpluses. Thus, the spatial globalisation of production became dependent on the transnationalisation of the financial system, the free flow of capital. At the same time, the inflation generated by the welfare state had to be kept low, while central banks fed sufficient money into the financial markets to guarantee liquidity and thus the security of securities trading.

To survive in the global market, states must free their national money from its limited local validity at least by giving their currencies convertibility. Convertibility here simply means that states confirm the sameness of their currencies as national legal money and as the general money-equivalent, and thus also establish the security that financial capital needs in order to employ international capital movements through the exchange of national currencies (cf. Decker et al., 2016: 116f.). By making their currencies convertible, states enter into a relationship based on mutual trust and bilateral obligations, without, however, eliminating their competitive relationship. The states affirm, on the one hand, that the capital relationship determines the various economic formations at the national level, and that, on the other hand, their respective national means of payment, which represent the abstract wealth of capital, are considered by law the only general equivalent in their own country (Ibid.: 120). Thus, states do not accept foreign money in their own territory as valid or as a general equivalent and, conversely, do not claim the validity of their national money as a general equivalent outside their own territory. By exchanging currencies, however, the national means of payment can function beyond national borders as a means of using foreign currencies, markets and resources.

A domestic central bank confirms the effectiveness of its own national means of payment as cross-border valid money by acting as a liquidity reserve for the exchange of its own currency for foreign currency and vice versa. This also guarantees the money quality of foreign currencies, i.e. the central bank accepts the currency that is considered sovereign in other nations as valid, thus proving the similarity of the foreign currency with its own currency; it also takes and gives foreign exchange in return, which confirms the quality and effectiveness of domestic money beyond national borders. Central banks, which record foreign exchange surpluses, usually invest them in near-liquidity bonds issued by imperialist states. So the German Bundesbank invests its surpluses mainly in fixedinterest securities of the U.S. Treasury (Ibid.: 144). In this way, central banks confirm the monetary quality of the currencies exchanged, but they in no way guarantee the respective quantitative equality of the sums of money, since these are subject to the constantly fluctuating exchange rates produced and regulated in financial markets. Foreign currencies as internationally usable solvency are sizes that can be changed at any time. The special quality of a currency, which represents the productivity and profitability of national capital accumulation, corresponds to the power of imperialist state, which is permanently valued by international financial markets; imperialist states, which leave the valuation of their money to financial capital and financial markets, assume that their means of payment are assigned the economically correct, the external value which is advantageous for the state.

The specific mode of movement of commodities and capital between imperialist countries was studied in more detail in the 1970s by a number of German authors, such as Klaus Busch, Christel Neusüss and Claudia von Braunmühl, using the term "modification of the law of value in the world market" (Neusüss 1975: 105ff.). In this context, a mechanism for balancing the different exchange rates between countries on the world market was identified, especially with regard to the relations between the developed core countries within the imperialist countries, excluding the developing countries. The prices of companies of the less developed countries in this context are thus transformed into average international market prices due to the devaluation of their currency. Exporting companies from economically weak countries can now gain new market shares on the world market with their cheaper commodities precisely because of the devaluation of the domestic currency, while the more expensive imports reduce the volume of foreign commodities at home, thus giving domestic companies greater sales at home. Under the pressure of the deficits in the trade balance, the less developed countries are simply forced to devalue their currencies, while at the same time the surpluses in the trade balance of the developed countries are reduced by the process of revaluation of their currencies (appreciation). The prices of the companies of the more developed countries are modified on the world market by the revaluation of their currencies and move towards the international average. In this process, the extra profits of those companies that produce with higher productivity erode as their national currency is revalued. The dominant positions of companies in a more developed country can now be threatened by local companies in the less developed country on world markets. Certain sectors in the less developed countries, which have higher than average productivity, can now, precisely because of this exchange mechanism, make extra profits in international trade, even in the more developed countries.

In reality, there is little evidence of such a self-regulation of currencies on international currency markets, which is supposed to take place through compensatory exchange rate movements, precisely because the relatively low productivity and profitability of a national economy is also reflected in a low valuation of its currency. Conversely, the higher capital productivity of a country's total capital compared with that of the total capital of a weaker competitor country is reflected in the higher exchange rates of its currency. The large companies of the more developed states are now integrated without exception into the world market and must therefore increase their productivity, for example, by reducing production costs while at the same time facing different national currencies - that is, the exchange rate of the currencies determines to some extent how the production prices, which are calculated in the domestic currency, can stand comparison with those of foreign competitors. The exchange rate of a national currency thus has the status of a business condition for those companies of a country that operate on world markets. With their international operations, the export-strong companies of an economically developed country increase the demand for its money and drive up its exchange rate, while countries with export-weak companies have to permanently fight against a foreign trade deficit that leads to a fall in the exchange rate of their own currency.

A strong currency indicates the superior capital productivity and quality of the production processes of the companies and the financial system of a country. The productivity of companies of a national capital location, which integrates the national total capital, thus also asserts itself in the exchange rates of the domestic currency. The low productivity of companies of a less developed country cannot be eliminated purely by currency manipulation, as described by Neusüss and others. Instead, the devaluation of domestic currency further burdens the balance sheets of importing companies, and only companies with above-average profitability are able to do better business on the world market as a result of devaluation. Cheaper imports, however, include for the highly productive companies of an economically developed country the reduction their production costs, while companies with below-average profitability can target the level of profitability of companies that are successful on the world market.

Thus, exchange rate changes cannot completely eliminate the advantages of companies with high productivity and/or low unit labour costs. If the sales abroad of the strong export-oriented companies with high productivity (measured in foreign currency that has been devalued) decline, this is more likely due to the low productivity of total capital and the low demand of the less developed country. Those companies have to check if the less developed countries can cope with price increases at all.

The successes of imperialist states in world markets, which private banks and other financial institutions process into permanent shifts in exchange rates, modify the conditions of competition between national economies. Access to the rest of the world's supply of goods is now cheaper for companies of the strong competitive countries and more expensive for those in the less competitive countries.

Only a relative stabilisation of exchange rates is achieved on international markets. Ultimately, the reproduction of differences in productivity and profit rates (between the companies of developed countries on the world market) remains decisive for economic power constellations, and thus there is no equalisation of national profit rates at the international level. The devaluation of domestic currency might have a certain protectionist effect for national capitals, but the companies of the countries with the highest international productivity have the power on the international markets to sell their commodities at lower prices than those of their less productive competitors, so that they not only realise extra profits, but can also steadily increase their market shares. This results in significant trade surpluses for the more productive countries, which are offset by the trade deficits of the less productive countries.

Is it at all possible to compare international and national competition? Companies that produce with unequal productivity compete in domestic markets in such a way that capital moves from one sector to another depending on productivity and profitability, until average production prices are finally established. The result of such a development should idealise average profit rates in all sectors, a tendency that goes in the direction of eliminating extra profits and intra-sectoral inequalities, by (a) generalising more innovative techniques within each sector and (b) eliminating companies that cannot modernise their production techniques to the point of reaching the average level of productivity. Such a relatively frictionless and ideal compensation process does not exist at the international level.[2]

---

[2] The traditional theory of international trade is based on two basic theses developed by David Ricardo: (1) free trade is regulated by the theory of comparative costs; (2) it leads to full employment in every nation. The first thesis states that a nation benefits from international trade if it exports a portion of the goods produced at low cost and imports an equally weighted package of production from abroad. In the long run, the values of imports and exports balance each other out, i.e. trade deficits and surpluses are always eliminated, and this applies to rich and poor countries alike. Empirically, of course, this is totally unsustainable, considering that large sections of the proletarian class, which

Exchange rates result from the assessment of the economic strength of currencies in their function as international means of payment, and this in relation to the economic power of a national economy. Important indicators of the economic power of a country and its companies (captured by numerical series and data) include the power of national fictitious and speculative capital and the amount of capital accumulation that a nation's companies can achieve. The use and valuation of national money on the world market then also reveal the international power-political significance of a nation's economy, i.e. its companies and its state. Exchange rates and their modulations also play an important role in the management of internationally composed securities portfolios; the risks created and regulated by them, in turn, allow for a further division of futures transactions.

The trade in the various national currencies gives rise to differences between the currencies, which not only affect their valuation, but also document imperialist power relations, inasmuch as the currencies which serve as functioning money on the international financial market, or even, like the dollar, as the reserve currency, not only represent the creditworthiness of the nation in which they are legal tender, but function as the dominant monetary symbols for global trade and credit. To financial capital, those currencies are per se considered money which redeem what states promise with the convertibility of their currencies, namely to be the designated "value", while the other currencies mutate accordingly into weak competitors of the currencies, which are used as real world money; the former however maintain their right as the sole legal tender within their country, nevertheless functioning for financial capital as locally useful.

The preferred funds for international financial transactions are therefore those currencies that can be used for financial transactions throughout the world. The central banks of all countries also use these currencies as their reserve currencies. Thus, the issuers of the financially

---

currently numbers about three billion people worldwide, are currently unemployed (well over one billion). Moreover, in today's global capitalism, trade imbalances are the rule rather than the exception. Keynesians therefore modify the standard positions of comparative cost theory by bringing into play oligopolies, economies of scale and differential elasticities of demand, technology and technological knowledge. This in turn gives state intervention a certain amount of leeway. For Anwar Shaikh, the fundamental evil of bourgeois theory is already present in Ricardo's theory of comparative costs (Shaikh 2016: 507).

strong currencies have the power to create international solvency themselves as needed, and this freedom is limited in particular by the number of such currencies, insofar as each of them can in principle be replaced by another, which means that their issuers must compete for support from the international financial industry. The economic power of the less developed countries is often based solely on the possibility of acquiring financial resources which the imperialist states constantly feed into the global economy.

Insofar as exchange rates reflect the average level of productivity in countries, companies with low profit rates are generally not adequately protected and are in danger of being eliminated by international competition. If these companies want to recapture their international solvency, they must either lower their production costs by increasing productivity, rely on a reduction in real wages or hope for sectoral national protectionism. If exchange rate fluctuations can protect the more productive industries of less developed countries to a certain extent, the less developed sectors remain relatively unprotected. However, the movements outlined here only affect the economic spaces of the developed capitalist countries and those of the emerging countries. John Smith points out that about 80% of world trade (measured by gross exports) is associated with the international production networks of transnational corporations, with about 60% of world trade, according to UNCTAD, consisting of trade in intermediate goods and services that enter the production process of goods and services for final consumption at various stages (Smith 2016).

None of this applies to the relations between the imperialist states and developing countries. These states can only protect national capital accumulation to a certain extent through measures such as foreign exchange control, capital controls and the nationalisation of the banking sector; but if they are in severe economic crisis, they should not become totally incapable of doing business with imperialist states, so that these states support the countries, which are weak in foreign exchange, with bilateral currency loans, so that they can continue to function as outlets for the export-strong companies of the imperialist states. With payment problems, and even more with the insolvency of a weak state, losses threaten also the trade of commodities of successful nations, as well as losses in the claims or foreign assets of the capital-exporting nations. Maintaining the solvency of weak states and rescuing or even restoring their creditworthiness - perhaps contrary to the pejorative judgement of financial markets - is therefore in the interest of imperialist states, especially the

U.S., whose currency still functions as the reserve currency for the global financial system. The states with the largest volumes of direct investment, trade sales, foreign credit and foreign assets are in any case integrated into the economic policies of the debtor countries and by no means leave the management of the national deficits of the underdeveloped countries to responsible governments. Rather, they are prepared to exchange financial aid for access to state property and the national disposition of the capital of the economically weak developed country. Strictly hierarchical power relations are maintained between the leading world economic powers and the many weak countries, which are notorious losers on the world market. In the event that insolvent states are no longer able to service their debts to several state financiers, the imperialist states then negotiate among themselves measures such as debt rescheduling and debt cuts; above all, with a view to ensure that no creditor state is favoured in the cancellation of debt, or benefits too much from its own credit assistance to the debtor.[3]

9.2   Capital Export

The companies of the developed nations are also expanding their economic power on the world markets by exporting capital. Today, direct investments abroad are still made primarily by companies from North America, Europe and Japan, but increasingly also by those from emerging countries such as China, Russia, India and Brazil. The export of capital from the leading developed countries prevents, on the one hand, the elimination of the less productive capital at home and, on the other hand, the more productive companies from benefiting from new extra profits or super-profits by transferring their monetary capital abroad. Super-profits or super-exploitation means, according to Smith, that the exploitation of

---

[3] While governments can still determine the level of national debt to a certain extent, the interest rate on government bonds is regulated on the international financial markets. And if certain states and their banks are considered particularly crisis prone, the capital market risk of both increases and the interest rates on government bonds rise. There are always financial players who push the devaluation of the wealth of entire nations with all available financial instruments by betting on and earning from rising interest rates, falling security prices and a decline in the currency. Losses can also mutate into a source of profits by means of derivatives trading. Traders make money from the insolvency of companies and from national bankruptcy, which they help to bring about themselves.

280   A. SZEPANSKI

the workers of the global South occurs less through an expansion of absolute and relative surplus value, but rather through the reduction of wages below the average value of labour power (Smith 2016: 10).

For a capital-exporting company, a certain amount of money in a foreign country acts as a capital advance with which it tries to increase its capital. On the one hand, the corresponding transactions indicate the company's power to generate investments in other countries; on the other hand, it must also be able to take into account the expectations of financial investors from all over the world. There are two forms of capital export: on the one hand, foreign direct investment, where the production process is moved abroad but remains as property within the company itself, and on the other hand, companies that outsource part or all of the production process to an independent supplier (independent in the sense that the leading company does not own any of it, even if it controls the activities in production in many respects).[4] Transnational corporations, which still have their headquarters in imperialist countries, are today the strongest drivers of the globalisation of production. Their structuring of production processes in low-wage countries thus takes two basic forms: first, the "in-house" relationship between the parent company and its foreign subsidiary, and second, an "arm's-length" relationship with formally independent suppliers.

In many cases today, direct in-house relationships with a subsidiary are transformed into business relationships with independent suppliers simply by signing some legal documents, without making any changes in working conditions or labour processes, the prices of inputs or the profits that accrue when the output is sold (Ibid). A western company can also buy machinery and pass it off as a capital contribution to a local company in emerging markets, where the machinery is installed. The local company can use the machinery as collateral to get a local bank loan and has the opportunity of bringing money out of the country.[5] This, however, is not

---

[4] Smith describes four types of direct investment: (a) the efficiency-seeking formation, which implies a reduction in costs, especially labour costs; (b) the market-based investment, which takes place mainly between imperialist countries themselves, and urges the proximity of production places to consumers; (c) the resource-seeking direct investment in the extractive (fossil) industries; (d) direct investment based on transfers of technology, which is almost exclusively between imperialist countries (Smith 2016: 70).

[5] Smith summarises that the South-North export of industrial goods should be read not so much as a trade but as an expression of the globalisation of production, and this in turn not only as a technical transformation of machines and other means of production, but as

the only way in which financial overrides transform production relationships when, for example, transferred profits being reinvested in financial assets is considered.

By exporting capital, the imperialist state gains a further increase in power as a result of the economic strength of its leading national companies in another country. By importing capital, the latter then agrees to the economic power of foreign companies in its own country without major problems. This aspect not only concerns the political sovereignty of states, since they are always to be understood on their own territories as capital locations and transfer points, that is, as economic authorities. Capital exports and imports lead to corresponding movements in the balance of payments of states, changes in their foreign exchange sums and requires certain regulations for liabilities. If the profits earned abroad are transferred into the domestic currency, the economic power of domestic capital is increased, and this naturally strengthens the validity of the domestic currency as an international means of payment (different in the case of capital flight). With capital imports, a country's own stock of foreign currency increases and, depending on its power on the world market, is used for further business or for foreign loans in order to incur further debts in foreign money.

However, it must also be emphasised that today there is a hegemonic faction of capital at the global level, i.e. transnational corporations and financial companies that drive the global economy. These corporations have internationalised markets through networks that transcend national boundaries. They operate largely independently of their original states, though they still have their headquarters there. On the one hand, transnational capital instrumentalises states all over the world, and on the other, every country is dependent on the circuits of transnational capital. In this context, states must provide positive conditions for this kind of capital accumulation, i.e. create both a positive climate for profits and repressive (and symbolic) rules for the proletariat that serve capital.

---

the development of a social relationship, namely that between capital and labour. International competition between companies to increase profits, market share and shareholder value proceeds in cyclical movements. An important feature of the neoliberal globalisation of production is the outsourcing of individual segments and links of production processes, the fragmentation of production and the splitting of global supply chains by means of logistics. Thus, the old notion of a North–South trade of raw materials for finished goods as an imperialist function has become obsolete (Smith 2016: 267).

To the extent that capital exports are financed with loans, the importing national economies mutate into investment spheres not only for foreign industrial capital but also for financial capital. Through crediting, financial capital provides internationally operating companies with further opportunities for gaining access to labour, means of production and resources in foreign countries, thus creating investment opportunities for themselves on the world market. Financial capital, which is already involved in and organises foreign exchange trading, now also claims the economies of other countries as an economic resource and addressee. It thus mediates and finances not only the trade of commodities, but also the export and import of capital; it acts as a lender and borrower of monetary capital with all functional floating currencies on the world market. Financial capital imports and exports monetary capital, participates worldwide in the trade of securities and derivative and transfers funds abroad and receives them in return, thus generating the world market as a specific financial space where major banks and other financial institutions decide in which currency monetary capital, be it credit, fictitious or speculative capital, is created and traded. To put it another way, currencies are now not simply involved in the relations of supply and demand for commodities, resulting in floating exchange rates, but are given the function of being available for further expansive operations of financial capital. The creation of credit, with which domestic banks are already making future wealth available, is being extended abroad by financing the export of capital.

By exporting capital, corporations in foreign countries participate in capital growth and accumulate foreign wealth, while at the same time, the national currency is strengthened in foreign investment as internationally recognised world money. In exporting capital, not only do companies make profits by exploiting foreign resources and labour, but the imperialist nation also increases its foreign wealth. With the import of capital, a developed economy and its imperialist state participate in a sum of capital, but it still remains at the disposal of the foreign capital-exporting company. For an imperialist country, the import of capital increases its solvency, thus increasing the potential for capitalist growth at home. Since capital import still remains dependent on the national sovereignty of the importing country, import is often influenced by strategic political considerations and occasionally, intended foreign investments in sectors and industries are prohibited because of security policies. The cross-border business relations that companies maintain among themselves and with their global customers are to a certain extent also political affairs of the state, giving to capitalist business and financial transactions a liability that other states cannot easily ignore or override by law. At the same time, the international financial markets are mutating into a quasi-supranational authority, where not only are companies participating in world markets continuously evaluated and regulated, but where information is always provided about the economic potential of a state as a capital location. The national debt of an imperialist country functions well as monetary capital if it is widely traded internationally as government bonds, with which the demand for its own currency increases.

It is not the state's responsibility to strengthen all companies in the country's export industry. Rather, only those companies whose profitability stands up to international competition with highly productive foreign companies are worthy of support, i.e. in particular groups whose size (profit mass) and profitability (profit rate) can stand up to international competition with other groups. Imperialist states constantly monitor creditworthiness with respect to the potential of their companies to transform every sum of money borrowed and invested into accumulating monetary capital. This requires a policy of growth that, on the one hand, creates favourable conditions for the accumulation of domestic capital and, on the other, shows international financial markets that the fictitious capital of one's own nation is profitable or at least secure. The negative effects of a too generous monetary and budgetary policy to support growth, which concerns the value of one's own national currency, must be avoided, i.e. the promotion of national credit creation must keep an eye on inflation. Any potential economic weakness, especially of the expected economic growth of a country, i.e. the possibility of inflation and a rising level of indebtedness of companies and the state, is identified, analysed and comparatively valued on financial markets by rating agencies and analysts. This is also done by permanently fixing the exchange rates of currencies and the interest rates at which companies and the state can obtain loans on the financial markets. As a result, states have long since ceased to be free in structuring their budgets, neither in the use nor in the procurement of their financial resources, which is why a permanent monetary policy is needed that influences the trade of national money on the foreign exchange markets in such a way that national money circulates as smoothly as possible internationally, while at the same time its external value remains stable.[6]

Exports of capital to the global South are characterised by a number of incentives for Western companies, such as deregulations or special forms of regulation, the appropriation of cheap raw materials and the exploitation of cheap labour in labour-intensive sectors of industry. The development of "export processing zones" can now be found in more than 130 countries, which alludes to the fact that industrial development is unevenly distributed but widespread in the global South. According to the World Bank, an export-processing zone is an industrial area, usually a fenced area of 10 to 300 hectares, specialised in production for export. It offers firms free trade conditions and a liberal regulatory environment (Smith 2016: 288). At issue here are duty-free imports of raw materials, intermediates and capital goods, flexible labour laws, long-term tax incentives and an infrastructure that in these zones is more developed than in other parts of the country. Especially in countries like China, where the price of labour is still relatively low, companies of developed capitalist countries still transfer parts of their production, i.e. massive capital imports occur in China, while the goods produced there are re-imported into developed countries. This is a special form of direct investment. The new form of globalisation is also based on an implicit pact between the financial capital of the leading countries and the economies of the emerging countries. While the latter also gain access to commodity markets in the West and receive a flood of direct investment from the large multinationals, the former countries have entered into agreements (TRIPS, Gatt, GATS) to protect the patents and property rights of domestic companies, create markets for services and open foreign markets for their own corporate controls. Emerging economies have been able to take advantage of competitive costs in wages, producing mainly "low-tech" consumer goods with imported technologies, then exporting them to the core capitalist countries and fighting weaker companies there.

---

[6] The industries of global South usually manufacture their products at relatively low profit rates, while at the same time, trade with industrialised countries is often asymmetrical enough, despite the integration of their own companies in international supply chains (industrial products versus raw materials or agricultural products). Samir Amin has identified a fundamental asymmetry between imperialist centres and the periphery, particularly in the fact that there is an unequal exchange related more to real wages than to the productivity of the different countries. According to Amin, unequal amounts of labour are still exchanged between the industries of different countries (Amin 2010: 134).

But they are now also increasingly investing in research, which, however, still relies mainly on creative imitation and adaptation, but is also intended to promote innovations that help reduce the technological gap between highly technologised core countries. In key industries such as robotics, IT, space, aviation and maritime travel, renewable energies and electro-mobility, China aims to catch up technologically with the core Western countries by 2035. Moreover, Chinese companies have increased labour productivity while still keeping labour costs low. We are now seeing the emergence of hypercapitalised centres in emerging markets and peripheries, while "third world zones" are emerging in the centres of the global North. All in all, it can be said that today, the capital of the twenty-first century increasingly acts as if the globe were its sole economic zone, integrating trade, circulation and production.

9.3 THE FINANCIAL INDUSTRY AND THE WORLD MARKET

The liberation of the financial system from the barriers of mere national money is an important component of the monetary interdependence of national economies on the world market and leads to a comprehensive internationalisation of the financial system. The rise of the transnational financial industry might be the most important historical development in the epoch of globalisation - this refers to the construction of a monstrous global complex, which leads to a new concentration of socio-economic power, including the mandates with which this industry points to states and other factions of capital. The owners, managers and directors of financial corporations sit today at the centre of the nodes of global economies. The global stock market, for example, has more than doubled in size from 2003 to 2017, passing the $100 trillion mark.

States themselves have to create certain conditions for the international transactions of the financial system by issuing rules for payment transactions between national payment systems; they offer insurance for certain transactions or provide guarantees for the regular payment of exports and grant licenses to foreign financial companies for business activities in their own countries. In addition, national central banks manage currency trading in accordance with the rules set by the national exchange rate. In order to smooth erratic price movements on the world markets, a whole range of other measures are installed. The balance of foreign trade and the balance of payments and exchange rate movements are important parameters that indicate the constant efforts of a national economy and its companies in the competition for the exploitation of monetary capital, which is circulating on the world market.

Companies that are limited in the growth of their own national market due to a lack of demand and therefore need to expand in the world market, need a developed banking system that organises the circulation of the respective national currencies. The services provided by private banks to exporting and importing companies are expanded with their own credit transactions, with which they take special risks for companies in foreign business, for example, by guaranteeing the creditworthiness of domestic companies to foreign business partners according to the rules of their country and at the same time save the rights of domestic companies against foreign business partners (Decker, Hecker and Patrick 2016: 126). Private banks do not function merely as service providers for export and import transactions, but above all as organisations for their own profitable credit transactions. They trade the arbitrage of currencies by buying cheaply across currency borders and selling expensively. With freely floating exchange rates, private banks, with their international money movements, constantly re-establish the valuation of currencies among themselves.

Speculative uncertainty or risk always remains part of the accumulation of monetary capital; this in turn is a resource for insurance transactions and derivatives trading. Various key figures, indices and parameters can become the object of financial speculation. The national differences between growth rates, interest rates, national debt ratios, degrees of inflation, exchange rates, etc. and their fluctuations, include a risk potential that is managed through the trading of securities and derivatives, i.e. a molecular evaluation of monetary performance and flow sizes occurs, which are fundamentally uncertain in their progression and therefore have to be hedged with a variety of derivative instruments (which can but need not be a profitable business for some companies). With these processes, the international financial system creates a sales volume of enormous dimensions and drives the accumulation of capital on a global scale and evaluates and influences the hierarchy of states and their currencies as well as that of transnational companies in global competition. A distinction can be made between the powerful nations, whose economies function more or less smoothly as both a source of credit and as an investment sphere for monetary capital, i.e. as successful financial centres, and the less powerful nations, whose economies do not have such capacities. Certain financial companies organise speculative endurance tests for countries where doubts about their creditworthiness arise, whether fundamental data such as inflation rates or the increase in public debt are precarious in relation to economic growth, or whether speculation on future growth in the territory in question is overheated, which is why financial institutions react with higher interest rates on government bonds. The power with which the financial industry functionalises states and corporations for its own business always exists in the form of currencies, which in turn are heavily influenced by imperialist states. In general, all countries must strive to make profits abroad for their companies to generate foreign exchange.

9.4   Imperialism

Financial capital and financial markets have played an increasingly important role within the world economy during the twentieth century. Over time, the constant monitoring of stock and foreign exchange rates and bond yields became increasingly important for large corporations and developed countries, especially at the international level. Today, the trade of fictitious and speculative capital, although it is racing at the speed of light in digitalised infrastructures around the globe, is still concentrated in local places, mainly in the major financial centres such as New York, Chicago, Hong Kong, Shanghai, Frankfurt, Paris, Tokyo and London. By financing the international trade in commodities, the export and import of capital, the expansion of securities and derivatives trading and global foreign exchange trading, the major private banks, hedge and investment funds are constantly creating new resources for themselves and their customers to increase their monetary capital.

In recent years, debates over the concept of imperialism have resumed, though in a very different sense than Lenin or Hilferding discussed twentieth-century imperialism. In *The City*, Tony Norfield summarises his own definition of imperialism, which is oriented to the actuality of the processes of today's world market: a small number of imperialist states today form a hierarchical alliance in the world market, which is simultaneously constituted by large multinational corporations that produce and trade enormous quantities of goods and services in the global supply chains and capitalise capital of all kinds and financial services. Economist Christian Marazzi also speaks of a historical period in which finance is "cosubstantial" with the production of commodities and services. William

I. Robinson, in turn, assumes the dominance of transnational corporations on the world market, especially financial corporations, which also invest deeply in media companies, industry, trade and the global military-industrial-security complex. This enormous concentration of economic power is translated into the centralisation of globally influential zones of political authorities that include the IMF, World Bank, WTO, G7 and G20 states, among others. Members of transnational capital also occupy important positions in national governments, especially in finance, central banks and often defence ministries (Robinson 2020).

Large international companies invest today in industrial capacities, but less in their own economies. The liberalisation of world trade, the collapse of the Soviet Union and the development of logistics enabled large corporations in the capitalist core countries to create new sources of profit and investment opportunities in the global South, while the prices of their inputs fall due to cheap imports from the South. The economic centres of power on the world market are thus based on a complex interplay between imperialist states, which through the provision of material and social infrastructure, are the starting platforms for developed capital, and the large transnational corporations, whose monetary capital constantly flows around the globe. In the last instance, states are now dominated by transnational capitalist war-machines (Lazzarato 2021). While the economic power relations between the leading capitalist economies (in total) remain strictly hierarchical, the relative power of the individual countries and their economies can always shift. For Norfield, the result is a division of the world based on the expansive exercise of economic, political and military power by states and their large corporations in accordance with the transnational power of transnational companies (Norfield 2016: Kindle-Edition: 189f.).

The leading imperialist states themselves must reach a certain economic scale in order to achieve a high concentration of capital and a developed and differentiated labour market at home, as well as favourable access to economic resources on world markets and, to a certain extent, control over international capital flows. The leading hegemonic power in the international geo-economic and geo-political comparison is still the United States, primarily because of its military strength and the dollar as the lead currency. Norfield specifically mentions five criteria that are decisive for a country's economic and political power position in the world market: (1) the size of a country's economy (an approximate measure is GDP); (2) the amount of foreign assets that a nation has at its disposal;

(3) the international power of its own banking sector; (4) the status of its currency as an internationally accepted means of payment; (5) the level of military spending (Ibid.: 1960ff.).

Finally, a country's position of political and economic power on the world market can only be identified if its economic and political relations with other countries are taken into account. Norfield concludes that today twenty countries occupy important and leading positions on the world market, particularly because of the strength and potency of their economies. The U.S. occupies the leading position in four of the five criteria listed above, and only in terms of the size of its own banking system and its services in the international context (interbank trade) is it surpassed by Great Britain with its financial centre London. Due to the high number of banks and direct investments related to foreign assets, the U.K. is in second place, even before Germany (ranked fourth), which is considered the leading political power in Europe. China ranks third as the leading "emerging market", which must be taken seriously by Western industrialised countries (Ibid.: 2060).[7] At the lower end of the scale are countries that are primarily interesting for both the Western industrialised countries and the emerging markets as suppliers of cheap raw materials, energy, food and labour (Moore 2015) and are therefore, for example, permanently monitored and evaluated on the commodity exchanges. A special role is played by the oil states, which, because of their unique natural product of oil, have gained a high share of the abstract wealth on the world markets and are now themselves trying to establish new locations for the creation of credit and for the trading of fictitious and speculative capital at an international level.[8]

---

[7] In a recent article, Norfield updated the ranking, putting China second. As he writes: "Five dimensions of international power can be used to gauge the status of countries. These show not only how the US is far more prominent in the hierarchy than suggested by a simple measure of economic size, such as GDP. They also map the relative importance of other countries and throw new light on a major geopolitical issue today: the rise of China" (Norfield 2021).

[8] Certain mechanisms for stabilising the latently endangered solvency of nations are institutionalised on an interstate basis. For countries with problems of their balance of payments, the IMF acts as a lender according to established rules. It takes money for this from a fund into which all of its participants pay according to a formula that reflects their economic strength. Each member has access to means of payment for its foreign obligations in accordance with its quota and to the extent of allocated special drawing rights. In recent decades, however, the IMF has focused its attention in particular on countries with weak economies, which are granted extensive loans to bridge phases of illiquidity

290   A. SZEPANSKI

The big companies of the imperialist countries and transnational corporations have important economic advantages on the world market (they can set prices, i.e. they can offer products, services and money capital at comparatively low prices and they produce their goods with the most effective and the cheapest technologies) and take, often underestimated, a powerful position in the networks of national economies and in those of the world economy, the latter also on account of their intensive relations with their own state. Indeed, imperialist states massively protect the property rights of their own companies (patents) and, through a series of political measures, strengthen their economic power in international trade and in the expansion of foreign direct investment. Last but not least, they secure, especially in crises, the solidity of their own currency and thus act as public insurance institutions for capital. The powerful financial companies enjoy permanent support from their national base, even if it is only the privileged access to their own currency that they receive through the domestic central bank. Politico-economic power relations differ on the world market with the differential accumulation of national capital, competition among transnational corporations and power struggles between different countries.

Today, the economic power of large corporations on the world markets particularly unfolds through global supply chains, i.e. through densely networked and transversal spaces constituted by infrastructures, information, goods and social actors and flow through money capital streams. These transnational spaces with their nodes, lines and borders are traversed by material and immaterial flows of logistics and flows of capital. Digital programmes, such as *Enterprise Resource Planning* (ERP), which

and restore their creditworthiness. For a number of national payment problems that go beyond short-term balance-of-payments difficulties, the IMF grants loans that far exceed the drawing rights acquired with membership and the payment of the national quota, as well as the regularly allocated special drawing rights. In return, the IMF is allowed to borrow from its solvent members. What was originally conceived as financial aid for the rapid settlement of deficits in the management of national foreign debt has developed into a supranational regime that decides on the budgetary, foreign trade and debt policies of numerous IMF members, especially in the category of developing countries. The goal remains the (re)establishment of the creditworthiness of the credited nations as part of the usable resources for the growth interests of the imperialist states. Loans aimed at the strengthening of the productivity of the national economy, but which are not considered lucrative for private financial institutions, are granted by the World Bank, a sister organisation of the IMF, which, like the IMF itself, ensures the integration of all nations into the world market.

converts and combines information on warehousing, production and human resources and are stored in databases into key figures, also open up new ways of calculating the supply chains by which a company is integrated (Lee and Martin 2016: 169). We can think here of outsourcing, the competition between different production places and the calculation of supply routes, for example, on the oceans, which are made possible on the basis of the valuation of different parts of a company. Logistics transforms the factory into divided and around the globe-distributed networks of production and circulation, which do not eliminate the territories of nation-states, but redesign them.

If, as we have already seen, foreign suppliers supply parts for a product that are assembled in the final production process in the factories of a corporation based in a developed industrialised country, the corporation does not have direct access to the suppliers. But if they are located in low-wage countries, they remain entirely tied to the production cycles of the corporations in rich countries (e.g. Foxconn). Based on UNCTAD data, Smith assumes that today, about 80% of world trade is conducted through the production and distribution networks of internationally operating companies, and it would therefore be wrong to focus in the analysis of world market relations and global supply chains only on the data available on foreign direct investment (Smith 2016: 50). UNCTAD estimates that about 60 per cent of global trade comprises intermediary products and services at various stages of production. Take, for example, the IPhone, which is designed and constantly redesigned in Silicon Valley, while the individual parts are manufactured and assembled in Asia (Foxconn) for production costs of about $225 and then shipped as a product to the U.S. ($85 transport costs), where it is finally sold for $650. Today, we are dealing with a super-exploitation of workers in the global South, orchestrated by certain transnational corporations, with profits constantly transferred to the northern imperialist countries. A large and still growing proportion of those workers integrated into global supply chains are now in the emerging markets. Much of global industrial production has thus been shifted from the North to the South, whether it be the t-shirts made in Bangladesh or the latest electronic gadgets in China; the stream of abstract wealth, which is created by Chinese and other low-paid workers and maintains and increases the profits and prosperity of companies and nations of the global North, does not appear in the economic data of Western institutes and economists. Smith argues here that outsourcing to foreign countries is a deliberate strategy of capital of the leading imperialist countries, shifting the entrepreneurial risk to suppliers and especially to countries where trade unions are weakly organised and where capital can therefore successfully pursue strategies to reduce wages and social costs, while at the same time intensifying the exploitation of workers in developed countries, which goes hand in hand with the expansion of employment in low-wage countries[9] (Ibid.: 22).

The power of the state depends also on the economic strength of multinational companies on the world market, which have extensive international trade and production networks. The state, in turn, supports companies by protecting property rights (patents) and negotiating certain economic agreements. Oligopolistic companies and imperialist states are therefore mutually dependent, while capital dominates in the last instance. What characterises a leading multinational company is not only its economic size and productivity, its degree of networking or market success, its global "value" for certain products or services, but also the backing of its own imperialist state and the advantages that can be derived from this membership. But today, the problem arises that some financial institutions are not simply too big or too networked, but are simply far too big to be saved by state subsidies in critical situations. These mega-corporations are permanently engaged in significant international business operations and have an enormous political lobby in their own and in foreign countries. As transnational corporations, they mostly continue to be related to a singular national economy, to the extent that they have a single national headquarters and from there expand abroad through hostile takeovers, mergers and investments. Powerful capitalist corporations, transnational companies and imperialist states are the key players on the world markets today, inasmuch as they can almost set all the important conditions for international trade, the financial system, cross-border investment flows and, finally, derivatives trading. However, the governments of imperialist states always set certain limits to the market operations of international corporations, and these limits are sometimes negotiated between the states themselves. Thus, products to be sold abroad may be subject to high local taxation and import tariffs, or they

---

[9] The one hundred largest multinational companies - Royal Dutch Shell leads in terms of sales, ahead of Exxon, Toyota and Volkswagen - have an average of 549 branches, with two-thirds of the branches located abroad. Siemens, for example, produces and today sells in more than 200 countries.

may not be sold at all because they fail to meet certain industrial and environmental standards abroad; exports to one's own country may be stopped, as the U.S. and EU do with their restrictions on certain agricultural imports from Africa; or conversely, foreign industries may be weakened by their cheap exports. Some companies profit from the restrictions on foreign products in their domestic countries and then expand their positions on the world market. But in return, they also generate income, employment and higher tax revenues for the foreign state. While certain companies that operate particularly intensively in the world market do not necessarily have the abstract wealth of their own nation in mind, imperialist states will always seek to promote both the expansion of their own companies and their own country as a capital location and ultimately the domestic economy as a whole. The more economic resources a country possesses, the more powerful is its state, and this in turn is to the advantage of its own companies and also to privileged parts of its own population.

When analysing the world market, the respective access of multinational companies to the internationally active financial industry must always be taken into account. Indeed, globally operating corporations require their financial services - consider here the stability of international payment systems, the role of foreign exchange in international trade, long-term investments, securities and derivatives trading, short-term loans and generally the exchange of money for money. The important functions of the financial system for the capital economy can today only be fully assessed in an international framework. While there is a differentiated division of labour within the financial system itself (i.e. bank lending, securities management, currency trading, stock and bond markets, etc.), its most important organisations and operations are concentrated in only a few developed countries. Financial capital generally arises from the necessities of the market economy of capital and is also an important instrument for the leading imperialist countries and their companies to maintain and improve their privileged status in the world market, with the financial industries managing assets and income from all kinds of countries. In the economically developed countries, it is not only the famous 1% of the super-rich who benefit from the financial status of their own country on the world market, but a much higher proportion of the population, with even workers and employees still holding financial securities that are in turn traded on the world markets. Also, financial institutions with a high turnover, such as insurance companies and pension funds, are mostly located in rich countries, since there are population groups there that are financially able to invest in such funds.

Easy access to one's own currency via a local central bank can significantly increase the economic influence of (financial) companies on other countries. Although a U.S. bank, which is located in France, for example, is subject to certain restrictions there, it can offer, due to its links with U.S. financial capital and the Fed, U.S. companies and also companies from other countries cheaper access to the dollar in France. Financial companies have a better chance of expanding on the world market if their countries already have a dominant position in global trade, direct investment and securities trading, and if financial transactions are to a large extent conducted in their own currency. The economic power also lies in the potential to grant large sums of credit and to get easy access to credit markets, which in turn means being able to borrow at relatively low interest rates anywhere in the world. All in all, this means to take an influential position in global financial networks. This depends also on the state to which a financial company belongs, since the state provides the technological infrastructure absolutely necessary to enable the economic expansion of the company.

Norfield cites three important factors that indicate how the financial sector plays a dominant role in the economy of an imperialist country and especially also in the world economy (Norfield 2016: Kindle Edition: 2926ff.):

a) The use of funds from abroad to lend to domestic companies and to the state. Today, this can be done in particular by U.S. financial companies (due to the dollar in its function as a global reserve currency) and by the London-based banking system.

b) The financing of investments made abroad by domestic companies in order to set up surplus value production processes abroad. This can be done through bank financing or through the stock markets, allowing further concentration of capital across national borders.

c) The appropriation of part of the globally produced surplus, as the major private banks and investment funds of the imperialist states extend loans and other financial securities to domestic and foreign companies and states. Each of these financial advantages of the companies of an imperialist state also depends on their privileged relations with certain other privileged states.

9.5 The Dollar as Leading Currency

The end of the dollar's convertibility into gold announced by Richard Nixon in 1971 was due in particular to the growing efficiency of German and Japanese companies vis-à-vis American companies, the rising costs of the U.S. war in Vietnam and the costs of the country's own welfare state. The resulting increase in the U.S. foreign trade deficit led to more and more dollars flowing out of the country than coming back in the form of exports, thus further increasing the demand for the dollar worldwide, while the U.S. gold reserves, which served to cover the dollar, did not grow at the same rate. Nixon's decision to abolish the gold standard also made it clear that material-value reserves such as gold are not simply replaced by non-material-value reserves, but rather, unlike gold, they can be multiplied, since they can be constantly re-produced and multiplied without much detour. After the end of Bretton Woods, the American government successively reduced the costs of the welfare state, intensified intra-capitalist competition between companies at home and then exported it to the world market through direct investment, and finally, and this is crucial, built the hegemonic U.S. financial system, which created a new global space for the circulation of financial capital and which also made it possible for large sums of over-accumulated capital to be absorbed and productively applied worldwide.

Today, the leading global reserve currency is still the U.S. dollar, which in 2013 was 90% of all global transactions. The U.S. uses the dollar for almost 100% of its exports and 90% of its imports. In 2013, EU countries used the Euro as the accounting currency for 2/3 of their exports outside Europe and for 50% of their imports (Ibid.: 2954). Commodities of all kinds on the world market are therefore still most often priced and paid with the dollar. For U.S. companies, this means that the risks associated with the volatility of exchange rates are lower than for companies in other countries. It is generally less costly and less risky for a company to use its own currency for financial transactions, and even multinational companies usually use only one country's currency for their business and that is the one in which the company's headquarters are located. When currencies are particularly volatile, it is especially important for a company to have a strong domestic currency for its exports and imports. Many wealthy individuals and companies in turn hold large amounts of dollars because the currencies of their own countries are unstable and the dollar is the most widely used and accepted currency in the world. Thus, more than

60% of the dollar circulated outside the U.S. after 2000 (Ibid.: 2984). This, too, benefits the U.S., but of course it also makes the dollar more vulnerable to the volatility of exchange rate systems.[10]

[10] The possession of a global reserve currency makes it possible the threat of inflation and currency devaluation and, if necessary, to use them effectively. A reserve currency can be aggressive, because it can lead to foreign trade deficits (Triffin dilemma) and to a debt bubble for the very state that owns the reserve currency. However, the debt bubble can mutate into a weapon that remains a kind of explosive. As Heiner Mühlmann appropriately puts it, one can detonate the weapon, but then you have to make sure that it does not blow up in your own country, but in other countries (Mühlmann 2013).

After the end of Bretton Woods, the free floating of currencies led to a increased demand for the dollar, which continued to act as the reserve currency, although this did not necessarily equate to the demand for commodities and services from the U.S.. Above all, the oil and raw materials transactions that were still processed in dollars worldwide, generated a constant demand for the dollar, and this was particularly evident in the 1970s in the case of the petrodollars, which flowed in large quantities to Wall Street, where they were immediately converted into government bonds, stocks and securities. Moreover, because the dollar could continue to be used as a privileged means of payment on a global scale, there were large dollar holdings by companies and private individuals around the world, who tried immediately to reinvest the money capital on Wall Street in funds, shares, government bonds, and later in hedge funds and derivatives, thus more or less voluntarily fuelling the creditworthiness of the U.S. and its financial industry. The military-economic complex also solidified the economic hegemony of U.S. capital. This constantly absorbed and recycled the flows of money capital from other states and foreign companies and recycled them by undauntedly boosting imports into the own country.

As long as the dollar continues to function as the global reserve currency and means of circulation, the hegemonic role of the U.S. economy on a global scale remains secure (supported by the military complex). However, at the beginning of 2000, the U.S. economic decline accelerated, especially vis-à-vis China, and the dollar's international strength also declined. While the world's central banks still held around 70 per cent of their currency reserves in U.S. dollars in 2000, this fell to just 60 per cent by 2010. In 2017, the goal was to reach the 50 per cent mark such that it cannot be completely excluded that a further decline will lead to a mass exodus from the dollar. Furthermore, the question must be asked how long the U.S. will be able to internationally hold the function of a hyper sovereign by successfully using its monstrous war capacity and the world's leading currency, the dollar (Ibid.: 111). This also makes it possible to devalue one's own currency, so that one pays back debts nominally but not in real terms. This is particularly important if one floods one's own markets with mortgage loans and sells the corresponding CDS abroad, which were paid with one's own currency, whereby the later devalued currency of the dollar leads to massive losses for the buyers of the CDS.

Today, the issuance of bonds, government bonds and loans must always be covered by CDS insurance. When banks grant loans, they take out CDS insurance, possibly also abroad, which means that the risk can be exported abroad (Ibid.: 59). It is precisely the combination of the world's reserve currency and the massive use of derivatives such as CDSs that enables the U.S. to export crises abroad or to transfer entropy. This happens in the context of the virality of CDS insurances, which, qua cloning, continue to develop

The decisions of the Fed continue to influence the global economy today, just as international money capital flows influence the financial industry in the U.S. The U.S. can reduce its external deficits by lending its own currency at low cost and as a low-risk financial asset while achieving high reflows/returns on assets invested abroad.

U.S. government bonds are risk-free debt insofar as they are affordable with the Fed's dollar issuance (or even with the collection of taxes). The Fed can also buy up circulating U.S. government bonds themselves. At the same time, government debt can generally be monetised relatively easily on financial markets (the repayment aspect recedes here), thus often creating an implicit compulsion for governments to make budget cuts (austerity), because new money has to be borrowed constantly by issuing government bonds, which implies further relatively risk-free investments for the private sector to make even riskier deals (Lee and Martin 2016: Kindle Edition: 147). This dollar-related option also opens up the possibility of increasing the financial liquidity associated with oil, because options can be used to hedge the price of oil and the dollar so that the price of oil can rise without the value of the dollar falling. Oil reserves now become a financial asset in themselves, becoming all the more valuable the more volatile the oil price.

With its loans and assets, the U.S. generates higher returns abroad than it pays foreign companies. If exchange rate effects are taken into account, the yield advantage of the U.S. in this area has been 3.3% since 1973 (Häring 2016: 173). The U.S. and its companies can also use financial resources around the world, and thus have easier access to financial funds on world markets than other countries and their companies, because the dollar accounts for two-thirds of all official foreign exchange reserves worldwide. Many countries have currencies that are closely linked to the dollar. From 2000 onwards, however, the U.S. recorded a growing currency deficit due to a strong influx of monetary capital, when Asian central banks in particular bought U.S. government bonds and securities denominated in the dollar en masse, and China's currency reserves

---

into differential chain letters, in which the time delay is integrated. The last buyers that enter the chain before a credit event such as insolvency occurs are the losers. For example, before the subprime crisis, U.S. banks sold their derivatives/CDS abroad on a massive scale to hedge unsecured mortgage loans, with CDSs having to be paid out when bankruptcies and insolvencies (especially in the US itself) occurred. If, in addition, the U.S. dollar is depreciated, then, with regard to the CDSs, which were previously paid with a currency that was later devalued, losses of foreign capital could also be expected (Ibid.: 111).

in particular, which were largely denominated in dollars, rose massively. The demand for the dollar was finally so big that interest rates on U.S. government bonds fell. This meant lower profits and rising prices on U.S. securities. This was one of the reasons for the crisis in 2008, but also indicated the dominant economic role of the U.S. in world markets.[11]

By issuing government bonds, the U.S. can avoid assuming certain risks that are otherwise inherent in currency trading. U.S. interest rates on government bonds may not be the lowest, but the dollar's share is highest in the international credit markets and the U.S. has the easiest access to these markets without taking particularly high exchange rate risks itself. It is also crucial that the U.S. has to pay relatively low interest rates in relation to the large amount of government bonds it holds. Although the value of the dollar may fall during crises, the U.S. generally holds little reserves of foreign currency, which again counteracts the fall of the dollar. The economically weaker countries and their enterprises, even if their own economic indicators are satisfactory, generally have to pay higher interest rates on the world market for their loans than the imperialist states and their companies, and cannot themselves take out long-term loans in their own currency. Often, therefore, they borrow in dollars and pay much higher interest rates than the U.S. and its companies. These loans in turn can be used to finance extra imports for U.S. consumers or direct investment abroad.

In addition, the cost to U.S. companies of paying interest on borrowings abroad is much lower than the profits they generate from their interest earnings abroad. The U.S. also continues to have positive net income, although foreign investments in the U.S. exceed U.S. investments abroad, which means that foreign investors hold higher amounts of assets (assets or securities) in the U.S. than U.S. investors abroad. In addition, the cash flows from abroad to the U.S., such as those made to buy bonds, are mostly managed by U.S. companies. Any company that repeatedly makes significant foreign business transactions must today hold a dollar account. It should also be clear that the U.S. is the world's largest exporter of financial services and U.S.-based companies receive the highest revenues. One way to take surplus value from foreign countries is

---

[11] Higher debt ratios in relation to GDP are characteristic for richer countries, especially those that hold a privileged position in the world financial system. Poorer countries have a less developed financial system and tend to have lower debt ratios, at least in relation to the size of their economies.

to acquire fees, revenues and commissions from service transactions and to manage financial services.

The appropriation of external value also takes place on international stock markets. In this case, the share capital of a company serves as a means of payment for the share capital of other companies (share swap, which takes place without cash flows). The mode and the profit that can be drawn from these movements are decided, among other things, by the global economic status of a country and the power of its stock exchanges. The stock market of the U.S. is the largest in the world, both in terms of the market capitalisation of the national and international companies based there, and the volume of trade, but other imperialist countries are today also listing more and more domestic and foreign companies on their stock exchanges. A company listed on an important stock exchange in a metropolis of an imperialist country has easier access to international money and investment funds and will therefore have easier access to new money capital. This fungibility of financial securities is an important feature of imperialist economies. The U.S. can impose economic sanctions against countries such as Iran and Russia because other imperialist countries that do not agree with these measures can be threatened to cut them off from the U.S. financial system if they do not agree with the sanctions. The U.S. thus comes closest to "full spectrum dominance" in the international financial system, especially in terms of its military-backed economic power and the role of the dollar as the still globally functioning reserve currency.

9.6   Global Value Chains and the Global Proletariat

Automation, whose application would not be possible today without the extensive use of information technologies, has been an essential technological component of the new international dynamics of capital accumulation since the 1980s. At the same time, more new jobs were created (especially in Asia) and masses of workers are expelled from production in the core countries of capital. This discrepancy is manifested today in the highly fragile integration of a global proletariat into the internationally networked supply chains of capital and its fluid production systems, making labour available to capital on a global level, but in some sectors increasingly superfluous, as automation and the use of algorithmic software intensifies. Digital-financial capital has created a planetary working class that works itself out of its jobs by connecting to ever more comprehensive systems of robots and networks - networked robots and robotised networks, reducing the human element increasingly to a variable residue. The technological basis for this is algorithms and invisible software operations (Dyer-Witheford 2015: 178). The accelerated automation of those production processes that are fully integrated into global supply chains has, however, only led to higher profitability in some sectors in recent decades, because often enough, the expectations of economic growth and high productivity advances associated with the new technologies have not been fulfilled (cf. Gordon 2013).

Robots were first used in the core countries of capital in automobile and steel production and machine construction, but also early in the pharmaceutical, food and electronics sectors. In addition to industrial robots, there is now an increase in service robots in certain centres of global production, although they do not operate fully automatically, but rather assist the human user. With the reduction of costs for the production of the elementary technical element of cybernetics, the microchip, a general reduction in the price of machinery was set in motion already early in the 1980s. When the technical composition of capital is increased, this does not necessarily lead to a corresponding increase in the organic composition of capital, but rather it could remain constant or even fall, which at least temporarily inhibits the tendency towards a general falling rate of profit.

Automated industrial investments currently refer to the following developments: machines produce machines that carry out their operations at ever increasing speeds; there are machines that suck in cheap labour and machines that completely replace living labour - Ballard's Crystal World, the before mentioned conglomerate of robots and networks, robotic networks and networked robots (Dyer-Witheford 2015: 36). The production of these globally functioning production structures and processes requires the use of extensive and comprehensive cybernetic systems and networks. Thus, while there has been a reduction in the production costs of microchips, there has also been an increase in the total cost of the extensive systems, which is required to produce the chips and other products. The chip-producing companies became bigger and bigger and at the same time more and more automated. In 1966, a new factory cost was $14 million, in 1995 it was $1.5 trillion, and today it is $6 trillion (Ibid.: 75–76). This is negative for new investments. In general, it can be assumed that in the analysis of unit costs besides marginal costs (of an additionally produced unit), the allocation for fixed costs must also be taken into account. Fix costs refer to the span and capacity of existing machine systems. In addition, utilised machine systems require during their existence permanent maintenance, repairs, conversions and upgrades. This is also valid for complex software systems and their cycles, which are subject to an accelerated process in the context of competition and today's cult of innovation, which leads to high costs when new systems have to be used (cf. Fischbach 2017: 36). A cost degression with increasing output can only be observed within the lifetime and capacities of automated machine systems.[12]

Today, many production processes run largely on a microscopic scale, for whose adequate perception the use of robots is absolutely necessary. Nevertheless, even in these areas one cannot do without human labour entirely, because at least during production stoppages and malfunctions, technicians and engineers must be present to correct them. Updating the software alone can generate immense costs, which even compensate the cost-saving effects of Moore's Law, so that the organic composition of capital also increases again. This increase can be compensated to a certain extent by tapping new sources of low-paid labour at the end of the world's electronically coordinated supply chains, by outsourcing production to low-wage countries and by activating unpaid digital work. George Caffentzis refers to a "law of growing dispersion of the organic composition of capital" and assumes that any increase in the organic composition of capital through the use of new technologies leads to the emergence of industrial strategies and areas in which the organic composition declines

---

[12] If a new era of technological innovation and economic growth is really dawning with automation, then we should also register rising rates of industrial investment and fixed capital. Meanwhile, economist Robert Gordon, in his book *The Rise and Fall of American Growth*, speaks of a rapid decline in net investment by private U.S. companies since the new millennium. The rate of net investment relative to the capital stock has been falling since the 1970s and has been falling dramatically since 2002 (from 1970 to 2002, we register an average of 3.2% net investment in the U.S., in 2013, it was only 1%) (Gordon 2013). If, in addition, according to the latest statistical measurement methods, financial expenditures in intellectual property also count as investments, i.e. legal titles for technologies to secure the flows of revenues, then, according to John E. Smith, the investment rates for new, more efficient production processes and new organisational methods should be set even lower. At this point, in contrast to the dynamism of industries with high and dense competition, which require constant innovation, Smith speaks of non-competitive sectors (anti-markets), in which market shares are obtained by securing property rights (Smith 2016: 63).

again (Dyer-Witheford 2015: 37). By outsourcing production, there is a transfer of value, for example, from the production of iPhones at Foxconn in China to Apple's factories in Silicon Valley, where few people are employed. When wage levels have already fallen below the reproduction costs of workers in the global South (super-exploitation) and cannot be reduced further, buyers and suppliers look for new possibilities of savings in other areas of the international supply chains (input costs, transaction costs, logistics, coordination costs, demand management, etc.). The result is increasing pressure on diverse suppliers, which reduce total costs, ignore health and safety regulations and extend the workday (Smith 2016: 69).

An important starting point for this form of so-called globalisation was the Toyotism that emerged in Japan. Dyer-Witheford summarises the essential elements of Toyotism as follows (Dyer-Witheford 2015: 49ff.):

1) There is a reprogramming of the labour force in the course of the use of cybernetic machines, which now "know" themselves when they have to stop their operations in the course of making production processes more effective. The prototype of this development was a self-activating machine used in the textile industry, which is based on the feedback loop and incorporates human labour capacities into its rhythm. Workers can now operate several machines simultaneously.

2) There is a redefinition of the worker who now not only has to obey, but is addressed by management as an active participant in production, for example, through the possibility of changing the speeds of the machines (Kaizen system), which, however, does not serve to slow down the speeds of the machines in principle, but stimulates more effective adjustments of the worker to the machine flows. Comprehensive teamwork is set up, the accomplishment of which is no longer bound to fixed times.

3) Inventory and operating resources are reduced by outsourcing to certain suppliers, for which the creation of electronic networks and logistical structures is absolutely necessary, insofar as this ensures that the necessary parts for manufacturing a product can be delivered on demand (just-in-time) to the major industrial centres. The fixed and circulating capital tied directly to the factories in the centres is thus decisively reduced.

4) Production is adapted even more precisely to the requirements of demand, making it much more heterogeneous and at the same

time more adaptive than in Fordism. This adaptation requires the frequency-calculated use of tools and machines, the establishment of flexible working conditions and servomechanical automation. The worker is integrated as a part of the feedback loop of the machines, as a sensory element in a purposeful process that serves to keep the biological and mechanical components of the whole system in a certain rhythm. When robots began to be used more intensively in the automobile industry from the 1980s onwards, the simultaneous growth of globalised capitalist production required the construction of complex logistical infrastructures, which in turn depended on fully developed cybernetic systems. While public attention towards the internet grew only slowly, the most intensive applications of cybernetic systems outside the military sector were in companies and on the stock exchange.

The just-in-time logic of Toyotism was significantly intensified by the integration of the fluctuating information flows into databases and networks. Suppliers often initially settled near the main production sites, but this was usually no longer necessary after a certain point in time due to the progressive development of logistics and containerisation.[13] Rather, it required the establishment of a worldwide system of direct investment and trade agreements and the infrastructural expansion of the cybernetic networks themselves, in order to facilitate the access of capital to areas with high resources of cheap labour, such as Mexico, Southeast Asia, China and India. Additionally worth mentioning is that in 2005, the automobile industry produced about 87 million cars, buses and trucks worldwide, a clear indication that capital today is by no means producing in a purely weightless, immaterial or clean way; on the contrary, it is constantly increasing the production of products made of metal and plastic, again driven by fossil fuels circulating around the planet (Ibid.: 54).[14]

[13] It should also be remembered that logistics is not simply a matter of global capitalisation and distribution, but an industry that is characterised by bio and necropolitical features and requires a militarised security industry.

[14] In a classic disqualification process, new structured programming techniques (object-oriented programming) have also broken the writing of software into modules or broken it down into relatively simple step-by-step tasks, with managers delegating tasks to programmers who work on them more or less simultaneously, while they are observed by team

304   A. SZEPANSKI

Today, the international production of capital is simultaneously permeated by the methods and systems of Taylorism, Fordism and Toyotism. In this context, it is also necessary to analyse the global supply chains within which transnational corporations organise their production of commodities, i.e. to arrange each operational element from a geo-economic point of view in such a way as to optimise labour costs, effectively manage access to raw materials and establish optimal distance to the sales markets. To achieve this, the various logistics chains must be developed into integrated, continuously functioning sequences. From the 1980s onwards, these supply chains were also responsible to a large extent for the technical composition of the global proletariat, especially in the eastern countries and the global South. From a technological perspective, these chains can be traced back to cybernetics. In the course of increasing computer performance, higher transmission capacities and more powerful software, telecommunications simultaneously became cheaper, so that it made sense to further dissect the factories and reassemble them on a global level. The transport routes from the globally distributed supplier companies to the headquarters of a company, which is usually located in the core countries of capital, are becoming more and more effective due to the standardised interfaces between the supplier companies, the headquarters and the customers, and at the same time the data traffic is constantly being improved through standards such as Electronic Data Exchange (EDI) formats.

The logistical global supply chains not only lead to changes in the technical composition of the global proletariat, but also today absolutely

colleagues who compare and review their work in regular control excursions to uncover irregularities. This is a programming proletariat that does not hack, but often tries to mask its proletarian status by signs of hacking. The work of this proletariat, in turn, cannot be thought of without a number of other types of work. One finds in the industrial processes of computer production the jobs of semiconductor production in clean white rooms, the jobs of making circuit boards, printers and cables in less clean rooms (sometimes at home) and the jobs of low-paid service workers. In Silicon Valley in 2000, there were about 65,000 electronic assembly workers, 40,000 workers not employed in assembly and 200,000 service workers, the latter often women and migrants (Dyer-Whiteford 2015: 67ff.). Global production makes it impossible to imagine the Silicon Valley dream factory without the production sites in Bangalore, Delhi, Puna and Hyderabad, where, for example, service workers in the computer industry earn $30 a month, work 12 h or more a day without any job security, and live in tents or in the slums near the cyber towers. The triadic pattern of lucrative high-tech capital, professional informational work and low-paid work is now replicating itself on a global scale.

require the Internet of Things. A decisive moment in this development was the introduction of the barcode by IBM in the 1970s; later, detailed cybernetic tracking systems, inventory control and screen-based systems accelerated and optimised transport and communication systems. As the logistics chains grew in length and complexity, they quickly generated a separate sector of capital production (Microsoft, Oracle, SAP, Epicor, etc.) (Ibid.: 84). It was a matter of tapping into the cheapest resources of labour at the world market level, producing goods at the lowest cost and moving them at maximum speeds from production to storage to points of sale, expanding new transport routes and dealing with current and future problems of the company organisation as quickly as possible.[15] The far-reaching changes in logistics and in globalised value chains have allowed deindustrialisation in the northern countries of capitalism to meet rural depopulation in the south and east of the globe, while at the same time triggering a new wave of originary accumulation in the metropolitan areas. In Asia, Latin America and Africa, migrants flocked en masse to the metropolises to work in the new information economies or migrated further to the leading industrialised countries to find jobs in the service sectors of the cities. At the same time, North American workers were increasingly outsourced to distribution companies, with Walmart replacing General Motors as the most employment-intensive company in the U.S.

9.7 THE GLOBAL PROLETARIAT AND THE DIFFERENT ZONES

Dyer-Witheford examines in detail the composition of the global proletariat (in its relationship to cybernetics), which he calls, together with Karl-Heinz Roth, a "multifaceted multiverse" (Ibid.: 126), which is composed of those strata that can still sell or rent their labour power to capital in order to secure its reproduction, and of a surplus population

---

[15] Walmart is the classic example of a gigantic supply chain that combines logistics with just-in-time production. In 2005, the data centres connected to Walmart tracked approximately 680 million different products per week, barcode scanners and pinpoint computer systems identified and stored more than 20 million customer transactions per day (Dyer Whiteford 2015: 84). Satellite communications linked the respective business centres directly to the central computer system and then back to the suppliers to ensure automatic ordering was as smooth as possible. Finally, the RFID system was introduced.

that is divided into those who work in the informal sectors of the subsistence economy and those who are denied any employment and have thus become completely useless not only for capital but increasingly for any kind of production.[16] The surplus population continues to grow in the informal sectors of the economy and in the minimal subsistence economy, while at the same time precarious wage labour is expanding in a diffuse service sector - for example, the mobilisation of women for paid and unpaid work in the reproductive sector and the escalation of underemployment and unpaid or insecure work. In the peripheries, in addition to the informal sectors that are still linked to the circuits of capital, there are also non-capitalist modes of production like slavery or subsistence economies. There are productions in which the labour force is integrated into the C-M-C cycle, the first commodity being the labour force itself,

[16] Marx already brought the concept of the relative surplus population into play. On the one hand, he speaks of the industrial reserve army as a cyclical phenomenon that is in or out of production depending on how capital accumulation is going. But Marx believes in a long-term tendency toward its growth, measured in terms of the total labour population. Now, if this reserve army grows in the long-run, a part of it must be expelled from it altogether and disappear from the official labour market, thus no longer used as variable capital.

William I. Robinson assumes three forms of the surplus proletariat: a floating, a latent and a stagnant surplus proletariat. The first two forms are groups that move in and out of the production processes according to the cycles of capital accumulation, being integrated by new forms of the division of labour (industrial reserve army). The third group is those structurally outside of the production processes. Marx tried to capture this group sometimes under the concept of the lumpenproletariat, although he could not of course have anticipated processes in which, for example, through the replacement of labour by technologies, but also other processes, the arrival of the surplus population would become a structural problem for the global economy. Beyond Marx's largely negative qualification of the lumpenproletariat, this is now a structural condition for the marginalisation of outlaws in the world capitalist system (Robinson 2020).

The surplus population has thus long since become a structural category of political economy; it is a huge population group that suffers from long-term underemployment, earns vital income in the informal economy of the slums of the megacities and is supplemented by international refugees, those who must flee wars, repression and natural disasters and dwell as migrant workers in the non-places of the world. The surplus population nevertheless correlates with the precariously employed who, under the new conditions of global capitalism, may well be subsumed under the category of lumpenproletariat.

Instead of migrating, the surplus population of the global South has concentrated in "planets of slums", as Mike Davis has documented in his book of the same name, where hundreds of millions of people live in total misery. The spectacular growth of urban slums is also a result of the depth of the rural crisis. As Davis notes, urbanisation in the global South continues its breakneck pace, despite falling real wages, rising prices and skyrocketing urban unemployment (Davis 2006).

which is bought for money and integrated into a production process whose products, if they are realised on the market, contribute just enough money to enable the purchase of the goods necessary for the reproduction of the labour force and a small surplus for the entrepreneur. This is a cycle that serves purely to satisfy the needs of the worker, while at the same time subsuming it to an accumulation of surplus, albeit minimally (Sanyal 2014: Kindle-Edition: 5014). At the same time, the worldwide outsourcing and offshoring of large companies is setting in motion a dynamic in which, eventually, even regions of the former peripheries are reaching a critical mass of industrialisation, in order to compete with the old centres of capital accumulation in Europe and the U.S. (e.g. some cities in the BRICS states).

The world's "economically active population" grew from 1.9 billion in 1980 to 3.1 billion in 2006 and is now 3.5 billion. This was by no means the result of global population growth alone, but a consequence of the deepening of global capital accumulation and markets. Almost all of the numerical growth in the labour force has occurred in emerging markets, which now account for 84% of the global labour force. 1.6 billion people work for various forms of wages, most of them precarious, and more than a billion are small farmers and, above all, a large number of people working in the highly fragmented "informal economy" (Smith 2016: 113).

The collective *Théorie Communiste* speaks today of three zones of the capitalist world market: (1) the hyperzones of capital with high functional capacities in the area of the labour markets and the places of production (finance, technology and research); (2) secondary zones with intermediate industries and technologies (logistics and communication); (3) crisis zones with information industries characterised by low-paid labour, or zones of non-capitalist or no labour at all. Non-capitalist production continues to grow today, although here surplus populations and surplus capacities are not linked to each other, so that the former cannot be productively used for capital. On the one hand, capital is based more and more on globalisation and the acceleration of circulation while, on the other hand, more and more people are becoming dependent on markets, but without the possibility of being able to sell their labour in a wage relationship. They are thrown into circulation, from which today class struggle and especially riots are increasingly occurring (cf. Clover 2016).

308 A. SZEPANSKI

While capital is largely unified through the various zones of the globe, especially through competition, this is by no means true of the compositions and movements of the labour force. In the first zone, highly paid wage labourers with good private risk coverage meet with those workers who are still bound to certain aspects of Fordism, while other workers have long since been struggling with precarious conditions. In the second zone, precarious, low-paid work is the norm, mixed with islands of contract-paying work, migration and lack of social risk coverage. In the third zone, the survival of the proletariat depends largely on humanitarian aid, illegal trade and mafia-like structures, as well as on agriculture, but also on small communities in which production is geared purely to satisfying basic needs (Sanyal 2014). However, this development must be understood as a volatile and porous process, interspersed with constant migratory movements of the global proletariat and the specific economic and technological restructuring of capital. In these geo-economic arrangements, which are only briefly outlined here, the proletarian class today is largely fragmented and fractalised, insofar as the conditions of social reproduction can vary from one zone to the next and also within one zone, and insofar as the basic relations between capital, intermediate layers and the proletariat manifest themselves in all zones, albeit at different scales and mixtures.

Dyer-Witheford summarises what is now called the global labour market in the following tendencies (Dyer-Witheford 2015: 133ff.):

1) The end of the global rural population due to accelerating urbanisation, the introduction of monocultures, the use of automatic harvesting machines and genetically modified seeds in industrialised agriculture, and, last but not least, due to violent land grabbing. In 1980, agricultural production was still responsible for 50% of the world's labour; in 2010, it was only responsible for 35%.

2) Today there are about 200 million migrants worldwide; some are seasonal workers in local places, others permanently nomadic. These migratory movements are completely geared to the needs of capital. The borders of the imperialist countries are not open and the migrants are scanned and/or kept away with the latest technologies; the workers themselves are regulated according to various differentiations (paid/unpaid, qualified/unqualified, permanent/temporary).

3) The working nomads. Not all members of the proletariat, now numbering about 3.5 billion, are paid for their work, or are simply

badly paid. Indeed, about half of the world's proletariat is engaged in activities that, if at all, at best secure subsistence, ranging from rural work to seemingly independent work in informal sectors. Even in the metropolises of capital, self-employment often implies nothing more than a precarious web-based activity in the various micro-enterprises, or even independent, contract-based work that remains fully integrated into global supply chains or franchises. These are activities that are well circumscribed by self-exploitation and/or new forms of mega-proletarianisation. In the global South, informal work often implies street work, day labour, begging and cheap advertising.

4) The existence of a neo-industrial proletariat. Contrary to what many social theorists have conjured up, industrial labour has by no means declined on a global scale; industrial output has tripled in the last four decades, rising from \$2.58 trillion to \$8.93 trillion, while the world population has not even doubled in that time.[17]

While a large part of industrial labour has indeed been outsourced from the U.S. and Europe, significant parts of industrial labour in the former peripheries continue to be applied expansively, but mostly at low wages, often without the existence of unions and in largely deregulated forms.

Since the 1980s, a decline or stagnation in real wages, an increase in the precaritisation of broad sections of the population and the

---

[17] However, the economic significance of these figures needs to be examined more closely. In this context, Lohoff and Trenkle refer to the material parameter of labour productivity (Lohoff and Trenkle 2012). They argue that for the relevant output of living labour, which materialises in the total value mass at a certain point in time, it is not the absolute number of hours worked that is decisive, but the socially average, abstract working time that is necessary on an international level. If, for example, five jobs in China could be replaced by a single job in the U.S., then in a global context only this one job with its relevant productivity would be included in the socially valid, global value mass. In fact, empirical studies would then have to examine the productivity differences in certain industries in the U.S. and China. However, especially when it comes to the problem raised by Lohoff and Trenkle of melting the living mass of value in the age of microelectronics, not only material but also price categories need to be examined - the organic composition of capital, profit rates, the ratio of interest rate and profit rate. In addition, the lower labour productivity of Chinese companies compared to those of the U.S. can be compensated, to a certain extent, by lower wages (rising value-added rate) in China, and this must be set in relation to the average profit rates and productivity differences on a national and international scale, whereby ultimately price and not material indicators count.

310   A. SZEPANSKI

flexibilisation of labour at all levels of production and services have been observed in the most important industrialised countries. The rapid increase in income inequality, new commodification of needs and the reduction of wages are now leading to new problems in the macro economically oriented management of aggregate demand and the regulation of class struggle. The fragmentation of production processes and the distribution of partial work to legally independent companies (outsourcing) generally leads to a weak organisation of workers, a reduction of wages, a deterioration of working conditions and an increase in the rate of added value. The risks of fluctuating capacity utilisation are shifted from large multinational companies to dependent supplier firms, while at the same time new transnational production networks are created.

5) There is a multiplication of work and an increase in services, the latter as an amorphous category that includes such diverse activities as highly complex accounting, consulting, doormen, the work of security guards and the work in fast food chains. Many jobs today (advertising, marketing, entertainment and communication) take place in the circulatory sphere, and we are also dealing with the feminisation of work in terms of the inclusion of more and more women in paid employment, while the differences in length and pay of work continue to exist to the disadvantage of women worldwide.[18]

---

[18] Worth considering also here is the problem of the middle class, who are particularly involved in the design of the machines and the training of workers tied to the new machines, and who occupy a leading place in the wage hierarchy. Technological development has created such layers anew, but it is increasingly destroying them. At the same time, the division of global employment into three sectors - agriculture, industry and services, and possibly its expansion through the information sector - seems inappropriate today, insofar as it is almost impossible to imagine a job that is not in some way connected to digitisation. There is a sharp increase in the number of workers who are extremely and closely linked to cybernetic systems, such as programmers, software engineers, network experts, web designers, system administrators in all kinds of sectors (finance, entertainment, marketing and administration) and workers in the new creative industries. The growth of digital-based work is often associated with the middle class and its well-paid wages and high status, but even this much-vaunted narrative can now be challenged by trends in globalisation, for example the "rise" of relatively low-paid programmers in India. A large number of the work related to networks today is standardised, precarious and poorly paid. Nevertheless, the growth of cybernetic capital has given birth to a new middle class, which mainly takes on surveillance tasks, psychological counselling and technological responsibilities for capital; for example, the team leaders, project

References

Amin, Samir (2010) *The Law of Worldwide Value*, New York.

Clover, Joshua (2016) *Riot.Strike.Riot: The New Era of Uprisings*, London.

Davis, Mike (2006) *Planet of Slums: Urban Involution and the Informal Working Class*, London.

Decker, Peter, Hecker, Konrad and Patrick, Joseph (2016) *Das Finanzkapital*, Munich.

Dyer-Whitheford (2015) *Cyber-Proletariat: Global Labour in the Digital Vortex*, London.

Fischbach, Rainer (2017) *Die schöne Utopie. Paul Mason, der Postkapitalismus und der Traum vom grenzenlosen Überfluss*, Cologne.

Gordon, Robert J. (2013) *Is US Economic Growth Over? Faltering Innovation Confronts the Six*, in: http://www.voxeu.org/article/us-economic-growth-over.

Häring, Norbert (2016) *Die Abschaffung des Bargelds und die Folgen. Der Weg in die totale Kontrolle*, Cologne.

Lazzarato, Maurizio (2021) *Capital Hates Everyone. Fascism or Revolution*, Cambridge.

Lee, Benjamin and Martin, Randy (eds.) (2016) *Derivatives and the Wealth of Societies*, Chicago.

Lohoff, Ernst and Trenkle, Norbert (2012) *Die große Entwertung. Warum Spekulation und Staatsverschuldung nicht die Ursache der Krise sind*, Münster.

Moore, Jason W. (2015) *Capitalism in the Web of Life: Ecology and the Accumulation of Capital*, London.

Mühlmann, Heiner (2013) *Europa im Weltwirtschaftskrieg. Philosophie der Blasenwirtschaft*, Paderborn.

Neusüss, Christel (1975) *Imperialismus und Weltmarktbewegung des Kapitals*, Gaiganz.

Norfield, Tony (2016) *The City: London and the Global Power of Finance*, London.

Norfield, Tony (2021) *World Power*, in: https://economicsofimperialism.blogspot.com/.

Robinson, William I. (2020) *The Global Police State*, London.

Sanyal, Kalyan (2014) *Rethinking Capitalist Development: Primitive Accumulation, Governementality and Postcolonial Capitalism*, London.

Shaikh, Anwar (2016) *Capitalism: Competition, Conflict, Crises*, New York.

Smith, John (2016) *Imperialism in the Twenty-First Century: Globalization, Super-Exploitation, and Capitalism's Final Crisis*, New York.

---

coordinators and consultants who form the management apparatus of capital, which has been reconstructed on a molecular level in the course of globalisation.

Sotiropoulos, Dimitris P., Milios, John and Lapatsioras, Spyros (2013) *A Political Economy of Contemporary Capitalism and its Crisis*, New York.

UNCTAD Trade and Development Report (2016) in: https://unctad.org/web flyer/trade-and-development-report-2016.

CHAPTER 10

Technology and Finance

Over the last two decades, a digital technical system has established itself on a global level, an ensemble of functional relations between technical objects, whereby relations are metastabilised by digital technology. Through their digitalised electrical networks and with the help of logistic networks across the globe (land, sea, air), technological infrastructures ensure the provision and flow of information and energy, and of monetary capital and financial instruments. Digital technologies, their infrastructures and their specific forms of mathematisation and modelling have also long since penetrated the global financial system in an extensive way. The globalisation of financial capital is inseparable from that of the technical system, inasmuch as the latter, determined in the last instance by financial capital, enables the global networking of urban financial centres and makes business accounting more effective.[1]

Thus, the employment of financial transactions and the computerisation of transnational monetary capital flows is now occurring due to high

---

[1] The intersection of the price system and its complexity in and as synthetic finance implies the addition of informatics to the financial system, which allows for the monetisation of everything (i.e. everything that counts or can be counted by capital) and integration into risk assessment as a mode of accounting in the form of credit scores, interest rates and liquidity premiums. For Jonathan Beller, information itself transforms into a capital asset; indeed, information is a form of money. Its operations by means of

---

© The Author(s), under exclusive license to Springer Nature   313
Switzerland AG 2022
A. Szepanski, *Financial Capital in the 21st Century*,
Marx, Engels, and Marxisms,
https://doi.org/10.1007/978-3-030-93151-3_10

314   A. SZEPANSKI

computing power, the transmission of information via satellite and the existence of low-friction communication networks in real time, that is, with an extreme speed of circulation of monetary flows. The process of decimalisation (the pricing of assets by means of decimal numbers and no longer by fractions), which has been taking place on the financial markets since 2000 and which is constantly reducing the spread between buying and selling prices (bid-ask spread), reflects the necessity of moving ever higher transaction sums in ever shorter time on financial markets by means of digital techniques, so that ever smaller spreads can be compensated. Traders usually hold the positions of the respective deal for only minimal periods of time, while realising only small spreads, so that high profits result in particular from the amount and the speed of the monetary

quantification, processed through sociality and through what is understood as computation (ubiquitous computing), ramify all notable social phenomena with ever-increasing resolution and granularity up to the present day (Beller 2021: 24).

Like an invisible hand with infinite digits, the universal generalisation of the world computer heralds an ever more granular accounting, whereby, as a consequence of this sociocybernetics, a calculus of risk and reward now accompanies all knowledge. Information serves as an instrumental proposition for the universality of calculation and for accountability; it serves as the medium of calculating capital - the means of generating and discounting a future income stream by means of a cybernetic interface that communicates with any phenomenon.

Beller rewrites the general formula for capital as M-I-C-I'-M'. M, of course, stands for money, C for code and I for image/information. The code here is not a stable entity, but a discrete moment in the movements of the discrete state of a computer (we could say all networked computers and the world computer). Replacing Marx's commodity C with I-C-I', we register the sublimation of the commodity form by the matrix of information. The image code, the network commodity, replaces what used to be understood as a commodity (ibid.: 102).

For Beller, the movement of information is not separate from price: it is itself a price movement, the result of financial transactions, and it will form future transactions in accordance with a price calculus. Indeed, information is to be understood as a series of computational changes of states within a series of discrete transactions, divided into ones and zeros (discrete states) that not only convey something, but are in fact financial transactions. In this sense, information is literally a derivative of knowledge - its cost is a premium paid to maintain liquidity.

Today, platform companies have a high attractiveness for financial investors due to various business advantages. For example, these corporations have little fixed capital to maintain and their means of production are mainly hardware and software. They follow the power law, i.e. the exponential growth generated by network effects. In the end, they can engage in a rabid externalisation of labour costs.

transactions. In today's high frequency trading (HFH), digital automation qua algorithms infiltrate almost every aspect of trading, from analysis to execution and back-end processes.[2]

The functionalisation of the HFH systems includes the fine-tuning of the programming as well as storage capacities, manipulation of individual data points and packages, maintenance of databases and selection of inputs, etc. Today, digital automation forms the technological basis of financial capital, unfolding in networks in which human actors act, at times, only as parts of the relays of the continuously flowing information streams. The open source platform "Iceland", which dates back to 1996, was an important marker for the development of electronic, automated trading. In this context, quantitative finance, which uses the methods of big data, computer science and artificial intelligence as well as genetic algorithms and theorems of game theory in its processes, appears to be important.

High frequency trading has an important influence on the structures and turnover of financial markets, at least in the U.S. It is estimated that HFH systems (approximately 100 companies) currently account for about. 70% of the equity market volume in the U.S., while they account for one third in Great Britain, and this figure is rising. Although it is significant that HFH is now responsible for a large share of market transactions in U.S. financial markets, it remains only a sub-sector of the activities of the dominant financial corporations due to the low profit margins.

The far greater part of financial transactions in high frequency trading today runs purely via machine-to-machine communications, which human actors can only partially observe due to their comparatively slow latency, so that the data and information streams flow at a-human high speeds

---

[2] Algorithmic trading can be divided into two processes: high-speed trading and high frequency trading. Here, we understand algorithms as dynamic entities that are connected to certain forms of knowledge in a complexly structured way. Through their black boxes, numerous outputs are produced from multiple inputs. The algorithms are characterised by a multiple opacity resulting from specific relations between a set of human and non-human actors. Algorithms are less to be understood as pure codes, but rather their codes are to be related to recursive routines and realisations of social relations, i.e. they do not extract and condense neutral information from the flood of data by means of certain processing rules, but rather these processes and inputs involve very specific selections, reductions of complexity and patterns and, last but not least, the evaluations of the programmers and discursive totalisations (Mau 2019: 163).

through invisible apparatuses (black box) and even the distinction between machine, body and image becomes fluid (cf. Wilkins and Dragos 2013). Although the composition of human and a-human entities varies in HFH systems, in extreme cases some financial companies are currently eliminating almost all human intervention in the automated financial transactions (except for programming), so that the data read self-referentially by the machines continuously flows back into the algorithms, which are controlling the processes. The monetary capital required to perform successfully on financial markets at these speeds is only available for large financial corporations, which can thus invest in computerised infrastructures and, of course, open up a very unequal financial playing field for speculators.

In HFH systems, the financial economy is thus made largely invisible by algorithms. Programmes permanently scan financial markets to see whether the indicators shown by the algorithms reach certain levels, which become effective as buy or sell signals. There are "volume-weighted average price algorithms" (VWAP) that, in conjunction with econometric methods, generate complex randomness functions to optimise the size of trading volumes and the length of execution times of monetary transactions (ibid.). One might think that an algorithmised random sequence is an infinite sequence of binary digits that appears random to any algorithm, but this contradicts the idea of randomness in probability theory, where no particular element of a sampled space is considered random. Algorithms attempt to identify and anticipate specific transactions, while non-adaptive, low-latency algorithms "process" the differentials of transmission speeds in global financial networks. Genetic algorithms are used to optimise the possible combinations of price fluctuations of financial derivatives and ensure the optimal fine-tuning of each parameter within a financial system (ibid.). The implementation of algorithmic systems in the financial economy represents a qualitatively new phase of the real subsumption of the machinery under capital,[3] indeed it indicates the transition from cybernetics to a new contemporary scientific technicity, called a "nano-bio-infocognitive" revolution, based on distributed networks and supposedly frictionless systems (superconductors, ubiquitous computing) (cf. Srnicek and Williams 2014). At the same time,

---

[3] The real subsumption under capital implies that every aspect of the production process - technology, research, markets, workers, means of production, etc. - is determined by the process of capital utilisation.

digital trading processes in financial markets remain integrated into a financial ecology of powerful dominant corporations whose employees feed and control the self-referentially operating robots (those that liquidate large positions and those that observe indexes) with programmes and information.

The importance of speed has always been essential for financial markets, but the technical infrastructures of the information and telecommunications industries today enable the machine processing of financial transactions even with a-human speed and the corresponding accelerations. To measure the difference between the speed of nerve cells and the speed of optical networks, the first one must be multiplied by a factor of 4 million. The speed of a nerve impulse within the network of our body is 50 metres per second, while the information speed of the fibre-optic networks, located at the bottom of the Atlantic Ocean, is 200 million metres per second. One can speak here of a new algorithmic governmentality of 24/7 capital, in which the actors no longer appear as individuals, but only as "dividuals".[4]

In HFH systems, the realisation of profits involves a continuous acceleration - financial decisions today are made in milliseconds, microseconds and even nanoseconds. The iX-eCute chip from Fixnetix Trades processes

---

[4] The dividual functions as a separateness in machine processes in a similar way to the non-human components, be they technical machines, organisational processes, semiotics, etc. The human-machine complex is a recurrent part of production, communication and consumption. In these human-machine apparatuses, in which the machine complexes increasingly communicate with each other even independently of the human agents, both components are recurrent parts of production, communication and consumption; processes that mostly aim at producing profitable inputs and outputs. Both human and non-human agents (agents are not persons and semiotics are not representational) function in machine processes as (moving) points within the connection, conjunction and disjunction of flows that flow in networks, be they economic, social or communicative networks.

Dividuals constantly change their functions, taking on the drive, transmission, transformation or tool function in the machine structures, functioning as raw material and product, as both a means and object of labour. In doing so, dividuals do not behave statically; rather, they are transformed and modulated in the machinic processes by the functionalities of looping and sampling, even glitching, and this refers both to the aspect of passively operating on oneself and to being operated on by the machines; to a certain extent, the dividual also activates these functions itself. One thinks, for example, of the typification or self-activated adaptation of one's own person to mass-produced entities or profiles. In this respect, the dividend is always also a type of ... (citizen, consumer, patient, producer, etc.) At the same time, the dividend remains coupled to a machinic "outside", more precisely sutured to the forces of the "outside", such as dispersed labour with the silicon of cybernetic machines or life with the exogenous factors of genetic engineering.

318 A. SZEPANSKI

trades in 740 nanoseconds. This chip can process over 330,000 trades in about 250 milliseconds. Consequently, HFH systems have long since reached the temporal depth of nanoseconds (1 trillionth of a second). The average daily volume of financial transactions on the NYSE increased by 300% between 2005 and 2009, while the number of daily trades increased by 800% during the same period (cf. Durbin 2010: vi–viii). For example, the programmes used for HFH remain profitable for only a short period of time, so they need to be constantly updated, with the fastest computer systems generating profits even for a short period of time, resulting in enormous costs for companies in reprogramming the systems. Although the profits generated by a trade in HFH systems remain relatively small compared to other financial investments such as complex derivatives, the investments generated by digital machines at least provide relatively secure income.

Profitable strategies in HFH trading must therefore rely on the management of speed differences, with for example electronic frontrunning, where special programmes identify financially strong buyers in the market and the high frequency traders then buy the sought-after shares in milliseconds on the various stock markets themselves and resell them to the original interested parties at a higher price. Although earnings per share are not high here, they are replicated millions of times due to the high transaction sums and are also considered safe. Frontrunning is usually financed by large institutional investors, such as investment, hedge or pension funds, so ultimately also by pensioners and small investors.

However, even the speed of light can still be too slow in high frequency trading in some respects, so that geographical distances again play a greater role, and this means that in a deal a trader in New York simultaneously offers to a trader in both London and Frankfurt, the trader in London is preferred because the signal sent at the speed of light takes longer to Frankfurt than to London. In order to go beyond existing speed limits, certain companies cut holes in visible and invisible walls to position themselves physically as close as possible to the "matching engines" of the central trading centres. Today, in order to further reduce latency, some U.S. companies are laying their communication cables through long tunnels to further reduce transmission times between Chicago and New York. The logistics company *Spread Networks* laid a dark-fibre line between the trading hubs of New York and in Chicago between 2009 and 2014, which reduces latency (delay insofar as it cannot be performed at the speed of light) by one millisecond, demonstrating that trading and quoting take place in time dimensions that far exceed the human capacities of perception. The imperatives of acceleration demand that companies increasingly eliminate every moment that disturbs transmission and trading. This is also the reason for the tendency towards the spatial concentration of financial companies in the highly networked financial centres of the world, while at the same time companies continue to pursue strategies of decentralisation that remain dependent on the simultaneity of digitality.

Wall Street is usually still seen as *the* central location of the global financial system, but it is precisely in cities like New Jersey and Chicago that much of the American financial system is physically located. HFH hubs such as the NYSE site in Mahwah are home to many of the largest "matching engines" (machines whose algorithms evaluate, compare, buy and sell transactions from around the world) (ibid.: 16). There is thus a specific physical concentration of the distribution systems of the global digitalised financial system. Since electronic signals flow over optical fibre cables with transmission rates in the gigabit to terabit range, the distance between the sender and the receiver of information is considered a key variable for the systems' temporal latency. The competition between financial companies leads to a rapid race for the shortest response times in the markets, which usually results with these companies locating their HFH servers as close as possible to the locations of stock exchange servers (co-location). The U.S. stock exchange IEX, on the other hand, has extended the route to its central computer for financial companies with a 61-kilometre cable, so that the data takes 350 milliseconds to shoot through the cables to the stock exchange. This is intended to both keep high frequency traders at a distance and to guarantee fair trading.

At the same time, technological innovations require a cloudy and at the same time dense information structure that absorbs, stores and passes on enormous masses of data and information. Consider here data on commodity prices, exchange rates, interest rates, indices, social factors, etc. with analysts, rating agencies and financial media, which are in constant exchange with financial institutions as well as the technology sector, acting as information marketing machines in these contexts. The technological-informational architecture of HFH systems thus plays an important role in minimising latency in the networks of financial systems, with a high proportion of data and information on current price movements today flowing not via the public internet but via one of the largest networks in the world: the "Secure Financial Transaction Infrastructure"

(SFTI). As part of NYSE Euronext, SFTI provides a private high-speed computer network for financial companies in the U.S., Europe and Asia. However, because the transmission of information is itself limited by the speed of light, physicists have long since begun to study planetary coordinates for optimal trading locations, while other researchers believe that the fibre-optic cables used to optimise HFH systems will eventually be too slow, and therefore propose to run the communication channels through the earth's core to bypass navigation on the surface. Privatised particle accelerators would then generate and encode neutrinos to drill a submolecular path through the earth and gain even minimal time spans over their competitors. The dromological aspect (Virilio 2008) of the HFH systems thus directly affects their technologies, logistics, infrastructures and locations and requires the transformation of the entire planet into a medium for the circulation of capital, whose technological *dispositif* in HFH is currently multiple network structures and algorithms.[5]

The diagram of a trading system consists of three main components: (a) trading strategies, (b) mathematics integrated into the software programmes and (c) technological infrastructure (Srnicek and Williams 2014). High frequency trading is considered a perfect example of distributive real-time systems, where patterns from the fields of complex event processing are used, including thousands of individual programmes that increasingly resist the concentration of processing in the computer's CPU by delegating crucial trading tasks to special hardware components

---

[5] Statistical arbitrage strategies and the risk-free profit allegedly based on them are founded on the simultaneous processing of price differences for similar or identical financial products in different locations or markets. Thus, the statistical significance of the movement of two financial assets must be recognised. Today, however, it is hardly ever a question of two financial assets, but mostly of complex systems, even multiple sets of correlations between a large number of financial assets organised and structured by different sectors, regions and markets. Arbitrage is supposed to be used to evaluate, exploit and finally eliminate anomalies in the markets in order to contribute to correct pricing and to provide sufficient liquidity. But arbitrage is precisely the result of computerised systems that automatically and simultaneously place and split enormous orders on all possible trading venues in order to successfully exploit specific price movements, so that dysfunctions cannot be ruled out. At the same time, the risk of infecting the entire distribution system of high frequency trading is increased when digital networks are interconnected through the functioning of arbitrage, so that the indication of a "wrong" price on a singular market can lead to a wave of false pricing. The increase in connectivity in the standardised HFH systems also corresponds to an increase in volatility, which contradicts the abstract demand for an efficient market, culminating in the fact that every investment in securities achieves the same price on all trading venues.

(cf. Durbin 2010: 8). The HFH has long since adopted GPU computing (graphic-processor-accelerated computing), where the GPU is used in conjunction with the CPU to accelerate financial trading. Parallelisation is considered the crucial concept of current GPUs, which is also being perfected in the discourses and practices of financial science. The software of financial systems remains bound to the modularity of the components to be managed and at the same time serves to connect companies to specific communication networks (ibid.: 101–102). Cybernetic feedback technologies would be inconceivable today without the modularity of digital machines, a structuring in which modules, all of which are without exception based on an identical design, can be reassembled without losing their autonomy. The mode of possible recombination of modular constellations constantly requires new flexible tests, with which the continuous feedback operates first and foremost. For this purpose, software engineers working in financial companies develop such systems with regard to the observation of elasticity, flexibility and profitability of financial events.

The HFH systems compensate for the low profits of an individual transaction by the high number of profitable transactions. The typical HFH trader generates his profits mainly through two strategies: (1) managing the difference between bid/ask prices and (2) probability-based analysis, which focuses on exploiting the difference in price movements (cf. Srnicek and Williams 2014). In the financial markets, both passive and active trading can be observed, where the former involves the placing of an order in the system without knowing whether another party is willing to occupy the other side of the deal; for this purpose, the HFH system provides programmes (Autoquoters) to generate precisely those decision-making processes. On the other hand, active trading consists in occupying the opposing side of the orders already listed in the order books, using the software "Electronic Eyes" (Durbin 2010: 28–29). If the profits result from the difference in bid/ask prices, then the risk consists precisely in that before the trader is even able to complete a round-trip trade (buy and sell or vice versa), the market prices may already have moved against him and he will necessarily incur a loss.

The implementation of learning algorithms in the HFH systems leads to higher and higher computer performance, flexible coding of efficiency and deeper expert knowledge. Within this network, an increasing diversification *and* security of trading strategies is to be achieved in the future, but at the same time the accident continues to insist, especially insofar as certain events seem to be statistically predictable (cf. Wilkins and Dragos

2013). In this respect, the accident is not so much the result of an incident, but rather an expression of the fact that the systems are working too perfectly.

One of the trading strategies used today is the collection of "slow quotes", which implies that an HFH trader makes his decisions faster than a market maker can adjust his quotes to the respective price changes. "Quote stuffing" in turn means that an enormous number of orders are sent to the stock exchange and deleted again in the next moment in order to drive market prices in the intended direction in the short-term and then profit from the countermovement in the next moment. *Nanex*, an expert in the study of trading anomalies and a provider of software for the real-time analysis of stock quotes, has thoroughly analysed these strategies.[6] Ecstatic trading traffic can be triggered by a single error in the algorithm, so systems must constantly undergo specific stress tests and quality checks, periodic updates and bug fixing. In 2003, a company went bankrupt in sixteen seconds when a "wrong" algorithm was set in motion (Srnicek and Williams 2014). The use of a particular algorithm has already led to an immense number of orders being placed in the system but not executed. According to *Nanex*, this algorithm alone had placed four per cent of all orders available at a certain time in the central quotation system of the U.S. stock exchanges (which adds up the orders existing on the various trading venues), affecting approximately five hundred securities and using ten per cent of the total bandwidth available for quotations, suggesting that the algorithm had tried to increase the response times of competitors by using its own enormous bandwidth. Thus, the flood of orders reduced the bandwidth of the electronic trading system for other participants in order to influence pricing. Some HFH traders programme algorithms that generate a four-digit number of securities trading orders per second for a single share and send them to the stock exchange, whereby the orders only become visible when they appear at the top of the stock exchange order book, i.e. when they lead to the highest bid or lowest asking price. However, the majority of trading is in the range of invisible noise.

HFH systems therefore repeatedly produce phenomena such as flash crashes or ultra-fast black swans at intervals (Taleb 2010). Take *Knight Capital*, for example, an algorithmic stock exchange trading company that lost $400 million in about 45 minutes due to the failure of a trading

---

[6] http://www.nanex.net/.

algorithm (SEC 2013: 6). A small deviation from the code, i.e. a tiny decentration in algorithmic feedback processes, was enough to cause the catastrophic event. Such errors are part of algorithmic systems from the very beginning. An update within the network can, for example, create a feedback loop that puts the entire system into an unstable state, or algorithmic feedback loops between subsystems create a situation in which algorithms that interact with each other switch each other off, resulting in unproductive operations, which ultimately has its cause in "distributed dysfunctions". One could now assume that "distributed dysfunctions" represent a process in which the algorithmic networks erroneously produce a higher form of the ultimate machine. The prototype of the ultimate machine created by Claude E. Shannon has only one purpose, which is to shut itself down; there is a chain of machines that perform algorithmic interactions in such a way that each machine shuts down its neighbour at the exact moment it has completed the process of recovery. While simple ultimate machines still rely on humans to pull the lever, algorithmically distributed dysfunctions today also perform this function. They thus create a stable instability whose unproductive and dysfunctional routines can only be terminated by a non-algorithmic intervention. For example, certain software defects or feedback loops can cause algorithms to flutter around limit values and put them into a state in which they constantly place and immediately delete orders. Although these phenomena are difficult to detect, it seems that many unusual market events are due to such unproductive routines (Cliff and Northrop 2012). To cite another example: an initial analysis of the 2010 flash crash suggested that unproductive algorithmic interactions might have been behind it. The term flash crash refers to a short but rapid price slump followed by a similarly rapid recovery in securities prices.

References

Beller, Jonathan (2021) *The World Computer: Derivative Conditions of Racial Capitalism*, Durham.

Cliff, Dave and Northrop, Linda (2012) *The Global Financial Markets: An Ultra-Large-Scale Systems Perspective*, in: Calinescu, R. and Garlan, D. (eds.), *Monterey Workshop 2012*, LNCS 7539: 29–70.

Durbin, Michael (2010) *All About High-Frequency Trading*, New York.

Mau, Steffen (2019) *The Metric Society: On the Quantification of the Social*, trans. Sharon Howe, Cambridge.

SEC.gov (2013) in: https://www.sec.gov/.

Srnicek, Nick and Williams, Alex (2014) *On Cunning Automata: Financial Acceleration at the Limits of the Dromological*, in: *Collapse. Volume VIII: Casino Real*, London.

Taleb, Nassim Nicholas (2010) *Der schwarze Schwan*, Munich.

Virilio, Paul (2008) *Geschwindigkeit und Politik. Ein Essay zur Dromologie*, Berlin.

Wilkins, Inigo and Dragos, Bogdan (2013) *Destructive Destruction? An Ecological Study of High Frequency Trading*, in: http://www.metamute.org/editorial/articles/destructive-destruction-ecological-study-high-frequency-trading.

CHAPTER 11

The Functions of Financial Markets for the Capitalist Economy

In contrast to some Keynesian authors who constantly describe of all sorts of dysfunctions of financialisation, in this book we assume rather that the neoliberal model of financialisation and its austerity policies have proven to be a relatively effective strategy for maintaining capitalist hegemony, at least for a certain period of time. Indeed, since the 1970s financial capital has succeeded in mobilising large sums of money and monetary capital on a global scale, of which, from an organisational and political standpoint, the following factors were responsible: (1) the flexibilisation and restructuring of the banking and financial sector and the liberation of monetary capital movements from state regulation and taxes; (2) the steering and control of monetary capital flows into the financial system; (3) the privatisation of parts of state infrastructure and the state security system (Operators of privatised infrastructure often have to borrow or issue shares themselves to finance their activities, and this in turn strengthens the financial system. Privatisation has also massively expanded the range of securities on offer, such as bonds, stocks, etc. All this can be positive for individual capital, but does not necessarily indicate a positive balance for total capital.); (4) a massive expansion of the credit system, the markets for government bonds and stocks and an enormous increase in the trade in derivatives and the concentration of large sums of money in investment banks; (5) new techniques of capitalisation are emerging with

© The Author(s), under exclusive license to Springer Nature
Switzerland AG 2022
A. Szepanski, *Financial Capital in the 21st Century*,
Marx, Engels, and Marxisms,
https://doi.org/10.1007/978-3-030-93151-3_11

325

the creation and issuance of derivatives of all kinds; (6) the transformation of the activities of traditional commercial banks is also taking place in this context, and this is leading to new correlations between commercial banks and other financial institutions such as insurance companies and investment banks. The shadow banking system, which is engaged in the intermediation of loans and securities, currently has a trading volume of $200 trillion annually. This is more than 50 per cent of all worldwide traded assets. The main players are hedge funds, investment banks, pension funds, insurance companies and money market funds. Players that are not traditional banks are granting more and more loans. The procurement of liquidity is favourable here and the restrictions are lower than in the bank-based credit system. Short-term assets are mostly used to finance the portfolios, so there can be a flexible mix of risk profiles and assets with different maturities.

In the shadow banking system, funds are often raised with repo transactions that have a maturity of one day. Repos are contracts under which securities are sold at a certain price in order to buy them back again at a fixed price plus interest. They can also be resold and therefore serve for the creditor as a collateral. The security still belongs to the lender, while the borrower receives all interest payments on the security during the term of the loan. However, the borrower has to pay a risk premium on the security. In good times, repo transactions increase liquidity, the possibility of turning securities into money. As a rule, the trading of repos is carried out by so-called shadow dealers/market makers, but they can also engage in proprietary trading. These market makers can be major banks, clearing houses or investment funds. However, these types of financial intermediaries cannot create credit like private banks, but have to provide their financing in other ways. Shadow dealers therefore need access to the money markets, otherwise they would have to finance the trades with their own capital or take out bank loans. And while the convertibility of bank loans is guaranteed to a certain extent by the state through various collateral mechanisms, in the case of repos it is private mechanisms and collateral, whereby the degree of their security varies. Deposit insurance protects the deposits of private banks to a certain extent, while securities in the repo business are protected by securitised loans or swap transactions (CDSs). The value of the collateral underlying the repos is determined on the market, with prices fluctuating, but a payout at par is still promised. In times of crisis, the price of securities can fall sharply because no buyers can be found, which has led the Fed to set up collateral structures for the shadow banking system as well. Repo transactions increase liquidity on the financial markets, with government bonds having the highest market liquidity, while other securities can massively fluctuate in price. If the market liquidity of these securities is high, risk premiums increase. Since the market for government bonds is limited, other assets are increasingly used as hedges, which are supposed to be as liquid as government bonds but are not, and therefore have to be hedged by swap transactions.

The safest repos are government bonds, which also have the lowest interest rates and the lowest risk premiums. The level of risk premiums and the quality of the securities used as collateral are decisive here. Repos are used both to hedge risk and to finance risky investments. In the shadow banking system, short-term loans are mostly balanced with long-term liabilities, non-liquid assets are made tradable through securitisation and a flexible system of risks and maturities and hedges are set up. In contrast to commercial banks, lending in the shadow bank system does not create money on deposit, but rather transfers assets and funds through the market. With the help of market makers, capital market-based loans are financed via the money market. Since the Covid-19 pandemic, central banks have once again provided repo facilities to the shadow banking system and thus a security structure.

Sotiropoulos, Milios and Lapatsioras have summarised the development on international financial markets through the following points (Sotiropoulos, Milios and Lapatsioras 2013: 118f.): (1) In order to drive forward comprehensive financialisation in recent decades, new forms of insurance for debts or promises of payment had to be developed. The insurance of debt has become an important process that massively influences the global financial system and its crises. (2) Non-bank systems that operate in the international money and capital markets are largely unaffected by the regulatory restrictions to which traditional commercial banks are subject, and they are also able to lend money at extremely low interest rates. The various strategies of the shadow banks have reduced the profits of commercial banks and thus also changed their accounting procedures. Commercial banks now have to take over certain functions of an investment bank and concentrate excessively on trading in fictitious capital and derivatives. (3) There are new correlations between the technological innovations that are taking place in the "real sector" of the economy and the innovations in the financial sector that affect derivatives and financial services. This creates new market and adjustment imperatives for all possible companies, which are linked to the destruction of

328   A. SZEPANSKI

traditional technological and economic structures. The securitisation of loans tradable on the financial markets (cf. Hartmann 2015: 72f.) has contributed to the creation of enormous liquidity potential, the reorganisation and unleashing of risks and the dismantling of old banking structures. Securitisation is to be understood as a technology that is used in particular by shadow or investment banks in order to surpass the traditional big banks in competition. In this process, loans and securities are bundled and packaged into a single security and sold on special markets. Through the different ways in which financial markets function, financial capital continues to differentiate itself in terms of sectors, areas of power, instruments and technologies. (4) The so-called deregulation of the financial markets involves the removal of certain restrictions on certain owners and on the movement of capital, on price and access controls to the financial markets, and finally, it also affects issues of corporate law; it leads to the facilitation of trading and manufacturing conditions for derivatives, to free interest rate movements, to the transnationalisation of payment flows and, last but not least, to the establishment of offshore centres largely removed from the control of state authorities. Even in developed economies, the authorities responsible for supervising the financial markets, complex monitoring infrastructures and supervisory organisations have tended to been reduced, where even the Basel control strategies with their capital buffers could not prevent risk assessments and lending from remaining largely in the hands of the private banks. In addition, the balance sheet regulations were liberalised and certain accounting standards were privatised. The liberalisation of financial markets has further led to the expansion of large banks that are highly involved in international transaction chains, making them systemically relevant not only in terms of the scale of their transactions, but also in terms of the connections and nodes they maintain within the networks of the international financial system. (5) The over-the-counter (OTC) markets, the various offshore financial centres and special purpose vehicles (SPVs), the various money and capital markets with their instruments (bonds, securities, swaps, etc.) and the hedge- and investment funds, or, in other words, the general development of the financial regime as a dense network of organisations, together with new regulating activities (liberalisation of contract law),[1] with which certain organisations are able to

---

[1] Katharina Pistor writes that it is precisely the wealthy asset owners who today claim freedom of contract, without taking note of the fact that these rights are guaranteed

circumvent state supervisory authorities, the monitoring of credit practices and other supervision - all this makes the global financial system as a whole much more complicated.

It was states themselves that drove the expansion of the shadow banking system. When government bonds have to be placed on the financial market, they compete with each other for the purchase of their bonds, and they also find buyers in the shadow banking system, which thus remains dependent on government bonds to secure its transactions.

With offshore centres, the governments of the leading capitalist countries grant large financial institutions a legal space separate from the national legal space, making financial capital virtually stateless, which implies the convergence of certain policies, tax avoidance and money laundering of illegally acquired funds that in turn can be transferred in accordance with the rules back to the countries where the investors are headquartered. The worldwide expansion of the financial sector would not have been possible without legal rules, which allow financial institutions to use the laws of their home countries at the international level or, if it is profitable to them, to use foreign law.

Greek economist John Milios claims that processes of financial capital today contribute to an intensification of the competition between companies, no matter what sector they belong to, by improving their mobility, which has the tendency to produce average profit rates and returns and at the same time to realise extra profits by increasing the control of the efficiency of companies (Milios 2019). The modern financial system constantly generates new normalising procedures of evaluation, calculation and valuation of companies, providing specific representations (theories, data, information, etc.), institutions (analysts, rating agencies) and mathematical methods and models for quantifying capitalisation. These processes include, on the one hand, the capitalisation of securities and derivatives traded on the financial markets and, on the other hand, new practices of control of capitalist enterprises, aimed at improving their profitability and maintaining capitalist power relations as a whole. A

---

by states. International leaders in this encoding of capital, Pistor writes, are the English common law and the law of the State of New York. It is of course no coincidence that these legal systems correlate with the financial centres of London and New York, where the important law firms are also located (Pistor 2020: 25–26). However, there is no central right of one world state, but powerful and privileged national rights that are linked by certain rules. Transnational corporations then choose the rights most favourable to them.

330   A. SZEPANSKI

company whose balance sheets, market capitalisation and prices (observed and evaluated in the financial markets), indicate insufficient exploitation, will quickly lose the "confidence" of analysts, rating agencies and, as a result, of investors/speculators, which can lead to restrictions on credit, the threat of hostile takeovers and a reduction in the company's market capitalisation. The company must minimally then expect more difficult financing opportunities on the financial markets due to the prognosis of its future profitability. For the financial system, this type of correction has the function, among other things, of immediately compensating capitalist investors who are still willing to invest in an endangered company in the future with higher risk premiums for the affirmation of increased risk, corresponding to the deteriorated future economic prospects of the company.[2]

Financial markets today are largely secondary markets, providing a very specific "contribution" to the calculation, evaluation and control of current and especially future strategies of companies, thus reinforcing at the same time the tendency for average profit rates of industrial companies. The function of synthetic financial instruments here is to calculate, insure and regulate efficiency gains and risks, i.e. as with interest rates, their allocative function is precisely to allow money capital flows to flow as rule-compliant and at as high a speed as possible, and to a certain extent to control the investment decisions of the functioning capital. Contrary to Keynes' assumptions, it is precisely the illiquid market, i.e. the capital that remains tied to factories and machines, that cannot satisfy the effectiveness of fluid fictitious and speculative capital, since capital does not necessarily have to be tied to a certain place for a longer period of time;

---

[2] Bichler and Nitzan argue somewhat differently on this point. They criticise the notion that risks and returns are positively correlated, and instead assume that the correlation is negative: the higher the power of a company, the lower the returns, because power is exercised here through strategic sabotage and this will cause resistance. Moreover, stock markets do not develop pro-cyclically. Stock prices will only move in the same direction as current profits if the market expands massively (capitalised power is high); but if profits are moderate or low, then stock market price movements and current profits can hardly be correlated. The countermovement between the stock markets and the underlying economy reflects the sabotage of capital accumulation, i.e. financial investors do not really care about real capital; they are indifferent to the means of production, to labour and knowledge, even to market efficiency. They are purely interested in financial capitalisation. Even the long-term growth rates of financial capital (stocks and bonds) and the real capital stock (measured in dollars) correlate, for Bichler and Nitzan, only negatively (Bichler and Nitzan 2013).

as the financial markets illustrate, it can circulate constantly as fictitious and speculative capital and look for better possibilities of exploitation. It is precisely the financial markets that generate a fluid structure for calculating the effectiveness of individual capital - they are to be understood as a kind of (fictitious) superintendence of capital movements, so that individual capital must permanently adapt its strategies to the respective requirements of financial markets. It should be noted that the control of companies by the financial system, however efficient it may be, is still a fictitious control, inasmuch as the calculation, prognosis and evaluation of future complex production processes of companies by analysts, rating agencies and financial markets always have to include a multitude of contingencies. But nevertheless, if one prices out the risk, the processes of production and circulation can be further intertwined, whereby the gap between present and future is then further closed. It is precisely the attempt to control these contingencies that requires very specific risk management and condensed economic power. It is important to bear in mind that the place of capital is not occupied by a single subject: on the one hand, the managers or functioning capitalists have an intermediary function, oscillating between the maintenance of factory discipline, which they must permanently supervise, and the recognition of market discipline, which is related to the increase in market capitalisation. On the other hand, it is the money capitalists outside the factories who constantly have their agencies monitor the performance charts of companies. In this context, the organised financial markets exercise a critical function: they reward the profitable and competitive companies and punish those companies that do not produce profitably enough.

Today, it is the major rating agencies that permanently assess the profitability, solvency and prospects of companies on a global level, using specially developed differentiated scales that range, at Standard & Poor's, for example, from AAA to D. These ratings have a direct influence on the share and bond prices of companies, and in the case of the latter, on the ability of companies to pay interest on bonds and to repay the bonds themselves at maturity. This is the evaluation of the capitalisation of promises to pay, which are represented in the prices and the level of interest (risk premiums) of companies. In this context, the rating agencies are to be understood as information machines that produce an ideological, mathematical and standardised knowledge that can be accessed today by certain market participants worldwide, which in turn has a disciplinary effect on the companies themselves, which now have to comply with certain standards in their business organisation, for example, timely accounting, documentation of solvency, quarterly reports, management strategies, valuation of loans, etc. Companies can only survive on the financial markets if they permanently submit to these ratings and can demonstrate sufficient creditworthiness in terms of transparency, economic efficiency and profitability. The focus is less on the company's past and more on its future prospects of success. If a company is downgraded in its ratings, it must expect higher interest rates on loans and price markdowns on its bonds. The three major private rating agencies (Moody's, Fitch and Standard & Poor's) are paid by the companies themselves for their credit ratings, so that they receive the standardised evaluations of the business management information of their own companies, which on the one hand subjects them to further disciplining, and on the other, opens up new prospects of success if the ratings are good. Today, globalised financial transactions of companies are hardly conceivable without these ratings. The international community of investors can now easily compare a company in Japan with one in Canada in order, according to the future prospects of success of both companies, to invest or not.

Holders of bonds and shares are particularly interested in the short-term calculated profitability of companies, which increases the pressure on their management to increase productivity and profitability immensely. If a company is dependent on financial markets and their instruments, methods and valuations with regard to its financing, then the suspicion of an inadequate realisation, both now and in the future, even if it may be unfounded, increases the costs of its financing, lowers its share and bond prices and thus reduces its economic power for manoeuvre overall (Sotiropoulos, Milios and Lapatsioras 2013: 153). A company's workers are then also exposed to economic restrictions, and they may face the dilemma of having to accept less favourable outcomes in the collective bargaining process or, through a militant standpoint, having to force the company into bankruptcy or a takeover. For workers, the latter option is almost always associated with a violent restructuring of their own working and living conditions. For the workers, it is therefore a question of accepting the power of capital unconditionally or of surviving with greater insecurity or even falling into unemployment. Thus, financialisation promotes and accelerates the need to restructure capitalist production processes, and as a result, today we are witnessing longer working hours, greater labour intensification and more layoffs, while workers' demands for real wage increases are continually being silenced due, of course, to the strong fragmentation of the working class, the dissolution of the classical factory and the phenomenon of transversal precaritisation.

The concept of shareholder value, which provides the short-term maximisation of a company's profitability and, accordingly, the short-term sale of its insufficiently profitable parts of the company and, in addition, constant internal restructuring, creates a flexible mechanism by which the operational logic of financial capitalisation penetrates the organisational structure of the companies themselves, forcing them to adapt, adjust and restructure on a permanent basis (Windolf 2017). Speculative capital can now abstract in a certain way from the body of the enterprise (it is now a purely quantitative expansion of capital) and at the same time search in the balance sheets for hidden profit opportunities in the company, for "values" that can be monetised but are not yet reflected in the share price. The shareholder value is the ratio of the derivative when it affects the environment of the company. The share price is the derivative, while the company is the underlying. The options on the share price are in turn a derivative on the derivative. The derivative ratio includes also phenomena such as the increasingly rapid change in the so-called core business of companies when they no longer meet the return expectations of their owners. The threat of hostile takeovers is also one of the strategies of financial capital, whereby takeovers are profitable for investment funds precisely when the value of the company is lower than its market capitalisation. It is then possible to offer to the shareholders of the company higher prices when they buy their shares, in order to gain control of the company, restructure it and sell individual divisions, or the company as a whole, profitably. This must also be seen as an attack on the management of a company, although it usually remains a threat of a hostile takeover because managers have long known that if they violate certain mechanisms prescribed by financial markets, they can expect the share-prices of their companies to fall and thus become victims of a hostile takeover (Ibid.). These rather virtual threats, which are countered by far fewer actual takeovers, nonetheless unfold a comprehensive global disciplining of companies.

The permanent "control" of companies by financial capital also includes their molecular evaluation of the performance flows at the internal management level, and this is done systematically through the use of mathematical and stochastic models based on algorithms that

334   A. SZEPANSKI

aim at evaluating and optimising particular procedures used within the company's production processes, in order to continue to develop specific strategies aimed at maximising short-term profits. The software Enterprise Resource Planning (ERP), which is to be understood as the operating system of a company, brings together information about warehousing, production and human resources management from databases, whereby not only intra-company interrelationships are objectified and made visible, but the entire supply chain, e.g. of transnational corporations, can be mapped across continents. On the basis of this software, parts of companies can be divested, production locations can be compared and employment hierarchies in the companies can be evaluated. Accounting, i.e. the control of the performance flows in a company itself, sets in its strategic handling of figures, new standards for the account departments and bookkeeping. This type of operation or optimisation is practically implemented by using a variety of instruments (algorithms, math and models).

These mechanisms constantly require new forms of organisation within companies themselves, often forming formally independent companies that remain the property of a single financial holding company. Thus, in the wake of the need to realise short-term profits, a rapid shift of investments from the less productive to the more productive sectors of a company seems to be more easily possible, since legally independent sectors can be reduced, enlarged or sold in the short-term. Another strategy is outsourcing, which may also be due to certain technical necessities (e.g. when only smaller companies are able to produce innovative products, but as the large companies fuel the competition between them and suppliers, further cost reductions can be achieved that compensate for the declining economies of scale resulting from the fragmentation of production processes) (Porcaro 2015: 30). The management and organisation of companies today is highly dependent on the respective financial holding company, institutional investors and shareholders, who are geared towards short-term profit maximisation and subject the returns on their investments to constant examination. In addition, institutional investors such as investment funds or hedge funds themselves are subject to specific controls because their investors are today more willing to withdraw their capital faster and invest elsewhere. Companies and certain parts of companies, which are already highly fragmented and sometimes outsourced for cost reasons, are now effectively capitalised: cost structures, buildings and machinery, the qualifications of employees and workers, technical know-how and especially future prospects of success are subject to constant assessment and evaluation on financial markets. The vertical disintegration of companies, the fragmentation of production processes and the global splitting of production are intensified by the management of the company, which is oriented towards the principle of shareholder value. With the parameter "expected profitability", the owners permanently put the future reproduction of the company itself at their disposal, whereby current production processes, parts of the company or business areas, wage levels, productivity, work organisation, real estate, research and fixed capital become the object of a very specific cost and profit calculation.

All this can be summarised as follows. The concept of shareholder value implies the financial decisive valuation of companies on financial markets at the same time as a decision on their future suitability as financial investments. Returns on capital are sought in order to reduce the risk exposure of investors and shareholders (plus the so-called performance commitment of managers) with a surplus and at the same time to increase the profitability of companies. While internal parameters such as the individualisation of compensation and distribution systems, flexibility of work, atypical employment relationships, efficiency of knowledge condensed in machines and labour and outsourcing production areas for the company, are constantly adjusted to conquer new business areas in the wake of ever more rapidly changing digital distribution networks (rapid obsolescence of new technologies, permanently aggressive marketing, changing consumer preferences, etc.). In this context, the performance of a stock corporation today always has to attest to the efficient accumulation of fictitious and speculative monetary capital, by taking advantage of the opportunity for structural innovation and potential mobility on the capital markets, in order to reduce dependence on the competitive conditions of one's own industry or to build up oligopolistic structures, which by no means excludes the possibility that innovations may also be blocked. In addition, large companies in industry or trade are starting to operate on financial markets themselves, so that the profits made may well be higher than in the actual business areas.

References

Bichler, Shimshon and Nitzan, Jonathan (2013) *Differenzial Accumulation*, in: http://bnarchives.yorku.ca/323/03/20121200_bn_da_ft_lexicon_web.htm.

Hartmann, Detlef (2015) *Krisen – Kämpfe – Kriege. Band 1: Alan Greenspans endloser "Tsunami"*, Berlin.

Pistor, Katharina (2020) *The Code of Capital: How the Law Creates Wealth and Inequality*, Princeton.

Milios, John (2019) *Value, Fictitious Capital and Finance: The Timeliness of Karl Marx's Capital*, in: http://users.ntua.gr/jmilios/8124-Article_Text-22400-1-10-20200311.pdf.

Porcaro, Mimmo (2015) *Tendenzen des Sozialismus im 21. Jahrhundert: Beiträge zur kritischen Transformationsforschung 4*, Hamburg.

Sotiropoulos, Dimitris P., Milios, John and Lapatsioras, Spyros (2013) *A Political Economy of Contemporary Capitalism and its Crisis*, New York.

Windolf, Paul (2017) *Was ist Finanzmarkt-Kapitalismus?*, in: https://www.uni-trier.de/fileadmin/fb4/prof/SOZ/APO/19-019_01.pdf.

CHAPTER 12

The Financialised Subject of Risk

Capitalist risk management today is not simply a form of calculating the future successes of capitalist companies, or a way of understanding the economic knowledge of the financial elites, but it also articulates and generates a comprehensively new dynamic of the socio-economic being of the entire population. Through the differentiated modes of operation of the financial system, monetary capital today defines almost all important social relations in the various socio-economic fields. In this context, American sociologist Randy Martin understands the concept of financialisation as a process in and with which current social and power relations are permanently generated, recalibrated and reconfigured by the financial industry. The financialisation of everyday life, studied in detail by Martin, structures the representation and valuation of the subject and even leads to the computerisation of the senses (Martin 2015). Additionally, the financial industry uses its power of naming through the use of very specific models, measurements, information and descriptions of the economic field as a hegemonic form of representation in order to achieve comprehensive symbolic legitimacy among the population and thus to enforce very specific logics of action. Thus, the financial system is to be understood as a multiple set of normalising protocols, indicators, ideologies and power techniques to permanently urge broad segments of the population to organise their everyday social life in an ego and productivity-oriented,

© The Author(s), under exclusive license to Springer Nature   337
Switzerland AG 2022
A. Szepanski, *Financial Capital in the 21st Century*,
Marx, Engels, and Marxisms,
https://doi.org/10.1007/978-3-030-93151-3_12

affirmative, flexible and, at the same time, rule-compliant manner. In the process, the speculator coagulates to become one of the most important leading figures of the current social economy, if he understands how to efficiently manage his job and business arrangements, his object relationships up to his private affairs, how to plan, coordinate and successfully realise his own future in the course of the self-valorisation imperative. Today, self-management is one of the big buzzwords of the coaching and marketing industry (invented in the higher management levels of personal finance), a performative trend word that permanently challenges the population to accept and pass the tests, evaluation programs and exams of the ubiquitous neoliberal assessment centres. The arbitrageur or speculator operates much more at the intersection of future projects, functions and initiatives than the classical entrepreneur, for example when the former writes contingent derivative contracts that are intended to make profits through the potential deviation from the fixed and expected prices, which in turn means that one can also profit from the losses or depreciation of the moves of other players. It is therefore always necessary to profit from the anticipation of other players' actions, to look over the shoulder to the competitors in derivative trading, so to speak, and to constantly diversify one's own portfolios according to the anticipated margins. In the field of financial war machines and the preventive security modes that accompany them, one must decide immediately, even before an action could vaporise, preferably now, and intervene before the enemy has even appeared, punish someone before a crime is committed, measure before an output has even been achieved and sell before the product has even been produced - all this also touches on the notorious, hyperactive, attention-deficit inducing disorder of subjects who are always acting inadequately according to the requirements of efficiency.

The possibility of benefiting from risk management resides in the continuous exploitation of arbitrage (the exploitation of the smallest differences), and this may also be considered one of the preferred ways of financialised subjectivation. Such a motivated arbitrage trade allows for the denial of dependence on social structures, which are now instead experienced and perhaps even celebrated as liberating competition that can be appropriated with individual sovereignty, as if it could be measured solely from the perspective of subjectively controllable inputs and outputs. However, current financialised biopolitics include not only the constant modulation of risk by subjects and their self-governing practices, but also the statistical sorting of the population around the average, or in other words, into those who are successful in the face of risk and those who are not. This is what it means to be at-risk. All rating, scoring and ranking procedures today are based on the average, or average measure, around which the winners, the over performers, and the losers, the underperformers, oscillate when they are put in relation to each other. While economic success is primarily propagated through the modes of operation of a collective contagion within the privileged middle classes and the rich elites, the permanent defeat of the wage earners, the precarious and the unemployed inevitably appears as a personal mistake. As if that were not enough, a financial industry has also developed that permanently evaluates, calculates and structures the responsibility, mobility and strategies of even the most disadvantaged people in relation to their own at-risk condition (from the granting of consumer loans to access to privatised public goods such as schools, education and health and to the management of death). Today, there is a constant expansion in the measurement of all types of services, the production of ratings, rankings, new queries and diagnostic tools, as well as indicators that process, using digital technology and infrastructures, to comprehensively monitor, illuminate and quantify the social life of the population. The indicators, which are produced using numerical series and data, induce non-hierarchical, quasi-invisible and, in particular, distanced forms of governance through the introduction of cybernetic ought-to-be-analyses, the quantification of information and the use of resources, and the fabrication of performance-oriented risk profiles, so that an exact and efficient governance, which is unprecedented in history, can be established that functions purely through numerical systems.

The control of contemporary risk subjects also requires profit-oriented insurance companies that permanently classify, normalise and evaluate their customers, and this clearly shows the risk subjects as dividuals,[1]

---

[1] According to Deleuze and Guattari, machinic enslavement divides subjects and recomposes them, thus making them more fluid, supple and variable, transforming them into dividuums. This kind of coupling between machine and human refers first to the cybernetic figure of communication, which regulates the intercourse between organisms and machines (Deleuze and Guattari 1992: 635).

In human–machine apparatuses, components are recurrent parts of communication processes mostly aimed at producing profitable inputs and outputs. Whereas disciplinary societies were structured around the relation of "individuals and masses", control societies articulate themselves through the dyad of "dividends and databases" - on the one hand, institutions of enclosure, on the other, processes of control operating in open milieus;

inasmuch as they are assigned specific figures relating to factors such as consumer characteristics, interactions, health, education and creditworthiness, which makes them into divided entities called dividuals. Insurance companies that use different forms of risk management and other financial instruments, convert the quantified elements, which are written in charts, into even higher quantitative categories in order to then constantly recombine the elements and create new incentive and allocation systems and achieve higher profits by increasing the performance, which the by-risk profiles documented subjects partly do themselves (Lee and Martin 2016: 539) insurance companies initially collect their data based on standardised risk definitions by sorting, hierarchising and pricing risk subjects according to criteria such as income, family origin, job, place of residence, gender and education. While the risk subjects are stubbornly occupied with their individual new formation in order to constantly reinvent themselves creatively and freely (and thus usually only adapt themselves to the fact that they cannot change anything about their situation in the slightest, or perhaps do not even want to), insurance companies regard them as rather stereotypical protagonists who live a quite ordinary life, under the circumstances of a "job advertisement that has come to life, a successful synthesis of all the character properties that personnel managers and elementary school teachers would like to see in a person" (Pohrt 1980: 98). While subjects willing to take risks, especially those from the middle class, constantly invoke liberation from the shackles of encrusted identities, they are at the same time scanned and classified extremely efficiently by insurance companies and other control firms. The

on one side, signatures and administrative numbering, on the other codes and passwords as conditions for access. However, there is now a third technology that uses both the signature as part of the political semiotics of the discipline and the codes in the open milieus or apparatuses of control. This technology is initially more focused on "individuals" conceived as indivisible spatiotemporal entities, but which, when it comes to their constitution, remain dependent on the mobilisation of a divisional material aggregated and algorithmically processed in the databases. These technologies thus do not belong entirely to individualisation qua disciplines, nor entirely to the divisiveness through the various procedures of control. Today, the dividuum primarily incorporates a statistical existence that is recorded, controlled and regulated by various private companies, opinion institutes and the institutions of the state. One classifies the dividuum as a biopolitical and genetic existence with the help of statistical procedures and probability calculation, respectively, and classifies them into different population groups. At the same time, risk profiles indicating the affective, physical and mental capacities of the dividuum are constantly regenerated, recombined and subjected to various tests.

upwardly mobile middle class - economically oriented upward, culturally oriented downward - even enjoys this and some of its representatives who perhaps occupy higher functions within the insurance companies themselves, succeed in outdoing each other in the high of hedging their lives, and this in the course of a speed-mongering spewing out of functions, formulas and slogans that mercilessly and at the same time gloomy ornament their own lifestyle. At the same time, the existence of subjects willing to take risks requires a control structure (statistics, tables and taxonomies) employed by the insurance companies, which classify and sort its clients according to risk categories for the purpose of establishing a proper risk profile. Self-optimisation processes and control structures are interdependent and mutually reinforcing. Today, companies and individuals are not so much checked for their creditworthiness by analysing the specific individual case, but rather on the basis of uniform quantitative indices, i.e. credit control by examining the individual case is replaced by the creation of standardised risk profiles. Thus, for the evaluation of consumers, the Fico Score was introduced, an algorithm that can be considered an important statistical tool for the control of the neoliberal subject. Scoring means attributing performance, efficiency, profitability or solvency to certain entities in order to classify them and make other assignments, while screening involves selecting entities from a larger pool and then establishing rankings of value. In both cases, this is now processed by machine algorithms.

Subjects are classified according to the criteria mentioned above, and points are then assigned to them that are weighted and combined to form a credit rating, to determine the credit allocation with the overall score. Statistical procedures are used to model the probabilities of servicing the loan or loan defaults by assigning credit ratings, which not only decide on the granting of loans themselves, but also on the conditions of the loans (terms, interest rates). Today, there is widely available data material on factors such as debts, market activities and the economic situation of subjects in general, which is used in risk calculation and evaluation, whereby the trend is to integrate more and more parts of the population into this process via credit risk colonialisation (Mau 2017: 64).

Insurance companies use the Fico Score to construct the credit histories of their customers; companies use it to check job applications and search for optimal locations; health insurance companies use it to make forecasts as to whether patients are taking their medication properly and regularly; and casinos identify the most profitable guests. Moreover, a wide and at the same time dense network of rankings, ratings and other evaluation mechanisms, which are carried out over numerical progressions and whose results are also visualised, now covers all socio-economic fields and also refers to almost all activities, moods and affects of the subjects, which in the case of the latter means that we are dealing with the design of aggregation and recombination of divided behaviours and attributes, i.e. an explicitly derivative logic, inasmuch as the subjects, through the mechanisms of ranking, screening and scoring, quantifying and monetising their risk profiles, are transformed into divided products, which in turn are evaluated by managers, analysts and others who paradoxically perceive themselves as individuals. In this context, a new regime of objectivity is generated, which not only makes differences and comparisons visible through quantifications, but also stages new hierarchisations and classifications. While ratings serve to assess and evaluate certain objects, i.e. facts, subjects and entities, by means of certain techniques, ranking places the objects in a certain order of precedence. The monetarisation and economisation of ratings and rankings leads to a permanent restructuring of the methods of increasing efficiency, the so-called performance-based allocation of funds and budgeting under the aspects of quantifying profitability increase or input–output matrices translated into figures, whereby increasingly areas such as education, health, prisons and even wars are also now affected.

Such a risk subject cannot remain passive, but must constantly behave actively and strategically within the framework of its risk management. Indeed it must construct its future in a calculating manner, whereby reward or punishment is the result of permanent management around its own calculated risks. Mirowski describes risk as the "oxygen of the entrepreneurial self" (Mirowski 2015: Kindle-Edition: 1912), which is itself a small "capital" that should be effectively and diversely utilised in all areas and situations of life, and this necessarily requires that risk be understood as constitutive for one's own life, job, family, insurance and consumption. Thus, the neoliberal subject of risk simultaneously transforms into a company, customer, product and raw material of its own life, while still dissolving the distinction between consumer and producer in favour of a subject that coincides with its own small capital. The neoliberal risk subject has to treat its personal characteristics, projects, skills and abilities like capital and assets that need to be nurtured, managed and increased, including liabilities, which of course also need to be managed. And of course, it is better to be on the side of the claims and assets than on the side of the liabilities, whereby in this context, insurance is a necessary institution, which is there to regulate the fluctuations and divergences that occur in processes of the exploitation of the self and that bounce to one side or the other. Finally, the neoliberal subject mutates into the game point of the simulation of derivative transactions, to which it is attached as if on a drip, while it must simultaneously maintain, consolidate and improve them in the highest degree of alert or flexibility. There is no fixed hierarchy between the various roles that have to be occupied, but rather they are taken up according to the momentary requirements, and it is precisely this kind of flexibility that requires the subjects' permanent self-control. Emotions, techniques and procedures change, and while who actually orchestrates this is not entirely clear, an integral must nevertheless continue to exist, however provisional it may be, if the neoliberal subject does not want to drift completely into the pathological and sociopathic.

In the course of financialisation, almost everything, from love, education to religion, is now seen under the lens of optimisation and profitability. This is complementary to the demands on the performance of companies (in terms of profitability) and governments (in terms of efficiency), which today often enough has to first and foremost convince financial markets. Finally, it is not least a question of the constitution of an investing subject: he should eat efficiently, i.e. he should even see food as an investment in his body, whereby obesity, one of the fastest growing diseases of civilisation today, is seen as the result of a wrong investment in the body. The motto is: respond to your precarious life by managing the risks, invest in health insurance to provide preventive care, respond to lack of solidarity by investing your time in a collectively practiced hobby or in a voluntary activity. Today, financialisation is also forming the transversal precariat and offers itself as a solution to its problems; precariousness is then not only a norm, but becomes a gift, a possibility for the financed subject to direct every ambition and effort towards living in the present, making quick decisions and privatising the future by investing in jobs, health and wellness, and by preferably insuring everything possible. In the financier we then find the leading figure for the elevated and leveraged precariat, whom all workers and employees should (and cannot) tirelessly emulate. This leads to a brave new life, characterised by maximum liquidity and quickly ready to assimilate to the most profitable situations.[2]

---

[2] Max Haiven gives a variety of examples that demonstrate the enormous influence of neoliberal finance on cultural and social life (Haiven 2014). He examines the Wall Street

344   A. SZEPANSKI

Since with the emergence of derivatives, the means of insuring against debt have become both objects of promise and profitability, we can no longer assume fixed positions of creditors and debtors in at least the wealthier segments of the middle class and the elites of developed countries. There will then no longer be the absolutely dominant creditor on the one hand, who occupies the capital position and, on the other hand, the exhausted debtor who marks completely the wage-dependent. If, for example, the liabilities of a debtor can be passed on from one creditor to a third creditor, and this kind of concatenation spreads in a global space, the positions of creditor and debtor involved are already no longer as clearly separated as, for example, in the former disciplinary regimes and those of sovereignty. They fluctuate, oscillate and exchange each other and are at the same time no longer easily observable. Debtors often understand debt purely as a dyadic personal relationship between creditor and debtor, where the creditor lends money and the debtor is contractually and morally obligated to repay. This view ignores the current forms of the chain of debts, insofar as they are not only an obligation but tradable assets, parts of a multiple security (e.g. CDOs). There are no longer any clearly identifiable zones in which the parasitic debtor can be precisely separated from its host, the creditor; rather, it is precisely the patterns of the last financial crises that have shown that, at a certain point, the weak parasitic debtor can even dominate or at least endanger the financial system in a certain way; it is then simultaneously the weakest and most powerful point in the financial system.

If the construction of debt today means the extension of the financial logic and strategies by which the subject is governed and governs itself, then derivatives are the flip side of the same process. While the axiomatic of capital apparently demands infinite indebtedness, in return it requires the construction of ever new forms of promises of payment and

---

banker, the much-vaunted "risk-taker" whose professional attitude towards the precarious makes him an extremely affective agent of a broader process of financialisation. At the lower end, he examines the objective victim, who is also "at risk" in a very specific way, namely the racialised sub-prime borrower, whose toxic debt allegedly poisoned the global financial system in 2007. Today, in the wake of austerity policies and the cult of branding, even Walmart is transforming its clients and workers into risk takers, neoliberal subjects and sophisticated financial actors who make the methods and practices of financial risk management their own. Moreover, in an era in which all aspects of life tend to be measured, quantified and speculatively managed, the nebulous term "creativity" takes on a supreme actuality; it includes a new discursive formation of financialisation.

money capital, especially when it comes to the modalities, technologies and methods of self-government and self-optimisation that are currently still organised by the biopolitics of neoliberalism. But one should not fall into the melancholy of imagining a universally and eternally indebted human being; rather, one should strictly refuse to accept the pathetic dialectic that permanently shifts the relationship between creditor and debtor back and forth. The reduction of the creditor-debtor relationship to that of a pure submission to capital must be resolutely opposed.

Capitalisation today constitutes a regime for regulating financial practices that go far beyond the binary practice of distinguishing between security and uncertainty, which culminates in the construction of risk. If in the past, social financialisation focused on important markers such as trust and anomaly, precisely to avoid disruption or accident, today risk is considered inevitable and its existence is even considered desirable, so that we must get used to living under conditions of the constant presence of risk. Today we have to consider at every moment the most current conditions of risk production and, at the same time, to examine the social relations that make possible capitalising on risk, in order to finally recognise risk as a central element of the government of the self and its economy.

The subject of financialisation is precisely the one that uses the present to calculate the future and speculate on future profits, while at the same time hedging risks and then blocking the dangers of this hedging over and over again by re-hedging them. The possibilities of loss and at the same time the hedging of this possible loss, with which even profit can be generated, are connected: loss and profit no longer constitute inverse proportional quantities, but one quantity now produces the other. This access to the future produces a method that looks rigidly and stubbornly at the future, at a future profit or at a hedge in the future. The future is thus equated with competitive success, and by insuring it while constantly reassessing fluctuating expectations of the future, it is possible to permanently redefine it. In this context, the derivative is anticipated as a price in the future, which of course has yet to happen, by calculating the price and discounting it to current values, and this is precisely how the contingent future is used to generate returns in the present. This way of managing the future affects the present, which is now itself divided and no longer the only one from which one started the calculation. To relate it to actors: their actions now have to include the future as a condition of their own actions, and thus current actions themselves are modified. Subjectivity itself becomes fluctuating; indeed, its evaluation takes place in the face of the naked axiomatics of money, so that there is no more time for the subject to incur something like a moral guilt. The current production of monetary debt through financialisation thus by no means requires a passive subject, but rather requires the production of an active subject who is no longer bound only to property and contract, but at the same time surfs on the incessant waves of risk evaluation, promises of payment, ratings and rankings. The financialised subject must now learn to perceive, evaluate and execute every possibility to improve its own life in order to oscillate in between a period of time spanning contracts and derivatives. The subject must constantly affirm that its life constantly oscillates between a debt to capital and the function of a creditor who creates his own life.

Debts are not directly inscribed on the body, but rather the addition of debts is inscribed in the brain again and again, and this via the mechanism of constant evaluation of productive possibilities. It is therefore not only a matter of evaluating debts themselves, but of increasing them with regard to one's own small capital and its possibilities and potentials. What is evaluated and shared here is thus less the potency to repay debt than a constant payment in the context of an evaluation of future possibilities. In this way, debt as a technology of power is finally integrated into a multiple dispositive of evaluation: it is the continuous process of evaluating the possibilities of valorising the subject, which is simultaneously organised and incessantly mobilised by certain power relations.

Today, the decisive factor in dealing with debt is no longer just its accounting or the tyranny of numbers, but also the management of risk, which consists in evaluating subjects according to their potential and determining the quantity of human capital they will potentially produce or accumulate in the future, for which purpose risk profiles must be drawn up and their addressees consequently classified according to arithmetical, hierarchical taxonomies; an incessant financial process produces the numbering (countability) of all the elements of life and social relations in order to constantly combine and compare the two areas, thus producing the endless repetition of the same thing. A constant government of debt is required: I manage my debt does not mean that I can manage my capital, and this is precisely why capital calls you today not only a debtor, but also a capitalising creator who intervenes transformatively in its own risk production in order to become an infinite and constant creator, which then mostly has to get by without reward. This kind of creator is a by-product of financialisation, which can even assume a proto-fascist authoritarian disposition. One tells the creator of small, fine debt capital that he can turn his life into a game of chance, but in which, and this is concealed, he never wins and is therefore forced to play the lottery until death. He is told that the market will bring him peace and prosperity; yet he sees a future ahead of him that, while not necessarily marked by poverty, is at least marked by permanent pressure and worries about his own living conditions. The financialised subject, who is both creditor and debtor, lives in an endless futurised now, which gently demands he focus his social imagination entirely on managing his own risks, leveraging their potential and maximising returns. Any perspective on the previously unknown is thus blatantly eliminated.

The singular relation between creditor and debtor can eventually expand to an expanding and chaining relation, but it can also be a relation of changing positions: every debtor can become a creditor and every creditor a debtor.

What does this mean for a resistant handling of debt? Instead of fixed positions and the perpetrator-victim relationship that lurks in the creditor-debtor relationship, we should strive to enrich the debtor with possible strengths that come from elsewhere: cancelling any consequences that lie in the debtor-creditor relationship, oversleeping payments of debt and creating differently structured communities. The debtor can actually show indifference towards his debt and thus act in an anti-disciplinary manner. The relationship between creditor and debtor is mobile in that attractions alternate with repulsions, and there are opposing tensions, and here too the boundaries are continually being shifted: a mobile field with no predetermined rules. Every moment is the fleeting moment of an invisible decision that is continuously renewed. Debt is then no longer about moral debt, but about relations that must be continually renegotiated, about strategies of changing tactics and about negotiations that go on and on and do not stop, but change, turn and perish. These are the minimal perspectives if the field of debt under capitalism is to be kept open.

References

Deleuze, Gilles and Guattari, Félix (1992) *Tausend Plateaus. Kapitalismus und Schizophrenie*, Berlin.

Haiven, Max (2014) *Crises of Imagination, Crises of Power: Capitalism, Creativity and the Commons*, London.

Lee, Benjamin and Martin, Randy (eds.) (2016) *Derivatives and the Wealth of Societies*, Chicago.

Martin, Randy (2015) *Knowledge Ltd: Toward a Social Logic of the Derivative*, Philadelphia.

Mau, Steffen (2017) *Das metrische Wir. Über die Quantifizierung des Sozialen*, Berlin.

Mirowski, Philip (2015) *Untote leben länger. Warum der Neoliberalismus nach der Krise noch stärker ist*, Berlin.

Pohrt, Wolfgang (1980) *Ausverkauf. Von der Endlösung zu ihrer Alternative*, Berlin.

CHAPTER 13

Financial System and Crisis

Reference to the generally negative characteristics of the financial system (excessive speculation) or to its recurring errors (the issuance of too many mortgage loans, flawed risk management, asymmetric information, etc.), sheds little light on the real causes of the global crisis of capital in recent decades. Mainstream economists have identified four main causes of crises: high debt, global imbalances, financialisation in general and the issuing of promises of payment for which people were not prepared (cf. Das 2015: 33). One also repeatedly points out the errors in the regulation of financial markets, for example, that the ratings of companies by the rating agencies, which were of course related to their own interests, were not correctly carried out from 2000 onwards; further mention is made of the dangerous use of CDSs by banks, which would have led to a reduction in their capital reserves; additionally mentioned is the lack of transparency in the OCT markets and the fact that investment banks were able to use their own models to assess market risks and the necessary reserves for risky investments from 2004 onwards, and so on. Other factors invoked were the rapid rise in housing prices, the issuance of prime loans and their securitisation, the incorrect valuation of collateral, the opaque relationship between SPVs and money markets (especially in the U.S.). Yet all of these explanations are not the real reasons for the so-called subprime crisis of 2007, but at best manifestations of the crisis-ridden development of the

© The Author(s), under exclusive license to Springer Nature
Switzerland AG 2022
A. Szepanski, *Financial Capital in the 21st Century*,
Marx, Engels, and Marxisms,
https://doi.org/10.1007/978-3-030-93151-3_13

global capitalist economy, which today is still represented by the neoliberal model, i.e. by the special organisation of capitalist social formations since the 1980s (cf. Milios and Sotiropoulos 2009: 164f.). Incidentally, many of these circumstances continue to exist even after the financial crisis of 2008; one need only think of the concentrated power of the three major rating agencies, the timid attempts by governments to regulate the financial industry, which can circumvent the regulations by creating new "loopholes" and exploiting empty spaces, the invention of new forms of derivatives and the complementary risk models, the success of which, however, remains dependent on the fragile and crisis-ridden accumulation of capital. Ultimately, the crisis of 2008 hit the working classes and their households particularly hard, separating them from their small fortunes and made their situation even more precarious.

The deepening of the financial system in the sense that today, at least in developed economies, potentially every existing sum of money can be capitalised and profitably invested as a promise of payment, is an important moment in the international expansion of capital, i.e. the global mobilisation of certain monetary potentials for the capitalist mode of production in order to further increase or at least maintain the profitability of capital. For some time now, additional players have been entering the world market, for example through the privatisation of state insurance systems, and this has led to a further mobilisation of sums of money that do not necessarily have to be invested directly in production, but are rather part of the capitalisation of future income flows and promises of payment. This will require an increasingly large non-banking sector within the financial system itself. At the same time, the pressure on so-called risk-free profits is increasing, which in turn leads to the issuance of new financial securities, thus integrating previously undiscovered markets into the world of credit, which in turn increases the risks that are now constantly fluctuating and migrating around the world.

An important aspect of the neoliberal model is its international character, in that the world market tends to be transformed into a single chart of profit. The international character of capital, combined with the expansion of new markets and the generalisation of risk management techniques to insure against risks of all kinds, has led to a deeper and broader distribution of risks since the 2000s. But risk management itself, since the first rumours about the lack of collateral for mortgage loans in the U.S. began to appear, no longer functions precisely, but rather indicates the planetary proliferation of risks. Today, the much-vaunted "wisdom of the markets" presupposes that the financial system evaluates each individual security, but this is precisely what has caused the loss of trust between the major players.

During the financial crisis of 2008, there was a virtual evaporation of liquidity in the credit markets because financial institutions hoarded capital instead of throwing it into circulation, as they feared counterparties in the derivatives business were insolvent, thus making the pricing of derivatives inefficient. The risk that banking institutions became insolvent was not only in realising low returns, but also in holding illiquid assets, which could trigger a chain reaction in which the liquid assets of "healthy" financial institutions could also be destroyed. This is often described as a "contagion", done by an objective, impersonal agent that operates independently from the social and sets in motion a deflationary spiral. Financial crises thus manifest themselves in a drastic reduction of liquidity resulting from a lack in buyers for securities, with the only means to end the crisis residing in the refinancing potential of central banks, in measures such as bailouts and quantitative easing, and in the issuance of new government bonds, which serve as collateral for new loans and thus initiate a further increase in lending. In this context, one has to assume a fractal chain of circulating risks, whereby a new bubble never develops where the last one burst before. The temporal structure of the chain of circulating speculative capital is characterised by two opposing forces and dynamics: the need to increase risk and the need to maintain the cohesion of the market. At the same time, these two aspects are interconnected, creating a structural-intrinsic tension that, in the logic of speculative capital itself, is leading to crises (LiPuma 2017: 156).

In temporal terms, circulatory financial capital perpetuates what LiPuma calls the "treadmill effect"[1] (Ibid.: 24). What may be rational

---

[1] It must be stated that time itself constitutes a form of abstract risk. Or, to put it differently, time is a ubiquitous form of risk that applies to every type of derivative. In production, agents minimise externally generated risk by extending time horizons. In contrast, an inverse set of risk conditions determines circulation. Since every derivative has an expiration date and the time period involved in it has no external referent, time is both a source and a quantifiable dimension of risk. For speculative capital, minimising risk means compressing or neutralising the effects of time, and this involves factors such as volatility, market instability and the emergence of contingent events. But this compression of time also possesses a qualitative effect: speculative capital generates an end in itself through the means of connectivity, the derivative; the derivative serves as a source of profits and its own reproduction. The resulting culture and economy of finance produce new social forms such as that of abstract risk, new technologies such as the pricing of derivatives

for institutional investors in the short run may be irrational and destructive for the financial system as a whole. The potential for errors inherent in the system cannot be reduced to individual actions or the dispositions of agents. Socially collective dispositions are created in the process, which steer the behaviour of individual actors in a particular direction. Securitisation strategies are inherently tied to a period of euphoria, from mortgage lending to derivatives. The structural dynamics of securitisation chains result in the need to constantly increase the leverage of portfolios by borrowing short-term money at low interest rates to raise the money to finance longer-term derivatives at higher rates. This was possible before the last financial crisis in 2008 because two cycles of leverage were related: homeowners leveraged their homes as financial assets and managers leveraged their portfolios, driving the two sewn-together markets into a mutually fuelled instability through two directional dynamics. If each high that is reached in the various financial markets represents a new plateau from which speculative capital seeks to eliminate the possibility of falling profits, then this is precisely what leads to the crisis as a systemic problem. In this process, two necessary tendencies conflict, namely the need to increase risk and the need to hold together the integrity of the market. These two opposing tendencies produce an intrinsic-structural tension that is sui generis social and, at the same time, intrinsic to the logic of speculative capital itself. This intrinsic logic does not imply that the market follows a linear logic and must collapse systemically, but it does establish the possibility of crisis processes that are intrinsic to financial markets.

The central argument LiPuma elaborates on the temporality of speculative capital is that derivative markets self-referentially set in motion a temporal progression by which abstract risk is pushed to a level where even small turbulence in markets can lead to systematic collapse. Thus, the propensity for instability that induces crisis also builds on the temporal dynamics of markets. There is a directional dynamic that points to increasing complexity and instability in markets, which LiPuma tries to explain with the treadmill effect. This must necessarily address the problem of time, namely the discrepancy between abstract time (of the

through mathematical models and new self-referential contractual arrangements. Factors such as self-referentiality, the compression of time and the monetisation of risk generate derivative markets whose construction of time bears no necessary relation to the markets of underlying or, for that matter, to the temporality of institutions, including financial institutions.

system) and the time of agents, times that are substantially different. Moreover, the financial field has a multiplicity of temporalities that are intertwined (Ibid.: 147).

Derivative markets are inherently unstable to the point that their volatility often rises to extreme levels. Their cycles move with increasing levels of leverage (growing risks), complexity and instability. These markets become increasingly unstable towards the end of a cycle. The more extensively extremely high profits are realised, the more speculative capital flows into the markets, forcing intense competition among financial corporations, which in turn drives the motivations of market participants to increase leverage (Ibid.).

Lucrative trades in markets today immediately attract huge flows of monetary capital, with sellers' yields falling as demand increases if certain market participants demand the same position. It is a characteristic of financial markets that there is a compression in time with which the acceleration of trades leaves a company's margins and returns more and more thin. The traders' response to this is again to increase their leverage, to which in turn the mass of traders must respond by applying the same strategies. An important point of the treadmill effect is simply that the market's progression requires market participants to constantly increase their risk appetite.

As long as investors expect asset prices to rise, these are liquid and can be sold at a profit. As soon as prices stagnate, however, investors try to sell the assets, which may only be realised at a loss. If a large investor wants to then sell a large number of assets, or a large number of small investors want to sell assets, this can lead to liquidity bottlenecks in the liquidation of the assets, which can result in panic actions and a related fall in the price of the assets.

Unanticipated risks, loss of confidence and massive construction and deconstruction of payment promises can therefore lead to gigantic swings in volatility that feed off each other. These swings in volatility are exaggerated when hedge funds, which are anyway highly leveraged, rely on long-term paper such as mortgage loans, but need quick money to invest in the short-term. Structurally, the temporality of financial money flows focuses on short-termism, indeed on the short-term that is immediately possible. This is also reflected in the permanent search of speculative capital for new arbitrage opportunities, a situation in which opposing positions neutralise the risks or the time lag between the beginning of the derivative position and the set expiration date. These mechanisms set in motion the directionality and compression of time, whether in terms of derivative positions or the attempt to exploit speculative capital as optimally as possible.

As we have seen, what may be rational for the players in the short-term in this context becomes a problem for the market as a whole. Financial crises are not simply consequences of random outbursts, as Nicholas Taleb assumed with his "Black Swans" (Taleb 2010), but they are results of a structural tension, stress or disturbance that is intrinsic to the temporalities of financial markets. In this context, external news may well accelerate crisis processes. The duration of the decline in liquidity, in turn, corresponds to the structural vulnerability of markets, to which highly leveraged derivative positions contribute, and which are particularly susceptible to accelerated liquidations.

In times of crisis, there is an increasing need for assets that are considered to be highly liquid and highly secure. Confidence about the future value of assets turns to uncertainty. It is a moment when Minsky's liquidity illusion becomes apparent. Assets are now becoming illiquid because there are no more buyers. If there is a greater selling of securities due to falling profit expectations, then higher collateral is required for repo contracts, for example, and the risk premiums on repo contracts also increase. Highly leveraged investors get into payment difficulties and have to sell even more securities to gain liquidity. We see a downward liquidity spiral as securities fall in price, risk premiums on repo contracts rise and more collateral is required. Repo contracts get more expansive and liquidity problems arise. As the prices of securities fluctuate continuously, the downward spiral can start rapidly, requiring monetary resources and central bank money to cover existing liabilities. Investors are forced at the end to sell securities at almost any price.

The financial system is unstable sui generis. It is pro-cyclical: either there is a lot of liquidity in the market and more are created, or there is too little liquidity and it is reduced even further. In times of crises, the private financial companies need the state and the central banks to stabilise the financial system as a whole. And if the shadow banking system plays an increasingly important role in providing liquidity, then it must also be stabilised more strongly.

Derivative markets create a social field characterised by the fact that investors must necessarily include the risk structure in their habitus. The systemic risk is then indicated in the loss of confidence in the solvency of counterparties and is realised as a mutual restriction of liquidity. A movement is set in motion whereby the realisation of a certain level of profitability becomes the base level of that timeframe to which future referencing will occur. No matter what happens in the markets specifically, the systemic dimension of risk, related to the market as a whole, can trigger a crisis. This is the modus operandi of finance and derivatives, insofar as risk is at the same time a concrete speculative and a socially generated activity that imbues the market with its systemic cohesion. In this context, the price decline of derivatives during a crisis is by no means due to mispricing; rather, the price of concrete risk expresses the temporality of systemic risk. It must also be noted that the market is not always liquid per se. Large orders of shares may amount to 100,000 shares, and these can only be settled over days or weeks.

Hyman P. Minsky is usually associated with post-Keynesian economic theory, more precisely with the American "school", to which authors such as Weintraub, Moore, Eichner, Kregel, etc. belong. In contrast to the European school around Kalecki, Robinson, Kaldor, Harcourt, etc., this school is more concerned with the monetary and financial processes of economics. For Minsky, investment is determined by profitability, and the so-called animal spirits depend on variables such as profit and interest rates. The key indicator here is the ratio of profit rate to interest rate.

With the help of Minsky's analyses (cf. Minsky 2011), it can be shown that, in addition to the existence of speculative bubbles on financial markets (phases of euphoria include phases of radical imitation and hyper-speculation, followed by panic phases, consolidation phases and phases of reorganisation), other factors must necessarily be added in order to trigger crisis processes at the level of total capital, not only the debt and credit economy, but rather factors that impair, disrupt and inhibit the already uncertain stability conditions of the capitalist economy as a whole. This is quite contrary to the assumptions of neoclassical economists, according to which it is, above all, the interplay of supply and demand on markets that sets and controls the price signals necessary for the formation of equilibria or that markets as self-organising systems strive towards the optimal state of equilibrium via cybernetic feedback loops.

Thus, the cycle of the extended reproduction of capital according to Minsky can be represented as follows: in stable production periods, which include positive long-term expectations of corporations, both their demand for financing and their investment volume increase, up to the point where companies completely abandon their risk aversion and at the same time increase their willingness to take on new debts, whereby the profits skimmed off in the companies, resulting from new investments, are used less to repay the loans and more for reinvestment, and in some cases loans are even financed with new loans. The gradual shift in the centre of fluctuation of market prices, or the length of time these processes take hold (the duration of a business cycle, which itself becomes a general determinant of the relationship between production prices and market prices), is also part of the so-called upswing, with a shift in the centre of gravity of market price movements in all sectors of production, until this centre of gravity finally determines the supply prices with which individual capitals compete.

It is the complex of solvent demand, price elasticity and debt financing potential that defines profit rates and profit masses and that determines capacity utilisation and investment in the various sectors and individual companies. During a boom, cost prices can rise significantly due to factors such as rising wages, increased prices for raw materials and rising interest rates (In this context, Sraffa has emphasised the problem that profit rates are needed to determine prices, and vice versa; prices are needed to determine profit rates, a problem that Marx poses anew).

In a boom, banks, hedge funds and other financial institutions are constantly creating new financial instruments or synthetic securities, while at the same time the indebtedness of companies is growing, and even in an already escalating boom, higher investments still lead to increasing profits, which at a certain point, however, are no longer sufficient to pay off the due part of the company's total debt. And finally, the effective money supply grows, while the rising prices of fictitious and speculative capital continue to increase the demand for securities investments, which is also serviced by banks, thus further increasing the supply of money and swelling the circulation of debt, further fuelling the attempt by companies to offset debt with risky investments and accelerating the increase in debt financing of companies.

At a certain point, the refinancing of companies actually becomes a problem because the cybernetic feedback system of the economy remains extremely euphoric despite the high growth of debt financing in companies, up to the very critical point, which Minsky defined as the Ponzi moment - when every further borrowing of a company is burdened with such high interest payments that they can no longer be serviced from the cash flow profits of the company, so that eventually assets are sold or new borrowed capital must be taken up in order to service the interest alone, thus triggering further cascade-like interlinkages of debt chains.

For example, the relationship between (expected) returns and scheduled loan obligations appears to be much more precarious from a certain point on; it requires either new loans to be taken out or further sales of assets, since banks are also constantly reducing their liquidity, partly because of the falling prices of securities plus the rising cost of their own borrowing. Since a large proportion of assets are now mark-to-market, i.e. asset prices have a direct impact on existing contracts, a fall in asset prices affects a large number of assets in real time. Since assets are the central nervous system of repo markets and the shadow banking system, their unsaleability in a crisis leads to a shortage of liquidity for all financial institutions. If the market makers, since they do not have access to central bank money, run into payment problems, the whole shadow bank system is quickly affected.

Although central banks can, according to Minsky, continue to supply the unstable and imbalanced markets with new liquidity due to the generally limited effect of their monetary policy, the only way to support and stabilise effective demand is through government deficit spending, which in turn decisively improves corporate situations.

A Ponzi scheme developed in the subprime mortgage industry by 2008. By passing on the credit default risks, banks were less and less interested in the creditworthiness of their customers. In addition, the subprime mortgages were only secured when real estate prices rose, but they started to decrease since 2006. Many subprime borrowers were no longer able to pay off their mortgages. As a result of the defaults, many smaller subprime lenders had to close or were taken over. Already in May 2007, subprime loans of about \$100 billion turned out to be bad debt. The private banks no longer trusted each other and the money market came to a standstill. Larger hedge funds had to file for insolvency. The insolvency of Lehmann Brothers was the final straw. The bank had a central position as a market maker in the transaction of derivatives contracts in the shadow banking system and therefore endangered the positions of many banks and investors on Wall Street with its insolvency. The story is well known. To prevent the credit crunch, the ECB, Fed and other central banks issued emergency loans at low interest rates. Governments started the well known bailouts and rescue measures. Interest rates were lowered, nationalisations occurred and a monetary policy of quantitative easing was pursued. Bad banks were set up to create liquidity and recapitalise banks.

It is the "sudden collapse of the marginal efficiency of capital" (Keynes 2018: 281) that leads to a jam in capital accumulation, all the more so because during a boom phase, the exorbitant increase in speculative transactions and debt financing artificially boost economic growth, while in the downturn, massive capital devaluations are imminent. This has a strong influence on the turnover times of companies with so-called productivity-sensitive components of fixed capital, but at the same time also prepares the ground for the new and important rationalisation process of the overall economic production apparatus. Neuralgic points of Minsky's theory concern, among other things, the vague determination of the relationship between equity and debt financing, Minsky's strong concentration on investments in fixed assets and the possibility of capital to circumvent the dependence of effective demand on investments and state deficit spending by expanding consumer credit, a possibility which he ignored but which has been increasingly realised since the 1990s. Ultimately, Minsky's irrepressible belief in the financial sovereignty of the state and his renunciation of a more detailed investigation of the integration of monetary capital into the structural movement of differential capital accumulation pose further problems for this theoretical approach.

In the end, how should we understand the relationship between financial crises and production? Sometimes financial crises open up a period of overaccumulation of capital, but sometimes they also mark the end of an overaccumulation crisis, and sometimes financial crises manifest themselves relatively independently of real economic cycles, i.e. they do not have a significant effect on the movement of industrial profit rates and on employment. In any case, the crisis movements of financial capital cannot be fully synchronised with the cycles of industrial profit rates, as traditional Marxist theory often enough tries to demonstrate, but the development of financial crises and their bubbles always has a certain autonomy. Carlota Perez has made an attempt to explain the connections: in the expansion phases, innovative companies have problems financing themselves because the companies that use the already established technologies absorb the available capital, while when these technologies have reached their highest efficiency and the profitable investment opportunities are lacking, there is sufficient monetary capital available. In the downturn phase, financial capital can intervene by financing new innovative projects or by modernising existing sectors, while unprofitable industries are liquidated (Perez 2002). However, the establishment of new technological-economic paradigms and productive forces remains an unstable process, since the realisation of new projects is contingent, regardless of the establishment of new institutional frameworks that support the new developments. Technological innovation remains inscribed in the movement of capital (Durand 2017 Kindle Edition: 1776).

It is also often assumed that due to the lack of demand or the impossibility of finding new investment opportunities, surplus capital simply migrates to the financial sector, where over time bubbles form or unproductive policies of purely monetary accumulation based on debt take place. In fact, a transfer of idle monetary capital to the financial sector has been taking place since the 1970s. One can think of the transfer of idle monetary capital from stagnant industrial zones in the Midwest (Ohio Valley) to capital-thirsty California, where new technology companies, financial institutions and the logistics industry were setting up. It was financial firms such as Salomon Brothers that created financial instruments such as mortgage bonds and collateralised mortgage obligations (CMOs, the packaging of various types of credit such as student loans, credit card debt, loans for home and car purchases, etc.) and organised their distribution in a self-referentially processing market in the U.S. (cf. LiPuma 2017: 129ff.). The derivatives were now no longer directly tied to production, but to the circulation of money flows on which their liquidity remained dependent, which in turn, spurs the multiplication of capital. The asset underlying the derivative is now integrated into an abstract relation. The derivative trades the volatility of this abstract relation, which in turn produces derivatives on this abstract relation (the CDS is a derivative that is the endless flow of the flows of CDOs and CMOs). What emerged was a speculative economy of circulation of CDSs and CMOs, whose thread to the "real economy" was that homeowners learned to treat their homes as financial assets. As Samir Amin insists: "Financialization then provides not only the sole possible outlet for surplus capital, it also provides the sole stimulus to the slack growth observed, since the 1970s, in the United States, Europe, and Japan. To roll back financialization would thus merely weaken yet further the growth of the 'real' economy" (Amir 2010: 65). With regard to the operations and strategies pursued by the financial industry, it should therefore be noted that they have their strongest effects precisely not in the circulation sphere and on consumption, but on investment. Take, for example, the dotcom boom and the corresponding hype on international stock markets. Not only did financial investments multiply, but real investments in the computer and telecommunications industries also increased. When the crash on the stock market occurred, investments in these industries in

360   A. SZEPANSKI

particular declined again, leading to a recession.[2] The role of derivatives
in the ensuing financial crisis consisted, among other things, in massively

---

[2] However, the influence of the financial sector on demand cannot be ignored of course.
Since the 1990s, the U.S. has been the world's largest importer of capital, with capital
import flows helping to finance its growing foreign trade and current account deficits.
For a long time, this influx of capital also served to finance the consumption of U.S.
citizens, whose wage income stagnated and who, as compensation, financed a growing
share of their current consumption with increasing debt. As a result, economic growth
in the U.S. was higher than in Europe or Japan. Since consumption accounts for 70% of
the U.S. economy and the U.S. is still the world's largest economy, accounting for about
30% of the world's national product, debt-driven demand also had a positive effect on the
global economy. While China focused its export industry of consumer goods strongly on
the U.S., Japan and Germany mainly supplied capital goods all over the world, but also
remained indirectly dependent on the steadily increasing demand for consumer goods in
the U.S. In a nutshell, speculation on financial markets supported the U.S.'s debt and
thus countered the tendency towards economic stagnation at a global level. When the
financial crisis broke out in the summer of 2007, international capital stopped financing
the consumption of U.S. households. Due to weakening demand, the U.S. economy slid
into recession at the end of 2007. It took about nine months until weakening demand
was reflected in the orders of the German export industry.

In *Cyber-Proletariat*, Nick Dyer-Witheford addresses the problem that the reduction
or stagnation of wage costs, made possible by automation and outsourcing, among other
things, raises the question of who should actually buy the products that flow out of
the global supply chains, a problem that has been increasingly answered in the U.S.
since the 1980s by granting consumer credit (Dyer-Witheford 2015: 169). It is also
possible to increase demand by increasing the number of workers, as has been the case
in China, when real wages are falling or stagnating, or by increasing luxury consumption,
as has been the case in the U.S., and by creating new social strata with considerable
purchasing power, as well as by increasing the number of actors (brokers, commercial
capital, real estate, etc.) who are responsible in advance for the realisation of the goods.
This does not solve the problem of realisation or overaccumulation. The latter can be
delayed by excessive prices and fees, higher taxes and radical austerity policies, but this
does not eliminate overproduction and the lack of profitable investment opportunities and
thus the overaccumulation of capital. In the context of the overaccumulation of capital,
it is precisely the rising costs of technological investments in complex and expensive
cybernetic systems and infrastructures that have partially compensated for the tendencies
that have counteracted the fall in the profit rate, which are based on the technological
innovations of cybernetics (microchips). The real estate sector illustrates what can happen
when the construction sector is lent large sums of money by banks and, at the same
time, mortgages are granted to consumers so that they can buy the terraced houses built
by construction companies. In this context, financial capital is an extremely important
juggler for postponing or compensating for the crises in question (and not just those
that caused them). Financial capital, which today is equipped with the best integrated
cybernetic systems, operates constantly in a field of insecurity that cyclically also creates
turbulence, with the new advantages of life gained by parts of the proletariat evaporating
in a matter of seconds.

fuelling the speculative boom from a certain phase onwards, with deals extending far beyond the U.S. and overcoming all local barriers. Nevertheless, derivatives were not the sole reason for the crisis, but they did give it a special intensity and a specific financial form.

Classical capital accumulation enters a crisis when functioning capital overaccumulates due to credit financing, whereby the production set in motion reaches its limits due to the falling rate of profit and can also no longer be realised profitably due to weakening demand and manifests itself as overproduction. An overaccumulation crisis can start with the bursting of a credit bubble. In this case, the production of surplus value and/or its transformation back into additional constant and variable capital is reduced and investment and employment of wageworkers slows down. In the crisis, overaccumulated capital and commodity capital are destroyed and devalued until capacity utilisation stops falling and investment processes stabilise again.

Economic growth requires, on the one hand, sufficient monetary capital and, on the other hand, higher employment and/or increasing labour productivity, which is always tied to a growing and qualitatively improved capital stock (gross fixed assets). The produced value mass is the sum of the transferred value of the means of production (constant capital), the value of the employed labour force (variable capital) and the produced surplus value. The slowdown of the investment growth and the decrease of the investment rate as well as the accumulation rate (growth rate of capital) are to be understood as important criteria of stagnant capital accumulation and dwindling investment opportunities. From the point of view of individual capital, it does not matter whether its utilisation arises from an investment in functioning real capital or in financial assets. In order to be able to assess the tendencies of accumulation, it is necessary to study all forms of capital. Since for companies, the profit as a whole count and not the coverage of the demand for commodities, it is ultimately irrelevant for the individual capital whether it achieves this profit with real investments or with financial assets.

In Germany, the macroeconomic savings ratio has fallen from 20 to around 10 per cent since 1970. This decline is largely due to the increasingly indebted state (negative savings) and private households, while the savings rate of the entire corporate sector, including non-financial corporations, has increased. The changed investment behaviour of companies in the productive sphere can be explained by the fact that returns on financial investments can be much higher in the relatively short-term compared to those in the productive sphere. This means that the expectations of shareholders and institutional investors, but also of management, for quick profits and bonuses are better satisfied than with investments with long and therefore uncertain realisation periods. This is due in large part to the growing global demand for capital in the emerging markets and the liberalisation of the international financial markets on the one hand, and a hyper-cyclical overaccumulation of productive capital in the highly developed countries on the other.

The investment ratio is the quotient of investments and gross domestic product. Its reduction can be explained by the denominator as well as the numerator. If we look at gross fixed capital formation in the numerator, no secular slowdown can be seen in Germany. Since the early 1950s, they have increased linearly - with the exception of crises. In other words, the decline in the ratio is due to the fact that the annual absolute growth in gross domestic product has been greater than that of investments. In important areas of the national economy, the ratio of production output to physical capital input has improved, i.e. the investment requirement per unit of output growth has fallen slightly in some areas as a result of capital-saving technical progress and increasing returns to scale. This development is reflected in a capital coefficient (ratio of gross fixed assets to gross value added) that has stagnated or even fallen in some cases compared to the past, particularly in the manufacturing industry, the information and communications sector and agriculture. In macroeconomic terms, this has slowed the growth of the capital coefficient, which has a dampening effect on the investment ratio. Finally, companies increased their investments abroad more than at home, so that the German stock of foreign assets has increased from 8 to 43 per cent of the gross domestic product between 1990 and 2012.

The generally low growth of the economy of the developed countries and the low profitability of its various sectors were also important reasons for the boom in the derivatives trade and for the rise of financial innovations. Conversely, derivatives, together with other aspects of the credit system, stimulated capital accumulation by reducing the transaction costs of companies, widening risks and releasing funds and payment promises for the generation of profits. However, when large amounts of credit are unable to be repaid, with myriads of other financial transactions behind them, this can become the trigger for financial collapse. This also leads to a self-reinforcing lack of confidence in the financial markets, to the point of a collective fear that the expected profits will remain illusory, and in this respect, the financial crises are always related to the "real economy". Contrary to the theses of the underconsumption theory, it is essential to emphasise that the arrow of causality runs from the production of capital to demand and not vice versa. It is therefore necessary to insist on the validity of Marx's thesis that "the rate of accumulation is the independent, not the dependent variable; the rate of wages, the dependent, not the independent, variable" (Marx 1996: 615). The dynamics of capital accumulation ultimately determines the effective demand and the respective level of employment, although Marx's critique of Say's law is not that there must always be a surplus of supply in capitalism, but that there is seldom an equilibrium between supply and demand, and this precisely because of the cyclical development of capital accumulation. Of course, crises are always symptoms of this tendency towards imbalance, but the essential characteristics of economic crisis are, on the one hand, processes of overaccumulation of industrial capital and the associated tendency for the general falling rate of profit, and, on the other hand, the surplus circulation of fictitious and speculative capital, which then circulates aimlessly around the financialised globe.

References

Amin, Samir (2010) *The Law of Worldwide Value*, New York.

Das, Satyajit (2015) *A Banquet of Consequences. Have We Consumed Our Own Future?*, London.

Durand, Cédric (2017) *Fictitious Capital: How Finance Is Appropriating Our Future*, London.

Dyer-Whitheford (2015) *Cyber-Proletariat: Global Labour in the Digital Vortex*, London.

Keynes, John Maynard (2018) *The General Theory of Employment, Interest, and Money*, Cambridge.

LiPuma, Edward (2017) *The Social Life of Financial Derivatives: Markets, Risk, and Time*, Durham.

Marx, Karl (1996) *Capital, Vol. 1* [1867], in *Marx and Engels Collected Works*, Vol. 35, London.

Milios, John and Sotiropoulos, Dimitris (2009) *Rethinking Imperialism: A Study of Capitalist Rule*, London.

Minsky, Himan P. (2011) *Instabilität und Kapitalismus*, Zürich

Perez, Carlota (2002) *Technological Revolutions and Financial Capital*, Celtenham.

364 A. SZEPANSKI

Taleb, Nassim Nicholas (2010) *Der schwarze Schwan*, Munich.

UNCITED REFERENCES

Abgabenordnung der Bundesrublik Deutschland (2021) in: https://www.ges etze-im-internet.de/ao_1977/.

Benanav, Aaron (2002) *Automation and the Future of Work*, London.

Bichler, Shimshon and Nitzan, Jonathan (2015) *Capital Accumulation: Fiction and Reality*, in: *Philosophers for Change*, http://philosophersforchange.org/.

Bourdieu, Pierre (2015) *On the State: Lectures at the Collège de France 1989–1992*, Cambridge.

Clover, Joshua (2016) *Riot.Strike.Riot: The New Era of Uprisings*, London.

Davis, Mike (2006) *Planet of Slums: Urban Involution and the Informal Working Class*, London.

Deleuze, Gilles and Guattari, Félix (1983) *Anti-Oedipus: Capitalism and Schizophrenia*, Minneapolis.

Deleuze, Gilles and Guattari, Félix (1987) *A Thousand Plateaus: Capitalism and Schizophrenia*, Minneapolis.

ESRB Report (2016) in: https://www.esrb.europa.eu/home/html/index.en.html.

Fischbach, Rainer (2017) *Die schöne Utopie. Paul Mason, der Postkapitalismus und der Traum vom grenzenlosen Überfluss*, Cologne.

Global Wealth Report (2010) in: https://www.step.org/step-journal/step-jou rnal-february-2011/global-wealth-report.

Gordon, Robert J. (2013) *Is US Economic Growth Over? Faltering Innovation Confronts the Six*, in: http://www.voxeu.org/article/us-economic-gro wth-over.

Guattari, Félix (1992) *Chaosmosis: An Ethico-Aesthetic Paradigm*, Bloomington.

Heinrich, Michael (2004) *Kritik der politischen Ökonomie. Eine Einführung*, Stuttgart.

Heinrich, Michael (2013a) *Begründungsprobleme. Zur Debatte über das "Gesetz vom tendenziellen Fall der Profitrate"*. Probleme des Beweisens und Widerlegens, in: http://www.oekonomiekritik.de/313Tend%20Fall.pdf.

Heinrich, Michael (2013b) *Wie das Marxsche »Kapital« lesen? Leseanleitung und Kommentar zum Anfang des "Kapital" Teil 2*, Stuttgart.

Krüger, Stephan (2012) *Politische Ökonomie des Geldes: Gold, Währung, Zentralbankpolitik und Preise. Kritik der Politischen Ökonomie und Kapitalismusanalyse, Band 2*, Hamburg.

Laruelle, François (1979) *La Transvaluation de la methode transcendentale, Bulletin de la societe francaise de philosophie 73*.

Luhmann, Niklas (1984) *Soziale Systeme. Grundriß einer allgemeinen Theorie*, Frankfurt/M.

Norfield, Tony (2021) *World Power*, in: https://economicsofimperialism.blo gspot.com/.

Sanyal, Kalyan (2014) *Rethinking Capitalist Development: Primitive Accumulation, Governementality and Postcolonial Capitalism*, London.

Smith, John (2016) *Imperialism in the Twenty-First Century: Globalization, Super-Exploitation, and Capitalism's Final Crisis*, New York.

Szepanski, Achim (2011) *Saal 6*, Frankfurt/M.

UNCTAD Trade and Development Report (2016) in: https://unctad.org/web flyer/trade-and-development-report-2016.

INDEX

A
accumulation, 1, 5, 9, 19, 27, 29, 30, 36, 42, 45, 48–50, 52, 61, 68–72, 80, 81, 84, 90–92, 96, 131, 136–138, 142, 146, 147, 155, 167, 179, 184, 186, 194, 210, 220, 221, 224–226, 228–234, 239, 240, 244, 247, 248, 251, 257, 264, 270, 271, 273, 277, 278, 281, 283, 286, 290, 299, 305–307, 330, 335, 350, 357, 359, 361–363

overaccumulation, 358, 360–363
actualisation, 17, 37, 41, 49, 51, 78, 91, 127, 170, 173
arbitrage, 48, 85, 109, 111, 114, 123, 124, 141, 142, 145, 286, 320, 338, 353
asset, 2–6, 19, 22, 23, 34, 63, 64, 69, 74, 78, 79, 81, 82, 90–94, 98–100, 105–110, 113, 115, 119–123, 125, 127–130, 134–139, 141–146, 148, 150, 157, 167–169, 171–173, 175–177, 185–193, 195–199, 201, 204–207, 210–214, 225, 228, 234–238, 243, 246, 250, 254–256, 259–265, 270, 272, 278, 279, 281, 288, 289, 293, 297, 298, 313, 314, 320, 326–328, 342, 344, 351–354, 356–359, 361, 362

generic asset, 107, 108, 111
synthetic asset, 107, 108, 167
Ayache, Elie, 167, 171–174

B
Bailout, 81, 225, 234, 235, 244, 251, 259, 351, 357
balance sheet, 8, 18, 69, 72, 86, 105, 109, 110, 116, 118, 128, 148, 186, 188, 193, 195–198, 205–207, 209, 210, 213, 225, 236, 237, 246, 248, 252, 254, 260, 261, 264, 265, 275, 328, 330, 333

© The Editor(s) (if applicable) and The Author(s), under exclusive license to Springer Nature Switzerland AG 2022
A. Szepanski, *Financial Capital in the 21st Century*, Marx, Engels, and Marxisms,
https://doi.org/10.1007/978-3-030-93151-3

368 INDEX

bank
central bank, 2–4, 7, 22, 61, 62,
81, 93, 95, 118, 180, 182,
184, 185, 187, 195, 196, 198,
200–206, 208, 212, 213, 225,
228–230, 233, 235–238, 240,
242, 243, 245–265, 272, 273,
277, 285, 288, 290, 294, 296,
297, 327, 351, 354, 357
commercial bank, 18, 61, 62, 68,
93, 105, 130, 180–186, 189,
191–208, 210, 213, 214,
225–228, 235–238, 242, 243,
245–255, 257–260, 262–264,
271, 326, 327
private bank, 2, 4, 9, 37, 62, 68,
69, 71–73, 81, 91, 95, 98,
105, 118, 128, 132, 179–188,
190–197, 199, 202, 203,
205–210, 212, 213, 225–228,
230, 234–236, 238, 240, 243,
244, 247, 250, 251, 253, 256,
258, 259, 261, 262, 265, 276,
286, 287, 294, 326, 328, 357
bank deposit, 5, 18, 59, 60, 93, 134,
183, 185, 186, 189, 191,
195–197, 201–205, 208, 209,
213, 226–228, 238, 245, 247,
265
Basel 3, 206, 207, 213
Bichler/Nitzan, 27, 48, 69, 70,
77–82, 107, 330
Black/Scholes, 110, 122–126, 155
bonds, 4, 5, 9, 35, 37, 62, 64, 89–94,
97, 98, 100, 107, 111, 117, 128,
135, 143, 144, 153, 156, 161,
175, 176, 180, 187, 190, 192,
197, 199, 204, 212, 214, 216,
217, 227, 236, 238–240, 242,
243, 253, 254, 256, 258, 261,
263, 265, 271, 273, 287, 293,
296, 298, 325, 328–332, 359

government bonds, 3, 4, 62, 72,
78, 79, 90, 96, 108, 117, 132,
135, 150, 154, 157, 175, 176,
187, 192, 202, 204, 224, 225,
227, 229, 230, 233–236,
238–243, 248, 251–261, 264,
270, 279, 283, 287, 296–298,
325, 327, 329, 351
borrower, 59, 62–64, 66–68, 73, 74,
94, 97, 118, 131, 180–182, 184,
186, 189, 191, 192, 195–201,
204, 205, 208, 235, 251, 255,
257, 258, 260, 262, 282, 326,
344, 357
Bubble, 156, 190, 234, 254, 296,
351, 355, 358, 359, 361

C
calculation, 6, 7, 12, 17, 19–21, 24,
27, 48, 51, 69, 79, 80, 83, 84,
86, 92, 96, 99, 100, 110, 112,
119, 121, 133, 140, 148, 150,
153–155, 160, 162, 182, 185,
194, 213, 230, 240, 245, 291,
314, 329–331, 335, 340, 341,
345
call, 3, 26, 33, 45, 48, 49, 96, 114,
122, 137, 143–145, 168, 169,
173, 195, 208, 232, 258, 305,
346, 351
capital
fictitious capital, 5, 8, 25, 34, 36,
77, 86, 89–92, 94–96, 99,
101, 107, 159, 179, 182, 189,
195, 196, 224, 225, 227, 232,
240, 241, 243, 246, 252,
262–264, 283, 327
financial capital, 5, 9, 66, 68, 81,
91, 96, 97, 100, 101, 118,
133, 137, 145, 147, 149, 151,
152, 156, 158, 170, 179, 188,
204, 209, 215, 216, 225, 227,

INDEX 369

228, 233, 235, 236, 241, 243,
247, 248, 264, 273, 274, 277,
282, 284, 287, 293–295, 299,
313, 315, 325, 328–330, 333,
351, 358, 360
industrial capital, 25, 26, 36, 47,
61–64, 67, 70, 94, 96, 190,
209, 224, 225, 233, 248, 282,
363
interest bearing capital, 5, 25, 35,
59–62, 64, 66, 67, 89, 94,
180, 232
money capital, 25, 31, 34, 35, 37,
49, 62, 66–70, 72, 91, 93–96,
106, 118, 135, 157, 160, 180,
192, 223, 235, 247, 259, 262,
269, 290, 296, 297, 299, 330,
331, 345
speculative capital, 4–6, 22, 36, 45,
72, 86, 89, 95, 96, 101–103,
105–110, 112, 121, 133, 135,
136, 149, 160, 161, 163, 168,
176, 179, 180, 185, 190, 209,
216, 225, 229, 245, 254, 255,
260, 277, 282, 287, 289, 330,
331, 333, 351–354, 356, 363
total capital, 1, 8, 9, 25, 31, 32,
37–44, 46–48, 51, 52, 61, 69,
71, 94, 96, 139, 140, 179,
205, 207, 211, 240, 275, 325,
355
capital export, 269, 279–282
capital flow, 2, 29, 47, 71, 96, 106,
115, 136, 157, 160, 223, 288,
297, 313, 325, 330, 353
capitalisation, 22, 27, 69, 70
cash flow, 8, 9, 65, 113–115, 122,
126–129, 151, 156, 157, 167,
179, 183, 186, 191, 198, 200,
205, 216, 298, 299, 356
circulation, 6, 8, 9, 14–17, 22–26,
29, 31–34, 36, 38–40, 47, 48,

60, 62, 71, 99, 109, 111, 112,
119, 121, 134–138, 140, 145,
161, 164, 165, 179, 199, 205,
208, 225–227, 232, 233, 245,
247, 249, 252, 257, 259, 260,
264, 269, 285, 286, 291, 295,
296, 307, 314, 320, 331, 351,
356, 359, 363
class, 36, 37, 78, 79, 84, 106, 107,
127, 130, 137, 146, 151, 152,
154, 158, 183, 217, 220, 221,
224, 230, 231, 263, 276, 300,
308, 333, 350
class struggle, 32, 43, 48, 86, 137,
147, 188, 220, 224, 229, 233,
307, 310
collateralised debt obligations (CDO),
108, 117, 118, 120, 126–132,
146, 344, 359
commodity, 5, 6, 9, 11–21, 23–27,
31–35, 38, 39, 43, 47, 51, 52,
60, 62, 63, 65, 71, 83, 93, 97,
99, 101, 106, 107, 110, 111,
113, 114, 120, 121, 124, 133,
134, 137–139, 141–143, 145,
151, 159–161, 179, 189, 193,
199, 210, 216, 217, 226, 229,
245, 256, 262, 269, 272, 274,
276, 278, 282, 284, 287, 289,
295, 296, 304, 306, 314, 319,
361
communication technology, 222, 307,
321
competition, 8, 9, 25, 29, 30, 32,
39–46, 48, 50, 68, 70, 85, 98,
99, 101, 131, 133, 154, 155,
164, 181, 182, 197, 202, 203,
205, 214, 215, 225, 226, 228,
233, 249, 254, 258, 262, 271,
272, 276, 278, 281, 283, 286,
290, 291, 295, 301, 308, 319,
328, 329, 334, 338, 353

370 INDEX

computerisation, 53, 85, 313, 337
contingency, 17, 37, 41, 42, 84, 96, 118, 132, 136, 167–173
corporation, 4, 7, 34, 35, 41, 42, 44, 45, 48, 62, 65, 67, 70, 72, 87, 95, 97, 98, 130, 143, 153–155, 179, 190, 204, 214, 221, 226, 229, 230, 243, 254, 255, 263, 269, 271, 272, 281, 282, 285, 287, 288, 290–293, 314–317, 335, 353, 355, 361
   transnational corporation, 64, 224, 269, 278, 280, 281, 288, 290–292, 304, 329, 334
credit, 2, 4–6, 18, 19, 22, 30, 35, 37, 38, 54, 59–64, 66, 68, 70–74, 89, 94, 97, 101, 105–108, 116–118, 128–132, 134, 135, 137, 142, 143, 145–147, 153, 157, 162, 168, 180, 181, 183–201, 204, 206, 208, 212, 225, 227–229, 234, 235, 237, 240–255, 260–263, 265, 269, 277, 279, 282, 286, 289, 294, 297, 298, 313, 325, 326, 329, 330, 332, 341, 350, 351, 355, 357–362
   credit creation, 68, 96, 105, 179, 182, 185, 186, 190–193, 195, 197, 198, 201, 203–206, 209, 228, 246, 247, 249, 251–253, 255, 283
   credit default swaps (CDS), 108, 116–118, 126, 127, 129, 156, 157, 296, 297, 326, 349, 359
crisis, 2–4, 6, 26, 28, 43, 50, 72, 79, 81, 90, 93, 118, 120, 127, 129, 132, 134, 146, 148, 150, 155, 156, 158, 160, 188, 198, 199, 205, 210, 212, 225, 234, 235, 237, 238, 241, 242, 244, 246, 247, 251–255, 257–265, 278,

279, 290, 296–298, 306, 307, 326, 327, 344, 349–352, 354, 355, 357, 358, 360–363
currency, 9, 20, 95, 209, 226, 237, 239, 242, 243, 246–249, 252, 258, 261, 272–279, 281–283, 285, 286, 288–290, 293–299
   leading currency, 295, 296

D

debt, 1–5, 18, 22, 23, 34–36, 54, 55, 59, 60, 64, 69, 70, 72, 74, 89, 90, 92, 96, 97, 106, 118, 122, 128, 129, 132, 133, 137, 144–146, 174, 184, 186–189, 191, 193, 196–201, 205, 206, 208–210, 212–214, 220, 226, 233–244, 246, 248, 249, 251, 254–256, 261–265, 279, 281, 283, 286, 287, 290, 296–298, 327, 341, 344, 346, 347, 349, 355–360
debtor, 1, 60, 64, 68, 69, 72, 73, 94–96, 108, 116–118, 122, 128, 132, 154, 180–182, 187, 188, 192, 195–198, 204, 207, 226, 229, 234, 237, 244, 247, 262, 279, 344–347
Deleuze/Guattari, 106, 107, 223, 339
derivative contract, 6, 106, 108–111, 114, 119, 120, 124, 131, 158, 159, 167–171, 173, 338
   synthetic derivatives, 120, 126, 172, 173
derivatives, 5–9, 19, 62, 83, 86, 93, 100, 101, 103, 105–113, 115, 119–123, 126, 127, 133–136, 143–149, 151, 154–176, 179, 182, 186, 189, 190, 203, 206, 207, 210, 212–214, 217, 247, 250, 253, 260, 263, 269, 271,

279, 282, 286, 287, 292, 293, 296, 314, 316, 318, 325, 327–329, 333, 338, 342–346, 350–355, 357, 359–362
dollar, 3, 54, 78, 105, 119, 261, 265, 272, 277, 288, 294–299, 330

F

finance, 2, 7, 9, 22, 53, 61–64, 69, 70, 81, 89, 92, 101, 107, 121, 122, 129, 133, 139, 144, 146, 157, 161, 163, 188–190, 193, 194, 214, 220–222, 229–232, 234, 235, 238, 239, 243, 245, 249, 256, 271, 282, 287, 288, 298, 307, 310, 313, 315, 318, 325–327, 338, 343, 351, 352, 355, 356, 360
financialisation, 7, 65, 102, 125, 136, 142, 146, 150, 151, 155, 156, 325, 327, 332, 337, 343–347, 349
future, 2, 5, 7, 17, 19, 22, 27–30, 35, 36, 43, 46, 48, 55, 62, 63, 69, 70, 72–74, 77–86, 89–103, 105, 107–116, 119–127, 133, 135–138, 145–150, 153, 154, 156–158, 160, 165–174, 176, 179, 180, 185, 186, 188, 189, 191, 193–195, 208, 209, 222, 223, 227, 228, 235, 236, 238–241, 243, 245, 248, 252, 253, 256, 263, 264, 277, 282, 287, 305, 314, 321, 330–332, 335, 337, 338, 342, 343, 345–347, 350, 354, 355
future contract, 113, 114

G

Global Value Chain, 299, 305

H

hedge funds, 8, 98, 154, 185, 214, 235, 257, 296, 326, 334, 353, 356, 357
hedging, 3, 6, 9, 70, 85, 107, 109–111, 114, 115, 118, 122, 123, 135, 139, 143–146, 154, 174, 176, 185, 212, 214, 257, 260, 286, 327, 341, 345
high frequency trading (HFH), 81, 85, 315–322
hype coefficient, 77, 78

I

imperialism, 287
income stream, 90, 94, 97, 120, 146, 150, 156, 158, 160, 314
infrastructure, 121, 153, 199, 207, 224, 226, 229, 232, 233, 235, 239, 244, 284, 287, 288, 290, 294, 303, 313, 316, 317, 320, 325, 328, 339, 360
interest, 3, 6, 9, 30, 35, 47, 54, 55, 60, 62–69, 71–73, 79, 80, 89–98, 101, 107, 116, 128, 133, 136, 137, 140, 147, 160, 176, 180–182, 184–186, 189, 192, 194, 195, 197–199, 201, 202, 204, 206, 208, 211, 212, 220, 228, 236, 238, 239, 241, 242, 248, 250, 253, 256, 257, 259, 262, 264, 290, 298, 326, 331, 349, 356
interest rate, 1–4, 9, 29, 30, 37, 43, 48, 64, 66–71, 73, 74, 79, 80, 83, 84, 90, 92, 93, 95–97, 99, 100, 102, 105, 106, 111, 113, 115–119, 122, 124, 127, 131, 136, 145, 146, 149, 156, 157, 175, 180–184, 192, 194, 195, 200, 202, 205, 211–213, 217, 233–235, 239–244, 247, 248,

372 INDEX

250–256, 259–265, 279, 283, 286, 287, 294, 298, 309, 313, 319, 327, 328, 330, 332, 341, 352, 355–357
investment bank, 185, 214, 271, 325–328, 349
investment fund, 7–9, 37, 83, 98, 128, 130, 185, 210, 214–217, 257, 287, 294, 299, 326, 328, 333, 334
investor, 3, 4, 9, 65, 72, 79, 82, 84–86, 92–95, 97, 100–102, 108, 110, 117, 122, 128–132, 134, 138, 139, 175, 176, 192, 199, 214–217, 236, 237, 240, 241, 251, 254, 255, 257, 280, 298, 314, 318, 329, 330, 332, 334, 335, 352–354, 357, 362

K
keystroke capitalism, 183, 195

L
labour, 5, 9, 15, 16, 25, 28, 32, 36, 38, 46, 50, 52–54, 67, 71, 96, 119, 133, 134, 139–142, 145, 146, 154, 159, 171, 189, 209, 229, 231, 249, 255, 270, 275, 280–282, 284, 285, 288, 289, 293, 299–310, 314, 317, 330, 332, 335, 361
labour power, 13, 24–26, 32, 34, 36, 46, 74, 139, 141, 142, 145, 147, 280, 305
Laruelle, François, 27, 37
lender, 59, 62–64, 66, 67, 73, 74, 94, 95, 118, 184, 192, 193, 196, 208, 235, 242, 247, 260, 282, 289, 326, 357

leverage, 2, 4, 81, 110, 120, 126, 160, 163, 207, 209–213, 343, 352–354
LiPuma, Edward, 81, 86, 108, 111, 112, 119, 133–135, 151, 160–162, 164–166, 351, 352, 359
liquidity, 2, 3, 6, 23, 37, 66, 81, 82, 87, 108, 110, 112, 124, 125, 133–137, 142–145, 151, 155, 157, 162, 164–166, 175, 184, 187, 188, 202, 205, 207, 212, 225, 228, 234, 242, 243, 245–248, 250, 252–254, 257–261, 265, 272, 273, 297, 313, 314, 320, 326–328, 343, 351, 353, 354, 357, 359
loan, 2, 3, 5, 6, 9, 34, 35, 48, 54, 60, 62–66, 68–74, 83, 92–95, 106–108, 116–118, 126–130, 134, 145, 146, 157, 160, 179–181, 184–192, 194–205, 207–213, 228, 232, 234, 235, 239, 242–244, 246, 247, 250, 251, 253, 255, 257, 260, 262–264, 278, 280–283, 289, 290, 293, 294, 296–298, 326–328, 332, 339, 341, 349–351, 353, 356, 357, 359
logistics, 167, 192, 220, 281, 288, 290, 302–305, 307, 313, 318, 320, 359

M
machine, 9, 28, 34, 52, 53, 63, 80, 82, 85, 96, 99, 103, 117, 138–143, 145, 151, 155, 189, 192, 209, 213, 220, 223, 232, 244, 280, 288, 300–303, 308, 310, 315–319, 321, 323, 330, 331, 335, 338, 339, 341

Malik, Suhail, 109, 113–115, 167–171

market

capital market, 2, 22, 23, 61, 62, 65, 68, 92, 95, 99, 101, 133, 184, 203, 214, 215, 227, 235, 236, 241, 253, 256, 257, 259, 260, 264, 279, 327, 328, 335

financial market, 3, 7–9, 23, 36, 45, 64, 65, 68, 74, 80, 81, 83–85, 87, 90, 91, 93, 94, 97, 98, 100, 101, 103, 111, 114, 116, 122, 124, 126, 128, 130–137, 143, 146–148, 151–156, 159, 165, 168, 171, 174, 189, 190, 195, 199, 205, 211–214, 233, 234, 240, 241, 243, 246, 247, 253–255, 258, 259, 261, 265, 270–274, 277–279, 283, 287, 297, 314–317, 321, 327–333, 335, 343, 349, 352–355, 360, 362

money market, 9, 23, 62, 68, 92, 156, 184–186, 204, 211, 212, 243, 248, 251, 259, 260, 326, 327, 349, 357

Marx, Karl, 5, 8, 9, 11–16, 21, 22, 24, 25, 27, 29–34, 36, 38, 40–42, 44, 59–64, 66–68, 70, 71, 77, 89–91, 95–97, 134, 137–143, 145, 147, 157, 159, 180, 306, 314, 356, 363

Marxism, 7, 38, 121

Meister, Robert, 81, 122–125, 134, 137–139, 141, 143, 144, 212, 234, 235, 243

Milios, John, 14, 33, 35, 42, 83, 113, 136, 148–151, 155–157, 159, 160, 226, 271, 327, 329, 332, 350

Modern Money Theory (MMT), 195, 226, 230, 236–238, 243, 249, 251, 253

money, 2, 4–7, 9, 11, 13–25, 27–29, 31–38, 40, 47, 50, 52, 54, 55, 59–64, 66, 69–74, 80, 82, 89–91, 93–97, 99, 100, 102, 105–108, 114–116, 118, 120, 122, 124, 127, 134–139, 141, 142, 144–147, 149–151, 155, 158–161, 166, 167, 170, 172, 173, 179–193, 195–209, 212–214, 216, 223–230, 232, 234–238, 242–265, 269, 271–275, 277, 279–283, 285, 286, 289, 293, 297, 299, 307, 313, 314, 325–327, 329, 344, 346, 350, 352–354, 356, 357, 359, 360

N

Norfield, Tony, 8, 9, 37, 107, 191, 210, 287–289, 294

O

option, 70, 91, 93, 95, 103, 105, 107, 108, 110–112, 114, 115, 122–126, 143–145, 168, 174, 184, 217, 236, 237, 260, 263, 297, 332, 333

P

power, 5, 6, 8, 17–21, 26, 29, 30, 41, 46, 51, 68, 77, 82, 84–86, 90, 94–97, 99–102, 107–109, 111, 135, 136, 139, 151, 153–155, 170, 171, 180, 181, 187, 188, 199, 205, 209, 212, 213, 215, 219–228, 231, 233, 239, 242, 245, 248, 249, 262,

265, 269, 272, 273, 276–281, 285, 287–290, 292, 294, 299, 314, 328, 330–332, 350, 360

power relations, 6, 79, 84, 137, 147, 149–151, 154, 220, 221, 260, 277, 279, 288, 290, 329, 337, 346

power technology, 7, 55, 105, 133, 148, 151–153, 155, 156, 346

production, 2–9, 24–26, 28, 31–39, 41, 42, 44, 46–48, 50–53, 61–64, 67–72, 77, 78, 80, 82, 84, 86, 89, 90, 92–94, 96, 97, 99–102, 107–111, 119, 121, 134–145, 151, 153, 154, 158, 160, 163, 165, 167, 188, 189, 194, 196, 199, 203, 209–211, 213, 215, 224, 230, 232, 233, 243, 264, 270–272, 275, 276, 278, 280–282, 284, 285, 287, 291, 292, 294, 299–308, 310, 314, 316, 317, 330–332, 334, 335, 339, 345, 346, 350, 351, 355, 356, 358, 359, 361–363

productivity, 1, 5, 29, 30, 32, 43, 46, 47, 52–54, 65, 94, 99, 131, 139–141, 171, 189, 193, 231–233, 271–276, 278, 284, 285, 290, 292, 300, 309, 332, 335, 337, 358, 361

profit, 2, 3, 6–9, 24, 26, 27, 29, 30, 32–34, 36, 41, 43–51, 62–72, 77–85, 92, 94, 96, 98–100, 102, 105, 108–110, 113, 114, 116–120, 123, 129, 132, 133, 137, 138, 140, 141, 144, 147–150, 154, 159, 161, 163, 164, 166, 167, 175, 176, 180–183, 185, 186, 188, 191, 194, 199, 200, 203–205, 207, 209–213, 215, 216, 221, 222, 225, 230–232, 241, 251, 252, 254, 255, 262, 264, 274, 276, 279–282, 287, 288, 291, 293, 298–300, 314, 315, 317, 318, 321, 322, 327, 329, 330, 333–335, 338–340, 345, 350–353, 356, 361–363

profit rate, 29, 30, 32, 35, 43, 44, 46–50, 61, 67–69, 71, 108, 140, 141, 194, 203, 209, 210, 217, 223, 251, 262, 264, 271, 276, 278, 283, 284, 309, 329, 330, 355, 356, 358, 360

proletariat, 16, 221, 281, 304, 306, 308, 309, 360

global proletariat, 299, 304, 305, 308

promise of payment, 18, 73, 80, 93, 94, 170, 197, 198, 350

put, 12, 18–21, 23–25, 27, 31, 37, 41, 59, 63, 79, 81, 86, 93, 97, 102, 114, 120–123, 127, 136, 143–145, 148, 150, 181, 191, 193, 205, 209, 211, 227, 228, 235, 247, 260, 282, 296, 323, 335, 339, 351

Q

quantification, 112, 137, 152, 314, 339, 342

quantitative easing (QE), 2, 3, 93, 208, 248, 254, 255, 258, 259, 351, 357

R

rating, 8, 118, 129–133, 153, 186, 187, 207, 234, 242, 255, 331, 332, 339, 341, 342, 346, 349

rating agency, 83, 130–133, 147, 150–152, 154, 207, 213, 214, 240, 283, 319, 329–332, 349, 350

INDEX 375

regulation, 8, 26, 32, 43, 66, 68, 81, 86, 132, 148, 185, 186, 205, 207, 213, 214, 226, 227, 247, 248, 251, 259, 270, 281, 284, 302, 310, 325, 328, 349, 350

relation, 5–7, 11, 12, 14–31, 34, 36–39, 41–43, 46, 48–50, 53, 59–62, 64, 66, 68–70, 78, 81, 82, 85, 86, 89, 92, 93, 102, 105, 106, 110, 112, 114, 119–121, 124, 127, 133–136, 138–142, 144, 146, 148–151, 154, 156–164, 166–168, 170, 171, 173, 175, 177, 181, 186, 187, 191–193, 195, 198, 201, 204, 208, 209, 211, 217, 220, 222, 223, 225, 229, 230, 233, 235, 240–242, 245–248, 262, 263, 269, 272–274, 277, 278, 280–282, 287, 289–291, 294, 298, 305, 307–309, 313, 315, 335, 337–339, 344–347, 349, 352, 356–359

repo transcation, 3, 184–186, 214, 254, 257–260, 326, 327

reproduction, 6, 8, 9, 15, 16, 20, 22, 25, 31–33, 46, 47, 51, 61, 67, 70, 71, 102, 119, 137–140, 146, 151, 160, 161, 163, 165, 182, 188, 220, 223, 276, 302, 305, 307, 308, 335, 351, 355

return, 4, 17–19, 24, 31, 36, 54, 60, 63, 69, 70, 77–79, 82–84, 91–93, 95–98, 100, 102, 107, 110, 116, 118, 120, 121, 125, 131, 134–136, 143, 145, 148, 149, 155–157, 161, 175, 176, 190, 203, 207, 209–212, 214, 215, 217, 229, 230, 236, 237, 242, 243, 250, 256, 261–263, 273, 282, 290, 293, 297, 329,

330, 333–335, 344, 345, 347, 351, 353, 357, 361, 362

risk, 4, 8, 9, 17, 32, 37, 45, 62, 68, 70, 72–74, 77–79, 81, 83–87, 90–92, 101–103, 107, 109–111, 113–120, 122–133, 135, 136, 143–145, 147–161, 164–167, 169, 174–176, 182, 184–189, 192, 194, 197, 198, 206, 207, 210, 211, 213, 216, 217, 225, 231, 234–236, 239, 241, 247, 248, 250, 251, 253, 256, 258, 259, 262, 277, 279, 286, 292, 295–298, 308, 310, 313, 314, 320, 321, 326–328, 330, 331, 335, 337–347, 349–355, 357, 362

  abstract risk, 7, 119, 149, 151, 155–159, 161, 166, 351, 352

  concrete risk, 7, 149, 151, 152, 155–159, 355

S

Securitization, 128, 326

security, 3, 7, 24, 35, 37, 49, 65, 66, 72, 73, 79, 80, 82–85, 89–97, 101, 105, 106, 108, 114–116, 126–132, 134, 137, 139, 144, 147, 150, 154, 156–158, 160, 176, 182, 184–187, 189, 190, 192, 195–199, 201–206, 212, 214, 225, 227, 228, 232, 234–236, 238, 240, 241, 243, 246–255, 257–261, 263, 272, 273, 277, 279, 282, 286–288, 293, 294, 296–299, 303, 304, 310, 320–323, 325–329, 338, 344, 345, 350, 351, 354, 356, 357

speculation, 1, 24, 36, 37, 85, 89, 90, 99, 105, 107–110, 114, 115,

119, 158, 194, 241, 255, 263, 286, 287, 349, 360

state, 1, 5, 7, 19, 20, 22, 23, 30, 41, 43, 48, 50, 53, 59, 61, 62, 65, 74, 81, 84, 90, 93, 95, 96, 112, 117, 118, 130–134, 136, 141, 146, 147, 153, 154, 157, 158, 180, 183, 186–188, 192, 195, 207, 209, 213, 216, 219–250, 252, 254, 256, 259, 261, 262, 264, 265, 269–279, 281–283, 285–296, 298, 307, 314, 323, 325, 326, 328, 329, 340, 350, 354, 355, 358, 361

stock market, 2, 4, 65, 86, 95, 98, 99, 101, 102, 113, 176, 215, 216, 256, 285, 294, 299, 318, 330, 359

subject, 16, 17, 20, 23, 26, 28, 29, 33, 35, 40–42, 50, 53, 73, 74, 83, 100, 106, 107, 120, 129, 148, 150, 152, 153, 158, 162, 168, 189, 206, 213, 220, 223, 226, 227, 230, 240, 249, 273, 292, 294, 301, 327, 331, 332, 334, 335, 337–344, 346

financialised subject, 338, 343, 345–347

surplus population, 142, 147, 305–307

swaps, 4, 105, 113, 115, 116, 129, 135, 157, 160, 261, 299, 327, 328

T

taxes, 65, 96, 145, 185, 188, 195, 199, 209, 219, 221, 224, 226, 227, 229–232, 235–244, 249, 252, 262, 284, 293, 297, 325, 329, 360

technology, 30, 37, 45, 46, 54, 140, 163, 209, 277, 280, 307, 313, 316, 319, 328, 339, 340, 359

time, 5, 7, 21, 24, 29, 32–34, 37, 41, 44–52, 60, 62–64, 66, 68–70, 72, 73, 77–83, 85, 86, 90, 91, 98, 102, 105, 106, 108, 110, 111, 113–120, 123, 124, 128, 129, 131, 134, 138, 140, 141, 144, 150, 155, 158–161, 166, 168, 170–174, 180, 185, 187, 189, 193, 195, 198, 200, 203, 205, 207, 208, 210, 211, 225, 228, 231, 232, 237, 243, 244, 247, 249–251, 253–255, 257–259, 273, 287, 297, 302, 303, 305, 309, 314–316, 318–320, 322, 325, 326, 330, 343, 346, 351–354, 357–360

Toyotism, 302–304

trade, 49, 85, 93, 95, 96, 100, 105, 106, 110, 112, 126, 135, 149, 164, 168, 171, 172, 184, 186, 213, 217, 224, 230, 234, 240, 256, 258, 260, 271, 272, 274–292, 294–296, 299, 303, 308, 318, 321, 325, 326, 335, 338, 353, 359, 360, 362

international trade, 2, 269, 272, 274, 276, 287, 290, 292, 293

tranche, 127–129, 131, 146

transcendentality, 39–42

U

underemployment, 306

V

value, 1, 3, 5, 6, 11–27, 30, 32, 34, 36–39, 44, 47, 52, 69, 73, 74, 78–80, 83, 85, 90–92, 96–102, 105–108, 111–114, 116,

119–121, 123–126, 129, 130,
132–134, 136, 138–147, 149,
150, 154, 157–161, 164,
166–168, 171–173, 176, 180,
191–193, 196, 205, 208, 212,
213, 215, 216, 225, 226, 228,
230, 233, 234, 237, 238, 241,
245, 249, 256, 257, 274, 276,
277, 280, 281, 283, 292, 295,
297–299, 302, 309, 310, 323,
326, 333, 335, 341, 345, 354,
361, 362

surplus value, 1, 5, 24–29, 32, 34,
37, 46–49, 51, 67, 70, 71, 80,
136–142, 158, 223, 224, 232,
233, 280, 294, 298, 361

value form, 12, 13
virtualisation, 17, 37, 41, 49, 51,
127, 173
volatility, 3, 82–84, 86, 87, 102, 103,
105, 106, 108, 110, 111, 115,
119, 120, 122, 123, 125, 126,
133, 135, 136, 155, 158, 159,
161, 162, 164–167, 170, 171,
173–176, 184, 187, 295, 296,
320, 351, 353, 359

W
world market, 8, 95, 132, 233, 243,
269–272, 274–277, 279,
281–283, 285–295, 297, 298,
305, 307, 350

Printed in the United States
by Baker & Taylor Publisher Services